FORGING FREEDOM

FORGING FREEDOM

BLACK WOMEN AND THE PURSUIT OF
LIBERTY IN ANTEBELLUM CHARLESTON

AMRITA CHAKRABARTI MYERS

THE UNIVERSITY OF NORTH CAROLINA PRESS

Chapel Hill

The paper in this book meets the guidelines for permanence and durability
of the Committee on Production Guidelines for Book Longevity of the Council on
Library Resources.

The University of North Carolina Press has been a member of the
Green Press Initiative since 2003.

Library of Congress Cataloging-in-Publication Data
Myers, Amrita Chakrabarti.
Forging freedom : Black women and the pursuit of liberty in
antebellum Charleston / Amrita Chakrabarti Myers.
p. cm. — (Gender and American culture)
Includes bibliographical references and index.
ISBN 978-0-8078-3505-0 (cloth : alk. paper)
ISBN 978-1-4696-1904-0 (pbk. : alk. paper)
ISBN 978-0-8078-6909-3 (ebook)
1. African American women—South Carolina—Charleston—History—19th century.
2. African American women—South Carolina—Charleston—Social conditions—
19th century. 3. Freedmen—South Carolina—Charleston—History—19th century.
4. Freedmen—South Carolina—Charleston—Social conditions—19th century.
5. Charleston (S.C.)—History—1775-1865. 6. Charleston (S.C.)—Social conditions—
19th century. 7. Charleston (S.C.)—Race relations—History—19th century. I. Title.
F279.C49N458 2011
305.48′8960730757915—dc22   2011015961

To the Lord,
through whom all things
are possible

CONTENTS

ILLUSTRATIONS, MAPS, & TABLES

Illustrations

Maps

Tables

ACKNOWLEDGMENTS

Thanking everyone who helped me to complete this project is a daunting task. This journey began many years ago, and I fear I will forget to mention someone. Still, I will try my best to extend my gratitude to all those who have guided me to this point.

I must begin by thanking my mentor from the University of Alberta. As I was committed to becoming a lawyer when we first met, the truth is that without Susan Smith's encouragement and support, which she still showers on me, I would not have gone to graduate school at all.

At Rutgers, I was fortunate to work with Norma Basch, Mia Bay, the late Dee Garrison, David Levering Lewis, Jan Lewis, Jennifer Morgan, and Deborah Gray White. In particular, Deborah, David, and Jennifer's influences on my work have been profound. Deborah's research captivated me as an undergraduate, and it was the chance to learn from her that brought me to Rutgers. Jennifer's scholarship on South Carolina drew me to Charleston and helped shape my analysis of it, and it was in David's African American History Seminar that the foundation for this project was laid. Deborah, David, and Jennifer also served as advisers, as did Suzanne Lebsock and Bernard Powers Jr. from the College of Charleston. I am grateful for everything they have done, and continue to do, to help me hone my craft. I am equally indebted to Clement Price, my mentor and cheerleader from my earliest days at Rutgers.

While at Rutgers, I received a Research Fellowship from the Rutgers Center for Historical Analysis (RCHA) to participate in the project "The Black Atlantic: Race, Gender, and Nation." By engaging in weekly conversations with Herman Bennett, Michelle Mitchell, and many others, the seminars at the RCHA helped to shape and conceptualize my work and enriched me beyond measure.

My time at Rutgers was made far more pleasurable by the stellar women and men I met in my classes. For their friendship and critical insights I thank William Jelani Cobb, Christopher Fisher, Tiffany Gill, Justin Hart, Peter Lau, Kelena Reid Maxwell, Khalil Muhammad, Aminah Pilgrim, Lisa Tarantino, and Stephanie Sims Wright. To Tiffany and Stephanie I am particularly indebted. Only they know how much.

I would not have been able to complete this study without the assistance I received from several organizations, including the Harvey Fellows Program through the Mustard Seed Foundation; two Research Fellowships from the Institute for Southern Studies at the University of South Carolina in Columbia; a Mellon Fellowship at the Library Company of Philadelphia; and the one-year leave that the Department of History at Indiana University extended to me at a critical juncture as I pushed to complete the project.

My time in South Carolina was truly a joy, due in large part to the wonderful personnel at the South Carolina Department of Archives and History in Columbia, and the staffs of the Avery Research Center, the Charleston City Archives, the Charleston County Public Library, the Charleston Library Society, the Robert Scott Small Special Collections Library at the College of Charleston, and the South Carolina Historical Society, all in Charleston. In particular, I must thank Harlan Greene, Yvette Lebby, Dorothy Richardson, Karen Stokes, and Deborah Wright for their unstintingly warm and liberal assistance. I would also like to thank Phil Lapsansky for his generous help during my residency at the Library Company of Philadelphia.

A number of colleagues at my first position in the Department of History at Kean University supported me intellectually and emotionally as I worked to finish the manuscript. In particular, I want to single out Burt Wailoo and Sue Gronewold and thank them for their wise counsel and friendship.

As I transitioned out of graduate school, I met a number of gifted scholars who have helped me in numerous ways over these last few years. For their encouragement, advice, and thoughtful critiques, I thank Leslie Alexander, Daina Ramey Berry, Nikki Brown, Victoria Bynum, Erica Armstrong Dunbar, Stephanie Y. Evans, Paul Finkelman, Kali Gross, Darlene Clark Hine, Lynn Hudson, Tera Hunter, Michael Johnson, Wilma King, Minkah Makalani, Jessica Millward, Jeffrey O. G. Ogbar, Nell Irvin Painter, Leslie Schwalm, Loren Schweninger, Nikki Taylor, Rosalyn Terborg-Penn, and Rhonda Y. Williams.

At Indiana University, I am surrounded by colleagues who share my passion for the histories of race, gender, freedom, citizenship, and sexuality. For reading drafts, helping me work through theoretical issues, providing feedback on a host of matters, and their collegiality, I thank Judith Allen, Claude Clegg, Wendy Gamber, Katie Lofton, Jim Madison, Emily Maguire, Marissa Moorman, Michelle Moyd, John Nieto-Phillips, Yeidy Rivero, Sara Scalenghe, Stephen Selka, Leah Shopkow, Micol Siegel, and Christina Snyder. Special thanks to my IU writing group: Kon Dierks, Matthew Guterl, Sarah Knott, Khalil Muhammad, and Kirsten Sword. Matthew, in particular, provided invaluable aid at critical moments over the last five years. I appreciate him deeply as a scholar and a friend.

My debt to the people at the University of North Carolina Press, who took a very raw manuscript and helped to turn it into a far better book, is substantial. My thanks especially to Thadious Davis, Sian Hunter, Mary Kelly, Beth Lassiter, Rachel Surles, Kate Torrey, and the two external (and originally anonymous) reviewers who devoted an extraordinary amount of time to helping me improve the manuscript: Leslie Schwalm and Janice Sumler-Edmond. Without their help, this project would be a much poorer contribution to the field of African American women's history.

Outside of the academy, many friends supported me in my efforts to finish the book without losing my sanity. Thank you to everyone at Grace Alliance Church in Piscataway, New Jersey, at Vineyard Community Church in Bloomington, Indiana, and in IU's Intervarsity Graduate and Faculty Ministry chapter. Thanks especially to Ruthy Brookman, Karen and John Costa, Tarez and Eric Graban, Kerilyn Harkaway-Krieger, Robynne Rogers Healey, Debbie and Mark Kincade, Joshua Krieger, Sandra Latcha, Robyn and Andy Mah, Cris and George Munzing, Mandy and Michael Nagyhetenyi, Paula and Blake Puckett, and Rebecca Martinez Reid.

My acknowledgments would be incomplete if I did not mention my family and all the encouragement they have extended to me over the years. Thank you to my parents, Sukla and Amal Chakrabarti; my sister, Anita Nila Chakrabarti; and my in-laws, Brenda Myers, David Myers, Janet Myers, Suzanne Myers Vaartstra, and Jay Vaartstra. Also a special shout-out for two young men who mean the world to me: Joel and David Kincade. For all the laughter you have brought into my life, I thank you. I hope one day you will understand how much I love you. Finally, my thanks to Spencer Myers for all his support and help over the last eighteen years.

This book is dedicated to the Lord, who "began this work" and then "carried it on to completion" as He said He would.

FORGING FREEDOM

INTRODUCTION

IMAGINING FREEDOM

IN THE SLAVE SOUTH

Sometime between 1800 and 1820, a black female Charlestonian by the name of Catherine petitioned the South Carolina General Assembly and asked the assemblymen to ratify her freedom. Originally the enslaved laborer of one Peter Catanet, Catherine was sold to a man named Dr. Plumeau for $300, "a sum far below her value," in order to enable "the wench to purchase her freedom." Catherine and Dr. Plumeau then entered into a contract, witnessed by Peter and his wife, which stated that Catherine would be manumitted when she had re-paid Plumeau her purchase price of $300. Catherine hired herself out and even-tually turned over the required sum to Plumeau, but when the good doctor died without mentioning the arrangement in his will, her troubles began.[1]

Upon his death, Plumeau's beneficiaries claimed to have no knowledge of the contract between Catherine and the deceased and tried to take possession of Catherine, who was already living as a free woman. She, in turn, initiated a lawsuit in the Court of Equity to avoid being returned to slavery. According to the petitions Catherine's guardian filed on her behalf with the courts and the state legislature, Plumeau "was capable of so despicable a transaction as de-frauding this negroe [sic] of her rights." Plumeau, it seems, had a habit of ob-taining "prime slaves" for low prices under false pretenses: he promised the original owner that he intended to free the said servant and then reneged on the deal, thereby defrauding both the original owner and the laborer. Catherine was fortunate that several white witnesses, including her former owner, testi-fied on her behalf. This persuaded the court that enslaved people had the right to enter into a contract as long as they had the permission of their owner. The court thus declared that Catherine's freedom contract was valid and, since she had fulfilled the terms of said contract, she was legally manumitted. Her free-dom was then ratified by the South Carolina General Assembly.[2]

Catherine's lawsuit is not unique: my research on Charleston uncovered similar legal dramas dating back to the 1790s. Indeed, a steady stream of the city's black women defended their rights as they perceived them, from the days of the early republic to the start of the Civil War. Asking the courts to formally recognize their freedom, defending themselves against false enslavement, petitioning the state assembly to repeal race-based taxes, and filing lawsuits to protect their property, Charleston's women of color used all the means at their disposal to protect their own definition of freedom. In doing so, they behaved in many ways like the black women who lived in Atlanta after the Civil War; women determined to enjoy a freedom of their own design as opposed to the more limited liberty that white Atlantans desired for them.[3]

It is this larger issue of the contested meaning of freedom that interests me. Exactly how are meanings of freedom crafted by different groups of people, and how are the rights of citizenship negotiated, and renegotiated, between people and the society in which they reside? The sources from Charleston reveal that ideas such as freedom, citizenship, and rights are always in flux and are definitively fluid, and that they are so precisely because people's imaginings, as well as their lived realities, of these constructs are highly individualized. To put it concretely, a person's understanding of notions such as liberty, freedom, and citizenship are dependent on their chronological context (the times in which they live), residential position (the place where they live), and factors of social space. Social space can include, but is not necessarily limited to, an individual's race, class, gender, religion, sexuality, language, nationality, and ethnicity.

What lies at the center of this study, then, is an examination of how black women in pre–Civil War Charleston struggled to live out their own vision of freedom. In the broadest sense, Forging Freedom is a social history illuminating the lives of free black women in Charleston, South Carolina, from the era of the new republic to the dawn of the Civil War.[4] At its heart, it analyzes the tactics that antebellum women of color utilized to obtain, define, and defend their own concept of freedom, tactics that included the acquisition of financial resources, building alliances with persons in positions of authority, and utilizing the state's judicial apparatus. Examining ideas of liberty from the perspective of those persons vested with the least formal power in the Old South, this study posits that black women used all the resources at their disposal to craft a freedom of their own imagining as opposed to accepting the limited confines of a freedom shaped for them by white southerners. And while the city's free black women were a diverse group in terms of age, wealth, marital status, color, and vocation, the common factors of urban condition, race, gender, and legal status worked together in critical ways to unify their experiences, shaping their identities and opportunities as well as the methods they used in trying to design their own freedom.

Discussions of the black definition of freedom have a rich literature, the majority of which is grounded in the Reconstruction Era.[5] There is less scholarship, however, addressing how free blacks in the early national and antebellum periods, particularly black women, envisioned freedom. Judith Schafer states in her discussion of New Orleans that freedom meant more to persons of color than just an end to physical bondage. It included not being under another person's supervision every hour of the day, keeping the fruits of one's labor, and walking unimpeded along the path to financial autonomy. She adds that freedom also encompassed the ability to maintain one's liberty by using the very legal system that worked to sustain slavery. And in her work on black women during the era of slavery, Wilma King posits that "the absence of physical, social, and spiritual shackles was as important as relief from racial discrimination and independence in making decisions leading to one's economic well-being." She concludes that "the dream of each black woman . . . was to enjoy 'Full Liberty to go and live with whom & Where She may Chuse.'"[6]

How do these definitions fare when measured against the experiences of black female Charlestonians? Research suggests that factors of place and social space meant that these women's visions of freedom differed from those of free men in New Orleans, for example, or from black women in the northern states. Similar to Schafer's subjects, however, for Charleston's black women, freedom meant more than legal manumission alone: it included earning a fair wage and attaining financial independence. And, like the women in King's work, black female Charlestonians sought to live where and with whom they wished, and worship as they pleased. Additionally, Charleston's women of color were committed to securing the emancipation and autonomy of their loved ones; choosing who, or if, to marry; overturning race-based taxes; acquiring property, particularly real estate and enslaved laborers; overcoming the occupational barriers of race and sex; and attaining upward social mobility for themselves and their children.

Seen from this perspective, it is apparent that while official freedom was certainly coveted, for black women, it was never an end in and of itself. More than a fixed legal category, or the simple flip side of slavery, freedom in the slave South was an *experience*. Manumission without the ability to improve one's social standing, acquire financial resources, and consolidate familial security was a poor imitation of liberty. It was the benefits of freedom that black women desired, and to see their visions become reality, they worked hard, constructed a variety of alliances with powerful persons, and sought the protections of the law that white Carolinians enjoyed as their birthright. Even when the judicial system was not oriented toward alleviating their predicaments, and it often was not, black women appealed to the courts and the state assembly in myriad ways to further their quest for a fuller freedom. This included signing petitions, creating trust agreements, submitting affidavits, and filing lawsuits. Thus, in language and behavior, black women drew on the ideas of citizenship in order to request equal protection under the law without necessarily demanding the rights of greater political participation.

On paper, there appeared to be no room for black women to engage in a debate about the nature of their rights. The law gave enslaved persons no such authority, and South Carolina's free people of color occupied a tenuous legal space. It is true that their marriages to other free persons were legal; they could purchase, sell, and bequeath property; lend money at interest; and work for wages. Coexisting with these rights, however, were policies limiting black freedom. Denied the title of citizen, free blacks were categorized as "denizens" of the state, a status halfway between citizen and alien. They also had no formal, political power, were barred from white-collar professions, and often had a ceiling imposed on their wages. Moreover, free black churches and schools were periodically outlawed or closely regulated, their freedom of assembly was regularly restricted, free black men over fifteen years of age had to acquire white male guardians, and, in addition to property taxes, all free black persons had to pay taxes on their own bodies (known as capitation or head taxes) simply because they were black.[7]

Charleston's free blacks also found themselves identified with those who remained enslaved: they were, for example, tried in slave courts for a variety of infractions and were subject to being picked up after dark by slave patrols. Additionally, they found themselves segregated in, or excluded from, a variety of institutions, including churches, hotels, restaurants, theaters, and even the municipal Poor House. Indeed, the old city workhouse was remodeled to create a building for indigent free blacks that would house them separately from poor whites, while Calvary Episcopal Church went so far as to provide white parishioners with a separate entrance, as well as raised seating, to differentiate them from black congregants, whether enslaved or free. Free blacks, then, had the right to work for what white people *chose* to pay them, at jobs they were *allowed* to perform, and were subject to onerous taxes without *any* of the benefits of representation, all while enduring public humiliation in a variety of social settings.[8]

Clearly manumission did not grant a black person unfettered access to equality. And, while subject to the same race-based restrictions as black men, free black women were further limited by their gender. Residing in a state committed to the principle of male rule, married women did not exist as legal entities apart from their husbands, most women could not speak on their own behalf in a court of law, and woman of all races were restricted from engaging in a number of well-paying trades, including carpentry and blacksmithing. In reality, then, black women's ability to acquire upward mobility, even more so than black men, required that they negotiate with those who had access to more power than they did themselves. Knowing that their autonomy was restricted, and realizing that building alliances with those in authority could help them create a fuller freedom, black female Charlestonians often forged social, financial, or familial bonds with men of stature in order to acquire the expanded liberty they desired. While pursuing these relationships, however, they came to realize that men were both a hindrance and a help in their quest for freedom. Although men were the gatekeepers to many of the rights they sought, black women also struggled against these same men's attempts to dictate and control other aspects of their lives, including oversight of their property and power over their children.

Despite the complications of partnering with men, some women were able to use these connections to acquire their legal freedom. Others were able to parlay such relationships, as well as their own hard work, if not into lawful manumission then into the accoutrements of a more meaningful freedom, including the acquisition of goods, particularly real property. In the pre–Civil War South, this meant houses, land, and bondspersons. And while it is unclear if slaveholding per se was a part of how black women in Charleston defined their freedom, owning laborers certainly enhanced a woman's ability to obtain privileges and acquire upward social mobility. In a society that glorified the possession of real property, those who garnered the most power and prestige were individuals who had attained the position of landowner, slaveowner, or both. A tragic irony that speaks to the fragile nature of black female freedom in early national and antebellum South Carolina, the ownership of certain black persons helped expand and solidify the freedom of other black persons.

Women of color, then, focused on accumulating property because they realized that money could help them obtain some of the rights denied to them on the basis of their race or their gender. For example, a number of well-to-do free blacks were able to avoid paying their head taxes . . . without penalty. Some used their financial position to gain entrance to elite churches, while others used their wealth as a platform from which to begin requesting equal protection under the law. The actions of these women, many of whom became litigants in lawsuits initiated to defend their property rights, suggested they believed that they were entitled to certain rights on the basis of their status as taxpayers, landholders, and slaveowners. Asking the courts and the state to entrench these rights, black women of means began articulating a concept of citizenship under which the protections of the law were to be extended to people on the basis of their socioeconomic status and contributions to society. In much the same way, their poorer counterparts asked the state to uphold justice and to honor those who were "loyal citizens," as well as those who displayed morally upright behavior. These women often filed suits and signed petitions utilizing the language of "virtue" or "helpless femininity" in defense of their personal liberties.

While Charleston's women of color thus used a variety of tactics to create autonomous spaces for themselves, they did not attempt to restructure the political order under which they lived. Instead, they used legal, economic, and social systems designed to deny them access to the full fruits of freedom to try to acquire a stronger position within the city's existing raced and gendered power structures. Aware that the factors of time, place, and social space limited their options, black women knew that they could never take the benefits of freedom for granted, and that the ability to collectively organize to demand their rights, which their descendants would attempt, was not within their purview.[9] Cognizant of their constraints, they thus worked as individuals from inside an inherently discriminatory system to shape the contours of their lives to better fit their own visions of freedom. Contesting barriers of race and sex in a multitude of ways, black women labored to secure the rights of freedom as they defined them, utilizing wealth, personal alliances, and the law to help them defend their liberty as they conceived it.

Living in a time and place that required them to make compromises, Charleston's black women struggled to achieve a meaningful freedom, beyond the confines of degrading work and continual poverty. Those who could thus worked to position themselves within the city's social and financial hierarchies in ways that allowed them to acquire power and pass it on to their children. Although some of these women adopted the elitist rhetoric of the society in which they lived, they also articulated new concepts of citizenship that defied traditional notions of rights being based on an individual's race or gender. It was this idea of an *earned citizenship*, as opposed to one based on the happenstance of birth, that these women passed on to their descendants. Many of those postbellum blacks, later identified by W. E. B. Du Bois as a "talented tenth," came to suggest that some black people had proven themselves worthy of civil rights by virtue of their patriotism, financial achievements, education, and respectability.[10]

Of course, not all black women were successful in their quest for expanded rights and privileges. Whether they won or lost their individual battles, however, what is important is that free black women in the antebellum South clearly believed that they were *entitled* to certain things, including the protection of their bodily freedom and the defense of their property, and they used every tool at their disposal to expand the parameters of their freedom. Savvy political actors, Charleston's black women refused to reside silently within the boundaries of a pseudo-freedom created for them by the master class that ruled the society in which they lived. Instead, they articulated their own visions of freedom in the face of societal superstructures created to both define and contain black women's rights. Utilizing a wide range of sources, including court records, family papers, legislative documents, probate data, parish registers, census materials, tax lists, city directories, organizational records, police ledgers, death certificates, legal case files, manumission books, and more, this study, then, does not simply add black women's voices to the story of one city; instead, and more important, it illuminates a pre–Civil War chapter in the narrative of black women's struggles for freedom, justice, and civil rights in the American South.

It is important to note that this project is, first and foremost, an analysis of free black women's lives in one city.[11] Focusing on one locale over seventy years allows me to paint a deeply detailed portrait of black female freedom in Charleston, while enabling me to illustrate and assess the changes to that freedom over time. *Forging Freedom* does, however, place Charleston's women of color within a broader context when possible in order to contrast their lives with those of black women in other cities in terms of manumission, employment, family structures, property ownership, and more. Using secondary literature on early national and antebellum free blacks in general, and black women in particular, I link Charleston where it is appropriate to other, urban centers across the South (specifically Baltimore; Petersburg, Virginia; Savannah, Georgia; and New Orleans) and separate Charleston when its experience is distinctive.[12]

Second, although black women take center stage in my work, comparative raced and gendered analyses are integral to this book. Where it is available, primary statistical data on Charleston's free black men and white women is used to illuminate the similarities and differences that existed between these two groups and the city's free black women with regards to rates of manumission, job opportunities, wage-earning potential, property ownership, and the accumulation of wealth. Additionally, secondary literature discussing free black communities in their entirety,[13] as well as works that compare the experiences of black and white southern women,[14] are utilized when appropriate in order to thicken the comparative context between Charleston's women of color, men of color, and white women.

Third, state law and the legal system are significant elements of this project. It is my contention that the law played a critical role in a black woman's ability to acquire freedom, in defining her life as a free woman, and in her responses to oppression. Black women in the late eighteenth and nineteenth centuries had a complicated relationship with the law, and while South Carolina legislation became increasingly hostile toward free people of color as the nation drew closer to civil war, black women continued to use the state assembly, the courts, and their own understanding of the law to protect their vision of freedom. I thus explicate those sections of state law that were especially relevant to black people and discuss how these laws developed over the seven decades of this study, which is integral to understanding both the change in black women's lives over time as well as their evolving definitions of freedom and the rights of citizenship.

Fourth and finally, while this book is an examination of free women, it discusses slavery throughout, particularly since many free black women had been enslaved at one point in their lives or were free by practice, but not by law. Additionally, evidence indicates that the tools black women used to escape slavery, as well as to find jobs and acquire property as free women, were tied to the nature of their enslavement. Moreover, when one considers how deeply the laws of slavery affected the lives of free people of color, and that most free women had loved ones who remained enslaved, it is fair to say that the realities of slavery continually influenced the story of freedom. Indeed, black women experienced a freedom constrained by the society in which they lived, and they continually worked to stave off reenslavement and restrictions to their freedom. Never completely free, their liberty was always contingent on their skills of negotiation within a system dedicated, at its core, to upholding black and female unfreedom.

Crafted as it is, then, Forging Freedom stands at the nexus of African American history, women's history, the histories of slavery and freedom, and the study of the (urban) South. Indebted to all of these subfields, my work also transforms the literature of each. Occupying the space between the history of enslaved women and that of postwar freedwomen, this project is a critical link in our overall understanding of African American women's history in the South. Studies of the post–Civil War South have posited that black women's experiences under slavery influenced the ways in which they later viewed the concept of freedom. Seeking control over every area of their lives, southern freedwomen struggled to dictate not only the terms of their labor but also their modes of dress, worship, and recreation.[15] Historians of slavery maintain that enslaved women undertook this sort of resistance as well, working daily to control their bodies, clothes, homes, worship style, and leisure time, all while still on the plantation.[16] Forging Freedom concludes that free black women in the prewar South were equally impacted by their experiences with slavery, interactions which affected not only how they saw freedom but also how they worked to bring their visions of freedom to life. The stories of antebellum free black women, then, are the next chapter in the history of enslaved women, and a precursor to the experiences of postbellum freedwomen in the history of southern black women's struggles for freedom, justice, citizenship, and autonomy.

The first full-length examination of Charleston to focus solely on black women, this study also contrasts these women's experiences with those of their black male counterparts, giving us a more complete picture of the city's antebellum free black community.[17] Analyzing black women's contributions to the economic, political, and social life of the city alongside the data available for Charleston's black men, it becomes clear that while more enslaved women than men were manumitted by their owners, when compared to free black men, free women of color had fewer occupational choices, they were more likely to be poor, and their success was more dependent on their building alliances with white benefactors. Offering a gendered perspective of how freedom was constructed and enacted by black people in one locale, Forging Freedom joins only three other monographs that focus on free black female communities in pre–Civil War America, namely those of Adele Alexander, Jane Dabel, and Erica Armstrong Dunbar. Given that Dunbar and Dabel work on northern cities, it is fair to say that this is a subject that demands more attention from scholars of the antebellum South than it has received to date.[18]

In addition to incorporating women's voices into the material on black Charleston, this project also distinguishes the experiences of black women from those of white women in the Old South.[19] While most examinations of early national and antebellum women include black women to some extent, the data in such monographs is still weighted more heavily toward white women. Gaps thus remain in what we know about free black women's lives. Integrating black women into the southern story, and contrasting their lives to those of white women when appropriate, this study reshapes our understanding of how gender, race, and agency intersected in the Old South, preliminarily sketching out the different kinds of freedom that were experienced by black and white women in the prewar era. In particular, the data from Charleston suggests that free black women not only were more likely to remain single throughout their adult lives than were white women but also worked outside the home for wages in larger numbers, were more likely to own real property, and were less likely to engage in collective social or political endeavors than their white female counterparts.

As I stated earlier, this book is, at heart, a local study. Due to the nature of my research, however, and having utilized the available scholarship on free blacks in other southern cities, I was able to compare black women's circumstances across locales in certain ways and draw select conclusions about the lives of free women of color in the slave South when appropriate.[20] The evidence suggests that while some aspects of free black women's lives were unique to the city in which they lived, such as the ability of Charleston's women of color to take advantage of local *feme sole* laws to expand their economic opportunities, others existed across state lines. In particular, the need to forge alliances with white persons of stature, and the utilization of the legal system to articulate, defend, and extend their rights, appear to have been hallmarks of black female behavior in urban slave centers across the United States.

Forging Freedom also reshapes our understanding of urban freedom and urban slavery in the early national and antebellum South. While this book is an examination of free black women, most of the women discussed herein were enslaved at some point, had enslaved friends or relations, or lived as illegally free persons. In reality, then, slavery was never completely absent from the lives of Charleston's free black women, and I discuss enslavement throughout the book. Indeed, the chapters on manumission, employment, and property ownership reveal that the unique nature of urban slavery, in addition to living in a city with a sizable free black population, provided women with opportunities to escape from slavery, acquire specialized job skills, buy property, live independently, purchase themselves and others out of bondage, and engage in a number of activities that were difficult for enslaved women to undertake in rural areas.[21]

Finally, this project speaks to the nature of political action. If political behavior is seen as mass organizing to secure legal or social change for an entire group, then Charleston's free black women were not political actors in the manner of their postbellum sisters. Progressive Era black clubwomen were known for working to "uplift" the less fortunate of their race as they themselves "climbed" the ladder of citizenship. Concluding that their own upward mobility was bound to the behavior and reputation of the black masses, clubwomen established numerous organizations dedicated to helping "degraded" blacks improve their work ethic, intellect, appearance, and morals. This was done so that all blacks could acquire the rights of citizenship, rights clubwomen felt they had already earned by virtue of their "respectability" but which they had not yet received because white people discriminated against all blacks based on the "inappropriate" behavior of a few bad apples. Hence the clubwomen's focus on reforming working-class and impoverished blacks. Since respectability was tied to *personal* behaviors such as cleanliness, hard work, and sexual morality, rather than wealth, even the poorest black person, according to clubwomen, could attain respectability . . . if he or she wanted to.[22]

Certainly antebellum women of color were concerned with shaping their public image, but their attention to individual progress differed from the community-wide, albeit elitist, focus of black clubwomen after the war. In the slave South, many free blacks who attained upward mobility did so in part by establishing cordial relationships with white persons at work, church, and in their neighborhoods. Such "personalism" was commonplace throughout the South, but it did not provide a black person with true security. As long as free blacks who aspired to better things stayed in their place, they would be permitted to own shops that served white clients, or rub shoulders with white persons at church, but they could never deviate from the appropriate code of southern racial etiquette. This meant that they had to be "respectable": they had to work hard; display public decorum, piety, and sobriety; and be unfailingly reliable and loyal. It also meant that they could never do anything that might bring them into ill repute. In particular, they had to appear not to sympathize with enslaved persons or the impoverished free black masses. For upwardly mobile free blacks, then, the fragility of their freedom was clear: they stood on a tenuous middle ground between freedom and slavery, a position dependent on white sufferance, which could vanish at any time.[23]

The reality of antebellum black women's lives thus did not allow them to engage in activism the same way their descendants would: free black women in the prewar South were never fully secure, legally, financially, socially, or otherwise. Agency, then, had its limits. Forced by circumstances to continually reinforce their own rights as individuals, Charleston's women of color were hard pressed to engage in activities not directly pertaining to their own betterment. They knew there was no such thing as too much wealth and no privilege that might not be taken away in times of social unrest or political upheaval. Realizing they had little time, money, or power with which to help the larger black community, they worked instead to shore up their own precarious positions and protect their families from encroachments on their always contingent freedom. Factors of time, place, and social space thus led to an inward-looking focus among Charleston's free women of color, as opposed to one of collective action.[24]

These were the circumstances, then, that led some black women to buy and sell other black people for profit, use forced labor to grow their businesses, ally themselves with white persons of stature, and distance themselves from people who could jeopardize their position in society. Realizing that their minds, skills, and bodies were all tools in their quest for the rights of freedom, and living where and when they did, many of Charleston's black women undertook certain, ostensibly personal, actions that furthered their acquisition of the rights and privileges of freedom and citizenship, actions which can thus be seen as political behavior. Positioning the accumulation of property, slaveownership, church attendance, and the choice of financial, social, and sexual partners as politically motivated actions, this study illuminates both the extent and the limits of black women's agency in the Old South and redefines our views of freedom and citizenship in the context of a raced and gendered slave society.

In crafting an examination of such a society, some of the thorniest issues I encountered revolved around questions of terminology, including how to refer to free people themselves. First, it is important to note that I treat both legally manumitted black persons and those who had no proper documentation, but who still lived as free people, as free people. My decision to do so was based in large part on the fact that Charleston's irregularly freed blacks behaved as free persons and city officials treated them as such: these persons of color owned real and personal property, earned wages, entered into contracts, and paid both capitation and property taxes. Additionally, South Carolina Justice John Belton O'Neall ruled in 1832 that evidence indicating a black person had lived as a free person for several years would establish the fact of freedom. A few years later, state judges concluded that illegally freed laborers had the right to own property. Declaring "there could be no slave without a master," the courts concluded that after an irregular emancipation, "until one is actually seized, the freed slave must stand on the footing of any other free negro." In other words, illegally freed persons of color were to enjoy all the rights of free blacks until and unless they were captured.[25]

In choosing to recognize irregularly manumitted persons as free blacks, I also had to decide how I would refer to those persons whose claim to freedom was not legally documented. This is a complicated matter. I object to referring to them as "nominal slaves" or "quasi-slaves" for a number of reasons.[26] First, my work complicates the very notion of freedom, emphasizing that freedom was not a static legal construct or a simplistic binary of slavery but an *experience*. I also believe that retroactively retracting the word "free" from people who believed they were free, and who lived as if they were free, perpetrates a kind of historical violence on the subjects of this project. Additionally, while persons who had not been legally freed could be reenslaved at any time, proper manumission was no guarantee against reenslavement: as my research reveals, "free papers" could not protect a person against the myriad hurdles the state erected to try to "legitimately" reenslave free blacks. The fragile nature of freedom for all free blacks in the Old South is thus foundational to this entire study.

Still, some signifier that reflects a person's undocumented status must be used, since there are places in this project where it is necessary to differentiate between those persons who were legally manumitted and those who were not. Recent studies on free blacks in the early national and antebellum eras utilize the terms "virtually free" and "quasi-free" for irregularly manumitted persons.[27] Given these precedents, and the fact that such language acknowledges an individual's day-to-day experience of freedom, as well as the extralegal nature of that freedom, I employ "virtually free" and "quasi-free" throughout the book, in addition to "free-by-practice" and "free-by-courtesy," to identify those persons of color whose freedom was not documented. I think it is fair to say that the language as it exists with regards to black freedom in the slave South is imperfect at best, and that these terms are not the only ways to describe those persons who did not have the legal documentation of freedom, but who lived as free people nonetheless.

With regards to identifying free persons in terms of color, I make it a point to refer to individuals as "black," "brown," "person of color," "negro," "mulatto," "Indian," "yellow," and so on, according to how they are identified in archival documents. There is, however, no consistency with regards to how a person is described in the primary sources: the same person can be, and is, referenced in numerous ways in assorted documents that were compiled at different times by various people. Apparently, what I have termed "individual eyeball estimates" were used by South Carolina's tax collectors, census takers, and the compilers of a wide range of local, state, and federal documents as the basis for determining how to describe persons of African descent.

In addition to drawing on the language from the primary sources where they are available in order to describe individual black persons, I refer to free persons of African descent more generally, or to free people as a group, as "free blacks" or "free people of color." These terms, in addition to "free negro" and "free mulatto," were regularly listed in all manner of public documents beside the names of individuals who were not socially constructed as white persons. These phrases were also used interchangeably by the church, the state, and by South Carolinians themselves, both white and black, when referring to persons of African descent. In the interest of simplicity and clarity, I choose to employ two of the most widely used terms.

The common use of "eyeball estimates" does, however, cause us to question how South Carolinians were constructing racial identity. How did white

Carolinians define a "Negro" in the years before the Civil War? Did they calculate a person's percentage of black ancestry, classify someone based on his or her visual appearance, or use another measure altogether? The fact is that while South Carolinians relentlessly distinguished between white and black in the public record, they refused to impose a strict standard on how to determine one's race. Indeed, the evidence suggests that some, if not all, white South Carolinians viewed race as both social and biological and thus somewhat fluid in nature. In 1835, Judge William Harper, in referring to a case he had recently adjudicated, stated that while the persons involved in the case had "Negro blood," to him, these persons were white. The judge stated that the grandfather of these persons, "although of dark complexion, had been recognized as a white man, received into society, and exercised political privileges as such; their mother was uniformly treated as a white woman; their relations of the same admixture . . . married into respectable families, and one of them had been a candidate for the legislature."[28] To categorize such individuals as "persons of color" after they had already exercised the privileges of whiteness was, to many members of the master class, unthinkable.

Race in South Carolina, then, appears to have depended in large part on the *performance of respectability*. To put it another way, racial classification was about a person's character: how an individual was both perceived by and accepted into his or her community. William Harper confirmed this, concluding that a man of color who was "a man of worth . . . should have the rank of a white man, while a vagabond of the same degree of admixture should be confined to the inferior caste." In 1848, Justice John Belton O'Neall upheld Harper's ruling, stating that an individual who had previously been received into society as a white person, and who had exercised all the privileges enjoyed by white people, could be regarded as being white. Since no statute or case law articulated what percentage of black ancestry made someone a "mulatto," and because the state assembly refused to legally define what made a person "black," race was not a fixed property in prewar South Carolina, and color alone did not determine a person's racial designation. The courts thus deemed various people white, black, or mulatto according to the facts of each individual's life, regardless of their actual heritage. Acknowledging that race was socially constructed, South Carolinians often gave themselves great latitude in determining a person's racial status and made decisions on a case-by-case basis, and many persons concluded that "not every admixture of negro blood" made someone a person of color.[29]

This flexibility of racial classification meant I had to resolve another critical issue: deciding which women were "black" for the purposes of my study. Similar to antebellum jurists, I examined the records that exist in reference to each individual woman and then, based on the sources, determined how to categorize a woman. Some women appear in the primary sources only once, making my decision cut and dried, if not necessarily conclusive. For others, multiple documents exist, both easing and complicating the situation. If all known sources classify a woman as white or as a person of color, I do the same. For women labeled in some documents as black and in others as white, I searched for additional information on the person in question in order to more accurately determine her racial status. Where it was not possible to make a definitive decision, I reference the ambiguity in the text or in the accompanying notes.

Readers will notice that all individuals in this project are referred to by their first names in second and subsequent references unless the sources do not provide a first name. I made a conscious decision to do this since archival records make it impossible to use surnames for all the women discussed herein. Antebellum documents almost never include surnames for enslaved persons, or they assign them the surname of their owner, a name that the laborer may not have accepted. The same situation often applies to documents regarding free women of color. For the sake of consistency and equal treatment, then, all persons, whether female or male, black or white, free or enslaved, are referenced by their first names when possible.[30]

Finally, a number of the women discussed in this study had sexual relationships with white men. Some of these interactions were nonconsensual, others were more complicated. There were some situations that were outright cases of rape, and then there were unions that lasted for decades and appear to have been based, at least in part, on affection.[31] As widely as these associations varied in type, so does the language I utilize to describe them, and the women involved in them. I cannot refer to each black woman who had sex with a white man as a rape victim anymore than I can label them all wives.[32] Instead, I evaluated the language on a case-by-case basis and refer to such couplings by a wide range of descriptors, including "affairs," "rapes," "faithful unions," "sexual encounters," "domestic relationships," and "marriages," depending on the available evidence. In the same way, I refer to the women in these situations as "wives," "rape victims," "sexual partners," "lovers," "domestic partners," "mistresses," and so on, when and if additional evidence exists to explicate the relationship. I do this in order to render as accurate an account of interracial sexual interactions as the sources will permit. There are, of course, instances where a lack of evidence makes it impossible to assign a term to a relationship or woman, and a number of unions that simply do not fit neatly into just one of these categories. I acknowledge these situations both in the text and the accompanying notes.

A seventy-year journey through Charleston's past, this project utilizes black women as its historical vehicle, interrogating their lives in order to explore the ways that urban women of color in the Old South imagined and crafted their own definitions of freedom. The first chapter sets the scene for the project by outlining the larger society in which Charleston's women of color lived and examining how the foundations of that culture arose. Including a brief overview of the history of the city from its settlement in the 1670s to the dawn of the new republic, this chapter illuminates how Charleston came to be a city of contrasts and contradictions, where the tension between rhetoric and reality with regards to issues of race and slavery (a tension that existed almost from the moment of the colony's inception) came to underwrite the script of black-white relations in the city during the nineteenth century.

Chapter 2 analyzes the various methods black women utilized to acquire their freedom and illustrates how their tactics overlapped with and diverged from those employed by enslaved men. While some historians have suggested that black women gained their freedom in large part due to the efforts of husbands, fathers, or lovers, this chapter demonstrates that women of color were active participants in securing their own manumission. They petitioned the state assembly, purchased themselves out of slavery, pursued nominal owners, became fugitives, engaged in extralegal trusts, filed affidavits with the courts, and entered into a variety of relationships with people who could aid them in their quest for freedom. Determined to see their families out of bondage, enslaved women succeeded time and again in "making a way out of no way."[33]

Chapter 3 examines the employment situation for Charleston's free black women, contrasting it with that of white women and black men. Lacking the skills needed to obtain certain positions, prohibited by race or gender from engaging in others, burdened by special licensing fees, and shackled to a reliance on a white clientele, a black woman's path to dignified labor and fiscal freedom was strewn with pitfalls. Determined, however, to both survive and thrive, black women turned "domestic" skills they had developed while enslaved into jobs as midwives, seamstresses, confectioners, boardinghouse keepers, and market women. Others engaged in occupations they were legally barred from practicing, including those of artisan, teacher, and land speculator. Working long hours, performing backbreaking labor for low pay, and allying with people who could help them advance their livelihood, some black women built careers that enabled them to attain the financial stability and dignity they felt free labor ought to signify.

Chapter 4 interrogates the connections between wealth, poverty, and rights for Charleston's women of color. Working to acquire their liberty and secure employment, black women came to realize that financial resources could help them fulfill their own definitions of freedom, including avoiding the payment of race-based taxes, attending the church of their choice, and educating their children. They thus strove to amass property, and while black women collectively never owned as much property as black men, both groups realized that social status and economic security in the Old South were tied to the ownership of real property, specifically land and laborers. Free people of color thus pursued the acquisition of these particular commodities. Black women understood that true freedom meant being able to live the way one wanted; that poverty made them vulnerable to sexual and racial harassment; and that property ownership increased their ability to dictate the direction of their lives. Some women thus became landowners, slaveowners, or both in order to bring their imaginings of liberty to fruition.

Chapter 5 reveals how one black woman worked from within the existing power structure to shape a life more closely in line with her own vision of freedom. Born into slavery in 1815, Sarah Sanders was purchased by Richard and Cecille Cogdell in 1830. In 1831, sixteen-year-old Sarah became pregnant with Richard's child. A few months later, Cecille died, and Sarah gave birth to the first of ten children she and Richard would have over the next twenty years. Richard never remarried and he, Sarah, and their children lived together as a family. And while Sarah died illiterate and enslaved, her children enjoyed a middle-class upbringing, including regular schooling and private instruction in piano. Richard even moved his virtually free black children to Philadelphia in the 1850s to ensure their freedom. Determined to secure for her descendants the privileges of liberty that white South Carolinians received at birth, Sarah's astute tactics of negotiation meant her children reaped the rewards of a fuller freedom.

Chapter 6 focuses on unraveling the complex matrix of race, sex, autonomy, and constraint in the lives of three women. The stories of Margaret Bettingall and her daughters reveal that black women often built various alliances with white men in order to gain access to greater rights. These men, however, were both gatekeepers and obstacles to the freedoms these women sought. The Bettingall women thus found that while their ties to certain men helped them improve both their social standing and their wealth, these same men also imposed on them a variety of constraints. Power in the Old South being legally, socially, and economically vested in maleness and whiteness, interracial relationships were rarely, if ever, equal partnerships. Like other black women, Margaret and her daughters came to realize that while their freedom entailed compromising with men in positions of formal authority, their choices lay within a corridor of options already constrained by those same men, who controlled the society in which they lived. What is impressive is how some women were able to work from within this inequitable system and reshape it in order to better fit their own definitions of freedom, equality, and justice.

It may seem extraordinary that black women had any agency in a city committed to upholding the precepts of patriarchal rule and racial slavery. It is telling that Charleston's women of color were able to utilize all the means available to them, within a social order stacked against them, in order to fashion as full a freedom as possible. The reality of their lives indicates that absolute power is as much a myth as absolute freedom, and that it is simplistic to think that white men had all the power in Charleston, and no one else had any. Clearly, the Old South was a continually contested site of power where autonomous spaces existed for women of color. The story, then, is less about the existence of such spaces and more about what black women did within them: how they pushed the boundaries of their lives as far as their abilities enabled them in order to articulate visions of liberty, rights, and citizenship that were uniquely their own.

PART I

GLIMPSING

FREEDOM

CHAPTER 1

CITY OF CONTRASTS

CHARLESTON BEFORE

THE CIVIL WAR

THE ANTEBELLUM CITY

White visitors arriving in Charleston in the mid-nineteenth century found themselves alternately fascinated, shocked, perplexed, and repulsed. As they disembarked onto docks teeming with black men hauling cargo, and pushed their way past dozens of black female vendors like Mary Purvis, selling everything from fresh fruit and oysters to clothing and homemade crafts, they wondered where all the white people were.[1] Somewhat disoriented, but continuing on, newcomers soon found themselves on Meeting Street, one of the city's main thoroughfares. Heading up Meeting, away from the water and toward the center of town, they walked by prostitutes of all colors who worked in the brothels along French Alley, between Meeting and Anson Streets. The women plied their trade at the boardinghouses near the water's edge, residences that were frequented by the sailors who were their steadiest clients.[2]

Hastening past this multiracial, rundown red-light district, tourists gazed around in confusion as they realized that the brothels and boardinghouses lay just steps from the elegant mansions on East Bay, home to the city's white elite. Here they paused to admire the architectural style of the homes, unique to Charleston. Known as "single houses," the dwellings were turned sideways, built to fit the long and narrow lots of the lower city, and situated with the long side facing the water to catch the sea breezes. One room wide and two or more rooms deep, with a false door facing the street front, the long side of a single house was an open porch that ran the full length of the house and overlooked an elaborate garden. Separate slave quarters and outbuildings dotted the yards of these homes, including kitchens, stables, livestock sheds, and outhouses, and each family's "compound" was surrounded by a fence or brick wall. New arrivals may have been shocked to learn that some of these houses were occupied by interracial families. The free black woman Margaret Bettingall, for example,

Map 1.1. Charleston, 1855. (Map by J. H. Colton; Historical Maps of
Alabama Collection, University of Alabama Department of Geography)

lived in this exclusive neighborhood with her longtime husband, wealthy white merchant Adam Tunno; their daughter, Barbara Tunno; and the couple's numerous enslaved laborers.[3]

The sightseers then likely continued their walk up Meeting Street, an attractive thoroughfare lined with South Carolina's trademark palmetto trees, until it intersected with Broad Street. At this point, they could have chosen to investigate Broad Street. Meandering down that famous roadway, newcomers found themselves strolling past the elegant Mansion House Hotel, owned by renowned pastry chef Eliza S. Lee, and the legendary Jones' Hotel, adjacent to aristocratic St. Michael's Episcopal Church.[4] While Eliza Lee and Jehu Jones were both free people of color, each owned substantial real property in the city, attended prestigious white churches, and their hotels, closed to the laboring classes (regardless of race), catered to a celebrity white clientele from around the state, the nation, and the world. Both establishments did brisk business throughout the year, and during Charleston's famous Race Week, they were filled to capacity.[5]

Doubling back to Meeting Street, most visitors continued up towards the center of town. Those who headed in that direction soon found themselves at the city's main intersection, where Meeting Street crossed Calhoun. Here they paused to gawk at Zion Presbyterian Church. Begun as the Anson Street Mission for enslaved persons, the church grew so rapidly that it relocated to the intersection of Calhoun and Meeting Streets, renaming itself in the process. Housed in the largest church building in the city, Zion's congregation numbered more than one thousand persons by 1861. Northern and southern whites alike were shocked at Zion's existence. They understood that St. Michael's and St. Philip's Episcopal Churches were elite white churches under white leadership but that each had some well-to-do, free black congregants. Indeed, many of the city's white churches had black parishioners, both enslaved and free. An independent black church, however, was shocking. How could white Charlestonians permit such a thing to exist after what had happened with the African Church and the Denmark Vesey conspiracy in 1822? How quickly they seemed to have forgotten.[6]

Shaking their heads in bewilderment, many new arrivals walked a short way down Calhoun and then turned onto King Street. The city's central business district, King Street was home to Charleston's most elegant shops. Here, in the heart of the city, free blacks, whites, and enslaved persons rubbed shoulders on their way to and from work; black servants ran errands for their masters; free women and men of color labored at their trades; and the elite shopped for a variety of imported goods with which to decorate their bodies and their homes. Amid such grandeur, however, tourists were puzzled to notice a vile odor. Looking down, they realized that the stately, shop-lined road was thick with a foul-smelling mud that threatened to suck the shoes right off their feet. The high price of imported paving stones meant that as late as 1825, many of Charleston's most fashionable thoroughfares remained unpaved.[7]

Continuing up King Street and heading for the old city line, appropriately named "Boundary Street," the more adventurous tourists crossed into Charleston Neck. Incorporated into the City of Charleston in 1849, the "Neck" had long been the city's low-rent "suburb." Limited job options and meager wages meant that many free blacks, newly arrived white immigrants, enslaved laborers hired out to city masters (but who lived on their own), and temporary white residents all lived in the Neck. There, rude little shacks, back-alley rooms, and window-less garrets offered the only housing many persons could afford. In particular, as poorly paid as most of them were, a number of the city's black workers, like free seamstress of color Sarah Blanch, were forced to live in the Neck. Teeming with flimsy wooden buildings prone to fire, lined with muddy, unpaved streets, and plagued by poor sanitary conditions, the Neck was home to many an unhealthy neighborhood.[8]

Not all the city's free blacks lived in the Neck, however. Unlike northern cities, Charleston did not practice residential segregation as a matter of law, and free blacks had homes on virtually every road in the city. Very few could be found on Meeting Street near the water, in the mansions inhabited by Charleston's leading white families, and many of the blacks who did dwell there were live-in servants. Midway through the city, however, Meeting Street gave way to well-tended brick and wooden homes where artisans and merchants of both races lived. Here, around Coming Street, lay the heart of the city's free black community. In 1861, Coming Street was home to 273 free blacks, more than any other street in the city. Comprising 18 percent of the street's population and occupying 23 percent of its dwellings, Coming Street's residents of color included members of some of the city's most prominent free black families. Jeanette Bonneau, property owner, slaveholder, and widow of free black school-teacher Thomas Bonneau, lived here, as did several individuals from the wealthy Weston and Dereef families. And further up Meeting, near Boundary Street, smaller, yet still respectable, wooden homes were inhabited by white laborers, enslaved persons, and free blacks of more modest means. Among the latter was Martha Evans, a free woman of color and greengrocer who owned a home near Reid Street.[9]

Mixed in throughout these racially diverse neighborhoods were those formed almost exclusively of urban enslaved laborers, enclaves where the lack of a white presence meant that blacks could come and go with more freedom and engage in activities they may have been banned from had they lived with, or near, white persons. If the city's new arrivals walked down Clifford's Alley, which ran west from King Street, between Queen and Clifford; or Grove Street, which lay above the Washington Race Course, almost at the northern boundary of the city; or perhaps Hester Street, just north of Grove, they would have immediately noticed the lack of white faces in these quarters, areas that had become havens for enslaved and poorer free blacks, away from the prying eyes, and control, of whites.[10]

Walking through the city's interracial and all-black working-class districts, sightseers passed a seemingly endless line of groceries and grog shops filled with enslaved laborers, free blacks, and working-class whites, all drinking, playing cards, gambling at dice, and gossiping. Although it was illegal for enslaved or free black persons to gamble, buy alcohol, or enter the premises of an establishment that sold liquor, some such businesses were actually owned by free people of color, including Sophia Cochran and Sarah Blank. Others were run by working-class whites who turned a blind eye to the law. Such open disdain for the master class's municipal directives, as well as the social familiarity across race lines evidenced in these grog shops, made many a visitor shudder.[11]

Newcomers were equally alarmed when the sun went down and they heard the ominous tattoo of drums. Concerned by the danger that black persons posed, white Charlestonians had long ago passed a curfew applicable only to persons of color. In 1822, in the aftermath of the Denmark Vesey affair, the city had also petitioned the state legislature for funds to construct a new municipal arsenal in order to ensure the white population's safety. Temporarily housed on Boundary Street, close to the many black districts in Charleston Neck, in 1842, the city established the South Carolina Military Academy, known as the Citadel, at its permanent, cannon-bedecked location in the heart of the city, at Calhoun and Meeting Streets. Charleston also established a police force to deal with its black population, a force 250 men strong by the 1850s.[12]

In the midst of this martial atmosphere, in a city where whites professed to understand that a well-trained military presence was essential for their survival in a slave society, visitors were likely confused by the number of black persons out and about after curfew had sounded, on their way to and from a variety of parties, balls, and horse races. Apparently, it was almost impossible to enforce the curfew. On the one hand, Charleston Neck, where so many black people lived, did not fall within the city limits until 1849, and it was thus infrequently patrolled by the city's police force until new jurisdictional guidelines were instituted in 1851. Even after 1851, however, blacks continued to walk the streets relatively unmolested at night, particularly in isolated neighborhoods.[13]

By the time recent arrivals reached their destinations, they were often overwhelmed, anxious to discover how it was that a city such as this had evolved: a place where carriages shared the roadways with pigs; where free artisans of color owned numerous shops while working-class whites struggled to find jobs; where prostitutes lived next to aristocrats; where the "master race" found itself awash in a tide of humanity mainly black or brown in color; where the fear of black rebellion was a daily specter, yet enslaved persons worshipped in their own churches and lived without white supervision; and where laws to control black persons were passed and ignored, seemingly in the same breath. Any longtime resident would have told them that to make sense of the contrasts, one needed to understand Charleston's history.

COLONIAL CAROLINA

Located about two-thirds of the way down the South Carolina coastline, Charleston sits on a narrow peninsula of low elevation, tidal land where the Ashley and Cooper Rivers come together to form the city's harbor. Hot, humid, and surrounded by malarial marshes, a frontier settlement was planted in this general area in 1670 by English colonists from Barbados. Funded by the Lords Proprietors (eight men granted a charter by the king of England to settle "Carolina") by 1680, the colonists had moved the seat of Carolina's government to the peninsula of land between the two rivers, where Charleston still rests today. Taking note of the region's rich soil, freshwater marshes, and river floodplains (all excellent for supporting agriculture) as well as the many mosquitoes (which contributed to the epidemics Charleston became infamous for) the settlers established trade relations with local Native Americans, began farming, and eventually asked the king to take over governance of the colony and dismiss the Lords Proprietors. The king thus made South Carolina, as it came to be called, a royal colony in 1719, after which it experienced slow but steady growth. By 1739, the colony's main outpost, "Charles Town," had grown from its original eighty acres to almost 160 acres, and by 1764 it had doubled in size yet again and boasted many new public buildings and private homes.[14]

Charles Town's growth from a tiny provincial village to a rich and vital commercial center was due in large part to its location on a fabulous natural harbor, which almost foreordained its coming prominence in the area of trade, first

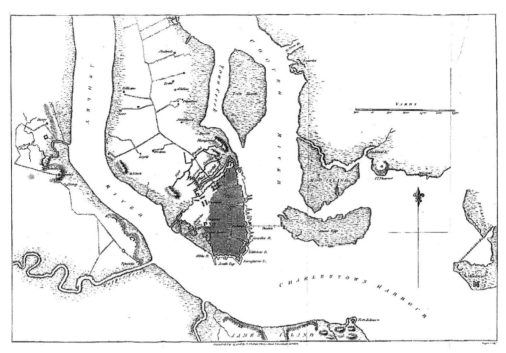

Map 1.2. *Charles Town Peninsular Area, Early 1700s.* (http://www.tourcharleston.com)

within the British Empire and later, after the American Revolution, with other regional centers of the early republic.[15] In fact, by 1742, the city's commerce exceeded that of either Boston or New York: hundreds of trading vessels cleared Charles Town's harbor annually, headed for the northern colonies as well as ports throughout Europe, the Mediterranean, and the Caribbean. Bursting with energy, its economy thriving, Charles Town was by 1776 one of the British mainland's four most important cities, and a trade nexus of the Atlantic economy.[16]

Charlestonians traded in all manner of goods in the late 1600s. European immigrants, particularly those who had come to Carolina via Barbados, hoped to make their fortune by large-scale plantation agriculture. In the early years of the colony's existence, however, they exported deerskins, naval stores, and lumber, although indigo did make for an early export staple. Not until Low Country residents discovered how well rice grew in this marshy region, however, did Charles Town undergo its massive growth spurt. Rice brought with it significant wealth and linked the city to staple crop agriculture, and as rice sales boomed, local merchants invested more of their profits in land, becoming both planters and traders. Indigo and rice, then, drove the economy of the Carolina colony in the early 1700s and made Charles Town a trade center, for as their income from rice grew, the colonists began importing a variety of other products, including wine, rum, and a wide range of English consumer goods.[17]

Concurrent to their investment in land on which to plant more rice, Carolinians poured vast amounts of capital into purchasing human beings to cultivate that crop. Already a major seaport, Charles Town rose to become a mainland center for the importation and distribution of enslaved Africans in the eighteenth century. This is hardly surprising, given that unfree labor was used in the settlement almost from its inception. As early as 1708, white Carolinians, most of whom were already familiar with African slavery from their experiences on Barbados, owned more than four thousand enslaved Africans. Four years prior to this, the colony passed its first comprehensive slave code, laws based almost entirely on those of Barbados. By the 1730s, the colony was importing about twenty thousand African laborers every decade, and the city's reputation as a major slave trading center was entrenched. The Seven Years' War, which began in 1756, only intensified this trend, as worldwide trade problems due to the conflict between England and France led to increased demand for "Carolina Gold," as the colony's rice was called. This meant greater profits, which meant more money invested in land and laborers, which led to the cultivation of more rice, which resulted in more money, and so on. By the 1760s, South Carolinians believed that they were living in a never-ending cycle of increasing prosperity.[18]

Tens of thousands of enslaved Africans continued to pour into South Carolina, and by the early nineteenth century the newly rechristened city of Charleston was second only to Baltimore in the mainland United States in terms of both population and commercial prominence. Rising to early celebrity on a foundation of white rice and black bodies, South Carolina, beginning the shift to cotton agriculture at the turn of the century, continued to engage in the foreign slave trade until 1807, capitalizing on its dealings in African flesh before the federal government abolished the Atlantic slave trade in 1808. Indeed, the colony imported forty thousand Africans between 1803 and 1807. And while most of the laborers brought into Charleston were resold to nearby plantations and Sea Island residents, a number of enslaved persons remained in the city. No other mainland region thus had a black population as large or as densely concentrated as the Low Country of South Carolina, all of which fueled white residents' fears of black uprisings in later years.[19]

It is fair to say, then, that as large-scale agriculture drove South Carolina's economy, the colony's commitment to slavery came to define its politics, social institutions, cultural forms, and everyday forms of intercourse. This was in large part a matter of demographics. Even before the American Revolution, the master class in Charles Town had power far greater than its numbers ought to have merited. In a city where enslaved persons and poor whites together comprised three-quarters of the population, the majority of Charles Town's eleven thousand residents in 1750 (over 60 percent) were people of color, both enslaved and free. And in 1776, the city boasted twelve thousand inhabitants, making it second only to New York City in size, but fully two-thirds of those Charlestonians were propertyless whites and enslaved laborers. A crowded, grimy, and disease-ridden urban center with a black majority, Charles Town, then, was home to nine out of ten of the mainland's wealthiest white persons, but it was also a place of widespread poverty, where 10 percent of the city's occupants owned more than 50 percent of its wealth.[20]

Those who rose to become members of Charles Town's white elite were an eclectic mix of persons. A major port of entry for free white immigrants in the eighteenth century, as well as a throughway for transient sailors, businessmen, and travelers, the city was a magnet for those hoping to make their fortunes in the "New World." Many of the earliest white immigrants were French Huguenots, who comprised one-fifth of the city's population by 1723. A large cohort of Irish nationals also made Carolina their home, enticed by a royal land bounty, as did a significant number of Sephardic Jews. Added to these arrivals were people who hailed from nations as diverse as Holland, Switzerland, Germany, and Scotland, as well as a group of French-speaking, Roman Catholic Acadians from Nova Scotia.[21]

Cashing in on the wealth that rice offered, by 1750, these diverse white peoples had given rise to a small but stunningly wealthy master class wherein a handful of individuals controlled fortunes in the hundreds of thousands of pounds. The men of this stratum flaunted their riches by building elegant mansions on the bay, purchasing carriages imported from Britain, and clothing certain of their enslaved laborers in aristocratic liveries.[22] They also outfitted their wives and daughters in imported fashions of lace and silk and bedecked them in jewels, publicly displaying the women of their families as yet another testament to their power, prestige, and hegemony. Many of these men even commissioned self-portraits, like the European nobility, while those who could afford it behaved like Old World aristocrats, fleeing pestilential Charles Town each summer to travel to the North or Europe. Others, who spent much of the year living on their plantations, owned private homes in town and came there to enjoy the city's famous sea breezes and take pleasure trips across the harbor to Sullivan's Island.[23]

As visitors arrived in the city's harbor in the last two decades before the Revolution, then, one of the first sights to greet their eyes was of these elite white women taking the air from the porticos of their mansions overlooking the waterfront, homes filled with imported mahogany and brass furnishings, mirrors, Turkish carpets, and Chinese accessories. These same ladies presided over the city's social season and were in large part the reason why Charles Town rivaled New York and Boston as a mainland center of society and culture by 1750. Dances and balls galore were to be had from January through March, and the city's elite frolicked in the Church Street Theatre, reputed to be the largest on the continent. Boasting of the many diversions their city offered, including eateries, plays, music recitals, and horse races, the city's wealthiest whites regarded themselves as the exemplars of southern gentility. Indeed, even after Columbia became the state capital in 1786, Charleston remained the social, political, and economic center of the state, as well as a resort for the region's wealthiest planters.[24]

In the midst of such wealth, however, the number of impoverished Charlestonians grew, as did the gap between the city's richest and poorest inhabitants. For example, more than one thousand Acadians entered Charles Town as refugees in 1756, fleeing the turmoil of the Seven Years' War in Canada. Thousands of women widowed by that same conflict also made their way to the city, arriving with numerous children and no money. As the number of orphans swelled, and the amount of desperate widows-turned-prostitutes escalated, the city was deluged by a wave of Irish indigents, all of which combined to stretch the welfare funds of the city's churches beyond their limits. Charles Town's relief rolls thus grew ever larger in the 1760s and 1770s, further revealing the disparity that existed between the locale's tiny, powerful, master class and its large, poor white community.[25]

BLACK CHARLESTONIANS IN THE EIGHTEENTH CENTURY

Charleston's economic dichotomy would only be exacerbated after the Revolution as working-class whites struggled to find jobs in a city where elite whites were used to hiring free black laborers and where enslaved workers could be rented for less money than whites would work for. Angered that the tradition of hiring enslaved persons and patronizing free black artisans undercut the position of white working-class men, few Europeans would immigrate to Charleston in the antebellum era.[26]

The lack of white migration to Charleston in the nineteenth century continued the city's pre-Revolutionary reputation as a place where the majority of the population was both black and poor. Indeed, Charleston's black residents, most of whom were enslaved, outnumbered its white inhabitants from 1790 until 1860 (see Table 1.1). The size of the city's black populace struck every new arrival, and none failed to comment on it. As Fredrika Bremer bluntly noted, "negroes swarm the streets."[27] And while the claim by some white visitors that thirty thousand black persons lived in Charleston was an exaggeration, the number of blacks who dwelled there, particularly free blacks, was significant. About 40 percent of the state's free blacks lived in Charleston in 1850, and on the eve of the Civil War Charleston had the fourth-largest free black population in the nation, behind Baltimore, New Orleans, and Washington, DC.[28] Additionally, Charleston was not only a city of poor and black persons but also a city of women: from 1820 onward, women, black and white, enslaved and free, comprised more than half of the city's inhabitants (see Table 1.2).[29]

Given the numbers, it is not surprising that slavery was a distinctive determinant in the lives of all Charlestonians. The outlines of urban slavery itself also played a role in shaping the attitude of white Charlestonians toward persons of color. As I mentioned above, many of the enslaved laborers brought to South Carolina in the 1700s remained in Charles Town, and they experienced a different kind of enslavement than those who worked on isolated plantations. Living in a bustling seaport where they could regularly interact with persons from around the world, and residing in close proximity to free blacks, working-class whites, and a multitude of other enslaved persons, bondspersons in the city were in a unique position to develop attitudes and engage in activities antithetical to slavery. Quick to seize every opportunity to enlarge their freedoms, urban enslaved laborers were able to acquire more independence than those who labored on plantations in the Upcountry.[30]

Certainly urban slavery was, first and foremost, about labor. Charles Town, however, had a more diverse occupational structure than did rural areas of South Carolina, and the jobs available to the city's enslaved women in the mid- to late eighteenth century included skilled positions such as seamstress, nurse, and pastry chef.[31] Black men worked in the city's rice mills and other manufacturing enterprises, while enslaved persons of both sexes were utilized as unskilled laborers. For black women this meant toiling as domestic servants, street vendors, and washerwomen, while black men, due to the city's location, engaged in maritime occupations like dockworker, boat pilot, and ship hand. Additionally, it was common for slaveowners who lived near Charles Town to apprentice their chattel to the urban center's skilled craftsmen: masons, blacksmiths, carpenters, and the like. Some of these trained bondspersons later opened their own shops, to the benefit of their owners, or their masters hired them out on an annual basis to free black and white artisans in the city who were both extremely busy and short on workers.[32]

TABLE 1.1. City Population by Condition and Race, 1790–1860

Condition and Race	1790	1800	1810	1820	1830	1840	1850	1860
Enslaved persons	7,684	9,819	11,671	12,652	15,354	14,673	19,532	13,909
Free blacks	586	1,024	1,472	1,475	2,107	1,558	3,441	3,237
Total blacks	8,270	10,843	13,143	14,127	17,461	16,231	22,973	17,146
White persons	8,089	9,630	11,568	11,229	12,828	13,030	20,012	23,374
Total population	16,359	20,473	24,711	25,356	30,289	29,261	42,985	40,520
% blacks	51	53	53	56	58	55	53	42

Source: U.S. Bureau of the Census, A Century of Population Growth.

Note: Charleston Neck's incorporation into the city in 1849 accounts for the dramatic population increase between 1840 and 1850. Also, while Charleston may have been the nation's fifth largest city in 1820, the city's population was static from 1820 to 1840 (Pease and Pease, Ladies, Women, and Wenches, 4). Given that the data for 1850 includes the residents of Charleston Neck, the population continued to stagnate after 1840 and actually decreased in 1860. This decline was due in part to the southwestern spread of cotton into the former Louisiana Territory, which drew many residents of the Eastern Seaboard South west to seek their fortunes (Powers, Black Charlestonians, 2).

This "hiring out" process, although lucrative, became controversial. Many enslaved persons began to procure their own work contracts and negotiate their hours, wages, and accommodations directly with potential employers, choosing to work for whoever provided them with the best deal. Most of these bondspersons also lived on their own and behaved, for the most part, as if they were free persons of color. In return for their increased autonomy, they sent a predetermined portion of their monthly wages back to their owners, most of whom lived in the countryside. Over time, a fair number of these urban slaves were able to save up enough money to purchase their freedom. Interestingly enough, the law stated that only slaveowners could legally hire out their workers. This law, however, was regularly violated as Charles Town's labor-hungry business owners chose to contract directly with enslaved persons, desperate to acquire as many skilled workers as they could find.[33]

In addition to the job training that many enslaved persons received in Charles Town, the city itself provided black persons with a diverse learning environment. This included opportunities to learn to read and write from friendly neighbors and employers, as well as in local churches and underground schools. Many of these eighteenth-century schools were run, as they would be in the antebellum era, by free black women.[34] Black residents of the city also had the opportunity to socialize with other persons of color, both free and enslaved, as well as whites of all classes. When the workday was over, black laborers might attend church or go to public rallies and lectures, and they had access to newspapers,

TABLE 1.2. Women as Percentage of City Population, 1820–1860

Type of Women	1820	1830	1840	1850	1860
Enslaved women	6,957	8,577	8,339	10,901	7,346
% of population	27.4	28.3	28.5	25.4	18.1
White women	5,330	6,502	6,203	9,774	11,662
% of population	21	21.5	21.2	22.7	28
Free black women	852	1,293	975	2,086	1,990
% of population	3.4	4.3	3.3	4.9	4.9
Total women	13,139	16,372	15,517	22,761	20,998
Total population	25,356	30,289	29,261	42,985	40,520
% women	51.8	54.1	53	53	51.8

Source: U.S. Bureau of the Census, *A Century of Population Growth*.

Note: 1820 was the first year that the federal census differentiated black persons by sex.

all of which helped keep them informed about what was happening in the world around them.[35]

Living in a city with a black majority, surrounded by black workers who were becoming increasingly well dressed, literate, skilled, and well informed, white Charlestonians worried that the city's blacks were forgetting "their place." In particular, they feared that they were losing control of an increasingly independent enslaved community. Then, in the late 1730s, three incidents ratcheted up the already mounting racial tensions. One was the now famous Stono slave rebellion of 1739, in which a number of white and black persons lost their lives. In 1740, the rumor of a conspiracy to organize a slave rebellion in Goose Creek Parish heightened white Carolinians' fears. It is no surprise that later that same year, the state legislature passed the "Act for the Better Ordering and Governing of Negroes and Other Slaves in This Province." This slave code would remain in effect with few modifications until the Civil War. Finally, in 1741, six months after the alleged conspiracy in Goose Creek, Charles Town suffered a fire that destroyed more than three hundred buildings as well as several wharves and untold quantities of trade goods. There was no evidence that enslaved persons were involved, yet white Charlestonians immediately assumed it was "slave arson," already believing that they were surrounded by enemies. At the same time, the fire provided some enslaved women with the chance to better their position: the woman Phillis, for example, was manumitted and given a modest inheritance because she saved her master's home from being destroyed by the fire.[36]

While they fretted about the perils of living surrounded by a sea of potential insurrectionaries, South Carolinians continued to import enslaved Africans into their state, to the tune of three thousand to four thousand persons a year. That number jumped to ten thousand a year by the 1770s, most of whom were women. Indeed, on the eve of the Revolution, Charles Town's enslaved women outnumbered their male counterparts twelve to one. An economic force in the city as the purveyors of critical foodstuffs, enslaved women's impact on the food supply unnerved white residents, who complained that these "disorderly" women continually raised the prices of almost every staple and were "insolent" to their customers to boot. Selling only to whom, and for how much they desired, some enslaved market women not only held their customers over a barrel but also used their industry to acquire enough money to purchase their freedom.[37] Black women, enslaved and free, would continue to dominate the ranks of Charleston's street vendors in the nineteenth century, leading city councilmen to pass numerous licensing regulations that attempted to restrict or eliminate black women's influence in this sector of the economy.[38]

Clearly, urban enslaved laborers enjoyed advantages their rural kin could not due to the practice of "slave hiring," independent living arrangements, and the intellectual, social, and recreational opportunities that a metropolitan environment afforded. These opportunities also allowed some enslaved workers to become free persons, and while most of Charles Town's free blacks were impoverished and not much better off than their enslaved counterparts, a small, propertied class of free blacks did emerge in these early years. Numbering only 4 percent of the city's free blacks in 1790, women nonetheless dominated this early group of "elite" free blacks as early as the 1750s. Hard-working artisans and tradespersons who lived above their own shops, some of these women were able to purchase real estate in the 1760s, positioning their families to play a prominent role in antebellum Charleston's larger free black community. Their descendants, who carried last names like Bonneau, Mishaw, Johnson, Weston, Holloway, and Dereef, would join with other blacks to become the standard-bearers of the city's antebellum free colored "aristocracy," a working nobility of skilled craftspeople who sported calluses on their hands but who managed to receive entry into the city's leading white Episcopal churches.[39]

CONCLUSION

Evidence reveals that the elements that made Charleston a city of contrasts in the mid-nineteenth century were already in place before 1790; indeed, they were in place well before the dawning of the Revolutionary era. Staggering wealth stood next to appalling poverty; silk-clad ladies of leisure walked alongside raggedly outfitted prostitutes; mansions grew up next to brothels; angry, working-class whites waged war on skilled black artisans; whites committed themselves to slavery and a race-based hierarchy yet gave enslaved persons the tools with which to live independent lives and acquire their legal freedom; and Carolinians refused to reduce the numbers of enslaved Africans they brought to their shores, desperate to make as much money as greed could envision, all while bemoaning the dangers of living in the midst of a black majority that might rise up and annihilate them where they stood.

Dependent on the labor of blacks persons but uncomfortable at that reliance; snubbing white laborers while professing the common cause of all white men against those who were not white; training and manumitting their favored servants and biracial kin while decrying the deleterious effects that miscegenation and a growing population of "uppity" free blacks had on those who were still enslaved; really, doing with the right hand what the left hand feared and despised, wealthy white Charlestonians created a tension between rhetoric and reality that came to underwrite the script of black-white relations in antebellum Charleston. As the city struggled to retain its colonial prominence in a new century littered with wars, embargoes, national panics, and bank failures, and its residents tried to compete with the rise of steamboats, canals, and railroads in the North and West, this tension revealed itself in almost every interaction that white Charlestonians had with enslaved and free women of color in the years after the American Revolution.

PART II

BUILDING

FREEDOM

CHAPTER 2

A WAY OUT OF NO WAY

BLACK WOMEN AND

MANUMISSION

In 1814, Sophia Mauncaut, a resident of Charleston, was accused by authorities of being an illegally freed black woman. With the threat of reenslavement hanging over her head, Sophia escaped the auction block by acquiring affidavits from four white Charlestonians, all of whom vouched that she was legally free. Philippe Barreyre, a local merchant, swore that Sophia came to Charleston in 1804 with her mistress, Josephine Catreuille, recently deceased. Joseph Dupont stated that he had known Josephine well and had advised her, when her financial situation was bleak, to sell Sophia. Josephine, however, informed Joseph that Sophia and her children were free people. According to Elias Pohl, Josephine had freed Sophia in Saint-Domingue but filed papers again in Charleston to ensure the woman's freedom. Elias claimed to have signed these new manumission papers in 1804, a story verified by Josephine's aunt, who had been present at this second manumission. Sophia Mauncaut thus avoided being resold into slavery, and secured the freedom of her daughters and their children, by acquiring the sworn statements of four reputable white persons who verified and validated her claim to freedom.[1]

This glimpse into Sophia's life highlights the central question of this chapter: How did Charleston's enslaved women make the transition to freedom prior to 1861, living as they did in a city whose white residents were dedicated to the continuation of racial slavery? Their very existence would seem to be an anomaly in a society that proclaimed persons of African descent were inherently inferior to whites, that black persons not under the control of some white person were a threat to peace and stability, and that black equaled enslaved. Despite these convictions, however, and the increasingly hostile attitudes that white Carolinians displayed toward free blacks as the century progressed, the number of free women of color in Charleston grew in size. Who, then, were these women? When did they arrive in the city, and from where did they come? By what means were they able to acquire their freedom? Which women were most likely to be manumitted, and why? What set free women apart from those who remained enslaved?

Enslaved women were divided by differences in age, color, occupational skill, and relational status as often as they were united by legal condition, race, and sex. As a result, they traveled a variety of roads to freedom. Despite their divergent personal situations however, black women did share certain common manumission experiences. First, they were actively engaged in determining their own fate. Hardly bystanders on the journey to freedom, women of color were as involved in working to emancipate themselves and their families as they were in their daily resistance to enslavement.[2] Records indicate that they purchased themselves and their kin out of slavery, became fugitives, "stole" their relations out of bondage, filed affidavits with the courts, drafted wills, engaged in extralegal trusts, pursued nominal owners, and built a variety of alliances with persons who could aid them in their quest for liberty.

Additionally, black women discovered that their sex hindered their ability to travel certain routes to manumission while providing them with other avenues to freedom to which enslaved men had little or no access. Thus, while some of their tactics for acquiring liberty, such as performing acts of heroism, overlapped with those employed by black men, fewer women than men were able to buy themselves out of bondage due to their limited job opportunities and the low wages that black women commanded in the labor market. At the same time, a number of women were able to access emancipation by establishing sexual alliances with white men, a method largely unavailable to black men. Analyzing the options available to them, and understanding the limits and opportunities that female gender provided them in the society in which they lived, black women did the best they could with the tools they had in order to find a way out of slavery.

Finally, enslaved women utilized the state's legal system, created to uphold slavery and protect the rights of white slaveholders, to sue for and retain their manumission, finding creative ways to reshape an unjust justice system so that it favored the rights of black people and black freedom. Like enslaved women in other cities, they found ways to make the law an autonomous force in the contravention of slavery and, in doing so, illuminated the tension between the law and freedom.[3] Using the legal system to acquire and safeguard their liberty, a system designed to keep them in bondage and reenslave them whenever possible, enslaved women proved time and again that they would do everything they could to make a way out of slavery and into freedom.

While this examination of black women begins in 1790, South Carolina's free blacks did not just "spring from the ground" that year.[4] The ways in which enslaved Carolinians acquired their freedom prior to this are difficult to trace, however: many eighteenth-century manumissions went unrecorded as owners and laborers alike believed it was unnecessary to formalize such deeds. According to Robert Olwell, those most likely to be freed before 1776 were women and light-skinned children, while adult black men were the least likely. He thus concludes that in colonial South Carolina, as in Louisiana, sexual or kinship relationships led to freedom for many persons. Sources from this early period also indicate that enslaved women in both South Carolina and Louisiana were set free for performing services of unusual merit, such as nursing their owner through a severe illness. Most of the women freed in such cases were manumitted by last will and testament after their owners had passed away.[5]

Other patterns emerged in the colonial era. Olwell maintains that while some servants purchased their freedom in these early years, more adult black men obtained their liberty this way than any other group in South Carolina. Additionally, although both black and white slaveowners allowed their laborers to buy their freedom, black masters apparently asked for less money, and enslaved persons sometimes used friendly whites or free blacks as intermediaries in their quest for freedom.[6] Not always trusting their masters to abide by their contracts, those in bondage would, at times, instead of buying themselves directly, ask someone else to purchase them using the enslaved person's money. Once the sale was finalized, the new "owner" would free the enslaved person and record a deed of emancipation for them. Olwell also discovered that after gaining their own freedom, many people toiled to buy and manumit their loved ones. Black women made it a particular habit to purchase and free their daughters, indicating their clear understanding that slavery and freedom were transmitted through black women's bodies.[7]

POSTWAR PATHWAYS

In comparing Olwell's conclusions to the years following the American Revolution, there appear to have been few immediate changes. Public records reveal an increase in the number of manumissions recorded in South Carolina between 1775 and 1790, suggesting that some slaveowners, like those in Maryland, freed their servants after being stricken by the Revolution's emphasis on the ideals of liberty and equality.[8] Carolina's women continued to find their way

TABLE 2.1. Free Black Population in Four Cities, 1810

City	Free Blacks	Total Population of City	Free Blacks as % of City Population
Baltimore	5,671	46,555	12%
Charleston	1,472	24,711	6%
New Orleans	4,950	17,242	29%
Savannah	578	5,215	11%

Source: U.S. Bureau of the Census, *Negro Population of the United States, 1790–1915.*

out of slavery after 1790, however, and in ways that, in the beginning, followed colonial patterns. Many masters did not register formal deeds of manumission for those they freed, and servants often did not receive a certificate of freedom on being released from bondage. Evidence of a master's intention to emancipate was usually enough to establish a person's freedom, and deliberate action, whether written or verbal, was all that was required to set someone free.[9]

Under such conditions, the growth of Charleston's free black population is not surprising. Only 586 strong in 1790, the city's free black community reached 1,024 ten years later, and climbed to 1,472 by 1810. And while Charleston's free population of color in 1810 was thus larger than that of Savannah, Georgia, which numbered 578 that year, it was far smaller than those of either Baltimore or New Orleans, which in 1810 numbered 5,671 and 4,950, respectively. Indeed, an examination of the overall population counts of all four cities reveals that Charleston had the smallest proportion of free black residents (see Table 2.1).[10]

The growth of Charleston's free population of color between 1790 and 1810 was still significant, however. One of the factors contributing to this expansion was natural increase. "Affidavits of Freedom," like those filed by Sophia Mauncaut (whose story begins this chapter), indicate that a number of black women who lived in Charleston prior to 1790 had children after they were manumitted.[11] Catharine, for example, was a "young mulatto woman" whose affidavit stated that she had been born free because her mother, a "mulatto woman" named Celia, had been manumitted by her owner, one James Guilland, in 1784, a few years before Catharine's birth. Sally Ford had a similar story. Born free in 1797, Sally stated that she was the daughter of a woman named Eliza, and that Eliza had earned her freedom in 1789.[12]

In addition to natural increase, migration played a significant role in the early growth of Charleston's black female population: free women of color came to Charleston from rural areas of South Carolina, other states, and foreign countries.[13] It was logical for black women from the countryside to come to Charleston, if only to find work. Jobs were scarce in rural areas: in many cases, field labor was the only option for recently freed plantation women. There was, however, more employment for women of color in urban areas, and a wider array of jobs, from fruit vendor to baker, seamstress to washerwoman.[14] This likely explains why forty-seven-year-old Becky Jackson took her eight children, left Cheraw, South Carolina, and moved to Charleston, where she worked as a washerwoman and rented a house on Alexander Street. One can also assume that she and other rural women went to Charleston, as they did to other cities, to gain access to churches, schools, and social activities, and to take advantage of the protections and opportunities available in a larger black community: in short, like black women after the Civil War, they moved to " 'joy their freedom."[15]

Prior to 1820, black women also migrated to Charleston from other states, particularly Georgia and Virginia. South Carolina did not outlaw owner-initiated manumission until 1820, while Georgians made freedom a legislative act in 1801, and the Virginia legislature passed two new laws in 1805. The first made it illegal for free black Virginians to carry guns; the second mandated that all newly freed black persons leave the state within one year . . . or be resold into slavery. The new laws reflected the impact that the slave rebellion in Saint-Domingue had had on the psyche of American slaveholders. Terrified that the "disease of rebellion" might spread across the water and infect the mainland, and attributing Saint-Domingue's rebellion to the island's free people of color, who had supposedly encouraged the colony's bondspersons to revolt, white Georgians and Virginians worked to reduce the numbers of potentially insurrectionary free blacks among them. This included attempts to prevent free blacks from the Caribbean from continuing to migrate to Petersburg and Savannah, where they were supposedly having "unsettling and detrimental" effects on the local enslaved and free black populations.[16]

These new policies in Virginia and Georgia, coupled with the greater economic opportunities that urban centers afforded to free blacks, led some women of color to head for cities like Baltimore.[17] Although Maryland's slaveholders saw free blacks as an incitement to "slave disorder" and made their elimination a priority by passing legislation that restricted manumission and mandating that newly freed persons leave the state, free blacks grew faster than any other segment of Maryland's population during the nineteenth century. The largest increase was in northern Maryland, around the city of Baltimore, where occupational and social opportunities drew in fugitives and free blacks alike, as did the fact that runaways could easily blend into the city's large free black community and escape detection by their owners.[18]

While some women headed north, another group chose to travel south, to Charleston. A native of Virginia, forty-year-old Chasey Travois evidently believed that South Carolina would be a good place to raise her family. Upon being manumitted, Chasey took her three children, left Virginia as state law required, and made Charleston her new home, as did Mary Allison. Born free in Virginia in 1798 to a white woman named Lydia, Mary likely found her economic and social opportunities to be greater in Charleston. Known for its diverse population and larger numbers of lighter-skinned free blacks, Charleston may have been a more comfortable environment for this free black daughter of a white woman than rural Virginia, with its strictures against interracial sex and predominantly dark-skinned free black population.[19]

CARIBBEAN CONNECTIONS

Clearly, not all of Charleston's free black women were native South Carolinians. Some were not even American-born, having come from Saint-Domingue after that island's 1791 slave rebellion ended with the removal of the colony's white slaveowners from power. Refugees from Saint-Domingue could be found throughout the eastern seaboard, but urban centers received the majority of the new arrivals, particularly port cities in slave states with thriving economies and well-established free black populations. Savannah, for example, saw a steady stream of black persons arrive from the Caribbean beginning in 1800. As a result, the city became home to Georgia's largest free black population by 1810.[20] Baltimore also received a number of black persons from Saint-Domingue, mainly enslaved runaways. The small number of free West Indian blacks who settled in that city quickly learned that, rich or poor, their freedom did not entitle them to the middle-class status in their new home that they had held on the island.[21] The bulk of Saint-Domingue's black refugees, however, ended up in New Orleans. Numbering more than thirteen hundred individuals, these new persons of color accounted for 90 percent of the increase in New Orleans's black population between 1791 and 1804. New Orleans received another influx of persons of color from Saint-Domingue in 1809, after that group's exodus from Cuba.[22]

Although Charleston never received as many black refugees from Saint-Domingue as New Orleans, their arrival worried white Carolinians nonetheless. The city's free black population almost tripled between 1790 and 1810, and white Charlestonians, like their peers in Virginia and Georgia, raised significant opposition to their new, often foreign-born, neighbors. In 1793, they sent petitions to the state assembly demanding the expulsion of all free blacks from Saint-Domingue now living in South Carolina. The legislature responded by prohibiting any further immigration from the Caribbean, but it refused to expel those blacks already in state. Believing that Saint-Domingue's rebellion was caused by traitorous free people of color, Charleston's white residents were appalled by the ruling. They gazed askance at the municipality's newly enlarged free black community, which now contained hundreds of black West Indians who could potentially bring down the city from within.[23]

Despite their fears, some of the city's newest residents posed no threat to those in power. Light-skinned and French-speaking, Marie and Joseph Langlois came from families that had been free before the Haitian Revolution and had occupied a middle caste in Saint-Domingue's social structure: below whites, but above those who remained enslaved. This was a position they tried to maintain in their new home. Joseph belonged to Charleston's premier mutual-aid society for men of color, the Brown Fellowship Society (BFS), open only to free "brown" men in artisan trades, and the couple owned black laborers. Émigrés like Mary and Joseph, then, like the family of prosperous Savannah pastry cook and businesswoman Aspasia Cruvellier Mirault, left Saint-Domingue *because* of the slave rebellion. Seeking to escape the civil strife then engulfing the island, these "free mulattoes" elected to leave a home now controlled by those who had once been enslaved and sought refuge in the slaveholding regions of the United States. They were thus rather unlikely to become threats to Charleston's ruling white elite.[24]

Of course, not all the black women who came to Charleston from Saint-Domingue were from this intermediate caste. Many were newly manumitted and had been freed as a reward for their loyalty to their owners during the revolution. This was Véronique's story. She earned her freedom in 1798 upon leaving Port-au-Prince, "in consideration of her faithful service . . . for never abandoning me during the revolution." Her owner, Gérard de Lacombe, executed a deed of manumission for Véronique in Saint-Domingue, but the papers were lost during the war. Gérard thus declared Véronique's freedom anew in Charleston in 1811 to ensure she would not be reenslaved. Similar concerns led Marie Yeuve to reissue manumission papers for Janette and her daughter, Louise Agathe: the originals, executed in Saint-Domingue, had been destroyed. It is difficult to know exactly why these women remained with their owners in the midst of the island's black uprising. It is possible that Véronique and Janette were truly attached to their owners. It is more likely, however, that they sized up the situation, decided the rebellion was unlikely to succeed, and concluded that their best bet for escaping the violence of the war and their enslavement was to remain "faithful" to their masters for just a little while longer.[25]

Some enslaved women from Saint-Domingue thus obtained their freedom before ever leaving the island; others labored in the United States for years before being manumitted. This was the case with Cyprienne, Cornélie, and Zémire, all of whom traveled to Charleston with their mistress, Marie Bois. While they served her "faithfully" in both the Caribbean and the United States, they had to wait until Marie died in 1812 before being freed under the terms of her will. The woman Cité was luckier. Originally from Saint-Domingue, Marie Le Prévost executed a deed of manumission for Cité in 1797. According to the deed, Cité, "une Négresse créole natif," gained her freedom due to "les grands et importants services" she had already performed for Marie. It is likely that these "important services" led to Cité's being manumitted within five years of her arrival in the United States, versus the twenty-year wait of Cyprienne and her sisters.[26]

A final group of women from Saint-Domingue appear to have been manumitted due to having conjugal or kinship relations with their owners. The wills of several white men originally from the island hint at these bonds: it is reasonable to assume that when an enslaved woman, her children, or both were set free by their male owner and left a substantial inheritance, a familial connection existed between the parties involved.[27] That Lucie and her son Baptist acquired their freedom and a significant amount of property from their owner thus suggests that Baptist was the son of the master. In the same way we can deduce that Adelaide was not just another field hand to Antoine Plumet. Upon his death, Antoine freed Adelaide and left her $1,200 and all the merchandise in his home, including his "silver plate, jewels, linens, and household furniture."[28]

If you contrast Lucie and Adelaide's manumissions to those in which enslaved women from Saint-Domingue received nothing but their freedom, it is easy to understand why some Caribbean women had an easier transition to freedom than did others. Most of the newly freed women who came from Saint-Domingue arrived as impoverished refugees and likely spoke little English. Additionally, many, including Mary Messive, had children to support: any financial assistance would have been of tremendous benefit to these women and made their segue to freedom less difficult. Of course, it is possible that the reason most of the slaveowners from Saint-Domingue did not bequeath any material goods to their former laborers was because they had nothing to leave them. Having fled the island in the midst of a civil uprising, these men and women may have had nothing but manumission to offer their former bondspersons.[29]

The influx of free blacks from Saint-Domingue, along with the steady rate of local manumissions and domestic migration, meant that Charleston's free black population increased rapidly after 1793, as did the worry of the city's ruling classes. Nervous about the addition of numerous Caribbean blacks to their populace, any one of whom could be a potential insurrectionary, white Charlestonians were equally troubled that a number of local slaveowners were taking advantage of the state's liberal manumission policies by freeing their aged and infirm laborers and dumping them in the city, where they had no savings or skills to fall back on. Municipal leaders thus grew increasingly agitated about the public cost of maintaining a growing number of free blacks who were elderly, decrepit, or both. Such anxieties had led Maryland to pass legislation in 1796 making it illegal to manumit persons who were infirm or elderly.[30]

In 1800, the South Carolina legislature followed Maryland's example and regulated manumission procedures for the first time. While no upper age limit was set on emancipations, individuals who wanted to free a laborer now had to appear before their local court of magistrates and freeholders. The court would not only interrogate the slaveowner but also question the enslaved person about his or her character and ability to make a living if freed. Were these people, in essence, *morally worthy* of freedom . . . and unlikely to become a financial burden on the public? If the court found the enslaved man or woman fit for freedom, it issued emancipation papers to the owner. The owner, in turn, was to give his or her former bondsperson a copy of the court's certificate, along with a formal deed of manumission. Both documents had to be recorded with the clerk of court in the district where the slaveowner lived. If any step in the process was omitted, the manumission became null and void.[31]

While the new process was cumbersome, manumissions were not overly hampered by the Act of 1800. Never intended to curtail all emancipations, it was hoped that the law would help prevent the freeing of persons who might become public charity cases. The law did, however, make it more difficult to liberate children, since their age meant they would be unable to support themselves. Some masters circumvented this hurdle by pledging to provide financial assistance to a child until they reached adulthood. Others apprenticed enslaved children to skilled artisans, stipulating that the child would be freed upon reaching the age of majority. This way, she or he would have a marketable skill when released from bondage. This is why Hagar was apprenticed to a seamstress at the age of six: when she turned sixteen, her training ended with her freedom. Hagar then had to provide for herself, but she was also in a position to find work in Charleston's garment trade, staffed largely by free women of color.[32]

South Carolina thus became something of a haven for free blacks prior to 1820. Although restrictive manumission laws cropped up in Georgia, South Carolina asked only that prospective free blacks provide evidence that they would not become a financial burden to the state. And while Virginians believed that "a man has almost as much right to set fire to his own building, though his neighbor's is to be destroyed by it, as to free his slaves," Charlestonians regularly looked the other way when minors and those without skills were freed in violation of the Act of 1800.[33] Even Louisiana instituted more restrictive manumission procedures in the early 1800s. After 1803, Louisiana outlawed the emancipation of any laborer less than thirty years in age, except in cases where the person had performed an act of extreme heroism. This negatively impacted the domestic growth of the free black population in New Orleans, although the influx of free blacks from other states and nations increased the number of free blacks in the Crescent City. In 1807, another law mandated that enslaved persons provide evidence of good conduct in order to secure their freedom (meaning they could never have engaged in criminal acts or run away), while the immigration of free blacks into Louisiana was prohibited and made punishable by fines and temporary sale into servitude. Compared to such measures, South Carolina's new law, the administration of which was left to local courts dominated by slaveowners loathe to strip other slaveowners of their rights (including the right to manumit their property), was mild. Black Carolinians thus continued to receive their freedom in large numbers after 1800.[34]

One thing that did change after 1800 was that more of the persons manumitted in Charleston were documented as being skilled laborers. This would have been prompted in large part by the new law, which required enslaved persons to prove that they could support themselves once free. And while the new requirements may have prevented some women from being emancipated (since enslaved men had more opportunities to learn a skilled trade than did enslaved women) the "Charleston County Index to Manumissions" indicates that women continued to dominate the ranks of the newly manumitted. The index lists the names of 245 men and women in Charleston County whose deeds of manumission were recorded between 1801 and 1820. Of those deeds, 151, or 62 percent, of the names are female.[35]

Evidently some enslaved female Charlestonians, then, exited slavery armed with the skills needed to find work as free people. Others took their talents and hired themselves out for wages while still enslaved, with or without the permission of their owners. Setting aside what they could, they approached their masters once they had acquired a sizeable sum and attempted to purchase their freedom. This was common practice in urban areas throughout the Old South. Enslaved persons in metropolitan areas had more opportunities to work for wages than those who labored in rural regions, and they were also more likely to have a skill to sell, which explains why most enslaved persons who bought their freedom lived in or near a city center.[36]

What did differ from city to city was the frequency of self-purchases. In Baltimore, the large number of owner-initiated manumissions meant that fewer people had to buy themselves out of slavery than in Charleston. Additionally, the prevalence of "term slavery" led more enslaved Baltimoreans to simply wait until their terms had expired to acquire their freedom.[37] In New Orleans, however, larger numbers of enslaved persons purchased their liberty than in Charleston. Spanish law allowed enslaved persons to approach their owners, negotiate a sale price, and then accumulate the funds by selling their extra labor. The legal code even stated that masters had to set a fair purchase price and that if they did not, their servants could petition the courts for help. Under U.S. rule, enslaved persons continued to have the right to contract with their owners to purchase their freedom. Masters, however, could now choose whether or not to permit their laborers to work for wages and could not be forced to enter into freedom contracts. Once they had given their permission, however, masters had to uphold a self-purchase agreement. Under both systems, significant numbers of women in New Orleans earned their freedom.[38]

For those female Charlestonians who were able to contract with their owners to acquire their freedom, how much they paid depended in large part on the relationship they had with their owners: an amicable relationship could result in a low price. Phillis Gunter, for example, turned over 120 pounds sterling ($546) to Frantz Jacob Foltz in order to buy herself and her "mulatto male child James" out of bondage. Contrast that with the good fortune of Lydia, who bought her freedom and that of her two daughters for five shillings (about $1) at a time when black girls sold for two hundred pounds (roughly $826) each. One wonders if Lydia's owner was the father of her children, which might explain his generosity.[39]

Most inexpensive self-purchases took place before 1800: manumission deeds reveal that only one woman was able to negotiate her freedom for a token sum after that year.[40] It is possible that the rhetoric of liberty that permeated the nation during the Revolutionary era led some slaveowners to free their laborers for minimal compensation prior to 1800. Whatever the cause, the fact remains that most women who paid for their freedom after 1800 labored for years to save the amounts required of them. Consider the situation of Nanny, who contracted with her owner, Barsheba Cattle, to buy herself out of bondage. We do not know how long it took Nanny to save the $550 demanded of her, or how many years Sally worked to save the ninety pounds (about $410) Jonathan McDowell charged her for her freedom. When we consider black women's low earning power, however, and the limited number of job options available to them, we can be sure that the money, "earnings and gains arising from her own labor and industry," represented years of sacrifice on Sally's part.[41]

Such struggles were not limited to women owned by white masters. Nanny's mistress, Barsheba, was a black woman, and Mira was the property of a black man named Dick Wragg. When Dick died in 1800, Mira, under the terms of his will, was permitted to sell her labor for wages. If she paid Dick's estate seventy-two pounds (close to $328) within six months of his death, Mira was to be freed. If she did not pay the full amount within the time allotted, however, she was to be sold. Estate papers indicate that Mira did hire herself out, but according to Dick's executor, "Mira had six months to buy her freedom and more than that amount of time has passed without her paying anything to the estate." Indeed, while Mira had been earning wages since Dick's death, she did not "seem disposed to pay any part of the same so your petitioner asks for permission to sell the wench Mira." Perhaps Mira was unaware of the terms of the will, and these were the tactics of an unscrupulous executor who hoped to sell Mira for more than seventy-two pounds. It is also plausible, given the low wages black women earned, that Mira had no money to give the estate after paying her monthly expenses. It is equally likely that Mira, now living on her own and able to command wages for her work, attempted to assert some control over the fruits of her labor and deliberately withheld her earnings, desiring to keep both the cash and her freedom. Certainly this is what the wording of the executor's petition suggests. The court, however, looked askance at a black woman taking charge of her life in this fashion and ordered Mira sold at auction in March 1801. Her fate is unknown.[42]

Despite the numerous financial, social, and legal obstacles that women like Mira faced, Charleston's enslaved women continued to find ways to escape from slavery. Willing to make almost any sacrifice to remove themselves and their loved ones from bondage, they, like black women in other states, labored long and hard to obtain their freedom.[43] The woman Betty, for example, was manumitted by her master, but her three sons remained enslaved. In 1818, however, Betty purchased the boys from Thomas Smith for $400. Acquiring the freedom of her children clearly mattered to Betty, as it did to the woman Betty Hambleton, who sought to free her daughter and grandchildren. While her daughter died enslaved, this Betty was able to buy and manumit her granddaughter, Betsey Grimes.[44]

Committed to bringing freedom to all their kin, black women in the nineteenth century, like their colonial foremothers, made a special habit of buying and manumitting their daughters, thus ending the generational legacy of bondage passed on through the black female line.[45] This explains why Polly labored for twenty-four years to save the 165 pounds ($750) her owner demanded of her. This quarter century of struggle enabled Polly to not only buy her own freedom, but also purchase her daughter, Beck, a sale that was finalized the same day that Polly made the last payment on her own manumission. And while we do not how long it took the free black woman Abigail Lee to acquire the sum of eighty guineas (close to $382), we can assume that 31 October 1800 was a momentous day for her. Having purchased the girl Rosetta from Mary Pinckney for the aforementioned amount on 24 October 1800, seven days later, Abigail, "in consideration of the natural love and affection I have for my daughter," freed Rosetta.[46]

Like black women, black husbands and fathers were also committed to seeing their families out of bondage, and a number managed to purchase their wives out of slavery.[47] Sarah Weston acquired her freedom when her husband, the free black butcher William Fryday, paid her master the sum of one hundred pounds ($449), but Lizzie's husband died before she was manumitted: a free black barber, Samuel Creighton left $1,000 in his will to purchase Lizzie's liberty. Clearly, neither women nor men waited for others to give them their freedom. Rather, enslaved persons of both sexes strove to divest themselves and their loved ones of the shackles of slavery, and they worked together to accomplish this when they could. A telling example of such cooperation is the marriage of Amelia and Peter Elwig. Amelia, purchased out of bondage by her husband in 1817, spent the next six years working alongside Peter so they could buy the freedom of their three children.[48]

Sadly, the hurdles free black women faced in the workforce meant that many of them were unable to purchase their children out of slavery. While some slaveowners sold children to their mothers for the nominal sum of $1, a fortunate occurrence for Margaret Wilson, others were forced to pay full market price to free their children from bondage. For Rebecca Parler, the costs were just too high. Rebecca was purchased out of slavery by her husband, Peter, a free black man. The couple then spent years trying to save enough money to buy the freedom of their daughter, Hannah. When Peter died in 1833, however, Hannah was still enslaved. Bess McIntosh faced an equally insurmountable purchase price for her daughter. Desperate to be reunited with her child but unable to save the amount required to buy her, Bess eventually freed the girl by "stealing" her away from her owner in 1825.[49]

The road to freedom was thus fraught with pitfalls and perils, and even women who did not have to purchase their freedom often discovered that their manumission came with strings attached. In 1798, for example, Benjamin Hicks executed a deed of manumission for Kate, "reserving nevertheless unto myself her personal services during my lifetime and provided also that during my lifetime she behaves herself as a good and faithful servant ought to do."[50] This vague, catchall phrase meant that Kate had to continually be on her best behavior to ensure she stayed in Benjamin's good graces: one misstep before his death could result in the cancellation of the deed, and who knew how long he might live? One also wonders exactly what "personal services" Kate had to perform in order to remain a "good and faithful servant." Nancy faced a similar situation. Her deed stated she would be freed in five years, provided she "faithfully cared for" her owner's daughter. Nancy likely ground her teeth in frustration whenever the child misbehaved during those five years: before chastising the girl, Nancy would have had to consider whether doing so would result in her own permanent enslavement.[51]

Even women whose deeds stated they would be freed after a fixed number of years, upon their owners' demise, or after a sum of money had changed hands, lived in a dangerous state of limbo: deeds could be canceled, wills changed, and money stolen. And, in places where delayed manumission was widespread, black people found their families composed of persons who were enslaved for life, some who were enslaved for a term of years, and still others who were free. The result: precarious family structures where any number of factors, including death, sale, breach of contract, or fraud, could separate people of color from their loved ones.[52] And since enslaved persons in South Carolina could not legally enter into contracts, it was dangerous to assume that the courts would decide in favor of a woman whose owner had reneged on a promise of freedom. Catherine, whose story I relayed in the introduction, was fortunate in that she had a white male advocate who helped take her case to court when her owner tried to defraud her of her freedom.[53]

While some women's woes were caused by their masters, the machinations of executors could also interfere with a woman's hopes and dreams. Grace, for example, believed herself to be a free woman. Originally the property of James Ryan, who "for many years previous to his death was very infirm and subject to frequent fits of severe disposition," Grace had nursed James for years and been "his most Confidential Servant." To reward her for her service, James left a will stipulating that Grace was to be emancipated upon his death. His executor, however, claimed that James died intestate and did not record Grace's freedom with the courts. Grace then found her freedom challenged by the executor himself, James's brother, Lawrence, who "endeavoured to Sell and dispose of your Oratrix, and threatens to sell her as a Slave in the Country." Seeking justice, Grace took her case to the Court of Equity in 1817 and asked the court to codify her manumission. While it is unknown if Grace won her suit, it is clear that she, like other women, discovered that black freedom in a slave society was a fragile thing; never fully secure, it required continual negotiation, both with the legal system and with the white men who helped build and maintain that system. Equally evident is that black women used every tool at their disposal, including their contacts with sympathetic whites and their access to the courts, to acquire the protections of the law to which they believed they were entitled.[54]

The perils that black women faced while transitioning from slavery to freedom were not due solely to the actions of dishonest owners and executors. Not all masters intended to defraud their laborers, but delayed manumission was still dangerous. Consider what would happen if the state abolished owner-initiated manumission between the date a deed was written and the date it took effect. Under those circumstances, a deed of "future manumission" would become worthless. This is what happened to Victoria. In 1807, Victoria's father, a free black man named Pierre, purchased her out of bondage for $50. A deed of manumission was then executed for Victoria, but it indicated that she would not be freed until she turned twenty-one.[55] The state, however, outlawed owner-initiated manumission in 1820: since Victoria did not turn twenty-one until 1826, she remained enslaved. The woman Nancy, whose owner had agreed to free her if she faithfully cared for his child for five years, found herself in the same predicament. The Act of 1820 also negated her manumission, which was not slated to take effect until 1822.[56]

OF MANUMISSION, MONEY, AND MEN

In a myriad of ways, then, enslaved women found their road to freedom blocked by both individuals and the state. Some women, however, were able to establish alliances with people who not only helped manumit them but also made financial provision for them. The rates of such assistance increased significantly after 1800, most likely due to the self-sufficiency requirement in the Act of 1800.[57] Prior to that year, most slaveowners appeared to believe that freedom was its own reward. Thus many early deeds were as brief as "Manumission of Grace, a slave, by Henry White." Indeed, of the forty-three deeds pertaining to women freed before 1800, only three made any financial bequests. The woman Tenah, for example, acquired a horse and some cows the day she was manumitted. More common, however, was the deed for Chloe: emancipated for "years of faithful service," Chloe's loyalty netted her only the manumission of herself and her two children.[58]

After 1800, more women received financial assistance of some kind upon acquiring their freedom, bequests that were usually listed as a reward for some past action, including years of faithful service, a deed of extreme kindness, unusual loyalty, or heroism. Antoinette, for example, received $100 a year for nursing Jacques Truelle through many severe illnesses, while the "mulatto woman Theresia," freed by Marie Gouvignon in 1803, inherited $300 upon Marie's death in honor of her "faithful service since her manumission." The woman Phillis's deed is unique: she won her freedom, and a modest inheritance, after saving her owner's home from "the great fire."[59] While it is likely that some of these women had the skills with which to support themselves, it is equally probable that others would have needed some financial assistance, whether due to their advanced age or because they had children to support.

While the aforementioned women all received modest sums of money upon their manumission, others were given substantial inheritances. The laborer of Charles Filben, Flora Filben was freed under Charles's will and received his household furniture, his clothes, his crops, and the use of his plantation for the duration of her life. She also inherited Charles's house and lot at 3 Union Street, a house and lot at 12 Dutch Church Alley, and four enslaved laborers. Additionally, all three of Flora's children were to be "decently maintained and educated" out of the funds in Charles's estate until her daughters turned sixteen and her son reached the age of twenty-one. Everything Flora inherited would transfer to her children upon her death. Interestingly, the will never mentions why Flora, Mary, Elizabeth, and John inherited the majority of Charles's ample estate.[60]

Charles was not alone in his generosity or his reticence. A number of men left significant bequests to women they had once owned without articulating their reasons for doing so. Jenny and her son Emanuel, for example, were manumitted by the will of Samuel Jones. Jenny also received all of Samuel's household goods, $200 in cash, a lot on King Street, the income from the lease on said lot, and an annual maintenance of $100. Then there was Dinah, a washerwoman, and her four children, all of whom were freed under the will of Charles Pinckney, a will written just weeks before his death. Dinah also inherited a large portion of Charles's estate, while her children were to be "suitably maintained" out of the proceeds of the estate during their infancy and eventually bound out to good trades.[61]

None of these wills indicate why the women and children in question were left such substantial inheritances, although it stands to reason that the legatees had a conjugal or kinship relationship with their former owners. The fact that none of the aforementioned testators had white wives or children, and that they not only freed these persons of color but left them the bulk of their estates, implies that the black heirs were members of these men's families. The fact remains, however, that these men chose not to explicate their relationships to these women and children. One wonders why, considering neither interracial sex nor interracial marriage was against the law in pre–Civil War South Carolina. There was thus no legislative barrier preventing a white man from acknowledging that he had a domestic relationship with a black woman.[62]

Men with legitimate families understood that their wives and children could contest their wills if they left an inheritance to a black woman with whom they admitted to having had an extramarital relationship. This likely prompted Paul Ravenel to take the care he did in constructing his will. First, Paul freed Elsy and her five children. He then stated that fifty acres of land was to be cut from his plantation, "upon which a comfortable wooden house is to be built, and the land and house given to Elsy for her life." Elsy also acquired "her mother Beck and father Bristol as well as five cows and calves and their increase during her life." Upon Elsy's death, all this property would pass to Elsy's children and their heirs. Finally, Elsy received $50 in cash. Paul left everything else he owned to his wife, Abby, and their two daughters, but stated that if any of his heirs refused to free "the aforementioned slaves," or did not abide by the terms of his will, that beneficiary would forfeit his or her share of the estate.[63]

The manner in which Elsy and her children were provided for indicates that they were more than just Paul's property. Paul strove to ensure that Elsy and her children would always have a home, and he gave Elsy ownership of her elderly parents, a considerate gesture that strongly suggests the pair shared a relationship beyond that of master and servant.[64] Paul may not have been able to openly declare the true nature of his relationship with Elsy, since he had a legitimate family, but he took great pains to ensure that she and her children (who we can assume were Paul's biological offspring) would be well cared for, and that his white family could not easily prevent his black family members from acquiring their freedom or their inheritance. This is yet another indication that Elsy and her children had a familial connection to Paul: in many slave societies, including that of Saint-Domingue, threatening to disinherit a white heir who interfered with a black family member receiving her or his bequest was commonplace.[65]

Paul's silence is understandable given his marital situation, but it does not explain why men without white heirs hid their connections to their black partners, children, or both. Their silence was likely based on the fact that they feared social ostracism if the truth were made public. While interracial sex between white men and black women certainly occurred in Charleston, and cross-racial relationships were legal, for a white man to publicly admit to having a black lover, or to having fathered a child of color, could open him up to "censure as infringing the rules of propriety and decorum."[66] The reality, then, was that a white man risked his good name and position in society if he confessed to being sexually involved with a black woman. His friends and neighbors may have known the truth and even acknowledged it behind closed doors, but while gossip or circumspect impropriety did not exclude a white offender from "good" society, a forthright admission of interracial sex could. Discretion, then, was the better part of valor. This would explain why Adam Tunno, merchant, slaveowner, and president of the prestigious St. Andrew's Society, never openly recognized the black woman Margaret Bettingall as his wife, or their daughter, Barbara, as his child. Certainly everyone knew that Adam had no wife other than Margaret (whom he lived with for forty years), that his daughter went by the last name Tunno, and that Adam willed a large portion of his estate to his black family, yet he never admitted his familial connection to the two women in the public record, not even in his will.[67]

Interracial sex, and the manumission of black women or biracial children, was hardly unique to Charleston. In Savannah, where the free black population was only 725 as late as 1860, over 68 percent of those free persons were listed as "mulatto." Although the methods by which census takers assigned color designations was subjective at best, the numbers still imply that sexual mixing between black and white persons was not uncommon in the Savannah area.[68] The census data from New Orleans is equally telling: by the late colonial period, "mulattoes" were 75 percent of the city's free population of color. Jane Dabel thus concludes that not only were many women in New Orleans manumitted because they were the mistresses of their owners, but sexual relations between white men and black women produced numerous biracial offspring who were then freed by their fathers.[69]

The reticence of Charleston's slaveowners about their sex lives was also common. While interracial sex occurred in all slave centers in the United States, only in New Orleans was it accepted and legitimized by individuals, the church, and the courts. By the 1790s, many men in New Orleans lived openly with their black mistresses and acknowledged paternity of their biracial children. Parish registers indicate that the Roman Catholic Church in New Orleans, in turn, baptized these illegitimate children and, even under U.S. rule, administered the sacraments to the enslaved and free black lovers of white men, and to their children of color. The courts also recognized such relationships. Under Spanish law, illegitimate children in New Orleans could acquire legitimate status if their fathers acknowledged their paternity before a notary. Under American governance, legitimacy could occur after the legal marriage of the natural parents. Such public tolerance, as well as the opportunity for legitimacy, was never available in Charleston.[70]

Charlestonians thus appear to have carved out a middle path between openly decrying interracial relationships and freely celebrating them, displaying behavior that suggested both their discomfort with and quiet acceptance of intimacy between the races. When Sarah was manumitted in 1801, for example, John Bull did not definitively state that she was his paramour. The wording of the deed, however, is indicative of the nature of the pair's relationship: "In consideration of the good will I bear towards my Negro Woman Sarah (well known as my House Keeper and confidential steward) for her obedience and fidelity . . . I grant and confirm unto . . . Sarah her emancipation and . . . bind myself . . . to pay . . . Sarah . . . 10 pounds sterling money . . . every year during her natural life."[71] The words "fidelity," "obedience," "confidential steward," and "House Keeper" are signal in this document. Between a man and a woman, the word "fidelity" implies sexual faithfulness and, when paired with "obedience," is strongly suggestive of the proper role a wife was to play in marriage: "to love, honor, and obey" her husband, forsaking all others. Add "confidential steward," which indicates that Sarah wielded some authority in John's household, being privy to his secrets and having charge over his property, and Sarah's position in John's life is more certain. That steward is paired with "House Keeper," is significant: like the word *domestique* in New Orleans, or the term *ménagère*, used in pre-Revolutionary Saint-Domingue, white male Charlestonians used "House Keeper" to refer to women who were mistresses of their homes, hearths, and beds, legal or otherwise. By using these terms together, John declared in language his neighbors would have understood that he and Sarah were involved in a domestic union akin to marriage.[72]

Due to the public silence surrounding issues of interracial sex, we may never know how many black women were freed due to their intimate relationships with white men. We are fortunate, however, that not all men felt the need to be as cautious as Adam Tunno. Thomas Branford Smith evidently believed that in death, at least, he could afford to be honest. In his will, Thomas stated that everything he had was to be sold and, "800 pounds placed in trust . . . for . . . Lindy . . . latterly emancipated by me. . . . All the rest . . . of my property . . . I give in trust . . . for . . . my son David, son of the aforementioned Lindy." When David, whom Thomas called his "natural son," turned twenty-one, he would receive his inheritance outright. Until then, David was to be bound out to a "humane mechanic" so he could learn a trade and thus eventually support himself.[73]

Thomas Smith may have been unusual in his candor, but he was not the only man who used his will to help his biracial children and the woman, or women, who bore them. Consider the situation of Peggy. The property of one Francis Dickinson, Peggy had a sexual relationship with a man named James Douglas. Upon James's death, Peggy inherited $500 to buy her freedom, while the couple's son, also named James, whom James Sr. had already purchased and released from bondage, received a bequest of $1,000. James Sr. also left the girl Mary, his daughter by Peggy, $1,000 so that she could procure her manumission. Additionally, James Sr. willed $500 to an unnamed child, "his son by Clarissa, belonging at present to Mrs. Crutier." The funds were to be used to pay for the boy's freedom.[74]

Clearly James had sexual relations with more than one enslaved woman, although the nature of these encounters is unclear. It is possible that both Peggy and Clarissa had long-term associations with James, although the fact that each woman belonged to other people would have made such relationships difficult to conduct. Of course, his connection to one or both women could have been a one-night affair or rape that occurred when he visited their owners' homes. There are clues, however, which suggest that Peggy's ties to James were more substantive than those of Clarissa. Although funds were provided to free all of James's progeny, Peggy was the mother of two of James's children, one of whom was named for his father and freed before James died. Peggy also received the means to secure her own freedom, but no such provision was made for Clarissa. In manumitting James Jr. before he died, and leaving a bequest for Peggy, James implied that Peggy held a more meaningful position in his life than Clarissa.

Unfortunately, we have no way of knowing how Peggy or Clarissa actually felt about the father of their children. If we contrast the manumission of these women, however, as well as of women like Lindy, who received an inheritance of eight hundred pounds from her former owner, and Flora Filben, who inherited Charles Filben's entire estate, with those of women like Chloe, who entered freedom with nothing but her body to her name, or Cyprienne, whose mistress gave her six dresses when she freed her, it becomes clear that some black women had a more difficult time in making the transition to freedom than did others. While emancipation was desirable, after years of unpaid labor, women who did not have to buy themselves out of bondage, and who received some sort of financial assistance, would have had a less difficult time moving from slavery to freedom.[75]

Clearly sexual intimacy was one of the avenues by which enslaved female Charlestonians accessed emancipation for themselves and their children. Additionally, it appears that some women were also manumitted with a modicum of property and thus found their path to freedom to be smoother than the one traveled by fugitives or those who had to buy themselves out of slavery. We cannot, however, conclude that a conjugal or kinship relationship with a white man always led to freedom, or to the acquisition of property. At best, we can posit only that black women who had sustained relationships with white men, and the biracial children of slaveholders, had a better chance of obtaining their freedom and inheriting property than did other residents of the slave quarters.[76] Indeed, it is fair to say that having children with a white man counted for more than sex alone, and that the children of long-term interracial unions were valued more, and received more material goods, than did the black women who were their mothers. We can also deduce that while more black men than women may have been able to buy their freedom, because they were more likely to have specialized skills that commanded higher wages, negotiating sex for freedom was an option more available to enslaved women.

This avenue to freedom, however, occurred under very coercive circumstances. Much of the sex between blacks and whites in the Old South was rooted in brutality, and the unequal power relations that existed between white men and black women makes it hard to describe relationships that were not openly abusive as being consensual. Indeed, it is difficult to use the term "consensual" when a society is so fundamentally unfree that a woman's best "choice" for acquiring the most basic of rights is to use her body as a tool of negotiation, and when we do not know if the women involved would have engaged in these liaisons had they already been free and had the full rights of citizenship.[77] Under such conditions, we must use words like "consent" with caution, although we also cannot categorize all interracial sexual intimacy under the rubric of violence. The slave South was not a place where white men were invested with hegemonic control and black women were absolute victims, utterly lacking in autonomy. Indeed, the length of certain unions between black women and white men, some of which continued long after a woman and her children had been emancipated, suggests that some women acquiesced to these relationships, if not at first then later, and if not out of affection for their partners then for the opportunities, protection, and power such a union could afford to them and to their children.[78]

Certainly Margaret Bettingall was able to use her relationship with Adam Tunno to forge a better life for herself and her daughter than they may have otherwise had. More than just a concubine, Margaret, who carried the keys to the Tunno estate clipped to her waist, was called the "head and front" of Adam's household. Even before Adam died, Margaret had acquired a sizeable personal estate, and the inheritance she gained at his death ensured her a place among Charleston's black elite. A communicant at St. Philip's Church, Margaret also had the ear of powerful white men and the wherewithal to purchase various members of her family out of bondage. The couple's daughter, Barbara, was manumitted by Adam while still a child and was raised by her parents in their mansion on the East Bay. Adam also sent Barbara to one of the city's best schools for black children, paid to educate his grandson, and bequeathed his daughter a substantial estate. Margaret and Adam's decades-long relationship thus not only benefited Margaret but also made Barbara one of the wealthiest black women in Charleston.[79]

Stories of women like Margaret should make us wary of generalizing about interracial sex in the Old South. Not all such encounters were abusive, nor were they all consensual; few such relationships would have been so uncomplicated given the factors of time and place, as well as the race, gender, and legal status of the parties involved. These interactions, then, serve to illuminate the fact that in societies where certain persons are, at best, only theoretically free, disenfranchised people develop techniques to help mediate unfavorable living conditions. In doing so, they come to realize that it is necessary to use a variety of methods to improve their positions.[80] In the Old South, enslaved women understood that their minds, skills, and bodies were all tools in the fight for freedom, and that their best chance of escaping slavery lay in utilizing all those assets in order to ingratiate themselves with persons whose social space imbued them with more formal, legal power than black women themselves had. Ingratiation could entail acts of loyalty, heroism, sex, or something else altogether. There were no guarantees, however, that their tactics of negotiation would be successful.

THE ACT OF 1820

As savvy as black women had to be to access emancipation in the early years of the century, they had to become even more creative in their pursuit of freedom after 1820. Until then, South Carolina had been something of a refuge for free blacks, particularly when compared to Georgia, Virginia, and even Louisiana.[81] Indeed, as the laws against free blacks grew more restrictive elsewhere, South Carolina's permissive manumission codes, coupled with natural increase and immigration, helped increase the state's free black population. Census records indicate that Charleston's free community of color grew from 586 in 1790 to 1,475 in 1820. The city's white population expanded from 8,089 to 10,653 during the same years, while the enslaved residents were 12,652 strong by 1820. Charleston, then, had a black majority well before 1820.[82]

Unwilling to decrease their slaveholdings, but concerned at the effects that a growing free black population could have on the security of their property, as well as on their ability to maintain control of the city's social order, white Charlestonians began demanding that free black migration into the state be restricted in the interest of public safety. In response to these fears, the state legislature passed the Act of 1820, which unexpectedly halted South Carolina's reputation for laxity with regard to free blacks. "WHEREAS, the great and rapid increase of free negroes and mulattoes in this State, by migration and emancipation, renders it . . . necessary for the Legislature to restrain the emancipation of slaves, and to prevent free persons of color from entering into this State: I. Be it . . . enacted . . . no slave shall hereafter be emancipated but by act of the Legislature. II. Be it further enacted . . . That from and after the first day of March next, it shall not be lawful for any free negro or mulatto to migrate into this state." The new law also made it illegal for free blacks already living in South Carolina to leave and then reenter the state, no matter what the reason.[83]

The Act of 1820 was a watershed in South Carolina history: from that day forward, anyone who wished to legally free an enslaved person had to petition the state legislature for a formal act of manumission. Both the lower and upper houses had to approve the petition for the act to pass, but since most legislators believed that there were already too many free blacks in the state, petitioning the legislature was a lost cause. A laborer had to perform a "heroic deed," such as revealing the plans of an imminent slave revolt, before the legislature would even consider granting a freedom petition. South Carolina's manumissions were thus brought to a screeching halt, and the growth of the state's free black population was abruptly checked. After 1820, many persons were freed only because their owners removed them from the state: the new law against free black in-migration prevented those manumitted in this manner from legally returning home.[84]

The 1820 law brought South Carolina into line with states like Virginia and Georgia. Indeed, Georgia wished so fervently to discourage the growth of its free black population that it not only passed legislation mandating that its freed laborers leave the state but also levied a $100 tax on all incoming free persons of color.[85] As for Louisianans, they soon followed South Carolina's example. In 1825, authorities there were permitted to expel any person of color they deemed "undesirable," while free blacks who left the state were prohibited reentry. In 1830, Louisiana passed a slew of new laws to further regulate the activities of free people of color and restrict their growth. Free blacks who had entered the state after 1825 now had sixty days to leave, and newly freed persons had to depart within thirty days or their former owners would forfeit the $1,000 manumission bond they were now required to pay for each servant they emancipated. Additionally, free blacks who had voluntarily left the United States were forbidden from ever returning to Louisiana, and free persons of color who had arrived in the state prior to 1825 had to register with the parish judge where they lived or at the mayor's office in New Orleans.[86]

Despite the fact that the Act of 1820 was similar to legislation in several other slave states, many Charlestonians were still shocked by its passage: they had never asked that owner-initiated manumission be outlawed, yet that is exactly what the assemblymen had done. A number of Low Country slaveowners were also angered by the fact that they were unable to free their laborers before the law took effect, since it became operational on passage. For those persons who had intended to free some or all of the laborers they held in bondage, but who had put off the "formality" of emancipation for one reason or another, their procrastination now returned to haunt them. For enslaved persons who had placed their hopes for the future in the promises of their owners, their pathway to freedom had just become far narrower and more uncertain.

Shortly after passage of the new law, slaveowners from the Charleston area began inundating the legislature with petitions requesting acts of manumission, prodded in many cases, no doubt, by enslaved persons themselves. One such plea came from Philippe Noisette. A renowned botanist, Philippe had, "under peculiar circumstances, become the father of six children, begotten upon his faithful slave . . . Celestine." He claimed that he had always intended to emancipate his family, but now found himself in a "distressing" situation due to the recent changes in the law. Presumably Celestine was "distressed" as well. After assuring the legislators that his family would never become public charges due to his wealth, Philippe asked that Celestine and their children be legally freed.[87]

Philippe Noisette was not the only Charlestonian shocked by the new law. John Carmille informed the State Assembly that some years ago he had formed "a domestic connection with a female named Henrietta and . . . has had by her three children. . . . Henrietta and her children are . . . in the condition of absolute slavery, the property of your petitioner. Your petitioner is aware that in making the above statement he is open to censure as infringing the rules of propriety and decorum. He has, however, no alternative but to make the present application or to remain indifferent to the present melancholy situation of his family who are dear to your petitioner." It is quite likely that the "melancholy" of his "dear" partner prompted John to file the petition: Henrietta's unhappiness probably made John's home life less than pleasant. John thus risked societal "censure," acknowledged his "domestic connection" to Henrietta and, after noting that his wealth would ensure his family never became public charges, asked the state to manumit his family. Like Philippe Noisette, John claimed that he had always intended to free his black family, and that the "sudden passage" of the "late legislation" had taken him by surprise.[88]

Neither Celestine nor Henrietta was freed by the state legislature. Indeed, the legislators appeared loath to manumit *any* enslaved person. Claude Rame, for example, claimed that he wished to reward Aurora for ten years of faithful service, and for her meritorious character, by freeing her and her four children. Although he agreed to support the family, Aurora and her children were denied their freedom. Likewise, Auguste Genty hoped to free Sophia, to whom "he ha[d] become greatly attached . . . on account of her faithful and affectionate conduct towards him." Despite the fact that Sophia was of high "moral character, capable of earning a living, frugal and industrious," and that Auguste could support her financially, the act, "which . . . Sophia has been anxiously expecting," was denied. Sophia's "anxious expectations" doubtless played a role in Auguste's decision to file this petition.[89]

The legislature likely rejected these petitions because its members could read between the lines: Aurora had served Claude for ten years and her oldest child was aged nine. As for Auguste, the terms "faithful" and "affectionate" would have been red flags to the legislators. These petitions were almost certainly denied, then, because they alluded to sexual relationships that violated "the rules of propriety and decorum." This does not explain why the assemblymen were unwilling to free Abba, however. A member of an old plantation family, Rebecca Drayton filed a petition on Abba's behalf. Abba had come to Rebecca from a close friend on the promise that when Rebecca died, Abba would be freed. Additionally, Abba had become dear to Rebecca, and she wished to reward the woman by manumitting her. Indeed, she felt "bound by her conscience" to do so and was "distressed" that the new law prevented her from carrying out her wishes. Despite such strongly moralistic language from the daughter of a Carolina "first family," a legislative committee recommended that "the prayer of the petitioner be not granted."[90]

The rejection of Rebecca's petition signaled that the legislature did not intend to manumit *any* bondsperson except as a special privilege under the rarest of circumstances. The Act of 1820, then, was not designed to slow down the rate of manumission: its aim was to *eliminate* it. The Judiciary Committee Report on the petition of John Walker made the state's position clear. John filed a petition on behalf of Ann and her three children. Despite his willingness to support the family of four, the petition was denied. The committee bluntly stated that "it is against the . . . policy of this state to emancipate slaves, and permit them to remain in the state. . . . The object . . . can be . . . accomplished . . . by sending his slaves either without the limits of the United States or to a non-slaveholding state."[91] This explains why only fifteen persons were freed by the South Carolina legislature between 1821 and 1838, one of whom was Peter Desverneys, who betrayed the alleged Denmark Vesey conspiracy to Charleston authorities in 1822.[92]

Enslaved South Carolinians and their owners, realizing that the state would be of no help in obtaining legal manumissions, now sought alternative routes to freedom. One option was for black laborers to travel to a state where they could be emancipated. For this reason Yaniki and her two sons, who were fathered by their owner William Doughty, left the state when William died. William had set aside funds to help pay for the family's transportation out of the state, and he also left each of his sons $2,000 in trust, the interest from which was to support them until they came of age. Phillis left Charleston under similar circumstances. Upon the death of her owner, John Hopkins, Phillis and her son traveled to Philadelphia, where John's executors were told to "immediately emancipate them." Phillis also inherited $2,600 worth of 5 percent stock as an annuity, plus $500 to help pay for her trip north.[93]

White slaveowners were not alone in utilizing these methods. We know that many black women, after securing their own freedom, labored to purchase their relatives out of slavery. Some, however, had never legally emancipated their kin due to the costly filing fees involved. The Act of 1820 was thus a horrifying surprise to "slaveowners" like Ann Scott. A "free colored woman," Ann had a daughter, Patty, who was born before Ann was freed and was "therefore still a slave." Ann had purchased her daughter and her grandchildren but had not legally freed them before 1820. When Ann died, Patty inherited her mother's estate, although she and her children were still enslaved. Aware of the problems this could cause, Ann directed her executors to use "all legal means available" to take her family north in order to free them.[94]

Moving to another state was, of course, not a viable option for every woman. Under the Act of 1820, free black persons who left the state could never return, nor could free blacks from other states migrate to South Carolina.[95] Many enslaved persons thus chose not to leave the state, since this avenue to freedom meant not only leaving behind any of their loved ones who were still in bondage, but also removing themselves from the only home they had ever known. South Carolinians thus began resorting to extralegal measures to access emancipation and remain in the state. While lawful freedom was certainly preferable, enslaved persons appear to have decided that the day-to-day experience of autonomy available to them after being unofficially manumitted was better than continuing to live as someone's legal property.

A freedom trust was the simplest way to circumvent the law. In a nutshell, a person sold or willed the servant they wished to manumit to a friend or relative "in trust," under the provision that the new owner allow the laborer in question to live and work where they liked, keep their wages, and enjoy all the rights of free persons. In short, they would be free-by-courtesy. This is what happened to Polly, once the property of Mary Smith, a "free negro woman." Mary left Polly in trust to the Incorporated Baptist Church, where she was to "have her own time and live without any interference from anyone." In the same way was Lavinia willed by her husband, the free black man George Logan, to her nephew William, "in trust that the profits of her labor shall be applied to her own support and . . . she shall in no way be liable for any of William's . . . debts." As the state continued to reject most petitions for manumission, such trusts became commonplace, and the number of black Charlestonians who were virtually free rose accordingly.[96]

While freedom trusts were risky, Charlestonians were fortunate that local authorities, many of whom were themselves slaveowners discomfited by passage of the new law, chose not to enforce the Act of 1820 when times were peaceful, which meant that the will of the master continued to reign absolute in most such matters. Indeed, many people did not even bother to hide their extralegal intentions: between 1822 and 1864, hundreds of Charlestonians actually recorded their deeds of trust with the secretary of state to ensure they would be honored. Typical was the bill of sale in which a woman sold two of her servant women to a friend for $1. She declared that since the law was opposed to manumission, she wished for the women to enjoy "full, free and undisturbed liberty" as if they had been freed. She also stated that if the ban on manumission were ever lifted, the women were to be legally freed.[97]

Considering how many trusts were recorded, it is likely that many more were clandestine, verbal agreements, conducted in private to protect all the parties involved. Secret trusts certainly existed in Georgia. The state of Georgia prohibited free blacks in Savannah, Darien, and Augusta from owning real estate. In order to circumvent this law, a number of free blacks entered into covert agreements with white men so they could acquire land. Essentially, they gave the man in question a sum of money with which to purchase a piece of property on their behalf. While the record would show that the owner of said property was the man in question, he was simply the front man for the purchase and agreed to be nothing more than a "paper owner." The real owner, and the person who would improve the land, pay the property taxes (via the paper owner), and make decisions concerning the sale or disposition of the property, would be the person of color who had supplied the purchase money.[98]

This was the nature of the agreement that Aspasia Cruvellier Mirault had with George Cally, and it explains how she was able to acquire lot 22 in the Pulaski Ward section of Savannah in April 1842. Aspasia's descendants, however, learned that verbal trusts were even riskier than those that were recorded. Contingent as they were on white men's honoring their word to a person of color, such trusts were fragile structures. When George decided to file a lawsuit in 1871 claiming that he was the true owner of lot 22, Aspasia's heirs' house of cards came crumbling down around their ears, and they found themselves battling to prove that Aspasia and George's arrangement was both real and valid. The problem lay in the fact that the original trust was not only illegal but also had only existed as a secret, verbal pact between two friends, one of whom was a black woman who had long since passed away.[99]

Charlestonians, like their counterparts in Savannah, used trusts to transfer property to one another, and they crafted trusts to bequeath property to virtually free persons. The law stated that enslaved persons could not own property, but it said nothing about property that was left to a free person, in trust for the use, benefit, and maintenance of an enslaved person. Consequently, people began using trusts to ensure the freedom of their laborers and endow them with property. In this manner Sophia was ultimately successful in her "anxious expectations" to live as a free woman. While his petition for her manumission had been unsuccessful, upon his death her owner, Auguste, left his executors two houses, all of his furniture, $500 and, "his wench Sophia forever, in trust that they will not, and shall not ever, in any way sell or dispose of Sophia nor require of her any services, labor, or wages, but will permit her to enjoy the furniture and $500 and to live in either house." The rental income from Auguste's other house was to be used to maintain Sophia, and after her death the property would pass to whomever she directed.[100]

In much the same way were Ann Jones and her nine children provided for by Ann's longtime companion, John Walker. Like Auguste's, John's manumission petition on behalf of Ann (and her then three children) was denied in 1825, but the couple remained domestically connected and had six more children together over the next fifteen years. When John died in 1840, he left his entire estate to his executors, "in trust . . . for . . . Ann Jones and her children . . . whom I acknowledge for my natural children and consider as free persons. If there is any doubt as to their free status, I give the said Ann and her children . . . to my executors . . . in trust, and command them to take such measures necessary to qualify Ann and her children to enjoy their bequest." It appears that John's executors adhered to his wishes, since Ann and her children continued to live in Charleston as free people after John's death.[101]

Black slaveowners also used trusts to transfer property to loved ones who remained enslaved. Molly Neyle, a free black woman, had manumitted her niece Barbara "years ago" but through "some cause unknown," the deed had never been recorded and was thus invalid. Since freedom was now "impossible due to the present law," Molly left Barbara and her future issue to John M. Hopkins on condition that John never ask anything of Barbara beyond $1 a month, which was to be used to pay the taxes due on Barbara's person. If it ever became legal to free Barbara, John was to do so at once. Molly also left half of her furniture and one-quarter of her estate to John, in trust for her niece. It is likely that Molly trusted John, a white man, to honor her wishes since he himself had a black female companion whose manumission he had arranged.[102]

Molly's situation was not uncommon. Charlotte Kershaw found herself the owner of her mother, Isabella, and her siblings, Harriet and Charles. In her will, Charlotte stated that she had never treated her relatives as chattel, nor had she ever allowed anyone else to treat them as such. She thus left them in trust to one William Kershaw, on condition that they receive as many of the rights of freedom as could possibly be permitted. They were to work for themselves, live where they pleased, and dispose of their time in any manner they saw fit. Charlotte then left her entire estate to her executor in trust for her family and declared that if it ever became legal to manumit enslaved persons in South Carolina, her family was to be freed and the trust voided.[103]

The success of such extralegal measures gave rise to a group of black persons in Charleston who were slaves in name only and accorded to them an economic independence that made them essentially free. Limiting such trusts and the resulting growth of the free black community proved difficult. Once released, virtually free persons vanished into Charleston's large, free black community and began behaving as if they were free: they found jobs, purchased homes, bought and sold property, and paid the head taxes required of free blacks. It was in this manner that Lydia Weston, illegally freed by Plowden Weston in 1826, came to be listed in the census as a free black woman. Allowed to live as a free person,

Nancy Weston, a virtually free black woman, lived in Charleston in the 1850s.
A member of the powerful free-black Weston clan, Nancy was likely related to Lydia Weston,
herself illegally manumitted by Plowden Weston in 1826. (Moorland-Spingarn
Research Center, Howard University, Washington, DC)

Lydia worked, paid her taxes, and conducted herself as a free woman in kind, and so became one in fact.[104] Freedom, then, was never just a legal category or construct but was, instead, a lived experience. And no matter how fragile it may have been, for many women, the benefits of virtual freedom were preferable to living in bondage, waiting for an official act of manumission that was unlikely to happen.

While it was slaveowners who drafted and filed these trust documents, it is clear that enslaved women actively pursued and often negotiated such arrangements. Some women, for example, approached free people of color they felt they could trust and asked these persons to purchase them from their current owners so they could live as virtually free people. Women in this situation gave their new "owners" the funds with which to purchase them, on condition that the purchaser of record allowed them to live as free people. It was on such terms that Maria asked Margaret Randall, a free woman of color, to purchase her from her current owner. On 18 July 1829, Margaret bought Maria for $200 from one Sarah McPherson. Two days later, Margaret relinquished unto Maria "all and every claim and claims of her wages unto me," and Maria vanished into Charleston's free black community.[105]

The chances of proving that a member of the city's free black community had been illegally manumitted were slim if the person in question had been freed by a trust. In order to prevent their reenslavement by outside forces, a quasi-free person's trustee could simply claim that the person in question was really their bondsperson. This gave a virtually free woman the protection of an owner on paper, but once the threat of reenslavement had passed, she could continue to live as a free person. Still, freedom trusts were a gamble: if a trustee chose to violate a trust agreement, the black woman in question had little legal recourse, since her freedom depended on her trustee's upholding what was, essentially, an illegal contract. And, even if a trustee were honorable, a woman still risked being reenslaved upon the death of her nominal owner if a dependable new trustee were not appointed prior to the original trustee's death. Such freedom was thus tenuous and always fraught with anxiety.[106]

As the doorway to emancipation narrowed in the 1820s, more black women began filing affidavits with the secretary of state to protect their free status. Many of these women did not have formal deeds of manumission and so risked being detained as fugitives or sold into bondage at the whim of the authorities. It was just such a situation that led Sophia Mauncaut, whose story begins this chapter, to file her affidavits in 1814. Like Sophia, Becky Jackson hoped to protect her children from future harassment. A washerwoman from Cheraw, South Carolina, Becky had moved her family to Charleston in 1813. Lacking freedom papers and new to the city, Becky likely worried she would be asked to validate her status, prompting her to file an affidavit of freedom. In 1822, William Minott gave a sworn statement that he had known Becky's grandmother and mother in Cheraw, and that both were free black women. Becky thus protected her children's future by having a white man confirm her family's free maternal ancestry.[107]

Such affidavits were even more crucial for members of Charleston's free black elite. Those with property and social standing had to secure their free status in order to protect their families' assets and rights of inheritance. Such concerns prompted Martha Inglis to file a statement attesting to the freedom of herself and her sisters, Catherine and Elizabeth. The wife of prominent free black hairdresser Thomas Inglis, Martha had two daughters, Claudia and Mary. As life for South Carolina's free blacks became more precarious in the 1820s, Martha took steps to secure her children's future. In 1824, planter Henry Rutledge signed an official declaration claiming that Martha and her sisters were the grandchildren of Lucy, a subject of the emperor of Morocco, who came to the colonies in 1775. He stated that Lucy and her daughter Susannah, the mother of Martha, had freely served one Sarah Smith for years and "had always enjoyed the advantages and privileges extended by the laws of this state to that class (Moors) of its inhabitants."[108]

While this affidavit would have allowed the Inglis women to live without the fear of enslavement, it is important to note that Henry claimed that Lucy and Susannah had never been enslaved due to their status as "Moors." Records indicate, however, that Martha's grandmother had been enslaved. A deed of manumission dated 20 June 1800 reveals that Susannah and her daughter Catherine, the daughter and granddaughter of Lucy, a "Morish" woman, were freed by one Sarah Smith, Charleston widow. Martha could not, then, claim a family line devoid of slavery: her mother and eldest sister had both been born enslaved. It is unclear why Henry swore that Martha's family had a heritage free of bondage. Perhaps neither he nor Martha knew the truth. What is more likely, however, is that Martha and Thomas, like other elite people of color, desired a lineage exclusive of slavery, believing such a history set them apart from those persons whose family trees led back to slavery . . . and all of its accompanying stigmas and shame.[109]

Although Martha was an elite woman of color, records indicate that black women from across the class spectrum sought to document their freedom and protect their families. Not all of these women had black mothers. Slavery was, of course, hereditary, and was passed on through the female line. Since it had always been illegal to enslave white women, and the enslavement of indigenous persons, legal during the colonial era, was outlawed under the terms of the U.S. Constitution, some women filed affidavits claiming that their mothers had been white or Indian.[110] Nicholas Lindenboom thus swore that Diana Beamer was the "daughter of a free Indian woman named Rachel Beamer," and Ann Garnier testified that Mary Bull, the mother of Charlotte and grandmother of Joseph, "was an Indian." And while sex between white women and black men was regarded by white southerners as gravely immoral, Ann Risher stated that the mother of Sarah Fox, "colored," was a white woman named Rebecca Fox.[111]

Other women filed affidavits claiming that they were not even black. Such a statement, if accepted, not only protected a woman's freedom but also exempted her and her descendants from paying the head tax required of free blacks in South Carolina, and removed the words "free black, negro, mulatto, or person of color" from beside their names, along with the stigma that accompanied such classification. This is likely why the Stapleton children were not content with William Gaillard's certification that their mother had been three-quarters white and one-quarter Indian. While this was enough to ensure their freedom, the family obtained yet another affidavit from one D. Gaillard, who stated that the Stapletons "were never known to have any negro blood." Betsey Findlay was also careful to provide the courts with evidence that she was descended from a Portuguese woman and thus "exempt from paying the capitation tax."[112]

Clearly, the 1820s were difficult times for free blacks in South Carolina, and black women had to become more ingenious in their pursuit of freedom as their legal options dwindled. The difficulties arose in part because white Carolinians were concerned that the state's growing free black population might one day incite enslaved persons to rebellion. Additionally, the very existence of free people of color belied the white South's stance that to be black meant to be enslaved. These anxieties were further exacerbated in 1822 by news of the alleged Denmark Vesey conspiracy. The resulting terror made life painfully difficult for free blacks throughout the state and in Charleston in particular. Municipal codes now barred free blacks from meeting in groups of more than seven without the presence of a white person; the African Church, where Denmark and many of his inner circle had communed, was destroyed, and its minister run out of town; and the names of free blacks and their businesses disappeared from city directories until 1830. All the privileges free people of color had long enjoyed, and had come to regard as their rights, were revoked as the city took on the air of a hostile, enemy camp.[113]

By 1830, however, peace had returned to Charleston: as memories of Vesey receded, the privileges extended to free blacks were restored. The legislature did not repeal the Act of 1820, however, so trust agreements continued to flourish. Thus, as court officials looked the other way, black women continued to obtain their freedom and inherit property, and the state assembly passed no more new laws aimed at regulating the free black population until the 1840s. This was at odds with what happened in other slave states in the 1830s. Louisiana, for example, dissolved its free black militia in 1834.[114] And, driven in part by the panic that swept the region after the Nat Turner Rebellion in 1831, Maryland passed legislation in 1832 that made it mandatory to remove newly freed laborers from the state. This was logical given Maryland's geographic proximity to Virginia, and that Maryland had the largest free black population in the country, a distinction the state was hardly proud of.[115]

THE ACT OF 1841

It seemed that South Carolina could again become something of a sanctuary for free people of color, which frustrated state legislators, concerned as they were with decreasing the potential for slave rebellions and maintaining state security. The courts' laxity in allowing trusts to continue unchecked thus led the assemblymen to crack down on both a populace and a judiciary that was ignoring the law. In 1841, angered by public disregard for the Act of 1820, and concerned by the growing number of propertied, virtually free blacks, the state assembly passed the Act of 1841. Intended to eliminate the loophole in the Act of 1820 that trust agreements exploited, the act mandated that any trust meant to keep an enslaved person in a state of nominal servitude only, or remove them from the state in order to free them, was void. The act also nullified trusts that left a bondsperson an inheritance or the right to own his or her time.[116]

The new act greatly restricted the ability of enslaved women to acquire their freedom. The only legal option now open to them was to petition the legislature for an act of manumission, but that body was not in the habit of freeing enslaved persons: in 1850, for example, only two servants were legally manumitted by the state.[117] Even the less appealing avenue, leaving the state (and thus one's friends and kinfolk) in order to be manumitted, had been closed off by the new law. Even if an enslaved person did leave, however, there was nowhere for them to go. No other state wanted free people of color, not even Louisiana, which in 1842 passed legislation banning entry into the state of any enslaved person entitled to future emancipation. This same law required free blacks who had arrived in the state prior to 1838 to prove they were of "respectful character," as well as to register and give a monetary bond guaranteeing their good behavior if they wished to remain. In 1857, Louisiana banned emancipation entirely.[118]

What is amazing is that, in defiance of the new law, black Carolinians, often by utilizing more circumspect language or secret verbal agreements, continued to use trusts to secure freedom for themselves, their friends, and their relatives. Restricting owner manumission thus led to innumerable evasions, and one jurist declared that the Act of 1841 had done more harm than good, since its main impact had been to cause "so many otherwise honest citizens" to break the law.[119] The sources support the beliefs of this jurist: many Charlestonians left blatant evidence of their trust agreements in the public records after 1841. In 1855, for example, Katy Ann Harleston and her daughter were sold to a new owner in trust for $5: the contract stipulated that the two women were to be treated as if they were free. Harriet O'Driscoll used similar language, leaving Sarah to her nephew, in trust that "he will allow her to have full and free use of her time and protect her in the enjoyment of any property she may accumulate."[120]

Virtually free women also continued to inherit property after 1841, in spite of the new law. In 1853, Diana was illegally freed by Jacob Wehlert and left the use of her former owner's furniture and house. She also inherited his gold watch and any money he had in his home. In similar fashion, the free black man Ishmael Mitchell left his daughter Phillis and granddaughter Lydia in trust to close friends, along with his house, lot, and any other property he possessed at his death. And Sarah, the sister of the free black man Natt Comings Ball, was left in trust to Natt's wife, Eliza. Sarah also received one share of Natt's Bank of South Carolina bonds.[121]

Into the 1850s, then, black women continued to bridge the gap between slavery and freedom, finding ways out of, over, and through bondage, even where there appeared to be no way. Trusts were established in Charleston as late as 1864, and virtually free persons who had been illegally manumitted before 1841 lived with some degree of security since the Act of 1841 was not retroactive. Those free blacks owned property, held jobs, and paid taxes, and city officials rarely took action against them. In such an environment a quasi-free woman like Hannah Gonzalez could openly purchase and sell black laborers, own land, and record bills of sale. Such freedom was fragile though, as persons who were free-by-courtesy could be arrested by city officials when and if the mood struck them. Traveling was especially dangerous: blacks who were free-by-practice needed to remain in localities where white people of good repute knew them and could verify their freedom with local authorities.[122]

While times remained peaceful, however, many white Charlestonians continued to look the other way and ignored the existence of the city's irregularly manumitted free blacks. As in New Orleans, it seemed that only those free blacks who showed a reckless disregard for the rules of appropriate conduct found themselves in trouble with the law. In New Orleans, police in the 1840s and 1850s sporadically enforced the numerous ordinances that applied to free persons of color and arrested only those who attracted undue attention through their unseemly behavior. This included everything from public drunkenness to vagrancy, prostitution, theft, aiding enslaved runaways, and wearing clothing above one's station.[123]

CONCLUSION

Times, of course, did not remain peaceful, yet as late as 1864, black women in Charleston continued to access emancipation. Looking back, it is clear that these women were a diverse group of individuals. Some were born free, others moved to the city from rural areas of the state, and a number migrated from places where life was more difficult than it was in South Carolina. There were women who were legally manumitted, a number who stole themselves and their loved ones out of bondage, and many who became virtually free persons through a variety of extralegal means. There were those who were highly skilled and women whose primary training was in the "housewifely arts"; some were biracial or multiracial and others were not. Just as there was no typical enslaved woman, there was no archetypal free black woman.

Black women also took advantage of situational opportunities to acquire their freedom, some of which were connected to the urban condition. A few, for example, had special skills and were hired out to city residents, which allowed them to earn wages and buy their freedom. Living in Charleston also gave some black women the opportunity to meet and marry free men of color who bought them out of bondage, while others used their residence in the city, and the ensuing connections therein, to ally with whites and free blacks who helped free them.[124] Southern runaways also headed for Charleston, where they could blend into the free black community and hide in plain sight. Another group came from Saint-Domingue and turned that island's civil conflict to their advantage, staying loyal to their masters during the revolution in order to later acquire their freedom. There were also a number of women who ingratiated themselves to their owners by nursing them through a dire illness or performing an act of heroism, debts that were repaid with manumission. A final group became sexually involved with white men, and in so doing, gained freedom for themselves and their families. Not only was there no representative enslaved woman, then, but also there was no generic pathway to freedom.

Despite these differences, there were also common threads that bound black women together. Most important was the fact that regardless of how they acquired their freedom, enslaved women were active participants in determining their own fate: they daily negotiated with individuals and the state in order to obtain and retain their freedom. They helped draft petitions, became fugitives, wrote illegal wills and trusts, pursued nominal owners, bought themselves out of bondage, "stole" their children, filed lawsuits, requested affidavits, and entered into alliances with a variety of persons who could aid them in their quest for liberty.

These alliances played a key role in a black woman's ability to access emancipation. No woman was an island, and a woman needed friends and patrons if she wished to see herself and her children escape bondage. And while negotiating with white people was complicated and risky, many enslaved women realized that those who aligned themselves in some way with white persons had the best chance of acquiring freedom. Consider the fact that women of any race could not speak on their own behalf in a South Carolina court of law. This meant that black women, even more than black men, had to be on good terms with at least one white man if they hoped to initiate a lawsuit, sign a petition, or file a freedom affidavit. For black women in the Old South, then, freedom, whether legal or virtual, meant forging partnerships with the very people who helped maintain the system of slavery they were attempting to subvert. Despite the issues involved with relying on people who could decide at any moment to renege on an agreement, however, some women were able to use their ties to white men of stature to acquire their freedom.

Black female Charlestonians also sought the protections of the law that white South Carolinians enjoyed as their birthright. Even when the law was not oriented toward alleviating their predicaments, black women appealed to the judicial system in their quest for self-determination. They not only filed lawsuits when people attempted to defraud them of their liberty but also recorded illegal trusts, wrote extralegal wills, drafted petitions, and persuaded respectable white persons to sign freedom affidavits on their behalf. In short, they utilized the state's judicial apparatus, which was created to uphold black slavery, to instead codify and defend black female freedom and autonomy. Whether they won or lost their individual battles, black women clearly believed they were entitled to their freedom, as well as to a legal recognition and protection of that freedom.

Clearly, enslaved women were savvy political actors who understood that time, place, and social space—namely, race, gender, and legal condition—limited their options in certain ways. Indeed, while they used many of the same tactics to free themselves that black men did, self-purchase was more available to enslaved men, while women found themselves more able to use sex to unlock the door to freedom. Enslaved women, then, learned a hard lesson early in life: their ability to negotiate better positions for themselves depended on their willingness to use all the tools available to them including their wits, connections, diplomacy, occupational talents, and bodies. Understanding the constraints of the society in which they lived, enslaved women thus worked to acquire freedom within the confines of a society that was committed to upholding the authority of those who were white and male.

Freedom, of course, was not the final chapter for enslaved women. It was, instead, only the beginning of a new set of struggles. Having navigated the obstacles that riddled the path to emancipation, black women discovered that life for free persons of color in Charleston held as many challenges as slavery. As they pursued gainful employment, worked to acquire property, and sought equal protection under the law, black women came to realize that despite having attained their liberty, legal or otherwise, they would continue to have to negotiate their freedom with those persons who wished to constrain black women's autonomy. They could never take their freedom for granted, living as they did in a society where people were always looking for ways to reenslave them, and since their very existence undermined one of the bedrock beliefs of antebellum white southern culture: that black equaled enslaved.

CHAPTER 3

TO SURVIVE AND THRIVE

RACE, SEX, AND WAGED

LABOR IN THE CITY

In the spring of 1835, Charlestonian Dye Mathews lost her husband of many years. A free man of color and an artisan, George Mathews left an estate that included his carpentry tools, a lot with several buildings on it located on Friend Street, and five enslaved persons. It is not surprising that George bequeathed his five grandchildren equal shares of his estate. His widow, however, received only her basic dower rights. George wrote that Dye "requires no provision as she is capable of maintaining herself and I know she will continue her kindness and protection to our grandchildren. She has a right of residence and home on the lot aforesaid." This same property was to be kept as a home for the couple's grandchildren until the youngest turned twenty-one years old. The five bondspersons, two of whom were children, were to be appraised and then permitted to purchase their time, but if they did not "avail themselves of this," they were to be sold so that each grandchild could receive his or her share of George's estate.[1]

The scant details of this will reveal that Dye and George were hard workers and very committed to their family: the couple had saved enough money to purchase their daughter and her then two children out of slavery in 1817, and they continued to care for all five of their grandchildren after their daughter passed away. That her daughter was not freed until later in life means that Dye herself had been enslaved when her daughter was born, although we do not know when or how Dye acquired her freedom. "Capable of maintaining herself," she may have purchased herself out of slavery by the fruits of her own labors, or George may have helped buy her out of bondage. We do know that George attained a measure of success as a carpenter: he was able to leave his family a home as well as five servants, and he bequeathed the tools of his craft to his two grandsons so they could train for a trade that would offer them stability and status. Certainly Dye's lifelong labor, her ability to "maintain herself," must have played a role in George's success, but her future held little prospect of rest: no longer a young woman, she would have to continue to work in order to provide for herself, plus care for her grandchildren, carrying on in her "kindness and protection to" them.[2]

Dye's story differs in some ways from those of many other free black women in that she was married to a skilled free black man of moderate means. In other ways, however, her life, particularly her tale of unceasing labor, both while enslaved and as a free woman, was reflective of the vast majority of antebellum black women. Due to their masters' generosity, a handful of women made the transition from slavery to freedom with relative ease. For most, however, work was a stark necessity: many newly freed women found themselves unemployed and homeless. In order to provide for their families, avoid being arrested under local vagrancy laws (which only targeted unemployed free blacks), and pay their head taxes, it was imperative that manumitted women find work as soon as they were released from bondage.[3]

The truth, however, was that Charleston's black women faced numerous obstacles in their search for jobs that would enable them to do all these things. It is true that South Carolina's free persons of color had the right to work for pay, and certainly the majority of black women in Charleston engaged in waged labor. Nevertheless, they did not have as many occupations to choose from as black men or white women, nor did they earn as much as either of those two groups. Free black women thus discovered that while low-paying, temporary, and unskilled positions were plentiful and easy to find, lucrative, steady employment was more difficult to acquire. Lacking the skills needed to obtain certain positions, prohibited by race or gender from engaging in others, burdened by raced-based taxes and licensing fees, shackled to a reliance on white employers and clientele, and faced with competition from white working women, the black woman's path to dignified labor and financial freedom was strewn with pitfalls. Poorly paid, and often forced by desperation to accept temporary positions, many women struggled to maintain their families and achieve a freedom beyond the confines of menial labor and continual poverty.[4]

White Charlestonians thus created a labor market intended to keep black women impoverished and dependent, able to do little more than put food on the table and pay their taxes, if that. This was likely not how enslaved women had envisioned waged work. For them, freedom included not being under a white person's constant supervision, keeping the fruits of one's labor, and having the ability to walk unimpeded along the path to financial autonomy. Such economic well-being depended on a black woman's capacity to overcome a number of discriminatory vocational barriers, make a decent living, and avoid the payment of unfair taxes. These things were crucial to a black woman's definition of a fuller freedom because dignified labor, lucrative wages, and the ability to save money would enable her to acquire some of the social privileges denied to her on the basis of her race and gender, as well as allow her to purchase property and buy her loved ones out of bondage.

Women of color, then, were determined not just to eke out a living and survive but to thrive. They did so first by drawing on skills they had developed while still enslaved, turning their abilities to clean, sew, cook, and garden into jobs as maids, seamstresses, pastry chefs, produce vendors, and more. Those who could also utilized their connections to successful black men and whites of both sexes in order to obtain financing for and attract clientele to their own businesses, or to engage in occupations they were socially or legally barred from practicing such as teacher, speculator, and planter. Finally, black women turned to the law to help protect their vision of freedom. As individuals and groups, they petitioned to overturn race-based taxes, worked to evade licensing statutes, and pursued *feme sole* status in order to retain control of their assets. Using these tools and tactics, a number of black women were able to overcome the obstacles arrayed against them and build careers that enabled them to attain the financial stability and dignity they believed freedom, and free labor, ought to entail.

BLACK WOMEN AND THE NECESSITY OF WAGED WORK

For the newly freed woman, her first few days in Charleston would have been both exhilarating and frightening. Even if she had previously lived in the city as an enslaved laborer, things had changed. She was now "free." What, however, did that mean? Would the dreams she had of freedom while still enslaved match the reality she now faced? Certainly she could now legally live on her own and be compensated for her labor. Indeed, Michael Johnson and James Roark state that in terms of their existing rights, the ability to work for wages was second only to free black Carolinians' ability to marry.[5]

Municipal records indicate that a large number of Charleston's free black women exercised this opportunity. Identifying them by the letters F.P.C. (free person of color), the 1819 city directory records the names of 244 black women, 101 (41 percent) of whom listed an occupation.[6] Twenty-six years later, the 1848 city census enumerated 546 "free colored women" in Charleston between twenty and eighty years of age, 322 (59 percent) of whom worked outside the home.[7] The numbers from the city capitation tax books are even higher. In 1861, tax collectors documented the names of 945 "free women of color" who lived in the city and recorded occupations for 758 (80 percent) of these women. This is significantly higher than the data from the 1860 federal census, in which 626 of the city's 1,251 "free negro women" aged fifteen to sixty-five years (50 percent) performed waged labor.[8]

Clearly many, if not most, of Charleston's free black women worked for wages. Indeed, some of those who appear not to have labored outside the home may have chosen to misrepresent their employment status to city officials in order to avoid paying the taxes charged to free black tradespersons living inside the city limits.[9] Additionally, a much higher percentage of the city's free black women than white women worked outside the home. According to the 1848 city census, of the 4,720 white women aged fifteen to eighty years who lived in Charleston that year, 516 (11 percent) listed an occupation, compared to 59 percent of the city's "free colored" women.[10] This compares favorably to both Savannah, Georgia, and Petersburg, Virginia. In Petersburg, for example, data from the 1860 census indicates that more than 50 percent of that city's free black women over fourteen years of age worked outside the home, compared to less than 10 percent of the city's adult white women. The evidence, then, suggests that the majority of free black women in the prewar, urban South were members of the paid workforce.[11]

Finding work was a necessity for most of Charleston's free black women: they had to make money to maintain their liberty. This is underscored by the fact that both the city and the state assessed capitation taxes on free blacks in addition to the taxes that all real property owners paid. From 1792 on, South Carolina charged every free black resident aged sixteen to sixty a $2 capitation tax on their persons. In Charleston, free black women fourteen to seventeen years of age were assessed another $3 for the city's capitation tax, while black women aged eighteen to fifty were taxed an additional $5. Such taxes were both socially humiliating and dangerous for black women: not only were white women never taxed on their persons, but failing to pay your "head taxes" could result in fines, arrest, imprisonment, and even a period of servitude.[12] A similar situation existed in Georgia, where as early as 1799, free black residents aged fourteen to sixty were taxed 31.25 cents per annum by the state. While this Georgia tax was nowhere near as onerous as the $2 tax charged by the state of South Carolina, the city of Savannah levied an additional tax of $6.25 on all free blacks residents of the municipality aged sixteen to sixty-five years, regardless of gender, unless they were carters, draymen, hucksters, or artisans. Persons in these trades, whether male or female, were assessed another $10![13]

These taxes were a serious hindrance to free black women's efforts at financial security, and thus undermined the stability of their freedom. Not only did they have to work in order to pay their taxes and avoid being jailed as unemployed vagrants, but the narrow range of their job options, and the low wages these occupations paid, made it difficult for free black women to both pay their taxes and have sufficient funds left to live on. Indeed, while the Charleston City Council demanded that free blacks work, as early as 1783 it also attempted to freeze the earning power of the municipality's free blacks by limiting their wages to a maximum of $1 for a full day's work. For anything less than a full day, a black worker, female or male, was to be paid 12.5 cents per hour. If a free person of color dared ask for higher wages and was convicted of committing such a "crime," he or she could be fined, and if necessary, jailed until such time as the fine was paid. While the wage cap was eventually lifted, free persons of color were regularly reminded how fragile the freedom to negotiate their labor was, and how easily it could be restricted, reshaped, or rescinded.[14]

The tenuous nature of black freedom was reinforced by the fact that one of the penalties for the nonpayment of head taxes was temporary enslavement. Free blacks from across the state thus decried the levying of these race-based taxes. In Charleston, free persons of color appealed to the state in an effort to overturn the city's capitation tax law as early as 1794. Their petition, signed by three women and thirty-one men, declared that the 1793 city head tax posed "a special hardship on those free persons of color with large families, and women scarcely able to support themselves." It was significant that the petitioners singled out women, whose wage-earning potential was less than that of black men, and that they requested the tax be repealed because it was an unjust measure against persons who were free and "loyal citizens" of the new republic and the state. The three black women who signed the petition, listed only as Mildred, Genelazier, and Catharine, thus not only believed themselves to be oppressed by the new law but clearly saw themselves as hardworking members of the young nation.[15]

Although this appeal was unsuccessful, black women continued to protest the head taxes. In 1806, free black women from Columbia petitioned the General Assembly, asking that it revoke the state's head tax. Politically astute, by 1806 black women had already learned that their position did not allow them to demand anything as citizens. Instead of petitioning as laboring members of the state or nation, then, they now played on accepted social images of female frailty and utilized the language of motherhood and iconic descriptions of virtuous, maidenly poverty to make their case. Crying that the tax placed "great severity upon the females of this class, especially those without fathers, brothers, or husbands to provide for them," the petitioners emphasized their defenselessness, begging legislators to repeal the tax so that "helpless females may not be sold into bondage on account of their poverty." Reports indicate that the assemblymen were sympathetic to the petition, although it was not granted.[16] Thirty-five years later, when Charleston's free women of color used similar arguments to ask that "female free persons of color be exempted" from paying the state capitation tax, South Carolina's legislators concluded that it would be "inexpedient to legislate on the subject."[17]

It certainly would have been "inexpedient" for the state to eliminate the head taxes free black women paid, since those tax dollars went into the state treasury. Still, the fact remains that numerous women were unable to pay their capitation taxes, a reality evidenced by the many names in the tax books with the word "destitute" written next to them.[18] Other women appeared unwilling to pay the head tax and pursued various methods to avoid doing so. Some simply ducked the tax collectors, while a number filed notarized affidavits stating they were not black and thus not liable for such taxes.[19] Then there were those women who used their ties to influential whites to avoid paying their capitation taxes. Hagar Cole, for example, was the daughter of the free black woman Margaret Bettingall, and the stepdaughter of Margaret's longtime partner, wealthy white businessman Adam Tunno. A resident of Charleston, Hagar regularly paid her property taxes, dues that were assessed at the same rates for all city property owners, regardless of race or sex. She did not, however, appear in the capitation tax books until 1840, when she was excused from future payments because she was "overage." Hagar was never penalized for defaulting on her head taxes, however, most likely due to Adam's position and influence in the community.[20]

Not all women who avoided paying their head taxes were as fortunate as Hagar. Refusing to pay the tax was risky: the state was as committed to collecting its money as some women were to not paying it, as Hetty Barron discovered. In 1840, the comptroller general of the state of South Carolina notified the tax collector of the city of Charleston that Hetty had "neglected" to pay her $2 state capitation tax for the year 1838. The sheriff of Charleston was thus commanded to find Hetty, take her into custody, and "sell her services" to recoup the money "necessary to pay the said Capitation Tax, together with the lawful costs and charges thereon." A warrant was duly sworn out for Hetty's arrest. Although we do not know if she was captured, it is sobering to realize how far the state was willing to go to make one free woman of color pay her head tax, even when the tax debt was less than the cost of pursuing her.[21]

Clearly, black women faced difficulties in their quest for financial stability. It is equally evident that they did not hesitate to fight the discriminatory legal codes that hedged them in, using the law itself when possible. They had to be willing to use every available tactic to defend themselves, particularly since most black women could not expect to marry a free black man who would pay their head taxes and support them. This was partly due to the fact that upon exiting slavery, black male South Carolinians discovered that high-paying jobs were difficult to find. First, they were prohibited from entering professions such as law, medicine, or teaching. Additionally, many lacked the training needed to find lucrative positions, while those with special skills, such as carpenters and bricklayers, found it hard to practice their crafts at times due to the availability of cheap slave labor and the protests of white artisans who objected to free black competition. Numerous black men were thus forced to take jobs that working-class white men shunned: occasional work as unskilled laborers. Toiling on the margins of the economy, black men's low wage-earning potential meant that black households in Charleston, as in New Orleans, often required the income of both husbands and wives in order to make ends meet.[22]

Due to the sexual imbalance that existed among Charleston's free blacks, however, many of the city's black women were not married to free black men. With a ratio ranging from 137 free black women for every 100 free black men in 1820 to a high of 169 women for every 100 men in 1848, black women were hard pressed to find a spouse in Charleston's free black community. Remaining single, then, or establishing marriages with enslaved men, which were not recognized by law, many of Charleston's free women of color headed their households alone. In 1830, less than one-half of the city's free black households were headed by both a man and a woman. Additionally, black women headed more than one-half of the free black homes in Charleston that did not list a spouse residing in the same household but did list children. Subsequently, the most common free black household in antebellum Charleston was one woman and her children. Few of the city's women of color could, then, count on having a man's income to help support them during their lifetime. Even as late as 1860, Charleston's free black women outnumbered free black men three to two.[23]

This imbalance was not unique to Charleston. Census data reveals that in Baltimore, women were 57–60 percent of the city's free black population during the antebellum era, while there were never more than 70 free black men for every 100 free black women in Petersburg, Virginia. In Savannah, Georgia, free black women—pressured by poverty, as well as a "continual shortage" of free black spouses, to work outside the home—regularly outnumbered free black men in the labor force. And in New Orleans, there were three times as many women as men among manumitted black adults. It should come as no surprise, then, that black women comprised 67 percent of the free black residents in New Orleans during the 1850s and made up the majority of the city's free black populace as late as 1860.[24]

The reality is that across the South, women were manumitted in larger numbers than were men, and free black women thus outnumbered free black men, particularly in urban areas. By 1860, women of color comprised 57 percent of the free black inhabitants in southern cities with populations of more than twenty-five hundred people, and in metro areas of over ten thousand persons they totaled 58.5 percent of the free black community.[25] Nowhere in the Old South, then, could black women count on having a black man's companionship or financial aid. Self-supporting, whether by choice or circumstance, a significant number of black women in every southern city were not just the heads of their own households; they were also the sole income earners for their families.[26]

Of course, the shortage of free black men meant that some free women married enslaved men. The children of such marriages were free, and enslaved husbands may have provided their wives with emotional support, but it is unclear how financially helpful black women found such relationships. Certainly some enslaved men were "nominal slaves," urban residents who hired their own time and were occasionally able to reside with their families and contribute to their households. Many, however, lived apart from their wives and children in another residence in the city, or on a distant plantation.[27] In such cases, an enslaved husband would have been less able, or unable, to provide support of any kind to his family. Additionally, even if an enslaved man did reside with his family, city and state officials would not have listed him as the head, or even the joint head, of such a household due to his legally enslaved status. The black woman in such a marriage would have thus experienced more legal, if not actual, authority in her household than the average southern wife. Add to this the very real fear that one spouse could be sold away from the other at any given moment, and it would have been difficult for such couples to enjoy what Whittington Johnson terms a "normal marital relationship."[28]

Manumitted with little or nothing in the way of resources and heading up their own households, often with children to support or purchase out of slavery, most black women in the Old South worked because they had to, and they began to work at an early age. Black girls were required to pay a $3 capitation tax to the city of Charleston once they turned fourteen, so unless they came from well-to-do families, girls of color entered the ranks of waged laborers as teenagers.[29] The reality of the freedom experience was that every member of a black household had to do her or his part if the family was to survive. Even women married to black men of means could not assume that their husbands could, or would, support them in life, or help to sustain them as widows. Consider the situation of Dye Mathews, whose story began this chapter. Although her husband possessed a laudable estate, Dye received nothing beyond the right to life tenancy in the couple's home and almost certainly worked to support herself until the day she died.[30]

Free black women's lives thus differed substantially from those of their white counterparts. White women, for example, were more likely to live in households with two spouses; while free black women outnumbered free black men, white women in Charleston were outnumbered by white men. In 1800, there were 91 white women in the city for every 100 white men, and by 1848, there were 98 white women for every 100 white men. As late as 1861, there were still 108 white men for every 100 white women aged twenty to fifty. White women had less trouble than black women in finding spouses, then, and marriage kept many white women out of the workforce. This was partly because white men had access to a wider range of jobs, and more lucrative jobs, than did black men, and were thus better equipped to support their families on a single income. Additionally, a number of married white women did not enter the labor force because it was considered inappropriate for "respectable" white married women, those whom Kathleen Brown terms "good wives," to work for wages. This might explain why only 11 percent of Charleston's white women were listed in the 1848 city census as laboring for pay, versus 59 percent of black women that same year. That 11 percent likely included many women who would have been forced to work by necessity: orphans, single mothers, widows, and the wives of poor men.[31]

RACE AND THE SOUTHERN JOB MARKET

The irony is that while most of Charleston's free black women had to labor for wages, it was difficult for them to find lucrative, steady work. It is certainly true that when compared to rural districts, where work prospects revolved almost exclusively around agricultural labor, southern cities offered free blacks more jobs, and a wider range of job options. Whether it was shipping and manufacturing work in Baltimore, industrial labor in Savannah's textile mills, or positions for skilled artisans in New Orleans, the belief that they could find work, buy homes, and make more money brought large numbers of free blacks to urban centers. Additionally, the increased autonomy and anonymity that came with living in a big city amid a substantial black community led numerous black fugitives to gravitate toward the South's urban areas as well, where they blended in and managed to live as free people for months, or even years.[32]

Many of these opportunities were only available to free blacks because hiring black people benefited the white community in some way. In some cases, black workers were in high demand because they were cheaper to hire and easier to fire, as opposed to maintaining enslaved persons year-round regardless of whether business was brisk or slow.[33] There were also those sectors of the economy in which white southerners refused to work, either because they felt those positions were degrading or because more profitable employment was available. These included domestic service and, in places where white men had more opportunity for professional employment, industrial work.[34] A strong economy, coupled with a shortage of white male laborers, also provided urban slaves and free blacks with job prospects.[35] In each situation, then, free blacks found themselves in demand because economic conditions, demographic factors, or social values necessitated their inclusion in the workforce, rather than because their white neighbors sought to include free blacks in their vision of civic society.

While cities thus provided free blacks with more job options than rural areas, people of color, both female and male, found their entrance into Charleston's labor force barred in various ways. One difficulty lay in the fact that many newly freed people came out of slavery with few marketable skills. Restrictions on black employment, however, presented an equally formidable obstacle. There were, for example, vocations that free blacks were prohibited from practicing, such as law or medicine. Municipal ordinances also forbade free blacks from selling alcohol or managing a billiard parlor, and in 1836 it became illegal for a black person, enslaved or free, to own or "loiter in" any establishment that sold liquor, including grocery stores. Additionally, free black Charlestonians faced special restrictions even in occupations that were open to them. Black "mechanics," or skilled craftsmen, for instance, were required to obtain costly licenses to engage in trades that white mechanics were allowed to practice freely.[36]

The regulating of free black labor was not unique to Charleston. From the borderlands of slavery to the heart of the cotton kingdom, free blacks faced a number of statutory limitations on their ability to work. Many counties in Maryland denied them the right to hold a peddler's license or operate boats, and nowhere in that state could free blacks sell meat or agricultural products without a writ of permission signed by a justice of the peace or three respectable (i.e., white male) persons.[37] Savannah barred free persons of color from all professional vocations including law, medicine, or drug making and dispensing and also forbid them from working as mechanics, masons, teachers, or boat pilots. Additionally, free blacks in Savannah who engaged in an array of vocations, from carpentry down to porters and laborers, had to purchase special licenses to practice their trade.[38] And after the United States took over governance of

Louisiana in 1803, free blacks in New Orleans discovered they could no longer own their own stores or work as carters.[39] In no state were free blacks permitted to own or work in any place where liquor was sold, nor could they retail liquor of any kind.[40]

These decrees make it clear that white southerners regularly used the law to complicate the abilities of free blacks to earn a living and to protect white people's exclusive domain over certain occupations. Additionally, black Charlestonians in the 1840s and 1850s found themselves competing for skilled positions with a growing class of white immigrant laborers. Faced with the prospect of unemployment, which could lead to homelessness, arrest, or indentured servitude, many free blacks found work only by agreeing to charge less for their services. This earned them the ire of working-class whites, many of whom refused to work for "nigger wages." As competition between black and white workers mounted, white laborers moved from asking the government to restrict black employment to physically taking their anger out on free blacks. In the last decade before the Civil War, Charleston's free blacks thus found themselves being assaulted by angry whites who hoped to drive them out of skilled trades. New laws, rising national tensions, and the hostility of local whites meant black Charlestonians who had opened their own businesses and done well for themselves earlier in the century now faced ostracism by the white clientele they depended on and, with it, possible financial ruin.[41]

This reliance on white customers was a difficult hurdle for free blacks to overcome. Whites decided who could buy land, open shops, or engage in certain trades. Free blacks thus had to ally with white persons in order to find and maintain jobs, as well as attract clients to their businesses. The southern economic system was, then, structured so that free black workers needed white patronage in order to survive. The need was not reciprocal, however, so blacks were always at the mercy of their benefactors. Blacks thus had to be cheaper, more reliable, more available, and more compliant in order to maintain the goodwill of those who could fire them, deny them credit, or stop purchasing from them whenever it struck their fancy.[42]

In many ways, a comparable situation existed in Baltimore. While the livelihood of free blacks there was humble, it was also reasonably secure: the city needed carters, draymen, coal handlers, domestic servants, and the like. This gave free blacks a modicum of independence and, as late as 1835, free black Baltimoreans were not legally excluded from any trade practiced by whites. In the 1840s, however, an influx of white immigrants revealed that free black workers could always be replaced. Unlike Charleston, which had numerous black artisans, Baltimore had always had enough skilled white workers, so free blacks worked mainly as laborers. Even those jobs, however, disappeared with the arrival of numerous working-class white immigrants, forcing blacks to accept lower wages and longer hours in order to keep their positions. In the 1850s, this led white laborers to physically assault black workers and those who hired them, resulting in the creation of new, exclusionary hiring policies in certain industries. Still, free black workers, particularly black women, were seen to be a necessary evil, a source of labor that the economy of the state could not do without. As one politician bluntly put it, if free people of color were pushed out of the labor force altogether, who would "supply the places of the free colored women . . . hired by the week, month or year as cooks or house servants in thousands of families throughout the state?"[43]

It is important to note that free blacks in the 1850s also experienced setbacks in a city seen as emblematic of black prosperity. Between 1850 and 1860, the white population of New Orleans grew from about 89,000 to almost 145,000 due to Irish and German immigration. This had a significant impact on the city's black residents: comprising 18 percent of its inhabitants in 1840, free people of color were a bare 6 percent of the New Orleans population by 1860.[44] And while some free blacks continued to prosper there, a larger number now competed against cheap white immigrant laborers in the unskilled sector of the economy. Indeed, black laborers, heretofore the majority of the city's waiters, hotel workers, and peddlers, were slowly replaced by New Orleans's newest white arrivals in the 1850s. Even black artisans experienced a decline in their hold on skilled crafts, and black tradesmen discovered new restrictions on their ability to obtain liquor licenses, open coffeehouses, and run billiard halls. While blacks in New Orleans still had more job options than those elsewhere in the United States and could be found working as engineers, doctors, merchants, jewelers, money lenders, and real estate brokers, in addition to practicing a variety of artisanal pursuits, their opportunities declined in the last decade before the Civil War.[45]

Clearly the 1850s were difficult times for free blacks across the South. In spite of the obstacles, however, some black Charlestonians managed to maintain their financial situations during these years. Ira Berlin posits that some employers set aside their prejudices and hired free blacks due to the shortage of white workers in certain vocations. Additionally, white employers who might have preferred to use enslaved laborers in their businesses often lacked the capital to purchase or rent such persons. Finally, a number of Charlestonians saw no reason to object if free blacks engaged in trades like barbering or tailoring: these were "slavish positions" that southern whites did not want, preferring to be served rather than to serve. Like their counterparts in Baltimore,

Savannah, and New Orleans, then, some free black Charlestonians managed to thrive well into the 1850s because the city's economic conditions, demographic factors, and social values necessitated their inclusion in the workforce.[46]

Another group of black Charlestonians experienced vocational success because of the tendency of slaveowners in the Lower South to selectively manumit favored workers, which translated into a better economic position for some of the region's free blacks. According to Bernard Powers, emancipators in cities like Charleston often prepared their enslaved laborers for freedom by training them in a marketable skill, teaching them to read or write, or giving them monetary support in addition to their freedom. These same white men and women, as well as their friends, relatives, and associates, then selectively patronized these newly freed tradespersons of color, ensuring that certain free blacks would acquire financial stability.[47]

Despite increased harassment from working-class whites in the 1850s, then, free blacks in Charleston still managed to obtain work, and wages remained competitive. And while the city's free men of color did not have equal access to all jobs on the basis of merit, there were more opportunities for them in the Lower South than elsewhere in the nation. Whereas northern black men were largely confined to low-paying positions as laborers and hucksters, Charleston's men of color could earn higher wages as carters, dray drivers, wood factors, and practitioners of a variety of artisan trades. Free black urban communities in the Lower South, Leonard Curry states, were comprised of the most talented and well connected of the formerly enslaved population. It is hardly strange, then, he concludes, that free blacks in cities like Charleston exhibited a higher incidence of vocational achievement than their northern counterparts.[48]

DOUBLE JEOPARDY AND THE BLACK FEMALE WORKER

One might conclude from this discussion that while the southern job market was undeniably marked by racism, slavery itself paved the way for free blacks to find employment in South Carolina. Certainly, white employers were used to slavery and were comfortable working with blacks. And despite the petitions of working-class whites requesting the elimination of free black competition in the labor force, the state legislature never fully prevented free blacks from making a living. The assemblymen likely understood that to do so could remove any incentive that free blacks had in upholding the state's inherently unequal social, political, and economic structures. Charleston's free blacks thus found themselves occupying an intermediate, although precarious, position in the city's labor market. They competed with enslaved persons, who were often cheaper to hire, but by working in positions whites disdained, or accepting less money than white workers, free blacks remained in demand as employees.[49]

The question is whether these conclusions, applicable to free black men, hold up when discussing black women; the two groups' labor experiences have not been systematically examined. Viewed from their perspective, it appears that black women found the labor market in Charleston to be an even more difficult place than black men did: there were many jobs open to them, but not a wide variety of jobs. Like their peers in other cities, Charleston's black women realized that the types of jobs available to black men and white women were more numerous than those offered to black women; that many of the vocations black women were permitted to practice were thought to require "slave-like" skills and were thus believed to be "peculiarly suited" to black people; that most of these jobs were also seen as being "inherently female"; and that the majority of these positions, being both raced and sexed, paid poorly. Entering a workforce shaped by assumptions about gender and race, Charleston's free women of color understood that while they owned their labor and could decide who to work for, their options as to what kind of work they could perform, and for how much, were limited.[50]

The city did offer black women a wider variety of practicable trades than the countryside. As Orville Burton discovered, most free black women in rural districts of South Carolina farmed for a living. Census data from 1860 reveals that 45 percent of Edgefield County's free black female heads of households listed agricultural labor as their occupation, and 39 percent of all free black female laborers in the area worked the land.[51] While not as vocationally limited as their rural sisters, then, many of Charleston's free women of color still found themselves classified as "unskilled labor." Forced by poverty to take whatever jobs were available to them, black women often worked in low-paying positions as day laborers, domestic servants, and washerwomen. For instance, the 1848 city census enumerated forty-five "free colored" female laundresses, twenty-eight house servants, and two laborers. Together, these women comprised 75 of the 322 employed "free colored" women listed in the census (23 percent). While things would worsen by 1860, when 33–37 percent of Charleston's free black working women labored in such occupations, the numbers reveal that even in 1848, twice the percentage of free black women (as opposed to free black men) worked at the bottom of the city's economic ladder.[52]

Many of Charleston's black women, then, ended up performing menial tasks for low wages, which was likely not what they had imagined of the freedom experience. In this they were like free black women in urban areas across

the South. In Baltimore, opportunities for black women were far more limited than they were for black men. Largely unskilled, black women in that city
often worked as domestics, and those who managed to escape cleaning other
people's homes still labored at jobs connected to household work: Christopher
Phillips concludes that after 1817, as many as nine out of ten of Baltimore's free
black female household heads were laundresses.[53] And in Savannah, one of the
most common vocations for black women was laundress. Indeed, Whittington
Johnson posits that free blacks in Savannah did not dominate any profession
except for that of washerwoman.[54] This speaks volumes about the raced and
gendered nature of work in southern cities. Not only was laundry work dirty and
physically exhausting, but it did not produce nearly as many success stories as
other jobs; it seldom allowed black women to earn enough to live, let alone live
well. This was partly because it only required marginal skills to perform, skills
that most women already had by virtue of doing laundry for their own families.
Additionally, so many black women took in wash to add to the family income
that the competition drove down the wages laundresses could earn.[55]

Washing clothes or performing domestic work did have some advantages,
however. For instance, women of all ages and skill levels could take in laundry
to add to their household earnings, and they could perform the work in their
own homes. Even the women of the Dereef family, one of Charleston's elite free
families of color, occasionally washed for wages: Abigail Dereef, the nineteen-
year-old daughter of wealthy wood factor Joseph Dereef, worked as a laundress
in 1860.[56] Another advantage to doing laundry at home was that women did
not need to find childcare, which protected their already slim salaries. Those
women who worked as domestic servants also found that they could, at times,
take their children to work with them, and they often came home with food
from their employers' kitchens, along with castoff household items and clothing. While such conditions replicated many of the realities, and much of the exploitation, of enslaved women's lives, the flexibility and money-saving features
of such positions also afforded some women opportunities not found in other,
higher-paying jobs, where they went out to work but had to pay for childcare.[57]

The free black woman's work situation was not entirely hopeless, then, and
those living in Charleston managed to engage in a number of occupations. In
fact, while many of the city's free black women were washerwomen, this was
not the single largest group of black female workers on record. In 1819, of the
101 black women in the city directory who gave a profession, 31 claimed washerwoman as their sole vocation while seamstresses topped the list at 34. Two
women listed themselves as both seamstresses and washerwomen, raising the

number of black women in those professions to 36 and 33, respectively. Thus as early as 1819, it appears that 36 percent of Charleston's free black female workers worked in the garment trade. Adding these seamstresses to the 16 women who were pastry cooks, mantua makers, cooks, bakers, or confectioners, we find that 52 of 101 of the city's working free black women who appear in the 1819 directory (51 percent) performed skilled labor, while manual laborers totaled 33 percent (33 out of 101) of the directory's black female workers. The remaining 16 women were nurses, midwives, school mistresses, bricklayers, and shopkeepers, all of whom could be classified as professionals or tradespeople (see Table 3.1).[58]

This trend continued on down through the century. In 1822, seamstresses again headed the list of black women's occupations recorded in the city directory, as they would in 1830 and 1835.[59] It was not until 1837 that mantua makers overtook seamstresses at the head of the list. Mantua makers, however, were also skilled artisans who earned a living with their needles: a mantua was a loose gown, commonly worn by women of the era.[60] Garment work in a variety of guises, from tailoress to dressmaker, mantua maker to seamstress, was thus the dominant occupation for free black women listed in the city directories (see Table 3.1). Additional sources indicate that this pattern held until 1861. Data from 1848 reveals that 63 percent of the employed, "free colored" women enumerated in the city census that year worked in "clothing-related" fields. In 1860 and 1861, almost 60 percent of the city's free black workingwomen on record toiled as seamstresses, mantua makers, or dressmakers.[61]

The work situation for black women in Charleston thus appears to run counter to conventional wisdom about the nature of black women's labor in the Old South.[62] The literature, which acknowledges that some free black women worked as artisans, cooks, and midwives, tends to view free women of color as domestic servants and washerwomen, first and foremost.[63] Certainly many black women in Charleston labored as maids and laundresses, but neither of these groups comprised the city's single largest bloc of black female workers on record, unlike in Baltimore.[64] In some ways, then, Charleston was more like Savannah. While the most common job for black women in that city was washerwoman, this was closely followed by seamstress, cook, and seller of small wares. And although most free black women in Savannah worked in "traditionally female jobs," 108 of the city's women of color who listed an occupation in 1823 did work that was business related: they were hairdressers, shopkeepers, and vendors of a variety of goods. As for seamstresses, while they were the second-largest group of waged workers among the city's free black women, they were the leading income earners. According to Whittington

TABLE 3.1. Black Women's Occupations, 1819–1859

Occupation	1819	1822	1830/31	1835/36	1837/38	1840/41	1855	1856	1859
Baker	1	1							
Bricklayer	1								
Cake baker/shop	1						1	1	
Confectioner	2	2	1		1				1
Cook	2	2							
Dressmaker						3	3	6	7
Fruits/vegetables		20				3	2	2	4
Fruit shop	5			2					1
Gardener		1							
Grocer		1					1		
Hotel						1			
Mantua maker	5	10	5	5	8	10	18	10	1
Mattress maker								2	
Midwife	1			1			1		
Milliner				1					
Nurse/dry nurse	6	6	2	1		2	1		2
Pastry cook	6	7	7	10	2	12	4	5	7
School mistress/teacher	2	4							
Seamstress/tailoress	36	33	11	27	2	7	12	3	
Seller in market/huckster	1								1
Shopkeeper	2	1		1					
Umbrella maker				1					
Washerwoman	33	18				2	9		1

Source: *Charleston City Directories, 1819–59.*

Note: Occupational terms used here are taken from the city directories. It is likely that listings such as "cake baker/shop" meant the woman in question owned or operated a cake-baking business, as opposed to working in a cake shop, but it is difficult to confirm this given the terminology used.

Johnson, Savannah's black community had a reputation for spending lavishly on clothes and groceries. Supplementing these black customers with a number of white clients, many black women found dressmaking to be a profitable venture.[65] It is unclear if Charleston's seamstresses were as successful as their counterparts in Savannah.[66] What does seem certain is that most of the city's laboring free black women worked in the garment trades.[67]

Certainly garment work was not the only vocation that Charleston's women of color engaged in. Utilizing skills they had developed while enslaved, Charleston's free black women turned a wide range of feminized household chores and "slave-like" pursuits into wage-earning occupations. In particular, they used their prowess in the kitchen to make careers in the food service industry. Some women, like Venus Deas and Roxanna Niles, were all-round general cooks, while others marketed themselves as experts in a particular type of food preparation. Ann Francis, for example, was a confectioner, Nancy Eden made her living as a baker, and dozens of black women worked as pastry cooks.[68]

Arguably the best known of Charleston's pastry cooks was Eliza Seymour Lee. Trained in the art by her once-enslaved mother, the woman of color Sarah Seymour, Eliza first sold pastries, then ran a boardinghouse, and eventually came to own Charleston's exclusive Mansion House Hotel. Eliza's cooking skills appear to have gone far beyond desserts, however. After the Civil War, two of Eliza's sons headed north to find work and began cooking for a living, using their mother's recipes. When news of their savory pickles and preserves reached the ears of an entrepreneur named Henry Heinz, he offered to buy the rights to Eliza's recipes from her sons. Family lore thus maintains that the recipe for "Heinz 57 Sauce" can be traced back to the kitchen of a free black woman.[69]

While few women attained the fame of Eliza Seymour Lee, pastry cooks were among the best paid and most successful of black female entrepreneurs in many southern cities. In Savannah, the wealthiest free black woman up until 1850 was pastry cook Susan Jackson. After several years, the earnings from the sale of her cakes and pies enabled Susan to open her own pastry shop. Over time, she acquired enough money to purchase several pieces of property in Reynolds Ward, one of the leading business sections of the city. She rented these buildings out to supplement her monthly income, purchased a number of enslaved laborers to help her in her growing business, and lived quite comfortably off of her investments until her death in 1860.[70]

Women like Eliza and Susan may have been unusually successful, but they were still representative of the larger class of free black women in the sense that they used food as the foundation for their economic security. Well-versed in cultivating and procuring food due to their years in bondage, many black women grew, acquired, and sold a variety of food products to hungry Charlestonians. Some even attained the titles of farmer or planter, labels generally reserved for white men. Jane Wightman, for example, owned a four-acre farm in Charleston, which she acquired from white businessman William Wightman, the father of her daughter. The most famous black farming family in the city was similarly biracial in ancestry. Margaret and Alexander Noisette owned substantial land in the Charleston area. Known for their advanced farming techniques, the Noisettes obtained some of their property, and much of their horticultural expertise, from their father and former owner, botanist Philippe Noisette.[71]

It was rare for a black woman to acquire the title of planter, and evidently those who did often obtained their land due to their connections to white men. This is not surprising: while chronically low wages made it difficult for black women to save the money needed to purchase farmland, another obstacle would have been the prestige accorded to planters in the Old South. In a society where respect was given to those who owned land and laborers, and where freedom was seen as a privilege reserved for whites alone, it would have been difficult for white southerners to live among black plantation owners. Unwilling to elevate blacks to the highest position on the social totem pole, and give them the respect that such rank required, whites may not have wanted to sell land to blacks. This would explain why the state of Georgia prohibited free blacks from acquiring real estate in the cities of Savannah, Augusta, and Darien after 1818.[72] It makes sense, then, that black female landowners often acquired their real estate via white men to whom they had social, sexual, or familial bonds. Such ties helped some white men overcome their aversion to seeing free blacks become landowners while giving the black women concerned the wherewithal to inherit or purchase plantation property.

While few black women became farmers or plantation owners, many women of color sold a variety of food and drink in cities across the South. Growing their own produce or utilizing their connections to rural enslaved persons, black women vended their goods in city markets, from baskets along the wharves, and from portable stands on nearly every street in and around urban centers.[73] No matter what state one lived in or visited, or whether these women were called hucksters, peddlers, or hawkers, travelers and locals in southern cities found themselves awash in a sea of black women selling everything from fruits and vegetables to oysters, candies, cakes, spruce beer, hot coffee, popcorn, peanuts, rice croquettes, clothes, and handmade crafts.[74] City directories indicate that many women, like Kitty Jacobs, were "Sellers in Market," while others, including Felicity White, sold fresh fruit for a living. A number, like Elizabeth Grant and Harriet Lazarus, were listed as "Hucksters," so we do not know what they sold, or where.[75] And in 1861, Mary Purvis had the distinction of being Charleston's only self-proclaimed "Oyster Woman." She undoubtedly had connections among the fishermen who worked at the city's bustling docks from whom she would have acquired her goods.[76]

The marketplaces and roadsides of southern cities were dominated by black women like Mary Purvis who hawked their wares to people of all backgrounds and ages come rain or shine. Indeed, their commanding presence in the area of food sales caused alarm among Charleston's white residents. Their concerns stemmed from the fact that black women's control over the city's food supply meant that they could, quite literally, hold its residents hostage by withholding goods from sale, driving up prices or even causing food shortages. Certainly black women were able bargainers, as many a woeful shopper discovered after encountering women who refused to sell "except on their own terms." This would explain why black market women in Charleston were, at various times, referred to by whites as "idle negro wenches," "loose, idle and disorderly," "insolent," "abusive," "notorious," and "impudent."[77]

These issues encouraged Charleston's city council to pass several bylaws that constrained the activities of black salespersons and became a financial hindrance to the economic aspirations of enterprising black female vendors like Mary Purvis. An 1807 ordinance aimed at limiting the mobility of black hucksters and centralizing the sale of food products in the city stated that a free person of color found selling goods anywhere but in the city marketplace would be subject to a $20 fine. In 1834, it became illegal to hire a free black person as a clerk or salesperson in any shop in the city. Shopkeepers who broke the law were subject to a $100 fine and faced up to six months in prison for each conviction. And finally, in an attempt to limit the number of black women engaged in food sales, as well as profit from those who did, the city council decreed in 1843, "It shall not be lawful for any free negro or person of colour, to open or keep within the limits of the city . . . any shop, shed, or stall, for the sale or disposal of fruit, without first obtaining a license . . . for which license every such person shall pay the sum of five dollars for each and every shop, shed, or stall, by him or her opened or kept within the limits of the City of Charleston; and every person offending herein, shall . . . pay the sum of twenty dollars for each offence."[78] Enforcement of the licensing laws was never absolute, "given their [white Charlestonians'] very real dependence upon the . . . marketeers to gather and distribute the city's food supply." The fact remains, however, that these laws were kept on the books and could be used by city authorities whenever, and against whomever, they chose.[79]

Similar legislation in Savannah mandated that all free blacks who vended small wares, were hucksters, or sold vegetables in the marketplace pay an annual licensing fee of $8. Despite this, so many black women took to the streets and markets to hawk their wares that the Savannah town council worried that there would not be enough black women available to help nurse whites during

Black female street vendors in Charleston, ca. 1879.
(Black Charleston Photographic Collection, College of Charleston Library, Charleston, SC)

the "sickly season of the year." Deeply concerned, the councilmen resolved to suspend issuing badges or licenses to free black women who wished to become market women or peddlers of any kind, and to arrest and jail every free black woman caught selling her goods without such a badge.[80]

Black female marketeers clearly made white southerners nervous, and they were evidently a force to be reckoned with. No doubt many a black woman thus chose to engage in this vocation for what it could afford to her. This kind of work allowed black women to be their own boss, set their own schedules, travel throughout the district, meet a variety of people, and earn a living. Exchanging information with sailors, conveying news from the countryside, transacting business with people of all colors, and deciding to whom they would sell, and for how much, these women had an autonomy many free blacks could not imagine.[81] Few hucksters would have become wealthy, however. Subsisting on the income earned from their daily sales, and vending their products from baskets atop their heads or portable roadside tables as opposed to established stores, market women and fruit sellers barely got by on their earnings and would not have been included among Charleston's free black artisanal, professional, or merchant classes.

Women of color could, however, pocket the money they made selling oysters and fruit and dream of acquiring their own store, which would provide them with more money than they made as street vendors.[82] There were certainly women to whom they could look for inspiration in most southern cities. This is remarkable, given that most black women labored long hours for low pay and considering the money that was required to open and maintain even small oyster cellars and cook houses.[83] Despite these obstacles, however, a number of Charleston's free black women owned or leased shops from which they sold a variety of goods and services. Nancy Burns had a fruit shop at 68 Meeting Street, while Mary Duprat and Betsy Henry operated cake shops, almost certainly selling items that they themselves had baked. Sophia Cochran had the distinction of being the city's only female grocer of color listed in the 1822 directory. According to city directories, no other black woman operated a grocery store in Charleston until Sarah Blank opened her establishment in 1855.[84]

Like other grocers of the era, Sophia and Sarah likely sold beer and hard ciders in their stores, in addition to hot foods and other goods. Although it was illegal for black people to buy or sell alcohol or spend time in a place that sold such beverages, free blacks were seldom arrested for selling liquor in otherwise legitimate cook shops and groceries, and for spending time in such establishments. Whether they sold alcohol or not, however, Sophia's and Sarah's shops, like other groceries of the era, would have been sites where people gathered to exchange news and socialize. Profitable ventures, these stores catered mainly to a black clientele, although working-class whites frequented such places as well. This must have given their owners a sense of independence, since they were not beholden to elite white customers for their survival. Additionally, the groceries would have provided blacks with a rare public space where they could gather and converse freely, away from the prying eyes of the master class. Sophia and Sarah, then, were undoubtedly well-known and respected members of the black community, in addition to being two of the best informed, privy as they would have been to all the news that passed through their shops.[85]

The preparation and sale of food and beverages clearly played a major role in free black women's lives. From growing and acquiring food, to cooking and selling it, the food services industry provided many a woman of color with her livelihood. For example, in addition to the occupations already discussed, a number of women turned their cooking expertise, as well as their housekeeping skills, into careers as boardinghouse operators. While some women only took in tenants during times of financial crisis, or opened up their homes solely to friends and relatives in need, others realized that housing boarders could be a lucrative venture in a busy port city where housing was at a premium. Women like Sally Graham thus leased, rented, and purchased buildings for the purpose of maintaining boardinghouses, lodges, or hotels.[86]

In addition to providing housing, most boardinghouse owners also cooked for their tenants. It was in this fashion that Eliza Seymour Lee, who began her days as a pastry chef, got her start in the hotel business. Eliza and her husband, the free black man John Lee, ran a rooming house in the early years of their marriage, and Eliza, whose skills in the kitchen were renowned, cooked for their tenants. Then her mother, "the free woman of color" Sarah Seymour, passed away and left most of her estate to Eliza, much of which was acquired from her white lover, most likely Eliza's father. This inheritance, when added to what Eliza and John had saved from their boardinghouse venture, allowed the pair to open what became one of the city's finest hotels: the Mansion House. Located on Broad Street, the Mansion House was frequented by elite whites from across the nation and around the world, and Eliza was known as a fine manager and an excellent cook. An entrepreneur who began her days laboring around hot ovens as a pastry chef, and who then spent many years cleaning up after the tenants in her boardinghouse, Eliza won her eventual success as a hotel owner through hard work and determination.[87]

In a city with only three hotels, it is worth noting that free blacks ran two of these establishments. The Jones' Hotel, owned by the free black man Jehu Jones, was the place to stay in Charleston. White slaveholders, businessmen, and foreign travelers of note all lodged there, and Jehu's wife helped maintain the hotel's reputation. Abigail Jones, like Eliza Lee, began her career as a pastry chef and was not only a "clever" manager but also an excellent cook. Her talents were passed down to her daughter, Ann Deas, who took over the hotel in 1833. By 1838, however, Eliza Lee owned the Jones' Hotel. British actress Frances Kemble visited Charleston in the late 1830s and stayed at Eliza's new hotel, describing it as "the best in the city." According to Frances, Eliza was a "very obliging and civil coloured woman who is extremely desirous of accommodating us to our minds." Eliza's "accommodating" attitude likely helped her to garner the glowing reviews so critical to success in an industry dependent on pleasing wealthy, and often capricious, white travelers. Managed by the "obliging" Eliza, and run by a well-trained staff that included several of Eliza's enslaved laborers, the Jones' Hotel continued to be Charleston's premier inn.[88]

Few women attained such success in the world of boardinghouses. Many, however, found the work profitable, whether they ran rooming houses full-time or were landlords in addition to holding down "day jobs." On Meeting Street, for example, near the city line, lay solid rows of small wooden homes in a neighborhood inhabited by hired urban slaves, newly arrived white immigrants, and free blacks and local whites of more modest means, mainly artisans and day laborers. The free black woman Martha Evans was one such resident. A greengrocer by trade, sixty-year-old Martha was also a landlord: she owned her own home near Reid Street and rented the adjacent property to a white male engineer from New York named Charles Huston. Martha was not alone in having a white tenant: some seventy-five whites in Charleston rented their homes from free black landlords in the 1850s.[89] Women like Eliza Lee and Martha Evans thus provided the city's newest arrivals, both white and black, as well as those too poor to own their own homes, with an invaluable service in this bustling port city that seemed to suffer from a continual shortage of housing.

While Martha Evans took in a white male tenant, other black women boarded children for money, including the children of wage-earning white women. Siblings Laura and John Moore, for example, resided with a free black woman. Abandoned by her husband, the children's mother, a white Irishwoman named Eliza Moore, was forced to take a domestic servant's position in a home where her offspring were not welcome. Lacking any relations to care for her children, unable to secure other (i.e., white) childcare on her meager wages, and prevented by residency restrictions from placing the pair in the city orphanage, Eliza asked her neighbor, a free black woman, to board Laura and John for pay. When "concerned citizens" discovered the situation, they complained about the arrangement to city officials who, in turn, removed Laura and John from the black woman's home and made special dispensation for the youngsters to reside in the city orphanage. While enslaved women were thus expected to care for white children as part of their unremunerated labor, white Charlestonians appeared to be less comfortable with free black women profiting from similar tasks.[90]

Pecuniary gains notwithstanding, boardinghouse operators, like seamstresses and pastry cooks, were still tradespersons or skilled artisans.[91] Some black women, however, exited slavery with talents that allowed them to operate as professionals. Several, for example, were able to use their knowledge of illnesses, ailments, and remedies to work as health care providers. Although their numbers were small (roughly 3–4 percent of all black working women listed in Charleston's directories in any given year) every directory and tax book contains the names of black women who made their living as medical practitioners. Most, including Clarinda Hamilton and Mrs. R. Baird, labored as nurses. And while no black female doctors are listed in the record books, each directory and census includes the names of black midwives. In cities like Charleston, with large black female populations, midwives of color like Molly Mathis and Dinah Buchanan would have been in high demand.[92]

Other black professionals in Charleston included teachers, community leaders who were arguably the most respected, and the best educated, members of the city's free black population. Although South Carolina, like Georgia, had outlawed black education by the 1830s, free blacks in both states set up clandestine schools for children of color in private homes in Charleston and Savannah. Indeed, large numbers of Charleston's black children could be seen walking the streets each morning carrying armloads of books, clearly on their way to school. While children in Savannah were not quite so brazen in their comings and goings, when times were peaceful the white residents of both cities looked the other way when black schools were set up in defiance of the law. This was due, in part, to the fact that many black teachers had strong ties to elite whites. Thomas S. Bonneau fit this mold. A member of the Brown Fellowship Society (BFS), Thomas worshipped at St. Philip's Episcopal Church, lived in a prosperous neighborhood on Coming Street, and, upon his death, left his wife, Jeanette, a home worth $1,000 and several enslaved laborers.[93]

Black women also played a significant role in educating free children of color, despite the legal obstacles and the competition they faced from free black men. The best-known schools for Charleston's black children were run by men of color like Thomas Bonneau and Daniel A. Payne, and black women found themselves teaching in gender-segregated facilities.[94] Still, there were always free black female teachers. As early as 1794, Amy Akin ran a boarding school for black children on Church Street, and in 1819, both Sarah Cole and Sophia Ives openly listed "School Mistress" as their occupation in the city directory. There was also Mrs. Stromer, whose school, founded in 1820, remained open until the start of the Civil War, and Amelia Barnett, who ran a school for girls on Mary Street. As late as the 1850s, Frances Pinckney Bonneau Holloway ran a school for free black children on Coming Street. The daughter of Thomas S. Bonneau, Frances was married to free carpenter of color Richard Holloway Jr., a man from a family as prestigious as her own, and with strong ties to elite whites. Frances's social standing was such, then, that she was able to teach black children openly, in defiance of the antiblack education laws, at a time when life was becoming very difficult for Charleston's free blacks.[95]

The reality of free black education in Charleston and Savannah was significantly different from that in New Orleans. Although black schools existed in South Carolina and Georgia, they were somewhat discreet due to their formally illegal nature. There were no buildings openly erected to house black schools, and free blacks understood that any time the goodwill of their white neighbors evaporated, so could their schools.[96] In New Orleans, however, black schools were conducted openly, and one even received government approval and funding. In 1847, the city agreed to the founding of the Catholic Institution for Indigent Orphans (CIIO), which opened that year under Principal Félicie Callioux, a free black woman. Established using funds that a deceased free person of color had left for such a purpose, the CIIO accepted orphaned free children of color without charge while free blacks who could afford it sent their children there for a nominal fee. Instruction at the CIIO, a coed institution, was conducted in both French and English, and children of all denominations were accepted as students. The school's five teachers were all free blacks and two, Madame Joseph Bazanac and Madame Adolphe Duhart, were women. And while much of the school's funding came from charitable contributions, as late as 1854, the CIIO received $2,000 from the state assembly.[97]

It is, of course, not possible to mention every occupation that antebellum black women engaged in. Those I have already discussed were the most commonly recorded, but free women of color did engage in other types of work. Some, for example, rose to positions of wealth and influence as rentiers. Deriving an income from buying, selling, and renting out land, buildings, and laborers, these women essentially speculated in human beings and real estate, activities long thought to be the domain of white men. For example, the wealthy widow of color Ann Mitchell loaned money at interest plus rented and sold enslaved laborers to a number of free blacks, including Richard Holloway, a skilled carpenter and father-in-law to schoolteacher Frances Holloway, mentioned above. When Richard died, he, in turn, bequeathed a number of enslaved persons to his wife, Elizabeth, laborers Elizabeth hired out for pay and whose combined wages helped support her and her daughters. At a time when black women could inherit bondspersons, and in cities where hiring enslaved persons to fill the economy's demand for laborers was common, a number of slaveowning black women became wealthy speculators.[98]

At the opposite end of the financial spectrum from Ann Mitchell and Elizabeth Holloway were impoverished women like May Flurney, the city's only black female bricklayer, and Ashley Bascombe, a mattress maker. And, as in any large city, there were those women who made their living as prostitutes. As the petitions against them indicates, sex workers of both races plied a thriving trade on the streets, docks, and wharves of the city, and since prostitution was not a crime in South Carolina, little could be done to stop such activities. Denunciations by the city's Ward 4 residents against "the mulatto wenches and prostitutes" who turned their neighborhood into "a constant scene of nightly brawls and riots" resulted in few arrests or charges, and streets like Clifford Alley continued to find themselves awash in sailors, plantation owners, and tourists, along with the women who serviced them.[99]

FEME SOLE STATUS IN SOUTH CAROLINA

It is a testimony to their determination that free black women were able to turn a variety of "feminine, domestic skills" such as cleaning, sewing, cooking, and gardening, into jobs as servants, seamstresses, pastry chefs, and produce vendors. Maneuvering the obstacles placed in their path, many women managed to earn enough to both survive and thrive. Some were aided in their endeavors by the fact that married women in South Carolina had a legal advantage not found in any other state: they could become *feme sole* traders. South Carolina recognized the right of a married woman to act as if she were single for the purposes of carrying out "business on her separate and exclusive account and benefit." In short, a married woman who became a *feme sole* (a single woman or woman alone) was an autonomous entity in the eyes of the law and could buy and sell goods or services and engage in legal contracts of any sort on her own, without her husband's approval. Unlike a *feme covert* (a covered woman), a *feme sole* could own her own property, had control over the wages she earned, could sue and be sued, and the profits or debts she incurred from her business dealings were hers and hers alone.[100]

By law, a woman automatically became a *feme covert* upon marriage. Early in the nineteenth century, however, the law in South Carolina was amended so that a man could consent to his wife's becoming a *feme sole* trader, despite her married status, by executing a written, notarized deed, or by simply allowing her to conduct herself as a *feme sole*, also known as "tacit consent." In 1823, the state assembly amended the law yet again, under "an Act to Regulate the Mode in which Married Women shall become Sole Traders or Dealers," and demanded that married couples henceforth formally register their *feme sole* intentions. A woman could still become a sole trader, but the law now required that "she give notice by publication in a public newspaper of her intention to trade as a sole trader, which notice shall be published at least one month, and if there is no newspaper published in the district, then the notice shall be published in the same way as the sheriff's sales." The new statute still did not require a husband to publicly declare his consent to his wife's separate business activities. It is not entirely clear if this meant that a woman could become a *feme sole* against her husband's wishes.[101]

It should come as no surprise that the vast majority of South Carolina's *feme sole* traders (83 percent) lived in the city of Charleston.[102] What is worth noting is that some couples formally executed deeds or registered their sole trader intentions before it became mandatory to do so, which suggests their desire to take every precaution in their business dealings. Such was the case with Sherry and Catharine Maria Sasportas. The only formal *feme sole* deed uncovered that concretely pertains to a free woman of color, Sherry and Catharine's deed was filed in 1817, six years before it became mandatory to do so.

> This Indenture . . . made . . . between Sherry Sasportas of the city of Charleston . . . Catharine Maria Sasportas a free mulatto woman his lawful wife . . . and Peter Smith, Esquire . . . Whereas . . . Sherry Sasportas hath considered . . . it will be proper and expedient for . . . Catharine Maria . . . to become a sole and separate trader . . . and to follow such lawful occupation and employment as she may think proper . . . he . . . hath and doth consent and agree that . . . Catharine Maria . . . shall . . . enjoy all the privileges and advantages of a separate and sole trader . . . and as relates to any occupation and employment she may pursue in as full and ample a manner to all interests and purposes as any sole and separate dealer . . . or femme sole . . . and . . . that the said Sherry Sasportas shall not . . . molest, trouble, or in any manner interrupt her . . . in such her sole and separate trade . . . occupation or employment or . . . dispossess or deprive her of any money, estate or affects and profits which she shall henceforth . . . acquire by her sole and separate trade . . . occupation or employment.[103]

Unfortunately, we know little else about either Catharine or Sherry. There is no indication what either of them did for a living, nor can we be certain that Sherry was white, although the fact that the deed makes no mention of his color suggests that he was considered to be a white man. As for his wife, an entry in the 1830–31 city directory lists a "free person of color" named Catherine Sasportes living on Alexandria Street in Charleston Neck. The federal census that same year reveals that this Catherine was between twenty-four and thirty-six years old and headed up a household of thirteen people, five of whom were enslaved. Whether these entries refer to the wife of Sherry Sasportas is unclear, and no other records for a Catherine/Catharine or a Sherry Sasportes/Sasportas have been located.[104]

Although the Sasportas contract was the only formal *feme sole* deed found that refers to a woman of color, public records suggest that other married black women behaved as if they were sole traders, deed or no deed. Barbara Tunno Barquet, for example, is listed in the 1830 census as the head of two separate households in the city of Charleston and the owner of several enslaved laborers. A married woman of color whose property should have legally belonged to her husband, John, Barbara's ownership of real estate and black workers (whom she rented out and sold) is indicative of her *feme sole* status. Her behavior seems to have run in the family: Barbara's half sister, Hagar Cole, although married to one Thomas Cole, also appears in the 1830 census as a slaveholder and the head of her own household. Additionally, in 1834, Hagar successfully petitioned the courts to have a white man appointed as the guardian of two of her children ... although her husband was still alive. Indeed, neither Thomas Cole nor John Barquet appear in the city's census records or court documents, although family papers and other public records indicate that both men were alive and residing in Charleston in 1830. Nor did either man file a *feme sole* deed for his wife. Instead, both Thomas and John appear to have permitted their wives to behave as single women via the practice of "tacit consent."[105]

Black female Charlestonians clearly took advantage of the state laws permitting married women to behave as sole traders. They bought and sold a variety of goods and services, owned their own property, and filed lawsuits and petitions with the courts, all without formal *feme sole* deeds. Whether this was always done from a position of strength, however, is debatable. Some women became *feme sole* traders because their husbands' debts were a liability to their families: men in financial trouble deliberately transferred their assets to their wives in order to avoid losing those possessions to their creditors.[106] Maria Lopez benefited from just such a situation. Maria, whose race is uncertain, was the wife of Jack Lopez, a free black man and a dray driver by trade. On 12 March 1822, Maria and Jack executed a *feme sole* deed for Maria. Jack then transferred all of his worldly possessions to his wife, "free from and discharged of all debts, dues and demands against him." His assets included "the buildings on a lot in Swinton's Lane, the buildings on a lot in Beaufain Street, four drays, one cart, five sets of harness, one four-wheel carriage and harness, two chairs on springs with harness, eight horses, one old negro man called Jonas with all my household and kitchen furniture."[107] It is important to note that while many men protected their property in such fashion, they also strove to ensure that their wives' business dealings did not adversely affect their own finances. The Sasportas deed, for example, stated that "the said Sherry Sasportas . . . shall not be liable to the payment of debt, or debts, or demands whatsoever which . . . Catharine Maria his wife shall or may hereafter contract or occasion by [illegible word] in carrying on her sole and separate trade, dealing, occupation or employment."[108]

Being a *feme sole*, then, was not always or completely empowering. Still, it meant that Charleston's married women of color were able to engage in practices denied married women in other states. This included everything from peddling fruit to owning their own shops: bakeries, restaurants, groceries, and the like. There was even a syndicate of black women in Charleston who operated an oyster emporium, and 80 percent of the city's hotel owners and boardinghouse keepers were women. Black *feme sole* traders could also enter into contracts and lend money on their own account. In 1838, Dye Waring, who had at one time been enslaved, loaned $1,600 to Abraham Moise, a Jewish attorney in the city of Charleston, "at 7 percent interest per annum, payable semi-annually." Abraham put up a lot of land he owned on the corner of Beaufain and Coming Streets as collateral for the loan. Dye, a married woman, filed papers stating that Abraham had discharged his debt to her in full as of 19 February 1844. *Feme sole* status, then, could and did give women in South Carolina, black and white, a financial autonomy that was unusual among married women in antebellum America.[109]

SHE HAD NOTHING TO FALL BACK ON;
NOT MALENESS, NOT WHITENESS . . . NOT ANYTHING

While some women were able to use the *feme sole* laws to their advantage, black female Charlestonians still lacked access to the variety of careers open to both black men and white women. From an early age, the city's black boys had a wide range of apprenticeship options that led them into occupations like barber, tailor, caterer, and carpenter. Some of these jobs were positions white men did not want (because they were seen as being "servile"), but they were, nonetheless, skilled trades by which black men could become financially stable. Black men still experienced economic constraints, however. Dependent on a white clientele, men of color were given protected status in a handful of vocations while being simultaneously prevented from engaging in more lucrative professions such as law or medicine. Additionally, due to their overconcentration in certain trades (45 percent of the city's free black men were carpenters and tailors in 1860, for example), black men were always vulnerable to redefinitions of "nigger work." In spite of these things, total economic disaster never struck

Charleston's free black men. Not only was there a shortage of white workers during the antebellum era, but most of the city's free men of color practiced skilled trades that were in high demand and commanded good wages.[110]

As a result of Charleston's social and economic terrain, many black men were thus able to open shops, engage in lucrative trades, and attain a measure of economic security. Some even expanded their businesses and hired other free blacks or enslaved persons to work for them. By 1819, free men of color performed over thirty different kinds of jobs in the city; by 1849 they toiled in over fifty different occupations. Laboring as they did in well-paying trades ranging from carpentry to tailoring, shoemaking to butchering, 59 percent of the city's employed black men could be classified as artisans. A group of (relatively) economically independent free black men thus emerged in Charleston in the years before the Civil War. And while 23 percent of the city's laboring black men worked in menial, low-paying positions (compared to only 16 percent of white men), only one-sixth of Charleston's working white men could be classified as artisans. In spite of the differential that existed at both ends of the spectrum, then, the social and economic situation in Charleston proved to be moderately advantageous for free black men.[111]

The situation was markedly different for the city's free black women. Data from the 1848 city census indicates that 322 of Charleston's "free colored women" held only fourteen different kinds of jobs, primarily low-paying positions as garment workers or washerwomen. "Colored men," by comparison, worked in forty-three different fields, many of which were in higher-paying trades like blacksmith, wheelwright, tinner, cigar maker, upholsterer, and carpenter. Black men also engaged in some of the same occupations as black women, working as cooks, fruiterers, and house servants, but the reverse did not hold true.[112]

By 1860, the economic gulf between black men and women in Charleston had widened. That year, the city's black men engaged in sixty-five different kinds of work spread across ten occupational classifications. Two-thirds of these were high-paying, skilled trades. Conversely, black women could only be found in eight different occupational classifications. The most highly skilled of these women were concentrated in four, low-paying trades, all garment related, including tailoress, seamstress, mantua maker, and dressmaker. Together, the women in these four occupations comprised roughly 57 percent of the city's black female laborers. The fact remains, then, that despite the increased employment opportunities the city afforded to black women (when compared to rural areas of the state), women of color were still twice as likely as men of color to be at the bottom of the economic ladder. In 1860, roughly 37 percent of the city's free black women labored in menial positions as domestic servants or washerwomen. That same year, less than 20 percent of the city's black men held similarly low-status, low-paying jobs.[113]

While cultural beliefs about appropriate male and female work thus barred them from achieving occupational equality with black men, long-standing beliefs about race and servile labor kept black women from attaining economic parity with white women. In the 1848 city census, 526 white women were listed as members of Charleston's labor force. These women worked in thirty-one jobs over six different categories. That same year, "free colored women" held fourteen jobs across four different categories. And while 230 white women worked, as black women did, in the needle trades, white women also had a foothold in professions black women were legally barred from practicing, like teaching, and they entered in large numbers into food-based vocations, a mainstay of black women's economic ventures. Charleston's labor market was, then, shaped by ideas about race and sex. Consider that in 1848, although all of the city's mantua makers, milliners, and seamstresses were female, the milliners were all white and over three-quarters of the mantua makers were black. That same year, black men could be found in forty-three occupations spanning ten categories, while white men held 188 jobs in fourteen categories, including some that were exclusively white and male: justice, religion, and fine arts. Taken together, the data indicates that Charleston's free black women were confined to certain trades based on color and excluded from other, more lucrative jobs due to gender. As important as race was to a person's economic opportunities in Charleston, then, so, too, was sex.[114]

Such racial and sexual segregation was the norm in cities across the South. Examining that city's apprenticeship records, Suzanne Lebsock concludes that the main economic problem facing free black women in Petersburg, Virginia, was a lack of job options. Black men in Petersburg had a variety of trades to choose from, black women very few, mainly low-paying occupations like seamstress and washerwoman. Some women were fortunate to enter freedom with specialized skills that helped them avoid such work, including nurses Jane Minor and Aggy Jackson, midwife Judy Denby, cupper and leecher Phebe Jackson, and baker Nelly White. Others used their connections to white men to become wealthy businesswomen. Amelia Galle, also known as Milly Cassurier, managed her owner's bathhouse while she was still enslaved. Freed in 1804 after bearing her owner a son, Amelia inherited the bathhouse upon John Galle's death in 1819 and became the city's most successful black female entrepreneur. Unlike Amelia, however, most of Petersburg's black women sewed, washed clothes, did housework, or stemmed tobacco for a living. And, as in Charleston, Petersburg's female labor force was divided by race and gender: there may have been black and white seamstresses, but all the washerwomen were black, tobacco plants hired black women, and cotton factories employed only white women.[115]

A similar situation faced black women in Savannah and New Orleans. While more free black women than men entered the labor force in Savannah, these women had more limited opportunities. In 1823, Savannah's *Register of Free Colored Persons* recorded the names of 108 free black female workers who toiled in only twenty different kinds of jobs; the same list contains the names of only forty-nine free black men who engaged in waged labor, but who worked in eighteen different occupations. And although fewer than 50 percent of the jobs listed by black men required a specialized skill, over 53 percent of the city's black male waged workers (twenty-six) practiced a skilled trade. The simple fact is that free black men in Savannah, while a smaller group, had more opportunities to find work in a variety of different, well-paying, skilled trades, many of which were closed to black women because of their gender.[116]

Black women in New Orleans fared little better. In 1850, only one-tenth of black male waged workers in that city could be classified as laborers, while the majority of free black women sweated in low-paying, menial positions as domestic servants, ironers, market vendors, and washerwomen. Additionally, fewer black women than men held professional positions: as late as 1860, forty free men of color were professionals in New Orleans, compared to only twenty-six women of color. Finally, from 1840 to 1857, black women in New Orleans could only be found in two different kinds of professional positions: boarding-house keeper and nurse. Sexism and racism thus curtailed jobs for women of color in New Orleans as they did in Charleston. Barred from jobs held by white women and black men, black women were allowed to work in vocations seen as extensions of feminine household duties, such as cook, domestic servant, or laundress, as well as those believed to require inherently "slave-like" skills.[117]

For free women of color, then, economic stability was an uphill battle. Not only did they have to compete with white women for work, but they were also locked out of higher paying positions due to their gender, and financially undermined by white Charlestonians who rented enslaved women to perform the same work that free black women did, but for less money. Discriminatory laws and societal assumptions about race, sex, and labor, in addition to chronically low wages, thus forced many free black women into poverty, and it is clear that class in antebellum Charleston could not be divorced from race or gender. Upward mobility was difficult for hucksters and washerwomen, and even free black entrepreneurs and artisans found their ability to prosper limited at times by their reliance on a small, impoverished black clientele as well as a well-to-do but fickle white one.[118]

CONCLUSION

Upon acquiring their freedom, Charleston's black women discovered that white South Carolinians had clear ideas about what freedom should look like for people of color, ideas that clashed with black women's personal visions of freedom. For women exiting slavery, freedom included the right to own their own labor. As we have seen, free blacks in South Carolina were "allowed" to work and could often "choose" where to work. Indeed, if they did not work, they would be unable to pay the taxes demanded of them and become subject to fines, imprisonment, or temporary reenslavement, a constant reminder of the fragility of the antebellum black freedom experience. Additionally, city and state coffers suffered if free people of color could not work, since free blacks were a captive source of tax revenue. Further, their dominance in certain, critical trades, including food production and construction, and the corresponding dearth of white workers to take their place, made free black labor crucial to Charleston's ability to function smoothly. The South Carolina General Assembly thus never completely prevented free blacks from making a living, knowing that to do so would hurt the state in tangible ways. Indeed, such punitive actions might have removed the only incentive that free blacks had to uphold South Carolina's racially divided and sexually discriminatory job market.

Despite the fact that black women's labor was essential to the overall health of the city's economy, however, white Charlestonians still had clear ideas about what types of vocations were appropriate for free people of color to engage in: it was necessary that free blacks work, as long as they remained in socially and financially subservient positions that upheld the traditional dominance of whiteness and maleness. Such deeply entrenched cultural beliefs meant that free black women faced numerous obstacles in their search for gainful employment. Most labored outside the home and performed waged work out of necessity. Usually single, and with children to support, the majority of black women, then, did not engage in paid work from a position of strength. And while they toiled at a variety of jobs, free black women never had as many types of vocations to choose from as free black men or white women, nor did they make as much money as either of those groups. Often exiting slavery without the training needed to be artisans (seen to be the purview of men), prohibited from engaging in professional (i.e., white) occupations, burdened by special licensing fees, and forced to pay race-based taxes on their own persons, black women discovered that their path to economic security was rocky at best. Add to this the hundreds, even thousands, of dollars that many women spent purchasing themselves and their loved ones out of slavery, and financial stability appeared to be an impossible goal.[119]

The reality was that black women in the Old South had the right to work for what white people chose to pay them, at jobs they were allowed to perform, and were subject to onerous taxes without the benefits of representation. It is a testament to their commitment to bettering themselves that some black women were able to attain a modicum of job security in the face of such obstacles. Whereas white Charlestonians crafted and maintained a labor market intended to keep free black women socially constrained and economically vulnerable, black women were determined to both survive and succeed. Taking advantage of skills they had developed during their enslavement, many turned their abilities to perform "feminine" household tasks into jobs as market women, midwives, mantua makers, and confectioners. Others used their education, wealth, and social connections to white persons to engage in occupations they were ostensibly barred from practicing, including teacher or land speculator. Some built relationships with white men, associations that enabled them to become entrepreneurs, acquire land, and even attain the title of planter. Through their never-ending labor and determination, then, many black women were able to develop careers that allowed them to achieve modest financial stability.

Black women also realized that they could never take their freedom for granted, and that they had to defend their rights as laborers in order to protect their vision of freedom. They thus signed petitions to repeal unfair laws, behaved as *feme sole* traders, filed affidavits, defaulted on their taxes, refused to buy special licenses, and used their connections to prominent whites in order to break the law, all in an effort to acquire and maintain those things they viewed as their rights as free workers and citizens. Whether they won or lost their individual battles, black women behaved in ways that suggest they believed they were entitled to fair wages and decent jobs, and that they ought to be protected, just like other citizens, from discriminatory taxes and restrictive legislation. They thus used the judicial system to both obtain and protect their financial resources so as to expand and maintain the parameters of their liberty, refusing to reside silently within the boundaries of an impoverished freedom erected by the South's master class.

Having acquired manumission, legal or otherwise, and secured employment, the next step for black women in building their freedom would be to attain property. Black women understood that a successful freedom experience was tied to their control of financial resources, without which they could find themselves reenslaved. It was not enough to simply be able to pay their rent and capitation taxes, however; such meager holdings would mean a vulnerable, narrow freedom, lacking in any real rights or privileges. Free blacks would have desired the more secure freedom that property ownership promised, as well as the expanded economic and social opportunities that it could afford to them and their children. Some concluded that such upward mobility meant allying with powerful whites, while others committed themselves to amassing certain kinds of goods, particularly real estate and enslaved persons. Women like Jane Wightman and Eliza Lee had already learned what could be achieved with the backing of white persons of stature, and the help of chattel laborers.[120] As the following chapters reveal, they were not alone in forging relationships with white persons in order to achieve their objectives, and those women who did so were generally able to acquire more privileges than those who eschewed or lacked white patronage.

CHAPTER 4

THE CURRENCY OF

CITIZENSHIP

PROPERTY OWNERSHIP

AND BLACK FEMALE

FREEDOM

In 1857, Eliza Seymour Lee initiated a lawsuit against fellow Charlestonian Henry Gourdin. A respected businesswoman, Eliza and her husband, John, had owned the city's two most illustrious hotels for decades, lodgings that catered to prominent whites from across the nation and around the world. By the 1850s, Eliza was a wealthy widow with ties to Charleston's white elites, and she oversaw her business affairs with the help of Henry Gourdin, whom she hired to help manage her finances. A prominent attorney, Henry appeared happy to take Eliza on as a client. Their relationship soured, however, when Eliza discovered certain irregularities with her portfolio. Confronting Henry and getting nowhere, and determined to protect her property rights, Eliza sued him for fraud and embezzlement.

The outcome of the case seemed certain: Eliza was a free black woman of the managerial class, Henry a white man from the professional class, and an attorney as well. Henry was thus vested with more economic and social status than Eliza, a woman of color whose race and gender placed her near the bottom of the southern power structure. One could thus assume that Henry would prevail. Eliza, however, clearly felt that she had the right to seek justice. She was intelligent, wealthy, and well connected, and her lawsuit indicated she believed that she was a citizen of the state of South Carolina and thus entitled to the protections of the law, regardless of time, place, or her social space. The courts evidently agreed: Eliza won her suit, and Henry was ordered to make restitution to his former client.[1]

It is true that Eliza was unusual in some respects due to her affluence. In other ways, however, what we know of her life and her lawsuit is reflective of the city's larger community of free black women.[2] As they worked to obtain their liberty and secure dignified employment, black women came to realize that money could assist them in fulfilling their definitions of freedom. In addition to providing them with the ability to acquire some creature comforts and rise socially, even modest wealth could help shield black women from some of the harsher aspects of discrimination. It could, for example, enable them to avoid the payment of certain taxes, gain entrance to particular churches, bring them into contact with people in positions of power and authority, protect their families, and educate their children. Wealth, and the connections that accompanied it, also allowed a number of black women to file (and win) lawsuits in various state courts. Women of color thus strove to amass property, understanding the connection between monetary assets and rights, and they used their financial resources to lobby for increased privileges for themselves and their kin.

All property was not created equal, however. Certainly black women acquired goods that improved their daily existence, including furniture, clothing, and jewelry. Possession of such material goods allowed women of color to represent themselves as belonging to a certain class, and aided them in the performance of respectable womanhood. In large part, however, they focused on obtaining those items that would help them solidify their always fragile freedom, expand their legal privileges, and rise in both wealth and social standing. Legally entitled to purchase real property, but never as wealthy as black men or white Charlestonians, black women understood that power, security, and status in the Old South were tied to the ownership of land and laborers. They thus pursued such acquisitions. Living in a society where they were always just steps away from reenslavement, free black female Charlestonians were rarely able to think about "the race." All they could do was utilize the options available to them in this time and place in order to give their own families the best chance at a fuller freedom. Poverty made free black women more vulnerable to sexual and racial harassment, while owning land and human beings increased their ability to dictate the direction of their lives, despite the social space to which their race or gender might relegate them. Those women who were able to purchase real estate and bondspersons were thus better able to shape their lives to fit their own visions of freedom.[3]

For free black women, however, buying real property was complicated by the occupational barriers they faced, as well as by the burdens of race-based taxation.[4] Laboring daily just to survive, a number of the city's black women still managed to acquire some assets by virtue of their toil. Another group inherited property from free black family members and added these modest resources to the fruits of their own labors, while still others acquired some of their possessions from white friends or relations. The methods by which Charleston's women of color acquired their wealth thus closely matched those of their peers in Savannah.[5] What these women understood was that in the slave South, men were imbued with more power and privileges than women, and white men had access to the most wealth and the highest status. Realizing, then, that the largest gains could be made by allying with men of stature, a number of black women entered into partnerships with men of influence, both black and white. Collectively, those who associated with black men were less affluent than those connected to wealthy white men, but those related to black men still fared better than their single peers. Thus, while being involved with a man did not guarantee a black woman an existence of comfort and ease, being single almost always condemned her to a lifetime of backbreaking work and poverty.

Additionally, for black women, being able to safeguard what they had toiled so hard to acquire was as critical as obtaining property in the first place. Even affluent women of color like Eliza Lee were not women of idle luxury, and most black female property owners labored long hours as seamstresses, washerwomen, and the like, until the day they died. They thus sought every avenue possible to protect their belongings and did not hesitate to demand that the state uphold their property rights in the face of corrupt persons and organizations who worked to defraud them of what little they possessed. Free black women thus protested against unjust laws, entered into premarital contracts, petitioned the General Assembly, and filed lawsuits to defend themselves as residents of the state. Shrewd political actors who understood that manumission did not grant them unfettered access to equality, black women not only used their wealth to position themselves as taxpaying citizens entitled to certain rights, privileges, and protections but also worked the legal system in order to defend their own image of freedom.

THE ACQUISITION OF CONSUMER GOODS

Dedicated to making their vision of freedom a reality, free women of color worked to purchase even small items that might ease their daily existence and allow them to perform a certain kind of social status.[6] That a number of women who were really quite poor died owning silk clothing, fine linens, and gold jewelry testifies to this commitment. Ann Bivet's estate, for example, was valued at only $42, yet at her death she owned four gold earrings, two gold necklaces, and four gold rings, in addition to her clothing and ornamental jewelry. The gold jewelry was worth $21, exactly 50 percent of her total estate. When she died, Margaret McWharter also left a small personal estate, appraised at just over $112. While she owned no taxable property, Margaret possessed several items that would have made her life more comfortable and enabled her to walk the streets of Charleston as a woman of respectable position. These goods included bed, home, and table linens, dresses and cloaks made of silk and lace, and a number of delicate petticoats and stockings.[7]

Such acquisitions might seem like foolish extravagances for women who were so desperately poor. Consider, however, how it felt for black women to wear what they wanted. Most had owned no clothing while they were enslaved beyond two work dresses made of the coarsest materials, while their mistresses were draped in silks, lace, pearls, and diamonds. For many black women, then, adorning their bodies with jewels and beautiful garments would have been an important expression of their freedom, a testimony to their belief that they were the equals of white women. In arraying themselves as they did, they made a ringing, nonverbal declaration that they had the right to dress as they wished, and as they wished to be seen: as ladies, not laborers. Much like the enslaved domestic worker, Ellen, who continually disobeyed her owner's reprimands and used her mistress's perfumes and cosmetics, an antebellum free black woman, in purchasing elegant clothing and other finery, "laid claim to a measure of possession of her own person, and a womanly person at that."[8]

The reaction of southern whites to black sartorial style suggests that they were discomfited by black people dressing as if they were the social equals of the master class. In 1822, the City Council of Charleston observed that the expensive clothing worn by many blacks was not only "highly destructive to their honesty & industry" but also "subversive of that subordination which policy requires to be enforced." The council then asked the state to pass legislation regulating the appearance of people of color.[9] In New Orleans, free women of color were forbidden to wear silks, gold, silver, pearls, mantillas, or slippers with silver bells. And if their hair was combed high, they were prohibited from placing feathers in it and had to cover said hair with a kerchief. The laws revealed that white southerners perceived personal adornment as a privilege for white persons alone. The fact is that the more leisure time a person has, the more time they have to care for their appearance. Stylish clothing and well-groomed hair were thus badges of nonslave status, while the head kerchief was an equally clear sign of one's racial status. Forcing women of color to cover their hair was, then, an attempt to return them, visibly and symbolically, to the status of "slave." Free black women who had become too clean and elegant, who competed too freely with white women, threatened the social order and were thus "retied" to slavery through the head kerchief.[10]

Of course, not all free black women chose to purchase fine clothing or jewelry with their hard-earned wages. Some acquired stocks or opened bank accounts instead. Of the fifty-two estate inventories known to belong to black female Charlestonians, eleven included stock shares.[11] Many of these shareholders were quite poor. Louisa Smith's entire estate, for example, consisted of four shares in the Union Bank of South Carolina, assessed at $200. Ann Wilson, in contrast, died with $2,700 in stocks, which made her one of Charleston's more prosperous women of color.[12] Most of the nine women of color who died with cash on hand lived similarly impoverished lives. Their money was usually on deposit at a local bank, and the majority of these accounts had small balances: Sarah Lucas, for example, had $25 at the Charleston Savings Institution. Less common is the estate inventory of Mary Williams, which indicates that she had $520 in an account at the Savings Bank of Charleston. These sums reflected years of labor and frugality on the part of both women. When one considers that their bank accounts comprised the bulk, if not the whole, of their estates, it becomes clear that neither Sarah nor Mary lived a life of ease.[13]

That black women worked extraordinarily hard in order to accumulate even a very small number of possessions is suggested by the fact that they listed their belongings, item by item, down to the very last tumbler. No matter how poor they were, or perhaps because they had so little, free black women in Charleston, like their counterparts in Baltimore, took great pains to leave amazingly detailed lists of their personal effects in order to ensure that these items passed on to the appropriate heirs.[14] Enumerating every item of clothing, each dish, tablecloth, blanket, and chair that they owned, a number of free black women also took the time to list their horses, cows, and pigs in their wills, carefully delineating how many of each animal they owned, and how this livestock was to be divided among their various friends and relations.[15]

BLACK FEMALE REAL ESTATE OWNERS

While most women of color owned little beyond the basic necessities of life, some, like Susannah Cart and Ruth Gardiner, left their heirs estates that included symbols of high social status, such as church pews and chaises. Like the majority of southerners, however, black women who could afford it invested in real estate.[16] Women of color placed a premium on owning real property, which not only indicated prosperity but also accentuated a black woman's free status and provided her with economic self-sufficiency. It was also an excellent way to earn the respect of white southerners and provided an opportunity for social advancement.[17] All of this would explain why otherwise affluent free black women had little or no cash on hand: they probably bought real property, tangible items of prestige whose value increased with time, as soon as they had accumulated enough money to make such a purchase. The city's probate records suggest this to be the case. Of the seventy free black women for whom wills, inventories, or other estate papers have been recovered, only five (7 percent) possessed both real estate and stocks or cash, while another forty-seven (67 percent) owned real estate alone: houses, city lots, farmland, and a variety of urban buildings.[18]

Municipal tax records support the data culled from the probate records. The 1859 list of taxpayers for the city of Charleston includes the names of 353 free blacks who owned some type of real, taxable property: horses, real estate, or enslaved laborers. Of these 353 persons, 306 owned real estate, and of those, 134 were women who collectively owned land, houses, or both assessed at almost $279,000, an average of $2,082 per woman. The following year, 309 of 371 free black taxpayers owned real estate. Of these 309 persons, 123 were women who together owned close to $267,000 worth of real estate, or about $2,170 per woman. Additionally, 245 original tax returns of free Charlestonians of color from 1860 reveal that 94 women of color possessed real estate of some kind, the assessed value of which was close to $163,000, or roughly $1,734 per woman. Evidently Charleston's free black women made it their business to purchase real estate if and when they could (see Table 4.1).[19]

Of course, owning real property did not mean that a woman was wealthy. There were many free black women whose taxable real estate holdings were little more than a shed or a shack and who were excruciatingly poor. This was the case with Bella Fenwick, whose personal goods, assessed at $27, were worth more than her $20 house. Rosina/Rose Dobbins fits into this category as well. Rose died possessed of an "old wooden building upon leased land situated in Pitt Street." She had no personal property whatsoever and died intestate, and her heirs and creditors were anxious to have the house, which "cannot be considered to be worth more than 150 dollars," sold in order to receive the monies owed to them. Given that sturdy wooden homes in Charleston cost around $1,000 while brick houses sold for roughly $2,000, neither Bella's nor Rose's property could be classified as (monetarily) valuable, although the buildings may have meant the world to their owners.[20]

Baltimore's black women were similarly impoverished. While there was the occasional Henrietta Gun, who possessed $18,000 in real property and $500 worth of personal goods, the more typical black female real property owner was like Harriet Berry, whose dilapidated 20- by 22-foot frame shack was appraised at just under $14 in 1831. The house was worth so little that the city chose not to assess taxes on it. Baltimore's free black men found themselves in a comparable situation. Since most of that city's free blacks worked in service occupations, as opposed to skilled trades, very few of them, female or male, acquired

TABLE 4.1. Free Black Real Estate Ownership by Gender, 1859–1860

Year	# FBW	# FBM	Total FBs	% FBW	% FBM	Amount Owned by FBW	Amount Owned by FBM	Difference
1859	134	172	306	44	56	$2,082/woman	$2,785/man	$703
1860	123	186	309	40	60	$2,170/woman	$2,651/man	$481

Sources: 1859 Tax List, at CCPL; 1860 Tax List, at RSS.

Note: FBW = free black women; FBM = free black men.

any real property. In contrast, Philadelphia's free blacks possessed more real estate, and more costly property, than their peers in Baltimore. Indeed, of the fourteen antebellum cities from across the country that Christopher Phillips surveyed in his book *Freedom's Port*, Baltimore had the lowest percentage of free black property owners, as well as the poorest black real property owners.[21]

Whatever their property was worth, the fact remains that women in Charleston controlled a significant share of the city's black-owned real estate. They did not, however, own more real estate than black men.[22] Indeed, although the city's free women of color outnumbered free men of color, not only were men the majority of Charleston's black real estate owners, but also as a group, they were wealthier than their female counterparts. In 1859, 172 of the city's 306 black real estate owners were identifiable as black men who collectively owned almost $479,000 in real estate, or $2,785 per man. This was $703 more per person than the average value of the property controlled by the 134 black female real estate owners that year.[23] The next year, there were 309 black real estate owners, 186 of whom were men holding real estate worth almost $493,000. Roughly $2,651 a man, this was $481 more than the average for each of the 123 black women who owned real estate that year.[24] Thus, not only did more black men than women own real estate in Charleston, but also black men possessed more valuable property than their female counterparts (see Table 4.1). This was due in large part to the vocational barriers the city's free black women faced, which would have made it difficult for them to save enough money to purchase real estate, prime or otherwise.[25]

The situation for black women in Charleston was thus comparable to the one in Petersburg, but less so than in Savannah or New Orleans. In Petersburg, census schedules indicate that 40–50 percent of all free black property owners throughout the antebellum era were women, but women controlled just one-third of the city's black-owned real estate.[26] By contrast, as early as 1820, Savannah's free black women comprised 58 percent of that city's free black real estate owners and controlled 57 percent of its black-owned real estate. Over time, women also became the majority of black real estate owners in that city who owned the most valuable property. Savannah's black women thus paid more in taxes than black men because they owned more real estate, and more costly real estate, the city's primary source of tax revenue in the nineteenth century.[27] And in New Orleans, the city with the largest and wealthiest free black community in the Old South, black women owned more property than either black men or white women up until 1850. Indeed, the U.S. government was shocked to discover upon acquiring Louisiana that over one-quarter of the homes and estates along the main streets of New Orleans were owned by free blacks, most of them single black women.[28]

Although these were impressive gains for people who had often begun life enslaved, the proportion of southern free blacks who owned property *decreased* over the antebellum era, as did the amount of property they owned. In Baltimore, only eight persons of color had acquired real estate by 1798, comprising 3.3 percent of all real estate owners in the city. The average value of the property they owned was $226, while the average worth of white-owned real estate that year was $1,479. By 1815, the fifty-eight black property owners in Baltimore were only 1.4 percent of the city's real estate owners, each of whom controlled an average of $150 worth of property. The average value of white-owned real property that same year also decreased, to $800, which was still more than five times greater than that owned by free blacks. And in 1850, black property owners in Baltimore comprised only 0.4 percent of the city's free black population, and only 0.06 percent of the city's population as a whole. Apparently even these minute numbers were threatening to white Marylanders, who asked the state in 1850 to prohibit free blacks from acquiring real estate or leasing it for more than a year. The measure failed, but the fact that it was even suggested illuminates the obstacles faced by black Baltimoreans who sought to acquire land and homes.[29]

Savannah's free blacks faced similar struggles. In Georgia, an 1818 state law prohibited free blacks in Savannah, Augusta, and Darien from acquiring real estate or enslaved workers. Although many free blacks still purchased land and laborers, it meant they had to find creative ways around this legal barrier. Most black property owners, like Aspasia Cruvellier Mirault, circumvented the law by establishing good relations with white men who acted as their trustees and secretly purchased real property for them using the black person's money.[30] Despite such efforts, however, data from city tax digests and census materials reveal that a higher percentage of Savannah's free blacks purchased property before 1830 than later in the century. In 1820, there were thirty-six free black real estate owners in Savannah who collectively owned property worth $31,250.

By 1848, the number of black property owners had risen to fifty-seven, but the assessed value of their collective property had dropped to $23,190. And in 1858, only forty-three free blacks in Savannah owned real property. Over the years, then, the number and proportion of free persons of color who owned property decreased: whereas 64 of Savannah's 572 free blacks owned real estate in 1823 (11 percent), by 1860 only 36 of the city's 735 free blacks (5 percent) controlled any real estate.[31]

A number of factors contributed to this decrease. After 1830, buying real estate became more difficult for Savannah's free blacks as a flood of European immigrants arrived in the city, driving up housing prices. Several black property owners also died intestate during these years, and their property was purchased by white persons, while other blacks, victims of the economic panics and depressions that swept the nation in the 1830s and 1840s, defaulted on their taxes and lost their homes. Savannah's racial climate also became more hostile toward free persons of color after 1830: fewer white men were thus willing to enter into trust agreements with free blacks, and others simply refused to sell real estate to free persons of color. Some free blacks were able to hold onto their property and bequeath it to their children, and the value of this property went up due to an inflation in real estate prices. There were also a few free blacks who increased the actual amount of real estate units they owned. Still, the overall picture of black property ownership in Savannah after 1830 was one of decline.[32]

Even persons of color in New Orleans experienced this downward trend. When the United States took possession of Louisiana, a number of white persons, alarmed by the wealth of the region's black population, demanded that free blacks in the new territory be prohibited from owning real property. While the measure did not pass, free black property owners in Louisiana were now required to pay property taxes, something not asked of them under Spanish rule.[33] Despite the new tax laws, however, the years from 1813 to 1830 were something of a "Golden Age" for free people of color in New Orleans. During this time, numerous free blacks purchased land and homes, and by 1836 there were 855 free persons of color in the city who collectively controlled almost $2.5 million in property, or $3,000 per property owner.[34]

Starting in 1837, however, the number of free blacks who owned real estate in New Orleans steadily declined. This was partly due to the national financial panic and bank failures of 1837, which led hundreds of free persons of color to sell the homes they had owned for generations. Five years later, a new law forcing recent black arrivals to leave Louisiana, and forbidding all contact with the Caribbean, led many free persons to flee the state. The free black population in New Orleans thus dropped from nineteen thousand in 1840 to only ten thousand in 1850 as those who could liquidate their assets and leave did so.[35] In 1850, free persons of color still controlled just over $2.2 million in real estate in New Orleans, but the heyday of black property ownership was over.[36] By 1860, the number of free black property holders in New Orleans had declined 32 percent since 1830, and the total value of the real estate they owned had gone from $2,465,000 to $2,628,000, a rate of increase that was significantly lower than the norm in light of the rising prices of property in the city.[37]

SLAVEHOLDING WOMEN

Unlike their counterparts in Savannah and New Orleans, Charleston's black women were never the majority of the city's black real estate owners during the antebellum era. However, while black female Charlestonians comprised only 40–44 percent of the city's black real estate owners, they amounted to 42–48 percent of the city's black taxpayers overall.[38] This is because in addition to real estate, Charleston's black women owned other types of taxable real property, particularly enslaved laborers. The first U.S. census noted that 155 free black families lived in Charleston District in 1790 and that 49 (32 percent) of the heads of these households owned enslaved persons. Craftsmen and shopkeepers, these "black masters" would have put their laborers to work in their fledgling shops and businesses.[39]

While the percentage of black slaveowners in Charleston would never again be as high as it was in 1790, it remained higher than the southern average of 2 percent. By 1830, roughly 12.5 percent of Charleston's free blacks owned enslaved workers. That year, 394 free blacks (out of a free black population of about 3,200) owned 2,078 enslaved persons (about 5.25 per owner). Of these black masters, 247 (or 63 percent) were women who collectively held 1,279 (62 percent) of the city's black-owned chattel laborers, or just over 5 per owner. In 1830, then, black women outnumbered black male slaveowners almost two to one, although the average black male master owned slightly more laborers than did his female counterpart. Census records from 1830 reveal that 147 black male slaveowners (37 percent) collectively held 799 (38 percent) of Charleston's black-owned bondspersons, an average of roughly 5.5 enslaved laborers per master (see Table 4.2).[40]

Although the percentage of free blacks in Charleston who owned enslaved workers was higher than that in other southern cities, black women still outnumbered black men as slaveholders in those cities, just as they did in Charleston. In Baltimore, for example, few blacks owned human chattel: most of that city's free blacks were unskilled laborers who could not afford to purchase enslaved persons. There were thus only five free black slaveowners in Baltimore in 1813, but all five were women, and they collectively owned six persons.[41] In Savannah, there were twenty-two black slaveowners in 1823, sixteen of whom were women. Collectively possessing fifty-eight servants, the majority of Savannah's black slaveowners, like those in Charleston, used their human property to help expand their businesses: the men were either in the building trades or personal services, while the women labored as seamstresses, pastry cooks, and washerwomen.[42] And in New Orleans, where the largest group of black slaveowners lived, 735 free blacks owned 2,351 enslaved laborers in 1830. In contrast to Charleston or Savannah, however, not only did a greater proportion of free blacks than whites in that city possess enslaved workers, but also they owned only one or two servants apiece. These laborers did not toil in their masters' shops but performed various domestic chores, including childcare.[43]

As the century progressed, records indicate a drop in the number of black slaveowners in Savannah and Charleston, as well as a decrease in how many persons those black masters owned. In Savannah, city tax digests reveal that the total number of black slaveowners increased early in the century from sixteen persons who owned thirty-two laborers in 1810 to twenty-two individuals who collectively controlled fifty-eight servants in 1823.[44] Between 1823 and 1837, however, while the number of free black slaveowners did not change, the amount of workers they claimed dropped to forty-four. The decreases of the 1830s became more dramatic in the 1840s and 1850s: in 1847, sixteen free blacks in Savannah possessed a total of forty-eight enslaved laborers, and in 1855, a mere ten free blacks held thirty-two enslaved persons. Thus both the number of black slaveowners and the sum total of servants they owned decreased in the 1840s and 1850s. By 1860, only nine black slaveholders lived in Savannah, and the nineteen persons they claimed ownership of were a drop in the bucket: 14,807 enslaved residents lived in the city that year. The one constant over time was that free black women in Savannah consistently outnumbered free black men as slaveowners.[45]

The losses experienced by Savannah's free black slaveholders in the late antebellum era were similar to the ones sustained by that city's free black homeowners, despite the fact that the demand for laborers remained high in Savannah and the prices of enslaved persons were subject to fewer fluctuations. Whittington Johnson concludes that the decline in black slaveownership was due in large part to the fact that white Georgians were unwilling to sell enslaved workers to free blacks because it made poor whites look bad. Indeed, white Georgians put pressure on the state assembly to terminate free black

TABLE 4.2. Free Black Ownership of Enslaved Persons by Gender, 1830–1859

Year	Total FB Slaveowners	# FBW	# FBM	% FBW	% FBM	Total EP Owned by FBP	# EP Owned by FBW	# EP Owned by FBM	% EP Owned by FBW	% EP Owned by FBM
1830	394	247	147	63	37	2,078	1,279	799	62	38
1859	109	61	48	56	44	281	157	124	56	44

Sources: 1859 Tax List, at CCPL; "Free Negro Owners of Slaves," 70–74.

Note: FBW = free black women; FBM = free black men; EP = enslaved persons; FBP = free black persons.

slaveownership altogether: it apparently reflected adversely on the institution of slavery to have free blacks owning enslaved persons when most of Georgia's white citizens could not afford to purchase them.[46]

Charleston experienced a similar decline in terms of black slaveownership. In 1830, 394 free black slaveholders lived in Charleston who collectively owned 2,078 enslaved persons. By 1859, there were only 109 black slaveholders in the city, and together they laid claim to 281 laborers. This means that while the city's free black population remained relatively constant between 1830 and 1859 at around three thousand individuals, the number of black masters decreased by over 70 percent while the amount of black-owned servants dropped 87 percent. The data from 1859 also reveals that 61 of those 109 black slaveowners (56 percent) were women who owned a total of 157 workers, or 2.5 per owner. The 48 black male slaveowners that same year (44 percent) possessed 124 of the city's black-owned enslaved laborers, also about 2.5 servants each. Black women thus outnumbered black male slaveowners in 1830 and 1859, but the differential between the two groups had dropped. Women comprised 56 percent of Charleston's black masters in 1859, compared to 63 percent three decades earlier, and both black women and men owned less than half the number of bondspersons they had possessed in 1830 (see Table 4.2).[47]

For black female slaveowners to outnumber black male slaveowners in Charleston is logical since they comprised the majority of the municipality's free black adults.[48] That they owned so many laborers could also explain why black women possessed less real estate than black men: they may have chosen to divert more of their assets to the acquisition of laborers than to the purchase of real estate. Enslaved persons were less expensive to buy than houses, so it would make sense for black women to purchase enslaved persons in lieu of, or prior to, acquiring real estate. This could explain why a number of women, including Nelly Wilson and Barsheba Cattle, owned laborers but not real estate, whereas it was rare to find a woman like Delia Wyatt, who owned two small houses but no enslaved laborers. Many of these women likely bought workers to help them expand their small businesses or hired them out for cash, allowing them to save enough money to eventually buy real estate.[49]

Of course, some black women owned loved ones whom they could not legally manumit. Of the forty-one wills attributable to black women, twenty-one (51 percent) refer to the ownership of enslaved persons. Four of these twenty-one wills (19 percent) indicate that the persons in question were relatives. Ann Scott, for example, was an affluent woman of color. In addition to a lot of land in Charleston with several buildings thereon, Ann also owned her daughter, Patty, and Patty's two sons, Jacob and Isaac, all of whom she had purchased out of slavery. Ann instructed her executors to use every means to free her daughter and grandchildren. If it was not possible to do so in South Carolina, they were to go up North and be manumitted. She then left her entire estate in trust for her enslaved kin, although Ann stated that if Patty preferred, everything could be sold and the proceeds given to her directly. Tenah Glen found herself in a similar situation but did not have to resort to a trust agreement with executors who might disregard her wishes. She was able to leave her enslaved son, Cudjo, to the care of his younger sister, Tenah's free black daughter, Mary Richards.[50]

Women like Ann and Tenah did not make up the majority of the city's black female slaveowners, however. Unlike Baltimore, most of Charleston's black mistresses owned enslaved persons as laborers. Large-scale manumissions in the Upper South meant that few free blacks in places like Baltimore had to purchase their relatives out of slavery or hold them as virtually free persons.[51] In Lower South cities, however, where owner manumission had been outlawed earlier in the century, and where financial resources were required to expand a person's freedom, black women used bondspersons to increase their wealth, often so they could purchase their own kinfolk out of slavery.[52] So it was that by 1850, the largest group of Charleston's black female slaveowners worked in the garment trades as seamstresses, mantua makers, tailoresses, and the like. Usually single, and with children to care for, these women supported themselves and were the heads of their own households. Realizing the value of using chattel labor in their economic ventures, they bought workers to help expand their small businesses, since hiring whites was not possible, and free black employees were more expensive than enslaved persons in the long run. It is quite likely, then, that Sally Johnson used her four servants in her pastry-making enterprise, while Barbara Barquet put some of her human chattel to work in her umbrella shop.[53]

Plantation owners and sisters Esther McIntosh and Charlotte Boon also understood the need for enslaved laborers. Residents of Charleston, both women inherited substantial property from a white man named Robert Collins. Robert had engaged in a long-term relationship with an enslaved woman named Sue and had nine children by her, including Esther and Charlotte. Upon his death Robert left Sue, now a free woman, and their children his 545-acre plantation in the parishes of St. Thomas and St. Dennis, along with the workers needed to maintain it. Both Esther and Charlotte knew it would be costly to work a plantation of that size without enslaved laborers, and neither woman attempted to free any of the human property she had acquired. Indeed, both women left their shares of the plantation, along with the bondspersons who worked the land, to their surviving relatives in order to keep the family's legacy intact.[54]

It appears, then, that many black women owned enslaved persons for pecuniary gain. Twelve of the twenty-one women whose wills referred to the ownership of chattel laborers (57 percent) indicated that they regarded their laborers as financial assets. Certainly Mary Douglas appeared to view at least one of her servants in this manner. A free woman of color, Mary owned an elderly man named William Irvine. A barber by trade, William was executed on 17 August 1832 after he was convicted of "stabbing, bruising, and wounding" a white man named John Cramer while in a drunken rage. In 1837, Mary, positioning herself as a property owner whose rights had been violated, petitioned the General Assembly and demanded that she be compensated for the loss of William at the hands of the state. The legislators awarded Mary $122. In a state dedicated to upholding the sanctity of private property and the authority of slave masters, and where numerous laws existed to compensate property owners for their losses, Mary's decision to press her rights as a slaveowner in order to recoup monies for the loss of a laborer, and the assemblymen's willingness to view her as a mistress entitled to restitution, made social and financial sense.[55]

Mary Douglas, like all women of color, understood that she needed to use all the means at her disposal to expand and protect her vision of freedom. For some women, this included the ownership of enslaved persons. Among other things, enslaved workers could be used to make a person's life, and the lives of their relations, more comfortable. This was of paramount concern to Juliet Eggart, who stipulated that her entire estate, including the "negro girl Celia," was to be used to provide an income to support her children. If Celia "misbehaved," however, she was to be sold and the money used to help sustain Julia's family. And while Jubah Warren was willing to manumit her enslaved laborers, her family's needs came first. Jubah gave her servant Grace to her sister Dianah and stated that all three of her sisters (Dianah, Nag, and Ceily) were to be supported "out of the

wages of my servants." Jubah's eighteen enslaved workers were to be manumitted only after the death of all three of her sisters.[56]

It is hardly surprising that Charleston's free women of color prioritized the
needs of their families over those of their laborers. In a society where their
very existence was seen as an oxymoron, free black women could rarely afford
to think collectively about "the race." Indeed, realizing that solidifying their
always fragile freedom was contingent on maintaining the goodwill of the
white women and men who were their employers, clientele, or kin, many of the
city's free women of color kept their distance from the enslaved. This ranged
from limiting their social interactions with enslaved persons to owning bondspersons themselves. In doing so, they reflected the behavior of free blacks from
across the Old South who realized that their advancement depended, in part,
on their distinguishing themselves from enslaved persons.[57] Understanding the
dependent nature of their own freedom, black women saw their world for what
it was and wrung from it what they could. Many thus became participants in
an oppressive regime in order to ensure that their own families became, or remained, free. They might treat their workers with a modicum of personal dignity, as Ann Walker did when she arranged a church wedding for her servant,
Sarah. At the same time, other black women, like laundress Grase Snipes, sold
off their laborers in order to purchase their own children out of slavery.[58]

Grase was not unique in distinguishing between her kin and her property.
Consider that Molly Neyle, who wished to free her niece, Barbara, left the young
woman a portion of her estate, part of the proceeds of which would come from
the sale of "Amy and her three children." Charlotte Kershaw also differentiated
between her "beloved relations" and her "two negro female slaves Sibby and
Jenny": both women were left to the "total management and Controul [sic]" of
Charlotte's relatives, who were themselves free-by-courtesy.[59]

This speaks volumes on the messiness of slavery and freedom in the Old
South. While formal manumission was desirable, it was not always the point:
more than a static legal construct or a simplistic binary of slavery, freedom was
an *experience*. The reality of life in Charleston was such that social connections
and financial resources allowed some black women to live as free people, regardless of the documented nature of their freedom. This, in turn, led other
black women to pursue such resources and connections for themselves and
their families, no matter what the cost. Women like Charlotte thus came to
possess their kinfolk out of compassion and love while simultaneously possessing other black persons who would help improve their own socioeconomic
status. The nature of slavery and freedom in Charleston also created a class of
women who, while legally enslaved, held other women as property, and it al-

lowed black female slaveowners to distinguish between themselves, their relatives, and their laborers, even when the slaveowners themselves, or members of their own families, were enslaved. Such psychological compartmentalization was a reality of life for free black woman in the slave South.

Owning enslaved persons or real estate did not, of course, guarantee a black woman a life of luxury. Obtaining such property was, however, requisite to a woman's ability to increase her financial and social standing, which could then bolster her demands for more equitable treatment by the society in which she lived. It appears, then, that while Charleston was a city committed to upholding patriarchal rule and a hierarchy of race, it was also a place where black women were able to negotiate autonomous spaces for themselves. Struggling to create lives that were more than nominally free, black women realized that white Charlestonians were willing to concede certain privileges to those who adhered to the principles of property ownership that whites held so dear. Using this to their advantage, black women pursued the acquisition of wealth, particularly land and human chattel, in order to bequeath to their descendants a more secure freedom than one limited by poverty and the fear of reenslavement. The tragedy lies in the fact that black female freedom in South Carolina was so tenuous that owning certain black persons became instrumental in solidifying the freedom of other black persons.

Although property ownership did not guarantee a black woman a life of ease, women of color who reached the ranks of propertied taxpayers were better off than most free blacks. They were also a minority among free blacks, black property owners, and the propertied class as a whole. Indeed, "they were as rare as rich women were among all women."[60] Although this makes them unique, it does not mean that we should not examine their lives. That any southern black woman was able to acquire property is worthy of investigation, considering the barriers such women faced. That some managed to purchase themselves and their loved ones out of slavery, acquire land and houses, and bequeath real and personal property to their children, is a testimony to their labor, frugality, intelligence, and determination. Indeed, propertied women are worthy of study partly because their lives were, in some ways, unusual. Their stories more fully reveal the complexity and range of black female life in the Old South and disrupt the notion that there was any such thing as a "typical" free black woman. Additionally, while property-owning black women were "rare," the constraints they faced in their quest for a freedom of their own design, and the strategies they utilized to try to succeed in that quest, were representative of the wider black female community in which they lived.

Examining black female property owners as a group, it is apparent that not all women of color came by their possessions in the same manner. The members of one group appeared to have acquired their property by hard work alone. In spite of the barriers they faced in obtaining gainful employment, free blacks in the Old South did have the right to acquire and retain real and personal property. Indeed, white southerners extended to them the privileges basic to the promotion of capitalist enterprise: the courts declared that "free Negroes, without any of the political rights that belong to a citizen[,] are still . . . regarded . . . as possessing both natural and civil rights. The rights of liberty, life, and property belong to them." With these limited rights, and the expanded job opportunities available to them in urban areas, some free black women were able to become property owners by virtue of their thrift, determination, and years of exhausting toil.[61]

Black female Charlestonians who acquired their wealth by virtue of their labors alone rarely owned large amounts of property, however. Single, or married to men with meager incomes, they, like their peers in Petersburg, were often newly freed, unskilled, older, and had children to support or purchase out of slavery. These women thus accumulated property against great odds.[62] Of the 142 free black female property owners in Charleston who appear in the probate records, 50 (35 percent) appear to have come by their property through years of hard work, frugality, and sacrifice.[63] Dollar values exist for thirty-six of these estates, twenty-one of which (58 percent) were worth less than $500. Grase Snipes, a free black washerwoman and mother of four, is representative of this group. When Grase died in 1812, her son John was still enslaved and her youngest child, Thomas, although free, was just an infant. After years of toil as a laundress, Grase died owning an estate worth $364. Three hundred dollars of this was the appraised value of her enslaved laborer, Dinah, and Dinah's unnamed child. Grase left all her personal effects, worth only $64, to her two adult daughters, Jane and Abigail, both free black women. Dinah (who likely worked for Grase in her laundry business) and her child were to be sold and the money used to purchase John out of slavery.[64]

Some free black women, of course, ended up in more comfortable situations. Most of these women did not come by their money solely due to their own labors but also inherited some property from spouses, parents, or other relatives, persons who had worked hard to accumulate and bequeath their wealth, and the privileges that came with it, to the next generation.[65] Elizabeth Holloway, for example, was the daughter of James Mitchell, a well-to-do free carpenter of color in the city of Charleston. Married to Richard Holloway, himself a skilled carpenter of color, Elizabeth inherited her husband's property upon his death in 1845. The estate included two enslaved laborers, the couple's home and lot on Beaufain Street, and other rental properties. Thereafter, Elizabeth appeared in the city tax books as the owner of real property assessed at $8,300.[66]

Elizabeth was not the only woman to inherit part of her estate from a black husband or father. The collection of 142 probate records refers to twenty-eight other women in this position (20 percent). Dollar values exist for nineteen of these twenty-eight estates, and of those nineteen, fourteen women (74 percent) received bequests in excess of $1,000. It is not surprising that black men's estates were, in general, more substantial than those of black women, since free men were able to engage in more lucrative occupations than free women of color. This explains how tinner William Pinceel was able to accumulate an estate valued at more than $3,200 by the time of his death. Comprised of five enslaved persons whose total saleable value was $1,500, a house and lot in Logan Street assessed at $1,000, and stocks worth almost $400, in addition to his tinning tools and household goods, the estate inherited by Ann Pinceel, William's wife, would have allowed her to live quite comfortably after his death in 1825.[67]

The city's wealthiest black woman likewise inherited some of her property from her black husband. Married to machinist Anthony Weston, Maria Weston was something of an anomaly in Charleston. According to the city tax books, Maria was the only free black woman, after the death of Jane Wightman, to control real property exceeding $10,000 in value: by 1859 Maria possessed real estate assessed at $41,575, in addition to owning fourteen enslaved laborers and a horse. Her tax bill that year was just over $675, the largest amount owed by any black person, male or female, in the city. By 1860, Maria's holdings included twenty-two human beings, ten lots of land, seven houses, three buildings on Mill Street, and a shop on Henrietta Street. And while no occupational listing has been found for Maria, other women of the Weston clan, one of the city's most prominent free families of color, were seamstresses and mantua makers. That Maria did not need to work is supported by the fact that, according to existing records, only thirty-six white Charlestonians possessed real property holdings superior to hers in value.[68]

Few black men left legacies the size of Anthony Weston's. Most free blacks, male and female, worked hard to accumulate even modest estates and pass them on to their loved ones. More common, then, was the situation of Rachael and Moses Wells. Moses was a skilled shoemaker during his life, but upon his death, his estate was only worth $503. This included several small lots and buildings in town, collectively valued at $450. Rachael thus inherited a relatively small estate from her husband, although it did pass almost entirely to her. Moses also made Rachael the executrix of his estate, an uncommon occurrence among free blacks in antebellum Charleston, which suggests that he trusted her ability to oversee his affairs. He may have also wanted to ensure that she was not cheated out of her inheritance by an executor who might not have adhered to her husband's wishes.[69]

A final group of black female legatees received all or part of their wealth from white friends or family members. Of the 142 probate records that refer to black women, 64 (or 45 percent) indicate that the source of a woman's wealth was a white friend, lover, or parent. Of these sixty-four cases, white women were the benefactors in only seven (11 percent). How generous these women actually were is sometimes difficult to determine, since estate inventories and assessments do not exist for all testators. Emily Benedict may have felt magnanimous in leaving to Mary, "a colored woman and my nurse while sick," a large mattress, two pillows, one looking glass, three pictures and "all my black wearing apparel," but it is unclear what financial gain Mary actually realized from this bequest.[70]

If an inventory exists, it is easier to determine the extent of a black woman's good fortune. When Marie Gouvignon died, she bequeathed to her former laborer, the "mulatto woman Theresia," $300 as a reward for services Theresia had performed for Marie after she was emancipated in 1803. Theresia's "mongrel daughter Eliza" received Marie's linens, clothes, and jewels, in addition to her bed and bedding. Considering that Marie's estate was only worth $709, $225 of which was the value of the woman Adelaide (freed under the terms of the will), Theresia's and Eliza's bequests were significant. Eliza's inheritance came to about $80, while Theresia received $300 in cash. The women thus inherited $380 of an estate worth $484 (after deducting the value of Adelaide). That Gouvignon had a cordial relationship with Theresia and Eliza seems clear. That she felt less for her other enslaved laborers is also evident. Although Adelaide was manumitted, she received no financial bequest to help ease her transition to freedom, and Marie instructed her executors to sell her two remaining workers in order to pay Theresia's inheritance.[71]

White women's kindnesses toward certain black women clearly did not extend to empathizing with black women as a group. Instead, their generosity was bestowed on those people of color with whom they had developed some kind of personal relationship. Their selective benevolence mirrored that of their male counterparts, who comprised the majority of white benefactors. Of the sixty-four probate records referring to women who inherited property from a white person, fifty-seven (or 89 percent) concern women who received a bequest from a white man. Additionally, thirty-five of these fifty-seven records (61 percent) pertain to women who definitively had either a physical or a kinship relationship with the men in question. We can conclude, then, that if a white male Charlestonian left an inheritance to a black woman, chances were three in five that the woman in question had a sexual or familial tie to him. Additionally, since 25 percent of all the probate records pertaining to black women (35 of 142) deal with the transfer of goods between white men and black women bound by blood or intimacy, we can posit that about one-quarter of the city's black women who inherited property acquired it from white men to whom they had some kind of familial connection.

These numbers are lower than those found in earlier works on Charleston, particularly those of E. Horace Fitchett, in whose studies black women appear almost exclusively as the concubines of white men, the mothers of wealthy "mulatto" men, or both.[72] They also appear to differ from those in New Orleans, a city with whose black community Charleston's has often been compared. While most of the research on the free women of color in New Orleans has focused on the Spanish colonial era, the general picture that emerges is of a city where large numbers of white men had open and lengthy sexual liaisons with black women, relationships that were publicly acknowledged and legitimated by both the Roman Catholic Church and the state.[73] These same men then left land and enslaved laborers to the black women with whom they shared their lives, and to the biracial children who were born of their partnerships.[74]

The continuing, quasi-legal practice of contract marriage (also known as plaçage) between women of color and wealthy white men, which was unique to Louisiana, led to the ongoing independence and power of free women of color in New Orleans. Property records from 1760 to 1800 reveal that during the colonial era, scores of free black women acquired prime real estate in New Orleans and passed generous estates on to their biracial children. Additionally, documents dated as late as 1850 indicate that well after the end of Spanish rule, white men continued to bequeath part or all of their estates to their black lovers and illegitimate children, whom they acknowledged as their offspring. While some of these men were bachelors with no legitimate heirs, others maintained both a legal white family and a plaçage black family.[75] These biracial children did well for themselves, and many went on to become wealthy businesspersons. Cecee Macarty was one such woman. The child of Henriette Prieto and her white lover, Cecee inherited $12,000 from her free black mother and used it to build up an import business worth $155,000. At her death, Cecee was the wealthiest woman in New Orleans, as well as the largest black slaveholder in the city.[76]

Although the two cities are often lumped together for the purposes of comparison to Upper South centers, the fact is that Charleston's free black community was never as large or as wealthy as the one in New Orleans. Additionally, while the probate records suggest that one-quarter of Charleston's black women acquired their property from their white lovers or fathers, interracial relationships were never legitimated in Charleston the way they were in New Orleans, and a larger proportion of New Orleans's black women benefited from such alliances. Additionally, not every black female Charlestonian who inherited from a white man became affluent. Despite the primacy of their social space in the Old South, white men were not guaranteed wealth. "The free black woman Sophey" discovered this after the death of Christopher Smith, with whom she had lived for "a number of years." Upon his passing in 1814, Christopher left Sophey his entire estate. When Sophey died, the estate was to pass to "a free boy, the grandson of Sophey," named John Shephird, also living with Christopher. Sophey likely appreciated Christopher's desire to bequeath her his worldly possessions, but practically speaking, she gained little from his affections. The day after his will was probated, Christopher's estate was inventoried, the total value of which was $44 in household goods.[77]

Other women who acquired smaller inheritances from white male testators appeared to have no familial connection to the men in question. Some men stated that these women were being given the bequest as a reward for past services. Apparently the "negro woman" Clara Hasell was to be supported by the interest arising from Martin Damascke's $663 estate as a reward for having nursed Martin during his "protracted illness." Similarly, Mary Smith, "a free negro woman," inherited Jacob Wulff's clothes, furniture, and five shares in the South Carolina Railroad Company as a reward for the "great attention" she had shown to Jacob. The household goods only came to $76, but the stock shares totaled a tidy $645. Mary's inheritance was only a drop in the bucket, however, considering that Jacob's estate was worth over $18,000.[78]

While many black women thus received modest sums from the white men they knew, others inherited more substantial property from white men who were either their sexual partners or their fathers. Upon his death, Onerine Pillot left his entire estate "for the sole use and benefit and advantage of my good friend Catharine Artho a colored woman." This included more than $3,000 in cash, stock shares, and household goods, and Catharine was given absolute control over her inheritance, except for Onerine's house and lot on Meeting Street. Given the right to live in that house for the duration of her life, she could not sell the property, which at her death would pass to her daughter, Maria Clara, whom Onerine referred to as his "adopted child." Onerine never admitted to having had a sexual relationship with Catharine, but the fact that he left her his entire estate, gave her life tenancy in his home (which a legal wife would receive as part of her basic dower rights), and referred to her daughter as his "adopted" child is highly suggestive, as is the fact that Catharine later changed her last name to "Pelot." Having inherited more than $3,000 in property, plus a home for life, Catharine Artho Pelot became an affluent free black woman almost overnight.[79]

Catharine's fortune, while impressive, pales in comparison to those of Tissee Cochran Lewis and Nancy Randall. Both women not only had long-term relationships with the white men from whom they later inherited but also bore these men children. For decades, Tissee made her home in Charleston County with Isaac Lewis, her former master and father to all six of her children. When Isaac died in 1851, Tissee and her children inherited an estate valued at almost $50,000, including more than $40,000 in stocks, a home on Sullivan's Island, and eight enslaved laborers. Nancy Randall was involved in a similar partnership with Thomas Hanscome. A wealthy merchant, upon his death, Thomas left over $150,000 to maintain and educate the eight children he had with Nancy. Additionally, Nancy personally received $15,000, her lover's furniture and linens, and the house Thomas had built for her before his death.[80]

Tissee and Nancy were not alone in inheriting substantial wealth from the white men in their lives. Jane Prevost, the daughter of Felice Causse, had a similar story. Whether Felice was white or black is unknown, but Prevost is referred to as "a woman of color" in various public documents. Early in the nineteenth century, Jane began a long-term relationship with a white man named William Wightman and bore him a daughter, named Margaret. Upon William's death in 1839, Jane inherited both of his houses on Chalmers Street, all his household goods, and $6,000 in cash. Their daughter received $20,000, while Jane's mother, Felice, was given $1,000. Thereafter, Jane assumed the surname Wightman and resided at 38 Chalmers Street, and by the time she passed away in 1853, Jane was a very wealthy woman. She died owning eleven enslaved laborers, a house and lot in Chalmers Street, several additional city lots, various personal effects, stocks, and a farm in Charleston Neck. The bulk of her estate was sold and the money placed in trust for her daughter, Margaret, who was living in Scotland with her husband, a white man named John McDougall.[81]

Jane Prevost Wightman was unusual in that she was one of only two black women on the city tax lists with real property holdings in excess of $10,000. The other was Maria Weston.[82] Most propertied black women, however, controlled estates assessed at $1,000 to $9,999. Roughly three-quarters of the city's taxpaying free black women fell into this category and, while not wealthy, could be classified as prosperous or affluent.[83] Many of the women in this tax bracket had also acquired their property as a result of their familial relationships with white men. The decades-long partner of John Walker, Ann Jones (who later went by the name of Ann J. Walker), and her nine children, whom John acknowledged as his "natural children," inherited John's $64,000 estate at his death in 1839. As late as 1861, the city of Charleston was still taxing Ann Walker's estate on $2,500 worth of real estate and two enslaved laborers.[84]

WOMEN, MEN, AND WEALTH

Examining black female legatees as a group, several things become evident. First, a key difference between women who received significant inheritances from their white lovers and those who inherited smaller legacies was the existence of children. Essentially, relationships that produced offspring generated larger bequests for black women than those where children were not involved. In short, the advantage lay with those women who could establish lengthy, familial connections to white men of stature. Black paramours who became common-law wives and mothers were more likely to obtain emancipation and the accoutrements of real freedom: education, wealth, legal privileges, and higher social status.[85] Consider the fact that most of the black women in Charleston ensconced in the wealthier tax brackets came by their property via their kinship ties to white men of stature. Indeed, it was rare to find women of color in the top tax category not connected to white men in some fashion: in 1850, the only free black woman listed in the tax books with more than $10,000 in real property was Jane Prevost Wightman, the longtime partner of William Wightman and mother to the couple's daughter, Margaret.[86]

Next, the advantages of interracial relationships were always greater for a woman's children than for the woman herself, from manumission, to education, to larger inheritances. Jane Wightman, for example, received $6,000 in cash upon William's demise; the couple's daughter, Margaret, inherited $20,000. Then there was the woman Fanny, who received the funds with which to purchase her freedom after the death of her lover, John Bonthron. Fanny also acquired a cash legacy of $1,000. Her two children by John, Margaret and James, were left a lump sum with which to buy their freedom, plus they received an additional inheritance of $6,000 apiece. Even Adam Tunno, the wealthy merchant who spent almost forty years of his life with the black woman Margaret Bettingall, differentiated between his partner and their child. Margaret, who died illiterate, inherited $1,250 upon Adam's death and may or may not have been legally freed. The couple's daughter, Barbara, was legally freed as a child, was well educated, and received $2,500 in cash, plus a share of her father's household goods, when he died. This was a significant legacy considering that Adam's estate was worth between $300,000 and $400,000 when he passed away.[87]

A number of black women were thus able to derive financial and social advantages for themselves and their children by establishing intimate relationships with white men. These rewards, however, grew out of the inherently vulnerable position that black women held in a slave society. In the Old South, a black woman's very color was a marker of sexual promiscuity, and her allegedly heightened sexual drive was an indicator of her "inherently bestial nature." Born to be whores as well as laborers, black women were seen as hypersexual beings, while white women were asexual creatures above such things as work or passion. One group's asexuality thus rationalized the sexual exploitation of the other.[88] It is true that some black women exploited the sexual ideologies on which their society was based in order to acquire certain benefits for themselves and their families. It is a testament to their determination to cross the freedom frontier, their willingness to make sacrifices in order to improve their children's lives, and their savvy skills of negotiation that these women were able to successfully navigate social and sexual relations that were extraordinarily exploitative and turn them somewhat to their advantage. At the same time, we cannot forget the numerous black women who were forced into interracial relationships against their will, and we must question how many of the women in "consensual" partnerships would have willingly entered into such liaisons had they had more options for upward mobility than what antebellum Charleston offered to them.

The evidence also suggests that black women who inherited their money from black men were, in general, less affluent than women who obtained their wealth from white men. Still prosperous, many of these women were educated, owned their own homes, and attended elite churches.[89] Jeanette Bonneau, for example, was the widow of Thomas Bonneau and owned a home worth $1,000 and one enslaved laborer. Well respected, Thomas had run a renowned school for free black children during his life and was a member of the exclusive Brown Fellowship Society (BFS). Additionally, Jeanette and Thomas attended aristocratic St. Philip's Episcopal Church, and their children all married into prestigious black families. Susan Dereef came from a similar lineage. While her estate was assessed at only $1,351, this included a house on Nassau Street and four enslaved laborers. Additionally, Susan was a well-connected woman. Among the oldest of Charleston's free families of color, the Dereefs attended St. Philip's Church, the men (many of whom belonged to the BFS) made their fortunes as wood factors, and their children married into other prominent black families.

TABLE 4.3. Free Black Women Real Property Ownership, 1859–1861

Year	# FBW Taxpayers	$1–$999	%	$1,000–$1,999	%	$2,000–$9,999	%
1859	134	38	28	52	39	43	32
1860	123	31	25	49	40	42	34
1861	122	26	21	55	45	40	33

Sources: 1859 Tax List, at CCPL; 1860 Tax List, at RSS; 1861 Tax Book, at SCHS.

Note: FBW = free black women.

Jeanette and Susan were thus elite women of color, although their wealth was less than that of a number of black women who acquired their property from white men of means.[90] It seems, then, that in Charleston, as in New Orleans, marriage to a black man did offer a black woman some wealth and upward social mobility, but not as much security or privilege as a relationship to a white man might.[91]

It is also apparent that the less taxable property a black woman owned, the less likely it was that she had a man, white or black, in her life. Hardworking laborers with children to feed, single black female taxpayers generally owned less than $1,000 in property (see Table 4.3). It is also unlikely that they attended St. Philip's Church or had male relatives in the BFS. Dianah Tresvant is a good example of one such woman. A free woman of color and a nurse by profession, Dianah lived on King Street from 1819 until the 1830s. By 1840, at the age of fifty-four, she had saved enough money to purchase her own home in Ward Two at 12 Orange Street. The house was assessed at $800, and Dianah paid taxes on it each year thereafter, up to and including 1861. That year she was seventy-five, too old to be liable for the capitation tax. She still had to pay her property taxes, however, which were assessed that year at just over $10. The 1861 tax book indicates that she paid her tax bill in full, despite not being employed.[92]

Many single black female taxpayers did not fare even this well. In 1861, close to 50 percent of black women who owned less than $1,000 in real property did not own even $500 worth, and of these, most owned only $50 or $100 in real property.[93] The sobering truth is that women who owned so little were, for all intents and purposes, as poor as those women who owned no real property at all and never made it onto the tax lists. Consider the lives of Emma Peronneau and Catherine Pritchard. A market woman by trade, Emma never owned more than $200 in real property. Her real estate holdings did not even include a proper house: her tax return for 1860, when she was thirty-eight years old, indicates that Emma's real property was a small shed at 1 Bee Street, located on land she leased from one Mrs. Shobel. Catherine Pritchard's situation was even more dismal. A washerwoman, Catherine owned only $50 worth of property. She never owned her own land, and her real estate in 1860, when Pritchard was forty, consisted of a shed on land on Hazel Street that she leased from a Mr. Chesborough.[94]

Of course a relationship with a man, black or white, did not guarantee a black woman a life of financial security. Some men simply had little wealth to give. Rebecca (a.k.a. "Beck") Parler discovered this firsthand. When her husband, the free man of color and dray driver Peter Parler, died in 1833, Rebecca, a virtually free black woman, inherited his estate. Since it was not possible for Peter to legally manumit her, Beck was left in trust to a friend so that she might continue to live as a free woman. Her inheritance consisted of $120 in cash (attained from the sale of Peter's horses and drays), $5 worth of furniture, and the right to life tenancy in the couple's house on Ratliffe Street. Although this hardly qualifies as a substantial estate, it provided Beck with a home, some furniture, and a little cash, which was more than most free black women could claim.[95]

Although partnerships with men did not ensure antebellum black women lives of wealth, or even comfort, black women with male partners still fared better than single black women. As industrious as black women were, occupational limitations and salary inequity meant that women who could form unions with men were more likely to get ahead, both socially and monetarily. Singleness, on the other hand, almost certainly doomed a black woman to a life of struggle and hardship. Perhaps this is one of the reasons why there were so few free black property owners in Baltimore: only 236 as late as 1856. According to Christopher Phillips, not only did free black women outnumber free black men in that city, but interracial relationships were few, and whites in Baltimore rarely made financial bequests to free black or enslaved persons. What little property black Baltimoreans owned, then, they had acquired as a result of years of enterprise, frugality, and sacrifice on their part . . . and their part alone.[96]

RACE, SEX, AND THE DISTRIBUTION OF WEALTH

Charleston's black women knew how pervasive poverty was, living as they did surrounded by destitute persons, both white and black, and even women of color who became property owners did not live lives of luxury. Hardly aristocrats, most of these women toiled their entire lives as market women, seamstresses, pastry cooks, and laundresses. Some made the journey from slavery to freedom to landownership in a single lifetime, and their wealth never compared to that of white Charlestonians. Data from the 1860 census indicates that the city's black taxpayers possessed estates worth an average of $5,400 while the estates of white property holders averaged $54,000. And while 20 percent of white Charlestonians were worth more than $10,000, only 1 percent of the city's free blacks ever attained such riches. Finally, free blacks comprised 15 percent of the city's population but controlled only 1 percent of the city's wealth. In sum, it was only in the context of a poor, free black community that black property holders could be seen as "elite": they were never the financial equals of their white neighbors, whose wealth always surpassed their own.[97] Charleston was not unique in this regard: in Savannah, white residents controlled more than $10 million worth of real property by 1860 while the city's free blacks never collectively possessed more than $50,000 in real property at any point during the antebellum era.[98]

This differential in real wealth between blacks and whites is even more noticeable if one compares white wealth solely to the holdings of black women. In 1859, black female property holders owned an average of $2,979 in real property across the Lower South. In 1860, this dropped to $2,695 per black female property owner, but women of color still owned more property, on average, than men of color throughout the region.[99] In Charleston, however, black women's holdings were much smaller. In 1859, the city's black male taxpayers averaged $3,600 in real property and free black women $1,640. In 1860, black women's estates averaged $1,709, half that of black men's estates, assessed at $3,411. Wealth, then, was highly concentrated in the hands of white Charlestonians, and among free blacks, a very few persons, mainly men, held much of the city's black-owned property, even though women were the majority of the city's free black population. Not only did very few of the city's free black women own real property to begin with, then, but those who did own property possessed smaller, and less valuable, holdings than their black male counterparts. This is not surprising, given the occupational difficulties women experienced in Charleston, and serves only to underscore how fragile black women's freedom was, and how contingent it was on their securing alliances with men, especially white men of stature.[100]

BLACK WOMEN, PROPERTY OWNERSHIP, AND THE LAW

Faced with such facts, black women did what they had to in order to amass wealth and "make a way out of no way" for their families, including allying themselves with men of means and utilizing enslaved laborers.[101] They also used every available tool to retain the wealth they had struggled so hard to acquire, including engaging in various forms of legal action. For some women this meant drafting marriage contracts, in certain ways akin to modern-day prenuptial agreements, in order to protect their property from their husbands. State laws throughout the antebellum United States dictated that when a woman wed, any property she had owned prior to her marriage automatically passed to the control of her husband. South Carolina, however, allowed couples to enter into marriage contracts, by which a woman could place the property she brought with her into her marriage in a separate trust estate to be administered by special trustees for the woman's "sole and separate use."[102]

Black women made good use of this special legal provision, just as they did with the opportunity the state gave them to act as sole traders.[103] Hagar Simpson, for example, owned a small city lot, one enslaved laborer, a horse and cart, and some furniture prior to marrying William Johnson. Before their wedding day, Hagar and William signed a contract that set aside all of Hagar's premarital property into a trust estate for her sole and separate use. Similarly, Sophia Smith asked her future husband, the free black goldsmith Francis LeFond, to sign a "conveyance in trust" wherein he promised not to disturb Sophia's personal real estate holdings. Hannah Norman apparently had little faith in such documents to protect her property: she turned all thirteen of her enslaved laborers over to friends before marrying James Miles. Hannah stated that if she were to die childless, her bondspersons would become the permanent property of her friends. Realizing that they could lose everything they had striven to gain by marrying a naive, careless, deceitful, or shiftless person, free black women did what they could to protect their property from their new partners.[104]

While some women safeguarded their estates by entering into marriage contracts, others filed petitions with the General Assembly to defend their property rights. In 1825, a group of free blacks from Charleston, comprised of both women and men, asked the state to repeal a new tax that affected Charlestonians who owned or rented homes "inhabited by negroes or persons of color" or who worked as "mechanics" or artisans. The tax, a hefty $10 per year, would be used to help pay for the municipal guard, which spent much of its time and energy harassing the city's black population. The petitioners stated that the new tax was unfair, unjust, and inequitable, and that it was, essentially, a surcharge against black property owners and artisans. Although the petition was not approved, it reveals that black women took their property rights seriously and were willing to present their arguments to the highest authorities in the state in order to protect these rights.[105]

The rejection of the petition also illuminates the obstacles that black women faced in their search for equity in the Old South. The persons who read the petition were white men, many of whom were from the rural Upcountry, locales with small or no free black populations. Often resentful of the power of Low Country planters, and fearful of Charleston's large free black community, many of the assemblymen in this post-Vesey era wished to expel free blacks from the state altogether, or reenslave them in the interest of state security. They were, then, hardly impartial. Additionally, free black women, many of whom were illiterate, had to rely on white men, who acted as their trustees, guardians, and attorneys, to articulate their arguments in said petitions, a tricky situation at best. Not only did black women need to maintain good relations with the white men who would file petitions on their behalf, then, but they also had to trust these men to construct documents that accurately reflected black women's thoughts and opinions.

Individual black women also filed petitions with the state to protect their property rights, although these petitions were rarely successful. Consider the case of Eliza Brown, whose mother, Sibby Gordon, died intestate in 1835 possessed of an estate worth $500. This property should have come to Eliza and her sister, Phillis, as Sibby's only surviving children. Instead, Eliza charged that the court-appointed executor, a white man named O. L. Dobson, had kept the property for himself. Eliza thus filed a petition with the General Assembly in 1838 to try to obtain justice. Claiming she was unable to work due to "disease" and that she was in dire financial straits and "dependent upon others" for her survival, Eliza said she could not afford to take the executor to court. She thus asked the legislators to uphold her rights and help her acquire her inheritance, which she requested be held in trust for her and her sister by one Thomas W. Malone. Several white citizens signed Eliza's petition and affirmed that "her story was true and her character good." Despite this, her petition was denied.[106]

Although the assemblymen gave no explanation for their decision, race, class, and gender, or the "social space" of both parties, would have played a part in the verdict. Consider Eliza's position as a destitute and ill woman of color opposing a respected white man: O. L. Dobson was a state assessor who would have been well acquainted with the legal system in general and property values in particular, enough so that the probate court judge deemed him a fit executor for Sibby's estate.[107] While South Carolina claimed that free persons of color had the same rights of life, liberty, and property that white Carolinians enjoyed, then, state legislators and judges behaved in ways that revealed that their protection of the rights of free women of color was erratic, even fickle. In reality they enforced black women's rights at their discretion. Assessing the reputation and status of each woman *and* her white advocates, as much as the facts of her case, the legal system determined which black women were and were not worthy of protection. Women who were destitute or had no sponsors (or less powerful ones) were easy to dismiss.[108] Time, place, and social space meant that women like Eliza Seymour Lee, who was wealthy and well connected, were able to obtain justice in the South Carolina courts; poorer women like Eliza Brown fared less well with the state assembly.[109]

In 1844, Myra Reid discovered what Eliza Brown already knew: that the General Assembly tended to deny the petitions of poor black women. Upon her death in 1834, Sarah Ferris, a woman of color, left her house and lot in Charleston to her husband, Ben Reid. His to use during his life, the property would transfer to one Sarah Ann Reid when Ben died. If Sarah Ann died without heirs, the property would pass to her mother, Myra (a.k.a. "Mariah") Reid, the petitioner. According to Myra, Ben was willing to relinquish the property to Myra and Sarah Ann before his death. Since Ben was enslaved, however, whether he had the right to transfer the property to the women was uncertain. Myra thus asked the legislature to pass an act allowing Ben to hand the property over to her and her daughter. Myra's guardian, John C. Miller, signed the petition on her behalf, and Ben's master attached his consent as well, as did the mayor and the City Council of Charleston. Despite the support that the Reid women had garnered from numerous illustrious white citizens, the assemblymen concluded that "at present the legal rights of the parties are unsettled." The legislators thus recommended that the petition not be granted. They appeared discomfited by the thought of allowing an enslaved man to first conduct himself as a free person (by claiming ownership of real property) and to then engage in actions (the transmittal of that property) that would benefit two free black women.[110]

While poorer women of color were forced to pursue justice with a legislature that was often unjust, black women of means bypassed the General Assembly and utilized the courts to seek protection of their rights. Certainly this worked for Eliza Lee, whose case opens this chapter, but she was not the only black woman who turned to the courts for help. The daughter of a black woman and her wealthy white lover, Barbara Tunno Barquet was a small-business owner and slaveholder. By the 1840s Barbara was a well-to-do widow who rented out her excess laborers for profit, loaned money at interest, and owned several pieces of urban real estate. She also held mortgages on various plantation properties, some of which were owned by elite, white South Carolinians. When one such mortgagee, James Hamilton, attempted to defraud Barbara of the $5,178 he owed to her, she hired an attorney and took him to court. Barbara knew how difficult it would be to win her case, since James belonged to one of the most powerful plantation families in the state. She was, however, a wealthy and well-connected woman. A landholding slaveholder and a taxpaying member of society, Barbara demanded more equitable treatment by the state in which she lived, and her suit suggested she believed that her wealth and social position entitled her to the same rights and protections as any other resident of the state. The South Carolina Court of Errors ultimately agreed with Barbara.[111]

While Eliza and Barbara sued individual white men, other black women took on entire organizations in an effort to defend their property rights. In 1833, a woman named Theressa Taylor filed a claim against the Roman Catholic Church of Charleston (RCCC). The former laborer of one Mary Watson, Theressa had inherited her freedom, some clothes, Mary's bed, and a benefit of $85 a year upon her mistress's death in 1796. The RCCC inherited the rest of Mary's goods, including her house and the land on which it stood. Under the terms of the will, the RCCC was responsible for paying Theressa's annuity out of the rent of Mary's home. In 1833, however, Theressa, now a free black woman, filed a petition stating that the RCCC had not paid her anything for several years. She thus asked that a court order be issued directing the RCCC to give her the money she was owed, which came to just over $349. It is not known if the order was issued or if Theressa received what she was due, but clearly this woman believed that her rights had been violated; that she was entitled to ask the state for help; and that South Carolina's legal system existed to protect the rights of all the state's residents, be they black or white, female or male, individuals or organizations.[112]

Elsey Pyatt felt the same way. A free woman of color, Elsey filed a petition with the Charleston County Courts in 1845 regarding an inheritance. What is interesting is that the defendant in this case was also a free black woman. Elsey's uncle, Peter Simpson, passed away in 1825 and left his "beloved wife, Hagar[,] . . . a free black woman," the whole of his estate, "for and during the term of her natural life, provided she . . . does not marry again." If she did remarry, Peter's executors were to take possession of his property and pay over to Hagar a one-third share of the estate.[113] Hagar remarried one William Johnson, so she was now entitled to only a one-third (or dower) portion of Peter's estate. According to law, the remaining two-thirds would have become part of Peter's intestate property, and Elsey, the daughter of Peter's late sister (Betty Simpson Hertsel Cooper) believed she was entitled to a share of this property. Elsey asked the court to issue a writ of partition forcing Hagar to turn over to Elsey her rightful share of Peter's estate, which included "a house and lot in Masyckborough, adjoining the city of Charleston." Hagar, however, would not consent to a division of the estate, claiming that Peter had no sister and that Elsey was thus not her late husband's niece. When Elsey filed a new petition, to which Hagar did not respond, the court granted Elsey's petition *pro confesso*.[114]

It is no surprise that Elsey filed this suit, or that Hagar refused to share her late husband's estate. In a city where most free blacks were poor, and where property ownership could make the difference between reenslavement and freedom, or between bare survival and the privileges that came with the accumulation of wealth, black women had to fight to acquire and retain what was theirs, regardless of whom their battles pitted them against. Far from behaving collectively, when it came to freedom, it was every woman for herself. Cases where persons of color tangled with one another over monetary issues were thus not uncommon, nor were they unique to Charleston. In New Orleans, a man of color freed his lover and their offspring before he died. He then left his partner and their children his entire estate. When the will was probated, however, another free woman of color appeared in court, claiming to be the dead man's legal wife and mother to his only legitimate daughter. This woman sued the man's lover and claimed the entire estate for herself and her child on the grounds that she had been legally married to the deceased. The courts in this case found in favor of the legal wife.[115]

CONCLUSION

Black women were not, of course, always successful in their quest to protect their rights. What is more important than whether they won or lost their battles, however, is that they used every available means to defend their possessions, understanding the link between the ownership of property and the accoutrements of a fuller freedom. All blacks in the Old South were subject to the authority of whites, but poverty made blacks more vulnerable to reenslavement. At a bare minimum, women of color needed enough money to be able to purchase some basic comforts and pay their taxes so as to avoid fines, prison terms, or sale into "temporary" servitude. Wealth, however, could help them to obtain additional protections and privileges. Property ownership thus became essential for black women: without it, they would be unable to negotiate upward social mobility and a more expansive freedom for themselves and their families. In pursuing financial stability, however, they faced a number of obstacles, including unjust taxes, low-paying jobs, the fraudulent actions of corrupt whites, as well as the hostility or neglect of the state. It is a testimony to their determination that some women of color overcame the hurdles placed in their path, acquired property, and then used their resources to shape their lives to better fit their own definitions of freedom.

In the pursuit of wealth, certain kinds of property became significant for black women, particularly real estate. The antebellum South was a place where land ownership was revered, and inventory lists suggest that whenever possible, black women invested in real estate, which would appreciate in value and enable upward social mobility. The wills of free black women also indicate that they never forgot the value of land, or how tenuous life was for free blacks in the Old South. Seeking security for their families, black women often instructed that the money they left their legatees be used to buy houses and other kinds of real property. Money could be spent unwisely, and stocks could become worthless. Real estate, however, would give their descendents enduring financial security and increased social standing.[116]

In the quest for security and respect, holding bondspersons became as crucial as the acquisition of land. Almost nothing inspired more admiration in the South than slaveownership, and no other investment promised a black woman as many positive returns. Owning chattel laborers put political and social distance between blacks who were free and those who remained enslaved, and elite whites were more likely to assist those women who upheld the principles of property ownership that they themselves held so dear. Finally, while not every black woman engaged in slavery for financial gain, many realized that their economic success depended on utilizing unfree labor. Always just steps away from reenslavement, free black women were rarely able to think collectively about what was best for the race. Instead, many became black masters, utilizing the limited options available to them in order to expand their businesses and give their own families the best chance at both survival and success.

Free black women often had little choice in this matter. Very few of them made it onto the city's tax lists to begin with, and those who managed to obtain real property controlled less wealth than Charleston's free black men. Most free women of color had no real property of any kind and thus found themselves at the bottom of the wealth index. Engaged in occupations that not only paid poorly but provided them with little opportunity for upward mobility, black women also faced sexual demographics in Charleston that meant a number of them would remain single for life or partnered with enslaved men who could offer them little financial support.[117] Struggling to support their children on their own, black women thus fought to amass real property and quite literally battled their way onto the city's taxpayer lists. The use of enslaved labor in their fledgling businesses was, sadly, one of the few ways out of the shattering poverty that the majority of southern free women of color were slated to suffer.

Occupational limitations and salary inequity in a city stratified by barriers of race and sex also meant that no matter how industrious a black woman might be, or how willing to engage in the practice of chattel slavery, it was men who held the most power in the Old South, power in terms of political clout, access to financial resources, enhanced occupational opportunities, and higher social status. Thus, black women who partnered with skilled, free men of color had a better chance of acquiring wealth and some of the privileges of citizenship than did a single black woman. While a relationship with a free black man did not guarantee a black woman a life of leisure, singleness almost certainly doomed her to a lifetime of poverty.

Equally important for black women living in Charleston was their recognition that while black men had more economic opportunities than they did, white men had the greatest occupational and social potential of any group in the city. Understanding the raced and gendered nature of poverty in the Old South, and the realities of time, place, and social space, free black women realized that those who allied themselves with white men of worth had the best chance of acquiring an expanded freedom. It is thus no surprise that many black women did what they felt was necessary to see their families clear of slavery: they engaged in long-term relationships with white men and bore them children. These women did more than make modest gains for themselves. The next two chapters reveal that their children were able to capitalize on their mothers' efforts and acquire the privileges of a more expansive freedom: legal protections, property, housing, education, and upward social mobility.

As Charleston's black women transitioned out of slavery and into freedom, they realized that white southerners were committed to maintaining economic systems and sociocultural beliefs that would continue the supremacy of patriarchy and whiteness. They also understood that while race and gender limited their access to many of the privileges of citizenship, white Charlestonians were often willing to concede certain rights to those women who appealed to the sanctity of property ownership. Astute political actors, black women used these insights to their advantage and utilized the judicial system in order to create autonomous spaces for themselves. Drawing on their position as property owners, black women asked the state to protect their rights. Whether they signed premarital contracts, demanded the revocation of unjust taxes, sued to recoup their debts, demanded the codification of their manumission, or petitioned to obtain their inheritances, black women clearly believed that the state had an obligation to defend their life, their liberty, and their property. Determined to enjoy an existence of their own design, Charleston's women of color refused to reside silently within the parameters of a pseudo-freedom articulated by the master class. Instead, as we have already seen, and the following chapters will highlight, they utilized all the means available to them in order to articulate their own visions of liberty in the face of a white superstructure committed to defining black women's freedom for them.

PART III

EXPERIENCING

FREEDOM

CHAPTER 5

A TALE OF TWO WOMEN

THE LIVES OF

CECILLE COGDELL AND

SARAH SANDERS

In 1831, Cecille Langlois Cogdell left her husband, Richard Walpole Cogdell, and moved out of the home they rented together on Broad Street. A middle-class matron and mother of five whose respectability had been demonstrated through her marriage, her church attendance, her ownership of enslaved laborers, and her social activities, Cecille had always appeared to adhere to the rules that governed the raced and gendered roles that South Carolina society afforded to her. As a result, she was rewarded by the church, the state, and her peers by being accorded all the rights and privileges of virtuous, middle-class, feminine whiteness. Why, then, did Cecille risk losing her position, along with the financial and social benefits that accompanied it, by walking away from her husband of twenty-five years?

Family papers reveal that Cecille left her husband shortly after their sixteen-year-old enslaved laborer, Sarah Martha Sanders, became pregnant with Richard's child. A few months later, Cecille passed away and Sarah gave birth to the first of ten children she would have with Richard. Thereafter, Sarah, Richard, and their children all lived together as a family in the house on Broad Street. And while Sarah died still enslaved in 1850, her children were privy to everything she had never attained for herself. From regular schooling to private instruction in piano, the Sanders children were raised in a manner befitting their father's white middle-class status, and when life in Charleston became dangerous for free blacks in the 1850s, Richard moved his virtually free children to Philadelphia, far from the threat of reenslavement. Determined to secure for her family the privileges of a more complete freedom, Sarah thus reaped for her children the fullest rewards of her sacrifices and astute tactics of negotiation.[1]

This chapter examines the ways in which two women worked from within Charleston's existing raced and gendered power structures to secure the privileges they desired for themselves and their children. Hoping to acquire the opportunities that white southerners, particularly white men, received as their birthright, Cecille Cogdell and Sarah Sanders each utilized their relationship with Richard Walpole Cogdell to try to shape their lives to more closely conform to their own visions of freedom. These alliances, however, were complicated at the best of times. While partnering with Richard gave Cecille and Sarah some of the liberties they sought, in a society that vested greater economic opportunity, political rights, and sociocultural authority in white men, their status as women meant their unions with him were fraught with inherent compromises that subjected them to new limitations.

In this way, Cecille's and Sarah's stories echo those of many other southern women, white and black, who allied themselves with men in order to attain a more expansive freedom. By making men their vehicle to upward mobility, many antebellum women found themselves indebted to their "benefactors," and thus living lives that were simultaneously freer and more constrained. In return for the bodily freedom, wealth, and social privileges these men helped her obtain, a woman's "patrons" often demanded her lifelong allegiance. This could entail an encroachment on her time, skills, finances, body, and more. Charleston's women thus realized that they were locked in a constant struggle for autonomy. They had little choice but to learn to negotiate with men, particularly white men, in order to amass the privileges they desired; if they succeeded, however, they often found themselves bound to the very persons to whom they had turned for help in acquiring their liberty in the first place.

CECILLE AND RICHARD

Cecille's and Sarah's stories begin with the man who linked them together. Born in Charleston in 1787, Richard Walpole Cogdell was only five years old when his father, George, died. He and his brothers were thereafter raised by their mother, Mary Ann Stevens Cogdell, in her residence at 1 St. Michael's Alley, also the site of her boarding school for young women.[2] Brought up in a close-knit, financially stable family, the Cogdell boys had an intellectually invigorating childhood. Richard's mother, who never remarried, was an amateur artist and teacher while Richard's older brother, John, was a sculptor and an attorney who practiced law across the street from his boyhood home. Uncle Harry, Mary Ann's brother, was a landowner, a musician, and a painter, and lived on nearby Tradd Street with his wife and daughter.[3]

In sharp contrast to his professional relatives, by 1809, Richard Cogdell was a clerk at the local Planters and Mechanics Bank, a rather humble profession for a man of his background. The exact reason for his employment at the bank is unknown, although it likely had to do with the fact that he had a wife to support: in May 1806, Richard Cogdell had married Cecille Langlois. His marriage at age nineteen was unusual, since white male Charlestonians tended to wait until they were well settled in their careers before they took on the responsibilities of a spouse. Richard's brother, John—ten years his senior—was more typical, marrying when he was older and better equipped to support a family.[4]

Why Richard married so young is unclear. Perhaps he and Cecille fell madly in love and wanted to get married right away. It is also possible that Cecille was pregnant when she married Richard. Premarital sex and conception were not unheard of in the Old South, and the fact that dates of birth are included in the family papers for all of the couple's five sons except the eldest, James Walpole, is suggestive. Impregnating and marrying Cecille at the age of nineteen may have cut short Richard's professional plans, explaining his modest position at the bank. A quick wedding, however, followed by a "premature birth," would have allowed both families to avoid the social stigma that surrounded cases of "bastardy."[5]

Continued examination of the family papers indicates that Richard and Cecille's marriage warrants further interrogation. First, there is the matter of Cecille's place of birth. According to their notice of marriage, Cecille and Richard were both natives of Charleston. Naturalization records, however, reveal that the bride's family came to South Carolina from Saint-Domingue. We do not have Cecille's birth records, but Maria Langlois, a white schoolteacher who lived on nearby Tradd Street, was born on the island. This Maria was Cecille's sister.[6] Maria may have been older than Cecille, but even if the Langlois Family left Saint-Domingue the moment that the revolution broke out in the French colony in 1791, and Cecille was born immediately after her parents' arrival on the mainland (as early as 1792), she would have only been fourteen years old when she married Richard in May 1806.[7] Even in the Old South, where white women married earlier than their northern counterparts, this would have been unusually young.[8] Thus, it is reasonable to conclude that Cecille was born before her family arrived in Charleston.

While the line in the marriage notice may have been a simple error, it is also possible that Cecille deliberately misinformed people about her place of birth because she wanted to distance herself from her neighbors, many of whom were refugees from Saint-Domingue and whose households created an expatriate community of sorts in her neighborhood. Among these settlers were Joseph, Antoinette, and Maria Langlois who, along with their enslaved laborers, lived down the street from Cecille and Richard. According to existing public records, however, Cecille and her sister were white, while Joseph Langlois and his family were black. The members of Joseph's household were all listed in the state's Free Negro Capitation Tax Books, and Joseph himself was admitted to Charleston's Brown Fellowship Society (BFS) in 1834, the highly regarded mutual-aid organization for the city's elite free men of color.[9]

It is possible that kinship ties existed between Maria and Cecille Langlois on the one hand and the Joseph Langlois family on the other, ties that kept Cecille from acknowledging her Caribbean birth. In addition to their common surname, the white schoolteacher and one of the black Langlois women had the same first name, Maria, and all the individuals in question were originally from Saint-Domingue. This is all circumstantial evidence, but the likelihood of blood ties between the families deepens when we examine the registers of St. Philip's Episcopal Church in Charleston. Within these books are the baptismal records for all five of Cecille and Richard's sons, including one in 1813 for their second child. The register states that Richard Clement Cogdell was born on 30 August 1812 and that he was the "Son of Richard W. and Cecille Cogdell." It also notes that Richard Clement was a "child of color."[10]

This document is nothing if not surprising. Two white persons had a "child of color." The question is, how? There are several possibilities. Richard Clement may have been adopted. The register does not mention this, however, and it was standard practice to note adoptions in antebellum church registers.[11] Perhaps one of the boy's parents was a person of color. There are no notations of color beside either Cecille or Richard Sr.'s names, however, which indicates that both the boy's parents were considered to be white persons.[12] Then again, maybe young Richard really was white, and the church recorder erroneously listed the boy as a "child of color." Given the legal, political, economic, and social limitations of free blacks in South Carolina, however, it is unlikely that Richard Walpole would have let such an error stand with regards to his son.[13]

If Richard Clement was a "child of color" and he was not adopted, then there is the issue of paternity. The register lists the name of the father as Richard W. Cogdell, and the child was named for his father and for two uncles named Clement, all of which suggest he was Richard W. Cogdell's biological son. It is possible that Cecille had an affair, and that Richard baptized the boy as a Cogdell to hide his wife's infidelity. It is unlikely however, that Richard would have given a child who was not his own two family names. Additionally, it is difficult to imagine a southern white man accepting a biracial child as his own flesh and blood, thereby accepting not only his wife's adulterous behavior but also her betrayal with a man of color. When white women had sex with black men and gave birth to "mulatto" children as a result of these liaisons, it was seen as a societal scandal. While it was understood, and even accepted, that white men had sex with black women, the reverse did not hold true. Certainly such relationships occurred, but middle- and upper-class women generally went to great lengths to hide such affairs, proof of which could lead to them being ostracized by their families and their communities. In Cecille's case, however, there is no indication that her son's birth was a scandal, that his arrival hurt her marriage, or that the couple tried to hide the child's existence. Instead, they had the boy baptized at their home church (one of the city's most prestigious, white churches) and had three more sons together, two of whom were also baptized at St. Philip's. Neither of these boys, however, is listed in parish registers as a "child of color."[14]

If infidelity cannot explain the baby's color, then, a final possibility is that one or both of the boy's parents were persons of African descent who lived as white people. We know that Richard W. Cogdell's grandparents immigrated to South Carolina from Scotland, and there is no evidence that they, or Richard's parents, were anything but white persons. Additionally, Richard appeared before Isaac Motte Dart, notary public, on 27 April 1802, and obtained a travel letter so he could visit his maternal uncle, Clement Stevens, in Jamaica. According to Dart, Richard, then fifteen years of age, was "a native of the City of Charleston, from native born parents of said state, and is a citizen of the free, independent United States of America."[15] In 1802, U.S. citizenship was a privilege extended only to whites, so there appears to have been no question about Richard's racial identity. Richard's adult life also reflected the privileges of whiteness: he worked in a bank, was a captain in the state militia, a city warden, a councilman, and a notary public, all positions that were forbidden to black men.[16]

This brings us to Cecille. Like her husband, no documents have been recovered proving she had African ancestry. It is possible, however, that Cecille was of African heritage, but lived as a white woman. Cecille's familial connection to Saint-Domingue, and her apparent attempt to hide that, is suggestive of this. Saint-Domingue, like most Caribbean colonies, had a large number of free persons of color. Often the descendants of white men and their black mistresses, many members of this group could trace their free ancestry back several generations and were extended protections, privileges, and rights beyond those accorded to enslaved persons. Highly skilled, lighter-skinned, educated, and often wealthy, Saint-Domingue's *gens de couleur libres* conducted themselves as a third caste, a group distinct from the (mainly) darker-skinned blacks of the island who remained enslaved.[17]

Considering Saint-Domingue's long history of interracial relationships, and the existence of a large number of *gens de couleur libres* in the colony, many of whom fled to Charleston and other U.S. port cities during the island's revolution, it is possible that Cecille, whose family was from Saint-Domingue, was of African descent and related to her black neighbors, the Joseph Langlois family.[18] This could be why Cecille identified herself as a native of Charleston, and not Saint-Domingue, and it would explain the coloring of her second son. We know that Cecille's neighbor, Joseph, was fair-skinned, as evidenced by his admission into the BFS.[19] Cecille, too, may have been lighter in color, what southerners called a quadroon or octoroon, light enough to live as a white woman until the birth of her second son called that whiteness into question.[20]

We cannot, of course, be certain that either Cecille or Richard were persons of color. Save for the baptismal document, there is no other evidence in the public records or family papers to indicate that the couple was anything other than white. While Richard Jr.'s baptismal record thus raises questions about "passing" and the socially constructed nature of both blackness and whiteness in the antebellum South, until further evidence is uncovered to the contrary, we must treat Cecille and Richard as white people, just as their contemporaries did.

Despite the notation on his baptismal certificate, young Richard's birth does not appear to have negatively affected his parents' marriage, or their social status. A respectable, middle-class couple who had one white child prior to the arrival of their second son, Cecille and Richard continued to live together as man and wife after the birth of their "child of color."[21] As for how they were treated by their peers, the Cogdells had heretofore always behaved as respectable people. Legally married, they regularly attended an elite white church and utilized unfree labor in their home, bondspersons whose work Cecille oversaw on a daily basis. As befitted her status as a middle-class matron, Cecille herself did not toil outside the home for subsistence wages, and her husband was employed at a job from which black men were barred.[22]

Having already fulfilled their obligation to behave as "persons of worth," Cecille and Richard, in return, continued to receive all the privileges of respectable whiteness after the birth of their second child. They still worshipped at St. Philip's Episcopal Church (eventually renting a pew there) and their social calendar included balls, horse races, and the theater. In later years, Richard received a captain's commission in the state militia, served as a city warden, a notary public, and a councilman. Additionally, the couple educated their three youngest sons at the prestigious South Carolina Society Academy (SCSA), and at least four of their five sons lived as white men, with the attendant rights of full citizenship, as opposed to the partial privileges of denizenship doled out to free people of color.[23] Cecille's and Richard's behavior, and the reciprocal actions of their peers, then, suggest that in South Carolina, whiteness, like blackness, was not only socially constructed but also a performance of respectability that was dependent on the actions of both the individual and the community in which he or she lived.

Social class appears to have been a performance as well. While the Cogdells attended balls and the theater, and purchased fine wines, furniture, china, and books, they were neither aristocrats nor truly wealthy.[24] Whereas elite white Carolinians owned real property—namely plantations, urban real estate, and enslaved laborers—Cecille and Richard rented their house and hired their workers by the month. The couple did not purchase their first enslaved laborer until 1817, eleven years after they were first married. As the pair did not own their own business or a plantation, the black workers they rented would have done housework, provided childcare, and performed general maintenance around their home.[25]

ENTER SARAH

At this point, it appears that Cecille and Richard's marriage, despite some early irregularities, had become routine, even mundane. This is not, however, the end of their story. Eighteen years after the birth of their son of color, the Cogdells' lives took a momentous turn. A bill of sale filed with the County Clerk's Office indicates that in August 1830, Richard W. Cogdell bought an enslaved girl named Sarah Martha Sanders. According to their receipt books, the Cogdells had not procured any new laborers since acquiring the man John in 1817, but since Sarah's purchase was never recorded in the couple's receipt books it is quite possible that others were left out as well. Family records state that Sarah Martha Sanders was born on 8 February 1815. If the date is correct, she was fifteen years old when Richard brought her home.[26]

Sarah's entrance into the Cogdell household led to significant changes in Cecille's life. The young girl, acquired in August 1830, became pregnant in June 1831. Cecille now faced an anguish that white women in the South had been dealing with for centuries: her husband had broken his marriage vows and had sex with a young black girl. It is almost certain that this was the situation that led Cecille to move out of her home. City directories reveal that in 1831, Cecille was living at the corner of Pitt and Rutledge Streets, near her sister, Maria, while Richard continued to reside at their house on Broad Street. Cecille's change of address is noteworthy. In the antebellum South, a white woman who left her husband, no matter what he had done, risked tarnishing her reputation and forfeiting the socioeconomic benefits that her marriage brought her. Given Cecille's position as a respectable, middle-class matron, it is surprising that she left Richard, despite the fact that he had impregnated Sarah Sanders.[27]

That Cecille left home because of her husband's infidelity is strongly suggested by a letter that Richard wrote. While the letter has no salutation, the contents are such that it could have only been written to Cecille: "From the charges you make against me, I will not attempt to vindicate myself—it would be an admission that it were possible for me to be guilty of them. . . . But . . . I forgive freely. That you may yet be happy . . . is my very earnest prayer. Farewell! I restore you to yourself. . . . You may find a more congenial, more complying mind, a truer heart never. . . . Henceforth be free—In your occasional visits, for I do not see how I shall be able to explain your total absence—you will find me the same—unchanged in manner or in feeling. . . . Farewell!! May the blessing of Heaven rest upon you and upon your children—May they requite you for all your domestic unhappiness."[28]

What, other than Cecille's accusations of infidelity, would have led Richard to write, "From the charges you make against me, I will not attempt to vindicate myself—it would be an admission that it were possible for me to be guilty of them"? It also made sense that Richard played the injured party: "But . . . I forgive freely. That you may yet be happy . . . is my very earnest prayer." Magnanimously "forgiving" her, Richard knew it was impossible for Cecille to truly be finished with him, despite his statement that she was to "henceforth be free." Had she left him permanently, the laws of *coverture* were such that Cecille would have still required Richard's financial support, and she would have had to return home to see her children. She could not have taken them with her, since the law gave fathers automatic guardianship of any of their children over seven years in age.[29] Cecille's three youngest sons, thirteen, ten, and eight years in age, respectively, still lived at home in 1830. Thus, when Richard wrote, "In your occasional visits, for I do not see how I shall be able to explain your total absence—you will find me the same," he was undoubtedly referring to having to "explain" her absence to their sons.

Had Cecille lived, these constraints might have forced her to reconsider leaving her husband. While white married women had status, their power did not include financial freedom or full legal rights to their children. Additionally, a white southern woman did not receive community support for leaving her husband just because he had had sex with an enslaved girl. In a society where sex between white men and enslaved black women was, in large part, expected, white women were taught to practice the "art of ignorance" when it came to the paternity of the "yellow" babies born in their households. If Cecille left

Richard because he had impregnated Sarah, even if by force, it is Cecille's behavior that would have been viewed by white Charlestonians "of worth" as inappropriate, not Richard's, and it could have cost her all of the privileges that her marriage had brought to her. As a respectable white woman, Cecille was, in short, expected to look the other way when her husband had sex with an enslaved woman.[30]

Richard understood the limits of Cecille's power, and she knew how precarious her position was. In a society where authority was based on both race and sex, women of all races had to learn the art of accommodation and were forced to acknowledge that they were bound to the very men whose positions had helped them attain their own rights and privileges. Cecille's marriage enabled her to acquire many of the benefits of respectability. Ultimately, then, it was Richard who had the upper hand if Cecille left him. This explains the wording of his letter, which suggests Richard knew he held all the cards. It was up to him to forgive her, or not, release her, or not, and allow her to see her sons, or not. Marriage to Richard had allowed Cecille to solidify her position as a white woman "of worth." She may have thus been torn between her rage and sorrow, on the one hand, and her need to retain her standing as Mrs. Richard W. Cogdell, on the other. The separation from Richard may have just been temporary, then, but a long-term decision was made moot by her death: Cecille Langlois Cogdell died in December 1831 with her identity as a respectable married woman intact.[31]

For all that her position as a white matron afforded to her, it is clear that Cecille's freedom was constrained in many ways. It was her sons who benefited the most from their mother's performance of respectability. Well educated and able to speak French and indulge in gambling, Cecille's sons lived like true southern gentlemen. One even fought a duel, and at least four of them engaged in careers forbidden to black men: George worked at the Charleston City Treasury; John practiced law; Charles was a clerk in the State Bank; and Richard Clement, the "child of color," became a lieutenant in the United States Navy.[32] The Cogdell boys thus acquired all of the rights and privileges of U.S. citizenship by virtue of their identity as white men. Exempt from capitation taxes, occupational restrictions, educational barriers, and political limitations, Cecille and Richard's sons experienced a fuller freedom than most antebellum Southerners.

Cecille did not live long enough to see her younger sons grow to adulthood. Her sudden death, however, also spared her a mother's grief: her eldest son, James, passed away shortly after she did, in February 1832. Just days later, on 1 March 1832, Sarah Martha Sanders gave birth to her first child by Richard W.

Cogdell, a son they named Robert. In less than three months, then, Richard had lost Cecille and James, and gained Sarah and Robert.[33]

SARAH AND RICHARD

What a moment in the Stevens-Cogdell family album. Richard's maternal grandfather, John Stevens, had believed that black women were incapable of virtue, and that interracial sex was both "horrid" and a "crime."[34] Then there was the fact that one of Richard's maternal uncles, the son of John Stevens, had apparently had sex with an enslaved woman and fathered a biracial child he never acknowledged.[35] Additionally, Richard's own mother, Mary Ann, daughter of John and sister to the man who had fathered a biracial child, believed that any white man who had sexual relations with a woman of color, "should be compelled by the laws of humanity to marry the person, black or mulatto, with whom such familiarity have existed." She also felt that a white man who had such a relationship ought not to have any "intercourse with genteel society or to appear in any public place of amusement on a level of equality with other citizens, and their seats in a house of public worship in a suitable place for such offenders."[36] And then there was Richard. He was, apparently, already the father of a "child of color" by his first wife. Now he had impregnated Sarah Sanders, an enslaved teenager whom he never freed or legally married but with whom he maintained a domestic connection for the next two decades and with whom he had ten children. How did white Charlestonians respond to this turn of events in the Cogdell household?

It seems that Richard engaged in this relationship with Sarah without any significant social consequences. Apart from Cecille's removal from their home, there is nothing to suggest that Richard's life was disrupted, or that his peers were dismayed that he had impregnated a young black girl shortly before his wife's death. Instead, in the year after Robert's birth, Richard's life appeared to proceed in a rather mundane fashion. He continued to work for the bank, was made a captain of the State Guards, gave the SCSA money for his white sons' tuition, and paid St. Philip's Church the $24 he owed for his annual pew rental. Winthrop Jordan posits that white Charlestonians had a more relaxed attitude (compared to other mainland regions) toward interracial sex during the colonial era, although they were not as accepting of it as people who lived in the Caribbean. In light of what we know of Sarah and Richard's story, Jordan's conclusions appear to hold true for the nineteenth century as well.[37]

Whether this relationship was accepted by white Charlestonians or not, it is still unclear if the union between Sarah and Richard was a violent tragedy or a consensual partnership. What we know about Sarah and Richard's relationship thus far is ugly. Sarah was black; Richard was white. She was enslaved; he was her owner. He was married when Robert was conceived; she labored alongside the mistress of the house. Sarah was barely seventeen when her first child was born; Richard was forty-four. In many ways, then, this fits the profile of a nonconsensual, violent sexual encounter, which it almost certainly was in the beginning.[38] It is less certain that it remained so when one examines the rest of the family papers, including letters written by the couple's descendants. We know that Sarah and Richard had nine more children together over the next twenty years, and that while Sarah was never manumitted, she and Richard lived together with their children and he never remarried. Additionally, although they were legally enslaved, Sarah's children by Richard were housed, fed, clothed, and educated by their father, and they, along with their mother, lived as virtually free persons of color.

It is difficult, then, to view Richard as only and always a sexually exploitative slaveowner, and Sarah as only and always a rape victim. It is equally challenging to see this as an affectionate union, although Sarah appears to have acquiesced to it at some point, almost certainly in order to improve her children's socioeconomic chances and choices. Instead, the evidence suggests that Sarah and Richard's relationship, like many, if not most, interracial unions in the Old South, was neither wholly coercive nor wholly consensual, but rather that it contained elements of both.[39] Yes, their relationship lasted until Sarah's death in 1850, and, yes, Richard recognized Sarah's children as his own and protected, educated, and provided for them. At the same time, while her connection to Richard gave her certain, material advantages, the limitations of the bond were formidable given that Sarah remained Richard's legal property until the day she died. It would have been hard to build a partnership based on consent and mutual affection given the intimidation that was likely present at the relationship's inception, as well as the unequal legal and social power dynamics inherent throughout its existence.

In terms of Sarah's enslaved status, the reason she was never legally manumitted is almost certainly because she did not meet Richard until 1830, and masters could not free their workers of their own volition after 1820. Under the conditions of the Act of 1820, Richard would have had to petition the General Assembly to manumit Sarah, and any children she had borne while enslaved, and it is highly unlikely that that body would have granted his petition. Laborers being freed generally had to perform some heroic deed to be deemed "worthy" of manumission, and they had to prove that they would not become a financial burden to the state. As far as we know, Sarah had no special skills, and she had young children with no visible means of supporting them. Additionally, the assemblymen had already turned down numerous petitions filed by white male Charlestonians requesting the emancipation of their black lovers and biracial children. Sarah was thus not a good candidate for legislative manumission, and Richard, whose brother was a former state legislator, would have known that.[40]

Had Richard been determined to acquire legal emancipation for Sarah and their offspring, he could have taken them to a free state. Under the Act of 1820, however, she and her children would not have been allowed to return to South Carolina, and it would have been difficult for Richard to go with them.[41] A middle-aged man, Richard was a bank clerk without a large fortune. His connections were all in Charleston, and what property he did own (including his enslaved laborers) he could not remove from the state. If his black family left the state without Richard, however, there would be no one to protect and provide for them. Additionally, the couple had to consider the needs of Richard's sons by Cecille, three of whom were still minors in 1832. If they had all gone to the North, Sarah and Richard would have found themselves in a strange city with several small children and no means of supporting them. Perhaps the only viable option, then, was to remain in Charleston, where Richard could provide for his family, and where Sarah and her children could live as virtually free people under his protection.

That Sarah and her children remained enslaved, then, does not necessarily mean that Richard did not care about them. Indeed, several clues suggest the opposite. For example, within ten days of Robert's birth in 1832, Richard procured a revolving steam washer for his home. Caring for a newborn would have significantly increased Sarah's workload. Either Richard understood this, and bought the washer of his own accord in order to help alleviate Sarah's burdens, or Sarah herself requested the machine. Cecille's death and Robert's subsequent birth meant that Sarah now commanded more power in the Cogdell household than she had previously, and her position as the mother of Richard's son, as opposed to simply being Richard's enslaved sexual partner, likely enabled her to negotiate for a variety of privileges. These benefits surely encompassed material purchases like the washing machine.[42]

The piano, which arrived just a few weeks later, was a similar acquisition. Whether Sarah played the instrument is unknown, but family papers indicate that her daughters received lessons as children, and that one became a fairly competent pianist. Apparently Sarah tried to ensure that her children had every possible cultural advantage made available to them. And while Sarah may have never played the piano that stood in her parlor, she certainly used the dinnerware that Richard obtained from Abraham Tobias on 23 December 1833. It is hard to imagine a widower with a house full of young boys picking out such an item for his own use. In light of the date on which the dishes were bought, it is fair to assume that Richard got the set as a Christmas gift for Sarah, in keeping with her position as the lady of the house.[43]

Taken together, these purchases appear to be the gestures of a man who cared for his partner, or at least wanted to keep her happy. They also reveal the new and more influential role that Sarah played in Richard's life. For example, all of the Sanders children were well educated, either by tutors or in one of Charleston's schools for free people of color. Certainly Sarah, who died illiterate, would have been anxious for her children to go to school in order to help improve their social standing. Additionally, the fact that the Sanders children attended school is significant, since an 1834 state law made it illegal to teach free blacks or enslaved persons how to read or write.[44] Sarah and Richard thus took a risk in educating their children. Of course, the fact that Richard's cousin-in-law, Lionel H. Kennedy, was the mastermind behind the new education law may have provided the family with some protection from the authorities.[45]

Numerous black Charlestonians daily violated the state's antiblack education laws and sent their children to school. The unspoken understanding between them and the city's ruling white elite was that as long as free blacks were circumspect, and times remained peaceful, they had nothing to fear. Thus, Charleston's black schools continued to operate after 1834, but did so knowing that those who turned a blind eye on black education today could condemn it tomorrow. Like every other privilege free blacks had, it was contingent on the goodwill of the white elite and could disappear during times of racial unrest.[46] In light of this, Sarah and Richard took a step of faith in educating their children. They knew their ability to do so without penalty rested on maintaining the sympathy of those in power, including Richard's cousin. Their efforts must have worked, since there is no record that they were ever harassed for sending their children to school.

The lives of free blacks were clearly ones of delicate balance, living as they did within a nebulous middle ground that depended on the largesse of paternalistic whites. They attended school, acquired property, ran their own businesses, shopped on King Street, and walked the streets with a modicum of dignity. These privileges could disappear in an instant, however: if people of color were disrespectful of white authority, offended the wrong person, or if a slave rebellion occurred, white Charlestonians would quickly rise to defend their way of life. In the process, free blacks could find themselves without any rights, privileges, or protections.

For Sarah and her children, things would have become particularly difficult if times had changed. They had no manumission papers, nor had they been freed before 1820. White Charlestonians would have known that the Sanders family was enslaved by law, but they would have also been privy to the intimate nature of Sarah and Richard's relationship. Sarah and her children were thus permitted to live as free people, but blacks who were free-by-courtesy could not wholly depend on this benign neglect, and living with such uncertainty likely took its toll on Sarah. With each child she bore, she would have worried anew about what would happen to her children, especially after she and Richard were both gone. Who, then, would protect them from being sold, and, if Richard predeceased her, how would Sarah herself avoid being put up on the auction block and separated from her children?

Sarah also would have understood that her family's security depended largely on the goodwill of Richard himself. Regardless of her new position in the Cogdell household, if Sarah's relationship with Richard ended, she could not move out or ask Richard to leave. Her children were not even hers to remove: they were, by law, Richard's property, as was Sarah herself. Had she and Richard had a falling out, or he met someone new, Sarah might have found herself serving again as his enslaved laborer, or he could have sold her, their children, or both. In short, Sarah and her children's continuing status as free people depended on Richard Cogdell's feelings, which could change in an instant. These fears could have kept Sarah from arguing with Richard, even when he angered her. They may have also kept her in a relationship with Richard, even if she no longer wanted him in her bed. Lacking even the limited rights of a legal wife, Sarah knew she had no recourse if Richard chose to renounce her or their children.

There is no indication that Sarah and Richard ever ended their relationship, but the uncertainties that plagued the lives of virtually free blacks like Sarah were only too real. What Sarah may have feared most was that Richard would die without having freed her or the children, or having made some sort of provision for them, leaving them at the mercy of his legal heirs. Sarah knew that she could not depend on Cecille's sons to protect her children. At least three of these boys grew up to become drunkards, gamblers, and debtors, and they went to their graves while still relatively young, taking their own lives or dying from conditions like dementia.[47]

A EUROPEAN EXCURSION

Sarah's fears were likely heightened whenever Richard left home for any length of time. Who knew what dangers might befall them during his absence, or if he would return safely? These worries almost certainly consumed her in 1844. By that year, Sarah had given birth to seven children, five of whom were still living. Robert, called Bobby, was twelve; Martha eight; Julia seven; little Sarah was almost five; and Cordelia was not quite three. It was then that Richard decided to quit his job and embark on a European excursion. Having recently come into a sizeable inheritance from the widow of one of his maternal uncles, he set off on a tour of the continent that lasted eighteen months, leaving Sarah and the children behind. By June 1844 he was in London, enjoying concerts in Her Majesty's concert rooms at Hanover Square. After a few months in England, he moved on to holiday in Paris.[48]

One can only imagine how Sarah felt about Richard's decision to travel to Europe at the age of fifty-seven, leaving her to manage everything by herself. Although Richard wrote to her and told her to contact "Mr. Whitney" for anything she might require during his absence, one wonders if this was enough.[49] Sarah was not quite thirty years old and had large burdens to bear. What if Mr. Whitney chose not to honor Richard's requests? How, then, would she purchase groceries, or pay the bills? What if the shopkeepers in town refused to extend her credit while Richard was away, or one of the children needed medical attention? Who would care for the children if something happened to Sarah while Richard was off playing the gentleman in Europe? The possibilities were endless and likely quite frightening.

As the months wore on, Richard visited the Tuileries and attended the opera while Sarah sat at home and cared for their five children.[50] One thus wonders how much sympathy Sarah felt for him when she received Richard's letter from Paris, dated 20 December 1844. Richard, it seems, had heard from his "child of color" by Cecille. U.S. Navy Lieutenant Richard Clement Cogdell was now being dishonorably discharged from his position. Richard poured out his grief and frustration in a letter to Sarah:

> My Dear Sarah . . . as I feared, Richard has been ordered to be dismissed from the navy, and unless the President chuses [sic] to soften the sentence, he is lost forever and my peace with it. Charles has not written me one line since the 12th of September. . . . He is ungrateful to keep silent. . . . If it was not for shame to see my old friends and enemies upon Richard's disgrace I would return immediately. I have no pleasure or peace. . . . It only remains for you to play false to make me abandon all hope. . . . I am almost always in my apartments and take no pleasure abroad. No person has had the power to charm me be assured. Women I never think of. The children I hope are well and behave. Kiss them for me

and say I pray for them all and hope to see them without being ashamed of them. I will not forget presents when I come home. . . . Keep pure and all will yet go well. Yours affectionately, RWC.[51]

The events leading to Richard Clement's dismissal from the Navy are not detailed in this letter, nor do we know how Sarah felt about this young man and his troubles. The letter does, however, give us some insight into Richard's personal thoughts, and his relationship with Sarah. Like other antebellum men, Richard knew that a man's standing in his community depended in large part on the behavior of his children, particularly his sons. The slightest slip on the part of a young man could tarnish his family's name, thus sons were continually reminded by their parents that they were to "never forget what is due your father's name."[52] It is no wonder, then, that Richard Sr. feared that his second son was "lost forever and my peace with it." Concerned with his own reputation, he went on to claim that it was only his "shame" at seeing his "old friends and enemies upon Richard's disgrace" that kept him from returning home immediately.

This "shame" at one son's indiscretions was reflected in Richard's attitude toward his other children. "Charles has not written me one line since the 12th of September which makes me quite miserable. He is ungrateful to keep silent." Frustrated with the situation of one son, Richard lashed out at another of his sons by Cecille. His children with Sarah also entered into his worries, prompting him to write that he hoped "to see them without being ashamed of them." It seems that Richard now feared that every member of his family might humiliate him.

His concerns extended to include Sarah, whom Richard hastened to assure of his affection. Claiming that their relationship was what sustained him through these dark times, Richard insisted that Sarah had every reason to trust him, and that he was having a terrible time without her: "I am almost always in my apartments and take no pleasure abroad. No person has had the power to charm me be assured. Women I never think of." One wonders if Richard wrote these words because he knew Sarah was upset that he had gone to Europe, leaving her to deal with everything alone. They may have argued about it before he left, or perhaps she sent word via "Mr. Whitney" that she was unhappy and needed him to come home. Certainly something prompted him to reassure her that he never thought of other women.

Richard was worried enough about his relationship with Sarah that he openly admitted his fear that Sarah might take another man to her bed: "It only remains for you to play false to make me abandon all hope of comfort in returning home . . . Keep pure and all will yet go well." Richard's anxiety about Sarah's fidelity highlights the insecurity inherent in their relationship. Like many domestic unions, particularly those that were not fully consensual, the partnership was plagued by doubts. Richard, apparently, was not confident of Sarah's feelings for him, which prompted him to write and tell her that her companionship was central to his life. It also explains why he hastened to assure her of his own faithfulness, since this might keep her from straying. The fact, however, is that while Richard was concerned about the constancy of Sarah's affections, she had far more to lose if their relationship ended. Richard could sell her, nullify her virtually free status, separate her from her children, or leave her destitute, and she would have no legal recourse against him. For both of them, then, but for Sarah in particular, the union was fraught with complications.

OF TENSIONS AND TRAGEDIES

Sarah and Richard were eventually reunited when he returned from Europe in November 1845, bearing gifts of expensive perfume. Whatever concerns either of them may have had about the other, they continued their relationship: their next child, Sophia Elizabeth, was born on 30 April 1847.[53] That was a taxing spring for the family. In February, in the midst of Sarah's pregnancy, Richard's older brother, John, passed away. In addition to land and money, John bequeathed to Richard "a Diamond Ring which had been left me in the will of my dear mother . . . with the design that the same may be kept by my brother in his family."[54] Richard's maternal grandfather, John Stevens, had left this ring to his daughter, Mary Ann, upon his death in 1772. Mary Ann wore the ring until she died in 1827, and then willed it to her eldest son, asking that it remain in the family. John, who died childless, passed the ring onto Richard with the same stipulation. In 1858, Richard gave this ring to his daughter, Sarah Ann Sanders. In this manner did the ring of a man who despised interracial sex and believed black women to be incapable of virtue come to reside in the hands of his great-granddaughter, a free-by-courtesy black woman who was herself the result of an extralegal, interracial relationship.[55]

For Sarah, pregnant in the spring of 1847, John's death likely heightened her own concerns about the welfare of her children. Richard was now sixty years old and had been diagnosed with asthma. What would happen to Sarah and her children when he died? Even if Richard did not worry about this, Sarah must have. It seems certain that she would have pleaded with him over the years to make some sort of provision for her and their children. Surely she and Richard both knew that from 1820 onward, other men in Richard's position had drafted trust agreements leaving their black families to white male confidantes on the understanding that they would allow their relatives to live as virtually free people. Richard had a number of close friends whom he could have asked to perform such a duty, including Alfred Huger. Indeed, he could have crafted a trust agreement that ensured the Sanders family their freedom and left them an estate that would be administered for them by that same trustee. If such a trust was ever executed in writing, it has not been uncovered.[56]

As the years went on, the situation had become more complicated. In 1841, the South Carolina state legislature banned the use of trust agreements that freed enslaved persons and left them property. Certainly many people continued to use "secret," verbal trusts, although such actions were trickier now than ever before. To make matters even more difficult, earlier in the century, Richard could have provided for Sarah and the children had he first taken them to a state where manumission was legal, and then given them property while he lived or left it to them upon his death. He would not have even had to admit that these were his own children in order to carry out such actions. The Act of 1841, however, not only outlawed trusts but also made it illegal to remove any enslaved person from the state for the purposes of manumitting them.[57]

Yet another obstacle existed that made it difficult for Sarah and her children to acquire any property from Richard. Not only were they enslaved by law, and thus not legally allowed to own property, but Richard also still had legitimate, living descendants: his sons by Cecille. By law, then, Sarah's children, Richard's "natural children," were not entitled to anything.[58] Had Richard tried to disinherit his white children by leaving the Sanders family his estate, or attempted to transfer property to his black family while he still lived, his legal heirs could have contested his actions, regardless of where Sarah and her children were living at the time, and even if they had been manumitted. Richard's only lawful choice, then, may have been to set money aside for his black children before he died, arrange for his white sons to use those funds to support their half siblings after his death, and hope that his wishes were honored when he was gone.

Although Sarah and Richard could not have known it, their situation would grow graver with each passing year. In April 1849, as Sarah gave birth to her ninth child, Miranda, South Carolina faced its worse crisis since nullification. The discovery of gold in California had prompted a mass migration west, and both sections of the nation wanted to see California, and ultimately the entire western region, join "their side" with regards to the issue of slavery. The rumblings of secession grew loud as U.S. Senator (and former vice president) John C. Calhoun fanned the flames of division in South Carolina, and Congress feared that war was on the horizon unless it could settle the issue of Western slavery. The resulting Compromise of 1850 poured oil on troubled waters, but this band-aid was soon ripped apart by public furor over the Fugitive Slave Amendment and the bloody warfare that erupted in Kansas.[59]

In September 1850, in the midst of this national uncertainty, the lives of the Sanders family were forever changed by a more personal tragedy. On 18 September, Sarah gave birth to her tenth child. Two days later, her body likely worn out from nineteen years of nonstop pregnancy, childbearing, and nursing, Sarah Martha Sanders passed away. She was only thirty-five years old, and she went to her grave knowing that her family remained in jeopardy. They had, up until this point, been well cared for, but Richard was unwell, and Sarah's six living children remained legally enslaved with no property of their own. Over the years, Sarah's savvy tactics of negotiation had acquired many things for her offspring, but they were still at risk, and she could no longer protect them.[60]

Sarah's passing was undoubtedly a shock. Richard, then sixty-three years of age, surely had not fathomed outliving his second mate. As he had done for Cecille, Richard purchased a plot for Sarah, and a headstone for her grave, and had the following epitaph placed on it: "Sacred to the Memory of Sarah Martha Sanders Who departed this life Sept. 20, 1850 Aged 35 years 7 months, Leaving 6 children to lament their loss. She was loved by All who knew her for her gentleness of character. Her infant daughter, 'Miranda' lies in the same grave. 'Thou Art gone to the grave, we no longer behold thee nor tread the rough paths of the world by thy side. But the wide arms of mercy are spread and enfold thee and sinners may Hope since the sinless has died.'" Four years later, the child Sarah had died giving birth to, a daughter named Florence, was placed in the grave next to the one occupied by Sarah and Miranda, and Richard was left to care for the rest of his black children without the help of their "gentle" and "sinless" mother.[61]

TRIALS AND TRANSITIONS

The 1850s proved to be years of great trial for the Sanders family. Richard raised his virtually free children alone while his white sons led disreputable lives. Richard Clement, Cecille and Richard's "child of color," never returned to Charleston after his dismissal from the Navy, and he appears to have predeceased his father. John Walpole, at one point a practicing attorney in Charleston, moved to Philadelphia and committed suicide in what was termed "a fit of insanity." As for George Burgess, his dissolute lifestyle of drinking and gambling finally caught up with him. Suffering from various ailments, and then diagnosed with dementia, George spent the better part of 1852 living with his maternal aunt, Maria Langlois, who cared for him until his death later that same year.[62]

The only one of Cecille's sons still alive after 1852, then, was Charles. Employed as a clerk at the State Bank as late as 1855, Charles never married and lived in perpetual debt. In 1853 he wrote to his father, claiming that he was in severe financial distress, and he asked Richard to bail him out . . . again.[63] Richard came to his son's rescue, but he also realized that Charles could not be trusted with the estate Richard had spent a lifetime accumulating. In 1856, Richard thus wrote the first of many wills. In it he left everything to Charles, as both custom and law demanded, but the funds were left to his son in trust with Elias Vanderhorst, Alfred Huger, John B. Irving, and Daniel Horlbeck, Richard's oldest friends. If Charles attempted to contravene the trust, everything Richard left would revert to his first cousin, Mary Ann Jane Kennedy.[64]

Having ensured that Charles would not squander a lifetime of work, Richard finally made some provision for his children by Sarah. Six days after Richard made out his first will, Charles wrote him a letter in which he stated that he would abide by his father's wishes and permit Sarah and Richard's children to "occupy the house belonging to you, and now occupied by them . . . in Friend Street . . . during my life on whatever terms you may please to suggest."[65] As late as 1856, then, Richard did not appear willing to remove his black children from South Carolina, but there was no guarantee that Charles would not turn his half siblings out into the street after his father's death, or sell them and the house to pay off his debts. There was no notarized deed, trust, or affidavit guaranteeing the Sanders children a right of residency in the house on Friend Street. There was only a letter acknowledging a verbal agreement between father and son that Charles could ignore if he chose. Still, it was more than what had existed while Sarah was alive.

While their futures were thus still uncertain, Sarah's children had more to worry about than just Charles. They would have been deeply concerned by the storm now brewing for all of Charleston's free blacks, particularly virtually free blacks. Since the alleged Vesey conspiracy, Charleston's free people of color had faced increasing restrictions and periods of repression, but in the 1850s, the city changed dramatically. For the first time in its history, Charleston had a white majority. New European immigration, the decline of slavery in older regions of the South, and the corresponding sale of enslaved laborers to states like Mississippi and Alabama meant that almost 60 percent of Charleston's population was white by 1858. Many of these residents were working-class people who resented competing with black women and men for jobs. With their numerical increase came new political power, and working-class whites now began maneuvering to force free blacks out of Charleston's labor force and, ultimately, out of the city itself.[66]

What kind of lives could Sarah's children hope to lead in such a city? Her eldest child, Robert, turned twenty-five in 1857 and would have been hardpressed to find employment: skilled craftsmen were increasingly unwilling to hire black workers in the face of opposition from working-class voters. Her older daughters, qualified to teach school in other parts of the nation, likely faced similar difficulties. Thus it was in the spring of 1857 that Richard, no doubt encouraged by his black children, decided that it was no longer safe to stay in Charleston. Shortly after his son, Robert, married Martha Julia Davenport at St. Philip's Episcopal Church in April of that year, Richard traveled to Philadelphia to look for a house. By the spring of 1858, almost eight years after their mother's death, all of Sarah's children were finally residing in the "free North," living with their father in the City of Brotherly Love.[67]

PHILADELPHIA

In hindsight, the Sanders family's decision to leave South Carolina was a wise one, although not easy or without pain. Although they would soon be joined in Philadelphia by a large expatriate community of black southerners, they, like all such migrants, missed their home and their friends.[68] The transition was most difficult for Richard, who was seventy years old when he moved to Philadelphia. In addition to leaving behind old friends, he was not in Charleston during the last days of his youngest son with Cecille, Charles. Maria Langlois, Cecille's sister, had cared for Charles's brother, George, during his final illness in 1852. In 1860, she wrote to Richard's friend Daniel Horlbeck about her care of Charles, who was now without the use of his legs and suffering from "mania." She stated that "every want and attention he can want shall be attended to. . . . It is a satisfaction to me that I am enabled to bestow on him those cares that none but one who is truly interested, would think of. . . . It is a truly painful duty."[69] Daniel forwarded Maria's letter to Richard who, having left this one son in order to protect the rest of his children, may have felt some guilt when reading Maria's words.

Moving to Philadelphia was not, however, enough to safeguard the future of Sarah's children. They were now free, but there was still the matter of financial provision. Richard thus took some steps to provide for his black children monetarily, including transferring several personal items to his daughter Sarah Ann. On 8 May 1858, in the presence of two witnesses, Sarah Ann received from her father, "A Gold Watch; A diamond Ring which was mine for many years; A piano made by Worcester; My music Box made for me in Geneva; My Cameo Miniature taken in Rome; My Garnet breast pin; My Gold stock Buckle; My Venetian Album; and My New Opera glass." The diamond ring mentioned was the Stevens family ring.[70]

Two years later, Richard updated his will. Charles Cogdell was ill and living with his Aunt Maria by then, and Richard clarified the terms Charles had agreed to abide by with regards to his black siblings. Richard left his entire estate, in trust, to the support of his son until Charles turned fifty. If, at that point, Charles was of "sound and disposing mind," the estate would pass to him directly, and Charles, upon his death, was to leave the entire estate to Sarah and Richard's surviving children. If Charles predeceased Richard, did not reach the age of fifty, or was not of sound mind, the estate would remain in trust until he died. Richard's executors were to then dispose of all the property and "make equal division of it" among his surviving children.[71]

Two months later, Charles passed away. His death removed the final hurdle from the Sanders children's ability to inherit their father's estate. Richard then wrote a new will to ensure that his surviving offspring by Sarah received their bequests: all of his property was left to Robert, Julia, Sarah Ann, Cordelia, and Sophie Sanders, "to be equally divided between them." Richard also noted that, "if any of the beneficiaries mentioned . . . should marry her property be settled in trust for her and subject to her disposition at death," thereby protecting his daughters' inheritances from the possible machinations of any future husbands.[72]

As the country marched to war, the Sanders family celebrated as Julia (Sarah and Richard's eldest daughter) prepared to marry. On 29 May 1861, Julia wed Edward Y. Venning at Protestant Episcopal Church in Philadelphia. Venning was born in Philadelphia, but his family was originally from Charleston. His father, Edward W. Venning, was a carpenter who had left Charleston for Philadelphia in 1830. Edward Jr. followed his father into the building profession and was the junior partner in their firm, Venning and Son. The Vennings were highly respected in Philadelphia's black community, and Julia's marriage was a sign that Sarah's sacrifices had borne fruit. Sarah had been, at best, a white man's illiterate and enslaved domestic partner; her daughter was a teacher, an accomplished and educated woman who married a man whose family ranked among Philadelphia's black elite.[73]

In 1863, shortly after Julia gave birth to her first child, Richard redid his will and left his estate to his children, "and to their heirs and assigns as ten

Julia Sanders Venning, the daughter of Sarah Martha Sanders and Richard Walpole Cogdell. This image of Julia, which captures her later in life, was taken sometime in the early 1900s. (Library Company of Philadelphia, Philadelphia, PA)

amounts in common to be equally divided between them." Richard probably rewrote his will in this manner in order to allow his grandchildren to benefit from his estate.[74] Unfortunately, as Julia settled into married life, her father discovered that he had little property to bequeath to his family upon his death. Having left his holdings in South Carolina after his move North, Richard's savings were then trapped there by the war, and the value of his property decreased daily. When the war ended, he was almost bankrupt. Many of his stocks and bonds were now worthless, and his lot on Friend Street had to be auctioned off because he did not have the funds to pay the back taxes. He became extremely agitated about his finances and worried constantly about providing for his children.[75]

In the midst of these woes, the youngest of Sarah and Richard's living children, Sophia Elizabeth, passed away in September 1865 at the age of eighteen. The next month, Julia Sanders Venning gave birth to her second daughter, whom she named Sophia Sanders after her recently deceased sister. Following his daughter's death, Richard added a codicil to his will passing Sophie's share onto his other heirs in equal portions. A few months later, in yet another codicil, he left his daughters Sarah Ann and Cordelia "all my household goods, jewelry, Silver, China, Pictures, Books, Piano, Bed and Bedding Linen and other Furniture." Julia was excluded from this bequest, likely because she was already provided for in terms of household goods due to her marriage to Edward Venning. Cordelia and Sarah were still unwed, however, and lived with their father, so they had more of a need for such items.[76]

While the sale of some railroad bonds eased Richard's pecuniary situation at this time, money was still tight for the family after the war. Thus, in 1866, Cordelia moved to Brooklyn and took up a teaching position in order to help ease the financial situation at home, leaving Sarah Ann to care for their aging father. In February 1866, "Delia" wrote to her father and advised him not to sell his lands in South Carolina. "I have heard that rents are so high in your old city that people cannot live there and are coming back north. You must not, therefore, sell your land. . . . Just think of the mean little rooms in Charleston renting for ten dollars a week."[77]

Whether Richard would have heeded Cordelia's advice is unknown. His health failing, he was bedridden for most of the year, and on 23 December 1866, Richard Walpole Cogdell passed away at his home in Philadelphia. He was seventy-nine years old. Sarah Ann, still living at home, contacted her siblings to inform them of their father's death and sent a telegraph to her father's friend Daniel Horlbeck in Charleston. Daniel, in reply, asked her to "send Body by first Steamer as Dr. Irving and self will see to Burial." The Sanders children knew that Richard had wanted to be buried next to his mother in the graveyard at St. Philip's Church, and they sent Richard's remains to Charleston on 30 December 1866.[78]

Daniel made the funeral arrangements and wrote Sarah Ann that "old Mr. Vanderhorst and others shall attend the burial . . . and Dr. Irving will be in town as I have written him. . . . My idea is to take the body . . . to the old church where he worshipped and summon his old friends to be present at the funeral ceremony." Daniel then asked Sarah Ann if she would return to Charleston for the funeral and suggested that all the surviving Sanders children should "come and live here in the South where are all your early friends and affections. All are now equal before the law on this scene there is no objection then. . . . Things are not as when you were here."[79] Whether the Sanders children attended their father's funeral is uncertain. We do know, however, that despite Daniel Horlbeck's pleadings, none of them ever returned to live in Charleston. Sarah Sanders had worked diligently to see her family escape from slavery. One could even say that she had, quite literally, given her life to this cause. Having finally left slavery behind them, it seems the Sanders children were not prepared to return to the scene of their mother's ultimate sacrifice.[80]

CONCLUSION

The lives of Cecille Langlois Cogdell and Sarah Martha Sanders are a rare glimpse into the benefits and drawbacks inherent in the lives of "negotiating women." For women in the Old South, compromise could have some positive outcomes. By constructing herself as a respectable white woman, Cecille Langlois Cogdell was able to acquire significant advantages for herself. She married a middle-class white man, lived in a reputable neighborhood, worshipped at a prestigious white church, owned and utilized the labor of enslaved persons, and lived and died as a white matron "of worth." As a woman in the antebellum South, however, Cecille also suffered from the limitations of her time, space, and social space. Near the end of her life, Cecille's husband had sex with their teenaged black laborer, which resulted in that same girl's pregnancy. Likely both angry and humiliated, Cecille appears to have left her husband due to these circumstances, although her society's acceptance of white male infidelity, as well as the social mores about proper white female behavior and the legal obstacles of *coverture*, might have eventually forced her to return to Richard had she not passed away. Having used her marriage to attain many of the privileges of respectability, Cecille was then bound, legally, financially, and socially, to the man who not only had hurt her but also had helped her attain the privileges and rights she desired.

It was Cecille's children who benefited the most from her tactics of negotiation. Raised in a financially stable and intellectually invigorating home, they received the education and upbringing that was due middle-class white men in the Old South. Educated, tutored in French, accustomed to traveling, and indulging in gambling, Cecille's sons were true southern gentlemen, evidenced in no small part by the fact that one of them was challenged to a duel. Financially aided by their father, their identity as white men also enabled them to vote, hold political office, and engage in profitable careers. Richard Jr. was an officer in the United States Navy, George worked in the Charleston City Treasury, John was an attorney, and Charles, the youngest, was a teller in the State Bank. Cecille's sons thus had all the rights and privileges of U.S. citizenship by virtue of their identity as white men. While such an identity was based in part on the happenstance of birth, the Cogdell boys also owed their privileges to their parents' ability to construct respectable identities for themselves, and to a community that acknowledged whiteness to be a performance based on social and biological components.

Sarah Sanders also practiced the art of compromise, although for her it was less of a choice than a necessity imposed by the circumstances of her life. Born enslaved, at the age of sixteen Sarah was impregnated by her married white owner. Although this relationship was almost certainly nonconsensual at the start, it continued with Sarah's acquiescence as she came to understand the benefits such a union could bring. Giving birth to ten children over the next twenty years, Sarah lived with Richard and their children as a family. Acting as Richard's wife after Cecille died, Sarah resided in a comfortable home, acquired a number of material goods, and spent the rest of her life living as a free woman. It was a limited freedom, however, since her manumission was not recorded and her partnership with Richard was not solemnized by either the courts or the church. It was, in reality, based solely on the continuing affections of the man with whom she shared her bed. Had Richard tired of her, Sarah's privileges could have vanished. Likely haunted by these fears, and limited by a myriad of legal obstacles, Sarah went to her grave uneducated, propertyless, and still lawfully enslaved. Her life thus reveals that for many, if not all, black women in the Old South, freedom was a fragile construct. Contingent on any number of circumstances, and the maintenance of unequal alliances with persons in positions of formal authority, freedom, far from being a simple legal category, was, instead, a continually shifting state of being or experience that had as many faces as enslavement.

Sarah's children had access to all that their mother never attained for herself. From regular schooling to piano lessons, Sarah's children were raised in a manner befitting their white father's middle-class station in life. And when the political climate in Charleston became dangerous for all free blacks in the late 1850s, Richard did something he had never done while Sarah lived: he took his biracial children to live in Philadelphia to try to protect them from the increased threat of reenslavement, and he eventually endowed them with his estate. It was there that Sarah's daughter Julia became a teacher and married into one of the city's most illustrious black families. Julia's daughter Miranda, in turn, became the first black female principal in Philadelphia. Another of Sarah's daughters, Cordelia, taught school in Brooklyn and in due course married William H. Chew, also the son of a respected black Philadelphia family. Cordelia's son Richard became one the first black students to attend the University of Pennsylvania.[81]

While the continuing story of Sarah's family is beyond the scope of this book, it is apparent from even this brief account that the compromises Sarah and Cecille made had the greatest impact not on their own lives but on the lives of their descendants. This is a reflection of the fact that while interracial sexual relations were not illegal in antebellum Charleston, they were also not fully accepted. In particular, white Carolinians did not seem ready to acknowledge the black women who partnered with white men as "real" wives, but they appeared more willing to accept the children born of such unions. Additionally, it is clear that the white men involved with black women valued the biracial children who were born of such alliances more than they did the women who gave birth to them. Thus, while Sarah died illiterate and enslaved, the "secret wife" of her owner, her children were all educated, propertied, and openly claimed by Richard as his flesh and blood. Indeed, both sets of children that Richard sired received more than what their mothers gained for themselves out of their relationships with Richard.

White men were thus both a hindrance and a help to Charleston's women. Enslaved women understood that the people who owned their bodies also helped maintain South Carolina's legal, political, economic, and social structures. Men of the master class were, then, both obstacles to and enablers of a woman's freedom. And if she were already free, white men could help a woman acquire wealth, respect, and many of the rights of citizenship for her children. White men, then, were the gatekeepers to the expanded freedom that Charleston's women desired. This meant that women often found themselves engaged in a myriad of alliances with the very people who constrained them in order to attain the privileges these affiliations could offer.

Although these relationships gave certain women some of what they sought, such unions also subjected them to another set of restrictions. By making white men their vehicle to a fuller freedom, women became indebted to their "benefactors" and were then subject to further encroachments on their bodies, their talents, and their time. In short, their "patrons" now held ongoing power over them. They could insist that, in return for giving these women their freedom, their wealth, and other privileges, the women now owed them their allegiance. Proof of their loyalty could entail many things, from financial aid to sexual favors. Southern women, particularly black women, often had no choice but to practice the art of accommodation if they wanted to attain the rights they desired. If they succeeded, however, they also found themselves bound to the very persons who constructed and helped maintain the inequitable system that forced women to seek male aid in acquiring these privileges in the first place.

CHAPTER 6

A FRAGILE FREEDOM

THE STORY OF

MARGARET BETTINGALL

AND HER DAUGHTERS

In 1842, Barbara Tunno Barquet became ensnared in the legal battles of a wealthy South Carolina couple. That year, Elizabeth Heyward Hamilton, a member of a powerful planter family, sued her husband, James, for violating their marriage contract.[1] Elizabeth brought an estate worth $100,000 into her marriage, and she and her husband agreed to place this property in a trust estate for Elizabeth's "sole and separate use." By law, James could not use the entrusted property to guarantee or pay his own debts. But he did just that. A land speculator and gambler, James, who had himself appointed guardian of his wife's estate, almost bankrupted the trust. In 1842, with creditors closing in, Elizabeth initiated a lawsuit to have James removed as guardian of her estate. She also named several of her husband's creditors, all of whom were seeking payment out of the trust, as codefendants in her suit. Seven of the debts were mortgages James had taken out on his wife's entrusted real estate. The holder of one such mortgage, in the amount of $5,178, was Barbara, a free black woman from the city of Charleston.[2]

How did Barbara, an affluent black woman, get caught up in the affairs of Elizabeth and James, members of South Carolina's white plantation elite? Considering the Old South's public commitment to racial and gendered hierarchies of power, how do we make sense of a court case wherein a powerful white man was financially indebted to a free black woman? What does the lawsuit teach us about Barbara as an individual, and about the broader experiences of free black women in Charleston and throughout the antebellum South? In order to answer these questions, and provide a wider historical context for the suit, we must step back from the 1842 legal action and examine the women in Barbara's family, including her mother, Margaret Bettingall, and her half sister, Hagar Cole.

It is important to note that Margaret, Hagar, and Barbara were different from the majority of Charleston's free black women. Wealthier than most of the city's free women of color, all three owned real estate and were slaveholders. Additionally, they were members of a racially mixed family and had access to white men of influence. The family also left records allowing us to resurrect their stories, fragmented though these documents may be. Finally, these women navigated an unjust social landscape in ingenious ways and acquired certain privileges thought to be outside the reach of both free blacks and women. They are thus worthy of study partly because their lives were, in some ways, exceptional. Rather than providing an example of the experiences that were "common" among free blacks, their stories more fully reveal the range of black female life and behavior in the Old South and challenge assumptions about what it meant to be a typical free black woman during the slave era. Indeed, the desire to define the "average" free black experience obscures the complexity of the world in which antebellum black women lived, a complexity these women's lives illuminate.

Although these three women were unique in some ways, the constraints they faced in their quest for a life of their own design, and the strategies they utilized to survive and succeed, were representative of the city's larger community of black women. In particular, Charleston's women of color understood that men were both a hindrance and a help in their efforts to secure greater liberty for themselves. The circumstances of black women's lives meant that men were the gatekeepers to the expanded freedom they sought, so they engaged in a multitude of relationships with men, both black and white, in order to attain the privileges these affiliations offered them, even as they struggled against the constraints these same men placed on them. The records of this one family thus allow us to delve into topics ranging from interracial sexual relations, to black female wealth, autonomy, and power, to the access that black women had to justice in the Old South. In particular, these women's experiences illuminate how Charleston's social, economic, and legal structures were designed to limit the freedom of black women, and how black women worked from within this inequitable system and reshaped it to better fit their own definitions of freedom and justice.

MARGARET AND ADAM

The story of this family begins with Margaret Bettingall. Much of Margaret's early history remains a mystery, including where and when she was born, and when she arrived in Charleston. We do know that by the early 1800s, Margaret was involved with a white man named Adam Tunno, a prominent Scottish merchant. An importer of madeira wine, Adam was both wealthy and well respected. Known for hosting elegant wine and dinner parties, he was also actively involved in the St. Andrew's Society, one of Charleston's most illustrious benevolent organizations, whose membership included government officials, prosperous merchants, and skilled artisans. Adam's social circle thus included men of power and influence, and his affluence enabled him to build a house on Charleston's East Bay, a home he shared with Margaret and their children: a daughter named Barbara, and a son who died in infancy. Margaret also had a daughter from a previous relationship named Hagar who resided with her mother and Adam until she married.[3]

Margaret and Adam lived together for almost forty years in a relationship that was, for all intents and purposes, a marriage. Margaret ran Adam's home, bore his children, and helped prepare the elegant parties for which he was known. Black friends and neighbors referred to Margaret as Adam's wife and considered them to be a married couple. White contemporaries called her the "mistress of Adam's household," or the "head and front" in charge of his premises. Regardless of how they referred to her, however, they all agreed that Margaret lived with Adam in the mansion on East Bay, oversaw the work of the many enslaved laborers who lived in the small dwellings scattered about the couple's yard, and carried the keys to the estate on her belt. These testimonials, when viewed alongside Margaret and Adam's wills, reveal that the pair had an enduring, conjugal relationship. These same documents refer to Margaret as "brown," a "Negro," or a "black woman," allowing us to identify her as a woman of color.[4]

Legally a person of color, Margaret was not a typical black woman owing to her wealth and social connections. In other ways, however, her life reflected the larger black female community of which she was a part. For example, like most black women in the Old South, Margaret was illiterate and left no records in her own hand. Indeed, the only document directly attributable to her is her last will and testament, a document she signed with an "x."[5]

Faced with these evidentiary obstacles, it is not surprising that there are unanswered questions about Margaret, beginning with her status as a legally free woman. That Margaret was a free woman is first suggested by the fact that she owned real property, which enslaved people were legally forbidden from doing, and because she left a will in which she referred to herself as a "free black woman." What is not clear, however, is if she had been born enslaved, and whether her freedom was legal or virtual. On the one hand, no manumission records have been recovered for Margaret, and her contemporaries stated that she had never been enslaved. Additionally, her daughter, Hagar, paid the capitation taxes required of free people of color, and no manumission records appear in Hagar's name, which implies that Margaret was free when Hagar was born.[6] On the other hand, on 20 August 1803, the legal emancipation of a child named "Barbary" was recorded in Charleston's manumission books: Barbary's guardian was listed as Adam Tunno.[7] This document suggests that Margaret was enslaved when her younger daughter was born, and that she lived her life as a virtually free person.

In addition to the speculation surrounding her legal freedom, there are questions about the exact nature of Margaret and Adam's union. No marriage certificate has been found for the couple, although records indicate that Margaret attended St. Philip's Episcopal Church, along with other elite blacks and wealthy whites. Acquaintances confirm that she was a communicant at St. Philip's, which she could not have been were she not Adam's wife, since the Episcopal Church did not extend membership to anyone leading a "wicked" life.[8] In short, had Margaret been "living in sin" with Adam, she would not have been allowed to take communion at St. Philip's. Family history states that Margaret, who was well known for her piety, was distressed when the new rector of St. Philip's refused to administer the sacraments to her for this very reason. This prompted Margaret to ask Adam to provide her with a document stating that she was his wife. Apparently Adam wrote a letter to this effect, which Margaret then presented to the rector. She was henceforth allowed to commune at St. Philip's.[9]

Whether the white community regarded Margaret and Adam as being legally married, however, is debatable. Black Charlestonians believed that since Margaret acted like Adam's wife, managed his home like a wife, and bore his children like a wife, she ought to be treated as such. The law supported this idea: the state of South Carolina did not forbid interracial marriage, as long as both parties were free, and decreed that marriage was a civil contract, requiring no written document or ceremony for its manifestation but only the agreement of the parties in good faith. Additionally, the courts ruled that common-law relationships became legal unions once the parties had cohabited for over thirty years. Under state law then, if she were a free person, Margaret's partnership with Adam would have qualified as a legal marriage at the time of his death, by which point the pair had lived together for almost forty years. And while white Charlestonians might have disagreed with the state's definition of marriage, and perhaps did not view Margaret as Adam's wife, they certainly knew that the couple shared a home, were involved in a long-term relationship, and had children together.[10]

The issues surrounding her freedom and marital status indicate that Margaret's liberty, like that of other antebellum black women, was both contingent and insecure. To live according to her vision of freedom and secure the manumission of her children, Margaret had to maintain a relationship of goodwill with a well-connected man. And despite her position in Adam's life, and the apparently consensual nature of their affiliation, Margaret would have lost the financial benefits she gained from her alliance with Adam had the couple separated. Additionally, if Margaret were not legally free, Adam could have gone so far as to sell her away from her children, or turned her over to the authorities as a fugitive slave. No matter what the scenario, Margaret's status, and that of her daughters, would have instantly changed. At best, such concerns would have meant that Margaret strove to keep Adam happy in order to safeguard her family's freedom. At worst, it could have kept her with Adam beyond the duration of any affection she may have had for him. Unlike legitimate wives, women in partnerships that had not yet achieved the status of legal union had little recourse if their "husbands" left them. Realizing, then, that their liberty was tenuous, and that they could not afford to upset their protectors, they had to walk a fine line in their quest for a freedom of their own design. In this, Margaret was no different from Sarah Sanders, the enslaved partner of Richard Cogdell.[11]

HAGAR BETTINGALL COLE

The fears that plagued free black women were only too real. Margaret's main concern would have been the freedom and financial security of her children, particularly Hagar, who was not Adam's biological child. Hagar lived with Margaret and Adam until she married Thomas Cole, a free man of color, with whom she had at least two children: a son named William, and a daughter, Mary. Hagar's husband was almost certainly the same Thomas Cole who in 1819 resided at 13 Maiden Lane and was a carpenter by trade. In all likelihood, Hagar's husband, a Charlestonian by birth, was the son of Thomas Cole Sr., himself a free man of color and a skilled bricklayer or brick maker by training. If so, young Thomas was a member of one of the city's oldest, and most respected, free families of color.[12]

It appears, then, that Hagar married into one of Charleston's most prominent free black families. This is significant considering the questions surrounding her mother's free status, and the fact that Hagar was not Adam's biological daughter. Charleston's affluent free blacks were careful whom they married. Deeply concerned with respectability, elite free people of color believed marriage was as much a matter of maintaining their wealth and free status as it was an affirmation of love or companionship. That Hagar was able to marry Thomas, despite the uncertainty of her lineage, thus testifies to the strength of her family's position. Whatever complications Thomas's marriage to Hagar may have created for the Cole family, especially if her own freedom was in doubt, it still connected the Coles to Adam Tunno, a wealthy and powerful white man who left Hagar a significant inheritance as proof of his affection for her, and for her mother.[13]

What we know about Hagar is limited by the fact that she, like Margaret, did not leave any personal papers. According to public records, Hagar resided on Archdale Street from 1821 to 1823 and paid her annual "head" taxes. She then disappeared from the capitation books until 1840, at which point she was excused from any further payments because she was "overage."[14] It is possible that Hagar did not appear in the capitation books for sixteen years due to recording errors. She was, however, listed in the federal census of 1830, but not in Charleston's capitation tax book for the same year, which suggests that she deliberately chose not to pay her head taxes. Certainly other free blacks in Charleston avoided paying these taxes without being fined, jailed, or re-enslaved.[15] Like them, Hagar was connected to a powerful white man, which may have enabled her to avoid paying a tax that penalized her simply for being black. That Hagar paid her city property taxes, dues that were collected from all real property owners and calculated at the same rate, regardless of a person's race or gender, supports this conclusion.[16]

Hagar's desire and ability to create a freedom of her own design transcended the evasion of capitation taxes. According to the city's public records, Hagar, despite her marriage, was in charge of her own business affairs and conducted herself as a *feme sole*.[17] For example, it was Hagar, and not her husband, who was listed as the head of the Cole household in the 1830 federal census, although Thomas was alive in 1830 and may have been living as late as 1860.[18] Hagar also inherited real and moveable property from family members, "free from the debts and liabilities of her husband, Thomas Cole," and paid taxes on real estate held in her own name.[19] Although no sole trader deed has been found for Hagar, that she owned her own property, paid taxes apart from her husband, and was listed by census takers as the head of her own household all suggest that Thomas "tacitly" agreed to treat Hagar as a *feme sole*.[20]

Hagar thus exercised significant control over her finances without the oversight of her husband, a situation outside the norm for most married American women of the era, white or black.[21] Her ability to live as a *feme sole* stemmed in large part from the fact that she had wealth and power of her own. Certainly her marriage to Thomas strengthened her social position in the black community, but Hagar was not financially dependent on her husband since she had her own money, given to her by her mother and stepfather. Additionally, Hagar had high standing in the city because she was Adam's stepdaughter. In all likelihood, then, Hagar was able to oversee her own affairs, regardless of whether Thomas "tacitly consented" or not, because of the position she occupied, and the wealth she acquired, as a result of her mother's long-term relationship with a powerful white man of means. The same could be said of other free women of color, including hotel entrepreneur Eliza Seymour Lee.[22]

ENTER BARBARA

Barbara Tunno Barquet proved to be as independent as Hagar and Eliza. Growing up with her parents in their mansion on Charleston's East Bay, Barbara was educated at a school for free blacks in the city, an education her father paid for. She thus improved on her mother's situation and died a literate woman, evidenced by her ability to sign her name to her last will and testament. Barbara was also openly acknowledged by Adam and other members of his extended white family as his daughter: Adam's nephew, John, for example, referred to her as his "Cousin Barbara," and Barbara went by the last name "Tunno" until she married. She also inherited a large part of Adam's estate at his death. By virtue of her mother's careful negotiations, then, and her father's money, Barbara was a free black woman of high social position.[23]

Barbara's status was reinforced by her choice of a spouse. On 6 July 1814, Barbara married an artisan originally from Saint-Domingue named Jonathan Pierre Barguet (also written "Barquet").[24] If wealth and white connections could lead to freedom and status for black women, light skin color and the practice of a skilled trade could do the same for black men. John came to Charleston from the Caribbean, was well educated, spoke French, and was an umbrella maker by trade. His status as an accomplished artisan and his French background elevated his standing among Charleston's free blacks, making him eligible for membership in the Brown Fellowship Society (BFS) in 1807. The BFS was Charleston's premier benevolent order for free brown men, and John's membership in that organization placed him firmly in the ranks of the city's free elite of color.[25]

Barbara and John thus had much in common, including the fact that they both went to St. Philip's Episcopal Church, the same church that Barbara's mother, Margaret, attended. Barbara, however, no more than twenty years old when she married John, was a first-time bride, while her groom had walked down the aisle at least once before. Although family records make no mention of this previous marriage, parish registers reveal that on 18 June 1813, a baptism was performed at St. Philip's Church for two boys named John Pincel and Joseph. The boys were the children of John P. and Mary Barquet, free people of color. Five months later, on 26 November 1813, another baptism was performed by the rector of St. Philip's Church for a boy named William. Since William was ill and could not be brought to the church, the ceremony was performed at the home of his parents, John P. and Mary Barquet.[26]

The father of John, Joseph, and William and the man who married Barbara in 1814 were undoubtedly the same person. Public records spell John's last name Burget, Barguet, and Barquet at various times, and parish registers indicate that Barbara and John knew each other at least as far back as June 1813, when John and Mary baptized their sons John Pincel and Joseph at St. Philip's Church.[27] The witnesses and sponsors of this baptism, all of whom were free people of color, included some of Charleston's most prominent black residents. Among the guests was William Pincel, from whom young John likely received his middle name; Thomas Bonneau, the head of an elite school for free black children in Charleston; and Barbara Tunno.[28]

Barbara not only knew John and Mary, then, but also knew them well enough to attend their sons' baptism. This is not surprising: John, Mary, and Barbara were all members of Charleston's free black elite, and they all went to the same church. Considering the small size of the city's prosperous community of color, this meant that the Barquets and Barbara Tunno would have moved in the same social circles and been acquaintances, if nothing else. It makes sense, then, that after Mary passed away, John asked Barbara, a woman who was his social equal and already a family friend, to become his second wife.[29]

What is not clear is why the family papers do not mention John's first marriage or his children by Mary.[30] There was certainly no shame in remarrying during the antebellum era. It was, if anything, quite common. Large numbers of Charlestonians died from annual outbreaks of malaria and typhoid, and nineteenth-century women regularly lost their lives in childbirth and from consumption. In fact, some southerners married several times over the course of their lives due to the region's high mortality rates, looking for companionship, financial stability, or a new partner to help them raise their children. Even if love, then, were not the principal motivating factor in John's marriage to Barbara, that should not have been a reason to hide the fact that he had been married once before.[31]

We know little else about John's first marriage, or about his children by Mary. The couple's three sons literally vanish from the record books after Barbara and John's marriage in 1814. Outside of their baptismal certificates, the only other mention of them is in the papers of the BFS. According to that organization's membership records, one Jonathan P. Barquet was admitted to the BFS on 4 November 1830. The 102nd man accepted into the order, this John joined the mutual aid society while his father, who was inducted into the society in 1807, was still an active member. John Sr. passed away sometime before 1844, but there is no record that he ever resigned his BFS membership or was expelled. No other records pertaining to John and Mary's sons have been discovered.[32]

It is curious that Barbara and John's eldest son, family historian Liston W. Barquet, never mentioned that he had half brothers. It is possible that William died in infancy and thus escaped Liston's notice: William was baptized at home because he was ill and may have passed away shortly thereafter.[33] But what of the other two boys, and John Jr. in particular, who joined his father's benevolent society in 1830? Perhaps Liston never mentioned him, or the other boys, because he did not know them: there is nothing in the records to suggest that John and Barbara raised John's sons from his first marriage. It is possible that Mary's relatives took the boys in after their mother's death and their father's remarriage.[34]

After their wedding, Barbara and John set up house at 113 Meeting Street and had seven children together, all of whom grew up speaking both English and French. The young Barquets attended St. Philip's Episcopal Church with their parents and lived in an environment of relative material comfort, the bulk of their family's wealth coming from their mother's side of the family. Adam helped Barbara maintain an affluent lifestyle for her family, giving her gifts of cash and real property over the years. He was also involved in the lives of his grandchildren. Barbara's oldest son, Liston, spent time with his grandparents and remembered his grandfather fondly. According to Liston, Adam paid his tuition at Thomas S. Bonneau's renowned school for free black children and ensured the boy was given a snack whenever he visited his grandparents.[35]

Thanks to her mother's relationship with Adam, Barbara was a woman of means by 1830. That year, Barbara headed up two households in Charleston, one the house in which she lived in Ward 3, the other a house in Ward 4. Between both dwellings, she oversaw the lives of twenty-two men, women, and children, thirteen of whom were free persons of color. Nine of these free people included Barbara and her family, but the identities of the other four, all of whom lived in the house in Ward 4, are unknown. These persons may have been boarders who brought in extra income for the family—a common practice among free blacks in Charleston and elsewhere. They may even have included John's sons from his first marriage. The remaining nine residents of Barbara's homes were enslaved. Affluent and well connected, Barbara not only owned valuable city real estate, then, but also was a slaveholder.[36]

Like Hagar, it was Barbara, and not her husband, who was listed as the head of these two households. And while no *feme sole* deed has been found in Barbara's name, she appears in a variety of public records under her own name and seems to have exercised significant personal authority over her finances: she purchased property, loaned out money, managed her own investments, and hired out her enslaved laborers for profit.[37] As was the case for her half sister, the key to this authority would have been Barbara's personal wealth and status, both of which derived from her position as the daughter of Adam Tunno. Since Barbara was not beholden to John for her economic security, her social position and family money made her one of the most autonomous married women in antebellum Charleston, black or white.

Such independence by a wife and mother was outside the norm for most elite free black families, which tended to be patriarchal in structure. This was due in large part to the shortage of free black men in Charleston.[38] The uneven sex ratio meant that free black women had fewer opportunities for marriage than free black men, which gave these men more power in selecting their mates and in exercising control over their households after they married. Thus, when free black women did marry free black men, their families tended to be more patriarchal in structure. Additionally, it is possible that some free blacks identified with the mores of the southern white elite, to whom they were often related, and that they thus adhered to (white) patriarchal family values. In some ways, then, Barbara and Hagar behaved in a manner that deviated from the cultural prescriptions of female submissiveness that dominated antebellum culture.[39]

That Barbara and Hagar acquired certain privileges in Charleston does not negate the very real constraints they would have faced in their quest for a freedom of their own design. It is clear that free people of color occupied a tenuous position in Charleston and in southern society in general: not enslaved yet "of color," free but not white, free blacks fit cleanly into no category in a slave society and were thus not fully accepted anywhere. Indeed, every privilege they had was always one rumor or rebellion away from being revoked.[40] Barbara, however, appears to have used her wealth, her connections, and her ambition to craft a full life for herself, despite the white South's deeply held cultural beliefs about black female intelligence, ability, and morality, and the corresponding social, economic, and political obstacles it erected to limit both free blacks and women.

Barbara's intellect, honed by years of managing her own money and renting out her servants, enabled her to run John's umbrella shop after his death in the early 1830s. Her business sense might also explain why the position of widow did not negatively affect Barbara's social or economic status, as it did for so many women. Indeed, while many antebellum widows quickly remarried, as much out of a need for financial security and protection as for love and companionship, Barbara remained single. Already prosperous, she was now a business owner as well, and remaining a widow allowed her to utilize the title of "Mrs.," with all its attendant virtues of respectability, while continuing to act as a *feme sole*, something a new marriage could have prevented.[41]

PASSING OF A PATRIARCH

Barbara likely wanted to remain a *feme sole*, since her financial position strengthened in 1833 due to her father's death. After battling the effects of heart disease for over a year, Adam passed away on 27 December 1832 at the age of seventy-nine, with Margaret and their daughter at his bedside. The estate he left included enslaved persons, cash, stocks, household goods, real estate, and more, and he was generous in his bequests to both friends and family. Of the $40,000 he disposed of in cash, $28,000 went to white relatives, friends, and business associates in the United States and Great Britain. Adam then wrote a codicil to his will and set aside the remaining $12,000 in cash in a special trust, stating that this money was to be kept separate from all the other obligations and provisions of his estate. In essence, he protected the $12,000 from any debts or liabilities that might have been attached to the rest of his property.[42]

The codicil is a carefully worded document. In it, Adam specified that the following legatees were "either under my protection, or my servants, my property," making an important distinction between the two different groups of people who would benefit under this section of the will.[43] Within the codicil, various free black men and women, including Hagar's son, Owen Chatters, were left bequests ranging from $100 to $1,200. Adam's favorite enslaved laborers also received monetary gifts between $40 and $200. The most substantial cash gifts, however, were left to Adam's black family. Margaret, "with her daughter Hagar Cole and children," received $2,500 in cash. Barbara alone received another $2,500 in cash. This sum was enough to purchase a brick home in an affluent neighborhood in Charleston, or two solid wooden homes in respectable neighborhoods.[44]

In addition to the monetary gifts outlined in the codicil, Adam left instructions in the body of his will about how to distribute specific household items. While most of these bequests concerned white friends and relatives, when giving away his portrait collection, Adam stated that his "niece with the five small pictures," was to go to "Mrs. B. Burguit." He then directed that all of his household goods, including his clothing, linens, furniture, dishes, glasses, kitchen articles, and silverware, be distributed evenly among his servants, "with Mrs. J. Harrison, Mrs. Burguit, and Hagar's family . . . also sharing in the distribution of these articles." Since his estate was worth between $300,000 and $400,000, the value of these household items added significantly to the money that Adam left his daughter and stepdaughter.[45]

The wording of the codicil raises many questions. In particular, why did Adam not name Margaret as his wife and Barbara as his daughter, referring instead to Margaret as "the free black woman Marg Bellingall" and his daughter as "Mrs. Burguit"? Charlestonians already knew that Adam had lived with Margaret for almost forty years and had a child with her, a daughter whom he had helped raise and educate and who went by his last name before her marriage. His peers were also aware that Adam had given money, bondspersons, and real estate to Margaret, Hagar, and Barbara over the years, and that he had paid to send at least one of Barbara's children to school. White Charlestonians thus acknowledged Margaret's place in Adam's life by calling her the "head and front" of Adam's household, while black Charlestonians referred to her as his wife. Adam had supposedly even provided Margaret with a document stating that she was his wife so she could continue to take communion at St. Philip's Church.

Why, then, was Adam's will so cryptically worded? The most likely explanation is that Adam was concerned about the social ostracism he could endure if he formally declared his familial connection to Margaret and Barbara. He would have been well aware that white Charlestonians were willing to ignore interracial relationships that were discreetly conducted, but that white persons who overtly acknowledged their black domestic partners found themselves censured for crossing established lines of propriety and decorum. In 1823, an editor for the *Charleston Mercury* newspaper bluntly declared that while this type of union existed, and often endured for decades, there was "not a white person in the community who would hazard a defense of it," and that a "white person so acting would be considered . . . degraded" for committing what was considered to be "an indictable offense against public decorum and public morals."[46] While such relationships were legal, then, they were not fully or openly accepted and rarely legalized.

Adam appears to have understood that he would have risked losing his clientele, his friends, and perhaps his presidency of the St. Andrew's Society if he openly proclaimed that he was Margaret's common-law husband.[47] Although his peers (really the whole city) knew the position that Margaret (and Barbara) held in Adam's life, they may not have accepted a forthright admission from

Adam that would have forced them to publicly acknowledge a black woman as his wife. This is likely why Adam referred to the woman who had stood by his side for four decades as "the free black woman Marg Bellingall."

It has already been established that a black woman's agency in the Old South was often constrained by her need to ally with white men, the very creators of the inequitable system under which she lived. Additionally, we have seen that a black woman's power was further limited by stereotypes about black female intellect and sexuality, societal definitions of respectability, and the fear of public censure. It appears that these same issues could, at times, hedge in even the freedom of white men. Margaret had been Adam's domestic partner for forty years. She lived with him, ran his household for him, oversaw their enslaved laborers, planned his dinner parties, and bore his children. For white Charlestonians, Adam's refusal to publicly state that Margaret was his wife, despite all these things, made perfect sense, but it is unclear if Margaret viewed the situation with such dispassionate detachment. She may have understood why Adam worded his will as he did. After forty years as the mistress of Adam's household, however, it is equally possible that Margaret was outraged that her husband listed her and their daughter in a codicil that included his enslaved laborers.

Margaret's one consolation may have been that Adam provided amply for his family of color, and that he quietly yet clearly differentiated between them and his servants in his will. Whereas those persons who were his "property" received small gifts ranging from forty to $200 and were mentioned at the end of the codicil, Margaret and her daughters were named first and received $5,000 in cash between them. Barbara alone received $2,500, more than any of Adam's white relatives, and Adam was sure to include his stepdaughter and her children in his bequests. Additionally, Barbara and Hagar benefited significantly from the disposition of Adam's household goods. By law, Adam did not have to leave anything to the free people "under his protection." That he singled out Margaret, Hagar, and Barbara, and left them large sums of money in a protected trust, testifies to the intimate relationship that Adam had with them, although he never declared this relationship publicly.[48]

LIFE AFTER ADAM

Of the three black women in Adam's family, it was Margaret whose life changed the most after Adam's death. She not only lost her companion of almost forty years but also had to relocate to a new residence at 19 Archdale Street. The mansion on East Bay, her home for decades, was sold in order to liquidate Adam's estate and fulfill the cash bequests he made in his will. Thus Margaret, like many antebellum widows, simultaneously experienced the emotionally taxing losses of death and physical dislocation. Unlike many widows, however, Margaret did not have to rely on her children or another man to help her out or take her in. She purchased a new home for herself and she, like her daughter Barbara, never remarried.[49]

For Barbara, life continued on much as it had before her father's death. Already affluent, Barbara became quite wealthy after she received her legacy from Adam's estate.[50] She continued to live at 113 Meeting Street and ran her late husband's umbrella business, a venture in which she likely employed some of the enslaved laborers she owned. Barbara also rented out several of her remaining bondspersons to augment her monthly income and, understanding the benefits of chattel labor in a slave society, passed still other servants on to her children to help increase their financial stability. In 1835, she sold a twenty-year-old man named Peter to her daughter, Margaret Humphries, for $1. The sum indicates that Peter was a gift, one that Barbara perhaps hoped would help her daughter and son-in-law, Joseph, build up their tailoring business: Peter's labor in the store might allow the couple to take in more orders and thus expand their client base. The gift appears to have worked: by 1840, the Humphrieses owned four laborers, including the man Peter, and business at the shop at 112 Queen Street was booming.[51]

Hagar also remained in Charleston after her stepfather's death. She, like Barbara, had inherited a substantial legacy from Adam, but things were not as secure for Hagar as they were for her half sister. In May 1834, seventeen months after the death of her stepfather, Hagar appeared in court to request that Edward Frost, a local white attorney, be appointed the legal guardian of her children, William and Mary Cole, "minors entitled to a personal estate within this state." Thomas Lehre, judge of the Court of Ordinary, upheld the request and made Edward responsible for the maintenance and education of the two children, and for the management of their estate, "for the better securing of the said estate for the benefit of said minors. I do hereby commit the tuition, guardianship and education of the said William Cole and Mary Cole to you . . . Edward Frost, charging you to maintain them . . . according to the circumstances of interest of the said minors during their minority, take charge of their estate, do such things as a guardian should, and render a true and faithful account of the said estate."[52]

This document is surprising. Why did Hagar terminate her husband's parental rights, and her own, and ask Edward to become her children's legal guardian? A *feme sole* with her own wealth, Hagar was more than capable of looking after her children's interests, so why did she seek a white male guardian for them? The only clue we have is that William and Mary were "minors entitled to a personal estate." This estate would have been the inheritance left to them by Adam Tunno. It is possible, then, that Hagar wanted to ensure that her children's estates were not accessible to their current guardian (their father) or to any creditors he may have had, so she gave Edward guardianship of her children to protect their inheritances. The courts would not have given Hagar legal guardianship of her children since her husband, their father, still lived. Indeed, one wonders what Thomas's reaction was to this loss of his paternal rights. It is unclear if he even had a say in the matter: his name appears nowhere in the guardianship records and the request was filed in Hagar's name alone.[53]

Hagar likely still had substantial control over her children's lives given that Edward Frost was also her guardian. Why Hagar had a guardian is unknown: under state law, only free black men over fifteen years in age were required to have white male guardians.[54] Perhaps she believed fewer people would try taking advantage of her if they knew she had a white lawyer to speak on her behalf. It is also possible that, as a woman of means, Hagar hired Edward to be her financial advisor as well as her representative in all legal matters, much like Eliza Lee did with Henry Gourdin.[55] Regardless of her reasons, Edward was evidently someone that Hagar trusted, both with her affairs and with her children. Still, she took a real risk in placing William and Mary's finances in Edward's hands. Had he been unscrupulous and bled their estates dry, Hagar would have been hard-pressed to fight him in court. With the problems Hagar and her family may have faced from Thomas and his creditors, however, giving Edward guardianship of her children might have been Hagar's best option.

This chapter of Hagar's life demonstrates yet again the constrained nature of antebellum black women's freedom. An affluent woman, Hagar acquired significant social power by marrying into Thomas's family. At the same time, her marriage gave her husband legal control over her person and her assets. The law also made him guardian of their offspring and thus gave him the right to any property those children might acquire while minors, or while they remained unmarried (as was the case with daughters). The only way to circumvent such spousal control was to establish oneself as a *feme sole*, which Hagar appears to have done. She then took extra steps to separate her finances, as well as those of her children, from Thomas: she acquired her own, white male guardian and gave up her parental rights to this same person. While Edward was a man Hagar apparently trusted, she still risked losing control of her children by turning them over to his oversight. That she did so despite these real dangers reveals how her liberty was hedged in by both race and sex. Socially and culturally, Hagar, as a woman, despite her wealth and power, had to marry. By doing so, she acquired both the badge of feminine respectability and the male "protector" required of all women in the antebellum South. As a black woman, however, she was then forced, by law, to retain a white male guardian in order to help safeguard her finances, and those of her children, from this same "protector."

Not all black women had to ally themselves with white men to protect their interests. A wealthy widow, Barbara, unlike Hagar, had no husband to threaten her financial independence. And while Hagar legally dissolved her rights to her children, Barbara became guardian to four free children of color in 1838. All four had inherited property under Adam's will in 1832.[56] Barbara assumed guardianship of the youngsters shortly before her mother's death, and after the children's parents had died. Margaret's will, written in May 1838, stated that she was leaving "to Barbara Barquet, in trust for Sarah and Margaret Reid, children of Margaret Cooper, deceased, 1,000 dollars. To Barbara Barquet, in trust for Eliza and Alexander, children of Matilda Lesesne, deceased, 1,000 dollars." The minors in question needed a guardian now that their mothers had passed away, and Margaret evidently wanted to ensure that their guardian would be someone she could trust to protect their inheritances. Barbara thus assumed oversight of the children in August 1838, three months after Margaret wrote her will.[57]

A MOTHER'S LEGACY

It is not clear precisely when Margaret passed away, or from what cause. Her will was proven in probate court on 13 January 1840, so she likely died in late December 1839 or early January 1840. Her passing meant that her daughters and several other free blacks received substantial inheritances for the second time in six years. Margaret, it seems, not only knew how to run a household but also had a head for finances and investments: she died with an estate appraised at just under $7,500. A sizeable sum, this amount does not take into account one of the four houses she owned, or four of her eleven enslaved laborers. These items passed directly to her children, so their value was not included in the assessment of her estate. Had they been, the value of her estate would have likely topped $10,000.[58] Margaret thus left her descendants a significant, and unique, financial legacy: the city's tax lists reveal the names of only two other free black women in the city who acquired real property holdings in excess of $10,000.[59]

Both of Margaret's daughters benefited handsomely under the terms of their mother's will. Barbara inherited $600 in cash, two laborers named Henry and Joe, and a share of her mother's furniture and clothing. Daughter Hagar received $100 in cash, the enslaved man Nelson, plus a share of her mother's

Will of MARGARET BELLINGALL

THE STATE OF SOUTH CAROLINA. IN THE NAME OF GOD AMEN.
I Margaret Bellingall, a free Black Woman of Charleston being of sound
mind and considering the uncertainty of life do make declare and pub-
lish this instrument of writing to be my last Will and Testament hereby
revoking all former Wills by me at any time made. It is my Will and desire
and I do hereby authorize my Executors hereinafter named or either of
them that may Qualify on this my Will to enter into and take possession of
all my real and personal Estate and sell and dispose of the same at private
or public Sale on the Terms they or him may deem most advantageous to
my Estate and I hereby authorize them or him to make[,] execute and de-
liver good and sufficient Titles in Law and in Equity to the purchasers of
the same or any part thereof except such parts and portions of my real and
personal property as I have hereinafter made a special disposition of in
this my Will. It is my Will that the funds or monies arising from the Sale of
my property together with any ready money I may die possessed of be appropriated first to the payment of my Funeral Expences and all just debts
the Balance to be appropriated to the payment of the following legacies
should there be sufficiency of funds to meet the several legacies[,] if not
and there should prove to be a deficiency a suitable proportion to be de-
ducted from each of the pecuniary legacies and in the event of a surplus a
ratiable [sic] proportion to be added to each of the pecuniary Legacies. To
my Daughter Barbara Barquet I Give six hundred Dollars also my Slaves
Henry and Joe. To my Daughter Hagar Cole I give one hundred dollars. To
my Grand Children Bella Dart, Susan Lesesne, Eliza Lesesne, and Owen
Chatters, to each of them I give one hundred dollars to be paid them as
soon as my Executors are in funds[.] To Barbara Barquet in Trust for Sarah
and Margaret Reid Children of Margaret Cooper deceased, one thousand
dollars. To Barbara Barquet in Trust for Eliza and Alexander Children of
Matilda Lesesne deceased one thousand dollars[.] To   in Trust
for Owen Chatters one thousand dollars. To the Trustee or Trustees of
Bella Dart and her Children one thousand dollars the same to be invested
in the purchase of a House and Lot if sufficient[,] if not to be invested
in Bank or other good Securities and the income Paid over to Bella Dart
until her Children respectively become of age when the principal is to be

divided equally between Bella Dart and her Children. To the Trustee or Trustees of Eliza Lesesne and her Children One thousand dollars upon the same Conditions and limitations as the Legacy to Bella Dart and Children[.] To Susan Lesesne and her Children by their Trustee or Trustees I give one thousand dollars upon the same conditions and limitations as the two foregoing Legacies. To my Slave Nelson I give twenty five dollars. To Thomas Horry Son of Owen deceased I give Twenty five dollars. To Hagar Cole and her two Children William Cole and Mary Cole, I give my House and Lot situated in Pitt Street, the portion of this property to which Hagar Cole will be entitled to be free from the debts and liabilities of her Husband Thomas Cole. To Adam Humphreys son of Margaret and Joseph Humphreys I give my Brown Slave Joseph. To Edward Frost in trust for Hagar Cole I give my Slave Nelson upon the same Condition as the foregoing bequest of a portion of the Pitt Street premises to Hagar Cole. To each of my Legatees and Servants I give a plain Suit of Mourning the expence of this bequest not to exceed three hundred dollars. To Barbara Barquet, Hagar Cole, Bella Dart, Eliza Lesesne, Susan Lesesne, and Owen Chatters I give all my household and Kitchen furniture and wearing apparel. Lastly I do hereby nominate constitute and appoint Arthur G. Rose and James G. Moodie Executors to this my last Will and Testament Executed by me at Charleston this Sixteenth day of May in the Year of Our Lord one thousand eight hundred and thirty-eight—

her

Margaret X Bellingall (L S)

mark

Signed Sealed declared and published by Margaret Bellingall as and for her last Will and Testament before us who in her presence and at her request and in the presence of each other have subscribed our names as Witnesses thereto.

W. P. Forbes. James Fife. Hugh Blair.

Proved before Thomas Lehre Esq O.C.T.D. on the 13 day of January 1840, and on the 20th day of January 1840 Qualified James G. Moodie Executor.

Will of Margaret Bellingall (or Bettingall), 1838. (Will Books of Charleston County, vol. 42 (1839–45): 67–69, South Carolina Department of Archives and History, Columbia) household goods. In addition to these items, Hagar and her children, William and Mary, inherited Margaret's house and lot on Pitt Street. Another bondsperson, the "brown man Joseph," was left to Adam Humphreys, the son of Margaret Humphreys. This Margaret was Barbara's daughter and the elder Margaret's namesake: Adam was thus Margaret Bettingall's great-grandson. Just as Barbara had sold the man Peter to her daughter and son-in-law to help expand their tailoring business, Margaret now used chattel laborers to financially benefit her descendants. Finally, in addition to gifts of enslaved persons, real estate, and moveable property, all of Margaret's grandchildren inherited sizeable cash trusts, as did the four children to whom Barbara had recently become guardian.[60]

On 23 January 1840, Margaret's estate was liquidated at auction and the proceeds from the sale of her houses, lots, and bondspersons went toward creating the cash trusts her will had outlined. Margaret's house and lot on West Street was sold to one Robert Henry, probably city merchant R. F. Henry, for $1,990. Laborers Sarah and Titus were purchased for $530 by L. L. Levy, one of the partners in the local clothing firm of Levy and Ancker, while servants Marian and Peter fetched $1,025 from a Mr. A. McDonald, almost certainly the grocer Alexander McDonald.[61] Margaret's home on Archdale Street was purchased for $840 by one Susan Lesesne (whom Margaret referred to in her will as her granddaughter) and her house in Bedon's Alley also remained in the family: Barbara purchased that property for $2,000. Hagar also purchased some of her mother's auctioned items, paying $570 for the enslaved woman Betsey and her infant. Finally, a woman named Isabella Simmons paid $400 for one final bondsperson, the man Dublin.[62]

Margaret left behind an estate that was admirable for any person of her time, male or female, black or white. This alone would have garnered her considerable, if grudging, respect from Charleston's white community. It is telling that both of her executors were white men: Bank of Charleston cashier Arthur G. Rose and Southwestern Railroad Bank employee James G. Moodie. Arthur and James knew Margaret well: as two of Adam Tunno's executors, they would have met with her several times in order to settle her late husband's estate. Both men thus had to have acknowledged the couple's domestic connection, and each had established a cordial enough relationship with Margaret that she later asked them to be her executors. Additionally, Barbara eventually asked James to become her financial advisor, yet another indication of his amicable and enduring ties to Adam and his family of color.[63]

A shrewd businesswoman, Margaret revealed in the construction of her will that she never forgot how tenuous life was for free blacks in Charleston: she instructed that the money she left her legatees be used to buy them houses and land. Money could be spent unwisely, and stocks could become worthless. Real estate, however, was a solid investment, the purchase of which would provide ongoing financial security for Margaret's family and increase their net worth. It would also improve their social standing, since antebellum southerners placed their wealth in land and houses and held in high esteem those who owned real estate.[64]

Margaret was a product of her time in other ways as well: a slaveholder, she bequeathed certain laborers to her children and sold others in order to make her heirs' lives more secure. Her concern was for her family's well-being, and she knew that owning enslaved persons was one way to guarantee her descendants' financial and social security in a slave society. Like other free blacks, Margaret realized that her freedom was dependent on the goodwill of elite whites, who always viewed free blacks with at least a modicum of distrust. Owing to the fragile nature of their freedom, then, free blacks could not openly denounce slavery, nor could they legally emancipate their enslaved property after South Carolina changed its manumission laws in 1820.[65] Instead, some free blacks sought to protect their own freedom, and their financial interests, by owning bondspersons and expressing no outward concerns about it. Black slaveowner-ship thus provided whites with evidence of free black loyalty; retained for free blacks the white patronage their shops needed in order to survive; and provided many free people of color with the means necessary to expand their businesses, as well as acquire wealth, some of the privileges of citizenship, and upward social mobility.

Realizing that free blacks walked a fine line between slavery and freedom, Margaret also understood how tenuous life was for free women of color in a slave society. Her will indicated her desire to ensure that the actions of men did not destroy the security of her family. First, she made certain that Barbara took guardianship of the four orphaned black children who would inherit under her will, aware that if Barbara were not named guardian, the court would ap-point whomever it wanted—likely white men of standing who may or may not have acted in the children's best interests. Even more telling was how Margaret strove to protect the inheritance of her daughter, Hagar, from Hagar's hus-band. At two different points in her will, Margaret stated that "the portion of this property to which Hagar Cole will be entitled to be free from the debts and liabilities of her husband Thomas Cole." Margaret Bettingall was no fool: she knew how easily a man could wreak havoc on a woman's financial security, no matter if he was white or black, legal husband or lover.[66]

Antebellum women in general understood that their status derived from their connections to men. Women of color also realized that they lived in a society that discriminated against both women and blacks. To combat the constraints of a legal and sociocultural system both racist and sexist, black women often bound themselves to the very persons responsible for creating this inequitable system, but they never forgot that these relationships were double-edged swords. While they used their ties to men to obtain the privileges of liberty, black women understood that these same men could make their freedoms disappear. Thus Margaret, who acquired power from her connection to Adam, worked to ensure that what she had labored so hard to gain would not be squandered by other men. And Hagar, who attained social prominence by marrying Thomas, sought to protect her children's estates from their father by turning them over to the guardianship of a white man, although by doing so she risked losing control of her children. Such risks illuminate the contingent nature of liberty for black women in the antebellum South: full freedom was truly out of their reach, their agency daily constrained by the society in which they lived. Limited in their choices, they did the best they could with what they had.

In retrospect, Margaret left her descendants more than just shares of a healthy estate. She was wise with her money, she understood the social climate of her time, and she shrewdly worked within the system to ensure the best possible outcome for herself and her family. She knew what it meant to be a free black woman in a society dominated by white male slaveholders, and although she engaged in some of the practices of this racist and sexist society, including the ownership of enslaved persons, she did not accept others, as evidenced by her efforts to protect her descendants from the patriarchal authority of men, both black and white. Using all the tools available to improve the condition of her family, Margaret was, at her death, still the same woman who so many years before had worked to retain the right to commune at St. Philip's Church. It was this legacy of agency, wisdom, and strategic negotiation that Margaret left her family, a legacy that would stand her younger daughter in good stead in the near future.

THE LAWSUIT

The years after Margaret's passing were tumultuous ones for Barbara, for this was when she was dragged into the legal battles of Elizabeth and James Hamilton. The link between Barbara and the Hamiltons was James G. Moodie. A friend of her father's, James Moodie became Barbara's financial advisor and guardian after Adam's death and helped her manage her portfolio. One of the properties she acquired on his advice was the mortgage on Rice Hope Plantation, property that Barbara thought belonged to James Hamilton, but which was actually a part of his wife's trust estate. Thus it was that a wealthy free black woman came to loan money to an elite, white male plantation owner. It may also have been at her guardian's suggestion that Barbara hired attorney Alexander Mazyck to represent her in responding to Elizabeth's "Bill of Complaint" in 1842. Interestingly, while all the defendants hired lawyers, Barbara was alone in asking that the debt owed to her be paid out of James Hamilton's personal funds rather than from his wife's trust estate. According to court records, Barbara stated that since the debt was James's, not Elizabeth's, repayment should come from his assets, not hers.[67]

Hamilton v. Hamilton played out in a number of stages over several years. In 1843, the court ruled that Rice Hope was, indeed, part of a trust estate. James had illegally used that estate to pay off his own debts and then defrauded his creditors by not informing them that they were purchasing mortgages on property held in trust. The trust estate was thus forever removed from James's control and placed in the hands of a new trustee, who was charged with managing it for Elizabeth's sole and separate use. Finally, while the trust was not to be held liable for any of James's personal debts, the mortgages on Pennyworth and Rice Hope plantations were upheld by the court. This was of small comfort to Elizabeth: she was unable to pay off the mortgages, so both properties went into foreclosure. The court then ordered that the plantations be sold at auction and stipulated that the proceeds from the sales were to be distributed to the mortgage holders in order of the dates of their liens.[68]

James Hamilton now arranged for the Bank of Charleston to buy Rice Hope at auction. The deal was that the bank would then extend enough credit to Elizabeth and James's two grown sons to enable them to take title of the plantation. The sons agreed to pay off the loan with profits from future rice sales. What happened next was fraud, plain and simple. To prevent excessive bidding, the bank bought the first two mortgages outstanding on Rice Hope and promised the wealthy holders of the large, fifth mortgage that they would be paid back before the holders of the smaller, third and fourth mortgages. The bank was thus able to purchase a plantation worth $60,000 for only $11,000, and Barbara, who held the third mortgage on Rice Hope, was swindled out of $5,178. Her response to such wrongdoing was not surprising, considering her history. Financially savvy, connected to influential people, the head of her own household, legal guardian to several children, a businesswoman, landowner, and slaveholder, Barbara followed the examples that her mother and her half sister had set for her: working from within the legal system to demand justice and protect her rights, Barbara filed a motion asking that the courts overturn the fraudulent sale of Rice Hope.[69]

We can only imagine the reaction of white Charlestonians when they heard that a free woman of color had challenged one of the most prestigious combinations of bankers, planters, merchants, and lawyers in the state. It was likely seen as an attack on the southern social system, which openly professed to place all women under the authority of men, and all black persons (enslaved or free, wealthy or poor, dark- or light-skinned) under the control of whites. If Barbara won her case, what might that do to the public image of the South's supposedly ironclad raced and gendered social hierarchy? Equally troubling was the possibility of a free black woman, even one as wealthy and influential as Barbara, winning such a high-profile case against an elite white man in open court, and possibly inspiring in other free blacks increasingly radical ideas about "their legal rights." More than just money was at stake, then.

These very concerns may have led the first judge who heard the case, William Harper, to dismiss Barbara's motion. A political crony of James Hamilton, William believed the "African negro . . . was an inferior variety of the human race" and "peculiarly suited" for enslavement. People of African descent, said William, could never exercise power in civilized society. As for women, William felt they suffered from an "infirmity, unsuitableness of character, or defect of discretion" that also made them unfit for the exercise of public power. In Barbara, then, William faced a plaintiff both black and female and, thus, by his standards, an individual who was doubly unfit to exercise power (i.e., undeserving of the rights of citizenship) in a "civilized society." It is thus safe to assume that both racism and sexism influenced William's decision.[70]

Undeterred, Barbara appealed William's ruling to the next rung of the judicial system. Upon receiving an equivocal decision from the Court of Appeals, Barbara continued on in her quest for justice and took her case to the superior constitutional court of the state, the Court of Errors. It was here, four years after Elizabeth had filed her original suit, that Barbara finally won her case. The South Carolina Court of Errors ruled that the first sale of Rice Hope had, indeed, been fraudulent, and it ordered that a new auction be held. Early in 1846, Rice Hope Plantation sold for almost $56,000, and Barbara finally received her money. Elizabeth's sons still managed to purchase most of the Rice Hope property on credit, and they held it in trust for their mother's sole use and benefit.[71]

The legal battles of Barbara Tunno Barquet and Elizabeth Heyward Hamilton reveal that both free blacks and women found it difficult to obtain justice in the Old South. Equity was not always attainable by women, even white women of privilege, because they were female in a social and legal system that upheld male authority as the foundation of social and civic order. Certainly this was the case with Elizabeth, who emerged from her lawsuit with only the residual proceeds of an indebted estate to her name, still married to the man who had literally brought her to the edge of bankruptcy. The reality was that while they claimed to protect a wife's property rights, antebellum equity courts were somewhat less than equitable for women. White women, like free blacks, occupied an intermediate position between white men and enslaved persons in South Carolina, and plantation mistresses often found that their privileges in terms of race were simultaneously constrained by the limitations of their gender.

Attaining equity was equally complicated for free blacks, who daily lived with the knowledge that they were people of color in a society committed to maintaining black chattel slavery and white authority. While Barbara eventually won her suit and collected the money owed to her, one cannot dismiss the roles that her wealth and influence played in her eventual success. Had she not been in a position to hire an attorney, or had the financial wherewithal to file a counter-suit and appeal the decisions that went against her in the lower courts, Barbara would not have won her motion. If you consider the miniscule number of free blacks in the Old South who had the social connections and wealth that Barbara did, it becomes clear that while the pursuit of equity may have been available to all free blacks, very few people of color would have had the means with which to successfully *secure* such equity.

THE END OF AN ERA

Winning her suit likely gave Barbara a deep feeling of pride. She, a free woman of color, had been vindicated in her demand for justice against a major financial institution and a family of elite white plantation owners. Her victory would have been another example to her descendants of their progenitors' determination, proving yet again that they came from a line of women who were shrewd and savvy strategists who never ceased fighting for their rights. Barbara had little time to enjoy her victory, however. Physically unwell, she wrote out her will shortly after the case was settled, and in February 1846, at the age of fifty-three, Barbara died from what her doctor diagnosed as a thickening or enlargement of the heart, also known as "hypertrophy of the heart." She was buried next to her husband in the BFS cemetery in Charleston.[72]

A document signed in her own hand, Barbara's will gives us some insight into her private thoughts. First, it reveals that Barbara, like Margaret, wanted to protect her daughter from the meddling of men. Barbara left her daughter, Caroline, "for her sole and separate use, my servant Phebe, not subject to the debts or contracts of her present or any future husband." Just as Margaret strove to protect Hagar's inheritance from Thomas Cole, and Hagar, in turn, gave guardianship of her children to Edward Frost to safeguard their estates, Barbara worked to protect Caroline from any man who might try to take advantage of her. Barbara learned an important lesson from the women in her family, and from her experiences in the equity courts. Seeing what James Hamilton did to his wife, and realizing that the courts did not always protect a woman's interests, even the interests of a white woman of privilege, Barbara strove to ensure that Caroline's inheritance was protected from potential male predators. It seems that Elizabeth Hamilton learned the same lesson: she, too, left her married daughter an inheritance that was set aside for her sole and separate use.[73]

Barbara also owned enslaved people, and she, like her mother, viewed her laborers as goods to be disposed of in the best interests of her family. Barbara named ten bondspersons in her will and divided seven of the ten between three of her children, without maintaining family ties among the enslaved. She also instructed that the remaining three laborers be left to all her children equally, stating that they could be sold in order to facilitate such a division. Estate papers indicate that the servants in question were auctioned off five months later for $1,350; the proceeds from the sale were divided among Barbara's children to fulfill the terms of the will. Any qualms Barbara may have had about the bondage of black people (and it does not appear she had any) were, then, overridden by her desire to ensure her children's security.[74]

Barbara's children benefited handsomely from her death. Even without the seven black workers she willed to them, Barbara left an estate valued at over $6,000. This included her home on Meeting Street, appraised at $2,500; several mortgages and bonds; five shares in the State Bank worth $445; two shares in the Charleston Bank valued at $194; laborers Diana, Bella, and Isaac; and $140 in household goods. Except for her silverware, some clothes, a few sentimental tokens, and the aforementioned seven enslaved laborers, all of which were distributed to specifically named individuals, Barbara's entire estate was left to her children and her granddaughter, Mary Louisa McKinlay, in equal shares. Mary Louisa inherited in place of her deceased mother, one of Barbara's daughters.[75]

CONCLUSION

Barbara's death closed a significant chapter in the history of her family, and in the history of black women in the antebellum South. The story of the Bettingall-

Tunno women illuminates how southern black women navigated a series of obstacles, first to obtain their liberty, and then to expand it on a daily basis, each right wrenched from a society unwilling to extend to them the full fruits of freedom. Black women understood that freedom did not grant them unfettered access to equality, and that blacks and whites had differing ideas about what freedom should look like for black people. Battling to shape the contours of their lives to better fit their own vision of freedom, black women thus engaged in a variety of personal acts to further their political agency. Regularly allying themselves with men and working within the system, women of color took lovers, owned enslaved laborers, married for upward social mobility, found guardians, and hired financial advisors and attorneys. Such tactics bound black women to the very individuals who were their greatest obstacles to true liberty even as they simultaneously improved these women's abilities to fashion a freedom of their own design.

The lives of the Bettingall-Tunno women thus reflect both agency and constraint on that agency and reveal that while free black women were incredibly hardworking and industrious, much of what they attained in their lives resulted from their tireless and astute negotiations with men. It was Margaret's forty-year partnership with Adam that allowed her to acquire wealth, power, and perhaps even her freedom. She ran Adam's home, owned real estate and enslaved laborers, and attended the most prestigious church in the city. Despite her social standing, however, Margaret's legal status as a free woman and a wife were never confirmed, and, unlike white women of comparable status, she went to her grave illiterate.

Hagar used her mother's relationship with Adam to make significant gains for herself. She married a man from an elite free black family, inherited property from her mother and stepfather, became a slaveholder, and used her position as Adam's stepdaughter to avoid paying her capitation taxes and to live as a feme sole. Despite her wealth and power, however, Hagar retained a white male guardian to protect her legal interests and handed over control of her children to that same man in order to protect their estates. Additionally, we do not know if Hagar was literate. No documents with her signature have yet been recovered, and being his stepdaughter may not have been enough to encourage Adam to educate Hagar, although white women of comparable socioeconomic standing would have received some type of schooling.

Barbara benefited the most from Margaret's relationship with Adam. In addition to receiving a top-notch education, paid for by her father, Barbara inherited a substantial portion of Adam's estate upon his death and her education, wealth, and social position enabled her to marry a high-status, free artisan of color and live as a *feme sole*. As a wealthy widow, Barbara also became the legal guardian of several free black children, owned enslaved workers, ran a successful business, engaged the services of both a white financial advisor and a prominent white attorney, and won a major lawsuit against the Bank of Charleston and a white man from a leading plantation family. Her children grew up in an affluent home, attended an elite church, were well-educated, and inherited substantial property upon their mother's death.

Despite her social status and wealth, however, even Barbara did not live a life wholly free from constraints. Like all free black women in the Old South, she was hedged in by both time and place and understood that she could never be completely free. Instead, her freedom, like those of other women of color, entailed continual compromise with the men who dominated the society in which she lived. Consider the lawsuit that Barbara filed. Unlike white men involved in similar litigations, or white women who were *feme sole* traders, Barbara had to hire a white male attorney to file her legal documents and speak for her in court: in the nineteenth century, the state of South Carolina did not permit free blacks, even those who were wealthy *femes soles*, to speak on their own behalf in a court of law.[76] White men, then, literally became the voices of white *feme covert* . . . and all persons of color. Male and female, rich and poor, *feme covert* and *feme sole*, free blacks were all legally silenced. Barbara's foray into the South Carolina courts, and her victory, is thus one more example of how Charleston's social, economic, and judicial structures were designed to limit the agency of black women, and how black women worked within this inequitable system to make their voices heard, and to create lives that better fit their own definitions of freedom, rights, and justice.

RETROSPECTIVE

Free black life in the antebellum South has long been a topic of research among scholars. Despite the lengthy historiography of the field, however, the lives of free black women in the Old South have largely been relegated to the shadows. From their efforts to gain their freedom to their involvement in the marketplace, from their attempts to acquire property to their forays into the worlds of litigation and finance, free black women played an integral part in the daily affairs of antebellum cities. Indeed, while Charleston's legal, political, social, and economic systems were created and maintained by white male slaveholders, black women, although invested with the least formal power in the slave South, left their own mark on these structures. Far from being inactive subjects in the drama of their own lives, black women were actors and agents who made significant contributions to the story of the pre–Civil War South.

First and foremost, Charleston's women of color navigated a variety of obstacles and made bargains with various groups of southerners in order to obtain their freedom. Once manumitted, however, whether legally or otherwise, black women realized that they would need to continue to renegotiate their freedom on a daily basis; that every step they took forward would have to be fought for within legal and cultural frameworks that were designed to deny them access to the full fruits of freedom. Rights that white Charlestonians took for granted—such as the ability to acquire property, attend the church of their choice, educate their children, or obtain gainful employment—were privileges black women would have to barter for throughout their lives. Freedom did not grant black women unfettered access to equality, and antebellum blacks and whites in the Old South had sharply opposing ideas of what freedom should look like for people of African descent.

Whether it meant acquiring affidavits to safeguard their freedom, petitioning to avoid race-based taxes, obtaining a character reference in order to take communion, or filing a lawsuit to protect their property rights, black women realized that their "freedom" entailed continual dialogue with those who held positions of formal authority in the larger society in which they lived. Armed with this knowledge, as well as their intellect, abilities, charm, and negotiating skills, women of color worked from within the system to try to shape the contours of their lives to fit their own visions of freedom. Their tactics were not designed to bring down the slaveocracy; instead, black women worked to ensure that they secured a place for themselves within the region's existing power structure. While not seen as citizens of the state, women of color nonetheless became political actors who daily lobbied those persons whose social space invested them with superior social and legal power in the Old South, all in order to secure for themselves and their families the privileges that white Charlestonians enjoyed as their birthright.

The need to negotiate meant that black women often had to make compromises in order to fashion for themselves the best life they could. Freedom was a dicey business for women of color in the antebellum South, so they utilized all the options that were available to them in order to get ahead. Understanding that their greatest opportunities lay in allying themselves with men, many black women engaged in a variety of relationships with men, both black and white, and used these partnerships to acquire the advantages that the South's legal and social systems would not have otherwise afforded to them. For some this included becoming sexually involved with a white man and using that domestic connection to gain power and respect for their families. For others it meant becoming slaveholders in order to acquire wealth, solidify their ties to the white leadership class, and protect their own precarious freedom. In short, constrained by the racist, patriarchal society in which they lived, free black women understood that their "choices" lay within a narrow corridor of options already limited by the white men who largely controlled the city in which they lived. They thus learned to do the best they could with what they had, making a way where there did not appear to be one.

It is hard to know how black women felt about making such compromises. What we do know, and can clearly see, are the choices they made in order to forge more secure lives for their families. This ability to negotiate, coupled with their determination to shape the conditions of their freedom to match their own specifications, allowed some women to leave their descendants a legacy of legal freedom, privileges, and wealth they might not have otherwise had. Indeed, many of the daughters and granddaughters of these shrewd and savvy "negotiating women" reaped the financial benefits of their ancestors' tactical compromises and learned from their examples how to acquire as full a freedom for themselves as was possible within the confines of a society unwilling to see them as anything other than lazy and lascivious laborers. The willingness of these later generations to negotiate had its limits, however: like Barbara Tunno Barquet and Eliza Seymour Lee, they refused to be taken advantage of. Wealthy and well connected, these women utilized all the weapons in their arsenal to protect their rights, despite the fact that their race and gender made them denizens (not citizens) and legal minors in the eyes of the state.

Black women understood that freedom in the slave South did not mean equality. It was, instead, a daily battle to shape the contours of their lives to conform to their own desires against a society intent on dictating the form that black women's lives would take. Charleston's social, economic, and legal structures were certainly designed to limit the freedom of black women. Black women, in turn, utilized opportunity, hard work, wealth, the law, and their connections to persons of stature to work from within the southern hierarchy of race and sex to shape their lives to better fit their own definitions of justice, freedom, equality, and citizenship. That they were so often successful is a testimony to their intellect, their determination, their courage, and their willingness to make sacrifices.

It may seem extraordinary that black women had any powers of negotiation in a society founded on patriarchal rule and based on racial slavery. If we view the Old South as a society where white men were invested with hegemonic control, then the ability to negotiate should not have existed for women of color. It is telling that black women were able to utilize all the means available to them, within a social order stacked against them, in order to fashion as full a freedom as was possible. Absolute power is as much a myth as absolute freedom, and it would be simplistic to think that white men had all the power in Charleston, and no one else had any. Instead, the slave South must be seen as a continually contested site of power where autonomous spaces did exist for black women. The story, then, is less about the fact that black women had the ability to negotiate and more about what they were able to do inside these contested spaces. It is the story of how they pushed the boundaries of freedom as far as their abilities enabled them, and how the power structure pushed back to try to shape black women's lives to fit the white image of what black freedom should look like.

DECADE OF CRISIS

Black women's abilities to push their freedom outward would change over the course of the nineteenth century and become increasingly restricted in the

1850s. The position of free blacks had always been precarious in the Old South. In a society predicated on racial slavery, black freedom existed only when and if whites felt secure enough to allow such an anomaly to exist within their midst; as sectional tensions grew worse, the sight of free blacks thus became intolerable to many white Charlestonians. Their central complaint was that free blacks were a bad influence on the enslaved population, who looked at free blacks and saw people who looked like themselves, but who worked for their own benefit and spent their money as they wished. Bondspersons then desired the same liberty for themselves and, according to the master class, became insubordinate and difficult to control. Additionally, if enslaved persons ever rebelled, it was feared that free blacks would make common cause with the rebels, since most free persons of color had friends and family members who remained enslaved.

Free blacks were now increasingly seen as a potential threat to the southern way of life, and many white southerners thought it best to excise such a dangerous anomaly from their midst. In the fall of 1858, working-class whites pressured Charleston city police to enforce the "slave-badge" law, which required all enslaved persons who hired themselves out for wages to wear special badges issued by the city and purchased for them by their owners. An enslaved laborer seen working without a badge could be arrested on suspicion of being a runaway. And while free blacks did not need badges to work, they did need to prove their legally free status in order to be exempt from wearing a badge. City police, however, began arresting any black person they saw toiling without a badge. This not only encouraged many slaveowners to buy badges for their laborers but also caused panic in the free black community since many individuals, even those who were legally free, lacked evidence of their freedom. Being picked up by the authorities for not wearing a badge could, then, result in enslavement for free blacks who lacked valid free papers.[1]

City police now began to more rigidly enforce the capitation tax laws as well. Free blacks in South Carolina had been liable for these taxes for years, but many free persons of color had managed to avoid paying them. In 1858, however, Charleston police, encouraged by the city's new, working-class white majority, announced that anyone claiming to be a free person of color had to provide evidence of having paid his or her city and state capitation taxes. Any free blacks found to be in arrears on their taxes had to pay their back taxes immediately . . . or face enslavement. The door-to-door campaign instituted by city police to uphold the law was a success: in October 1858, fifty-three persons were arrested for failing to pay their capitation taxes. Only five arrests had been made in the previous four months for the same offense.[2]

Despite the far-reaching nature of this crisis, many free blacks, and the white men and women who were their kinfolk, patrons, and guardians, believed that this, too, would pass. They were reassured by the words of men like Alfred Huger. Postmaster of Charleston, member of an aristocratic family, and a lifelong friend of Richard W. Cogdell, Alfred spoke out against the new laws in December 1858, stating that there was no "better intermediate class in the world" than free blacks: "They are respectable . . . our natural allies, tho they can never be our Equals. . . . They work faithfully and more economically than those white men who would supplant them. . . . [They are] worthy and pious people who acquire property by their own industry and who, having no votes, are not bought and sold as is the case with their persecutors[,] . . . do not inflict injury upon the Public[,] . . . are easily managed and controul'd . . . and are disfranchised forever . . . yet paying their taxes with punctuality and humility." For free blacks, such paternalistic condescension was preferable to the alternative being practiced by Charleston's new white working-class regime. They hoped that calm and rational-thinking men like Alfred Huger would bring some sanity back to the city.[3]

The days of paternal benevolence, however, appeared to be drawing to close. News of the incident at Harpers Ferry in late 1859 led to increased fears of insurrection in Charleston, and several southern legislatures debated proposals that would have forced all free blacks to leave their home states forever, or be enslaved. The South Carolina legislature alone considered twenty bills to restrict the privileges of free persons of color, and while none of the measures passed, they were not dismissed and could be reconsidered at any point. Fearing the future, free blacks began to leave Charleston in large numbers for places as diverse and distant as Haiti, Canada, and Liberia.[4]

THE END OF THE BEGINNING

For those who chose to remain, the situation continued to deteriorate. In August 1860, Charleston police began going door-to-door in the black community. They demanded that every individual provide proof of their freedom, including those persons whose families had been free for two or more generations. Even elite persons of color found that they were not exempt from such harassment and began to worry about their long-term survival. Later that same month, the Charleston Courier reported the arrest of sixty to seventy black people for working without wearing the proper badges. Those arrested argued that they were exempt from wearing the badge because they were free people. The courts, however, ruled against them, stating that only those blacks manumitted before 1820, or those born of women who were free before 1820, were legally free. Horror now struck the black community, many of whose members truly believed they were free, but who could not produce the documents to prove it. Faced with the auction block, many free blacks now rushed to purchase badges, hoping to retain their positions and their property through secret trust agreements with elite whites friendly to their cause.[5]

Despite the mass hysteria in the midst of this reenslavement crisis, the city's free black elite continued to reach out to white friends, patrons, business associates, and relations for help. Calling on the mayor of Charleston to protect them, free blacks stood up to the police, lobbied friendly state legislators, and circulated a petition among the city's white elite, asking them to oppose the new, anti–free black laws that were being advanced in the General Assembly. Their efforts to utilize the age-old bonds of patronage proved ineffective, however. The politics of secession had strained the bonds of elite white paternalism beyond the breaking point, partly due to the growth of Charleston's working-class white community. As their political leverage as a voting bloc grew, working-class whites pushed for the reenslavement of free people of color. Elite whites, fearing the loss of these working-class white votes, now hesitated to speak out on behalf of free blacks.[6]

As free blacks continued to be arrested, many persons of color realized that they could no longer rely on their alliances with elite whites to protect them. Hundreds of free blacks now decided to abandon the South. By November 1860, roughly eight hundred free people of color had left Charleston and headed for Philadelphia with the help of white friends and business associates, joining the Sanders family, who had fled there in 1858. These new migrants arrived with their skills and letters of recommendation, but little else: leaving as hastily as they did, many of them sold their property in South Carolina at a loss or simply left it behind, along with friends or family members who were unable or unwilling to come with them.[7]

Free persons who left Charleston in the late 1850s appear to have been wise, although such decisions were not easy or painless. They were lucky to have escaped while they still could. In 1859, South Carolina legislators began debating whether to allow the temporary sale of "vicious and/or vagrant free persons of color," and discussed whether free blacks as a class should be reenslaved. Life became so difficult for free women of color that several of them petitioned the state assembly requesting that they be allowed to enter a condition of slavery. The words of Lucy Andrews speak to the deep despair that many black female South Carolinians must have felt in the days leading up to the Civil War. The sixteen-year-old daughter of a white woman and an enslaved man, Lucy had an infant of her own to care for, and no steady employment. Forced to "wander from place to place to seek work and shelter," in 1860 she petitioned the General Assembly, stating that she desired to enter a condition of slavery, "seeing that slaves are better cared for and happier than your petitioner is in her miserable free condition." Isolated from both enslaved blacks and free whites, Andrews had nobody to provide for her, or protect her, and she begged for the right to become a slave and choose her own master. After three such petitions, on 12 December 1861 the assembly passed a bill permitting Lucy and her then two children to become slaves.[8]

Clearly South Carolina was no longer a "safe haven" for free blacks, if it had ever really been one. And while many an illegal trust continued to be transacted, and dozens of black women assured themselves that their hard work, their connections to the white community, their respectable demeanor and wealth, as well as the shield of legal justice, would protect them from the worst, to other black persons in the late 1850s and early 1860s, the truth was all too apparent: life was about to change drastically for Charleston's free people color, both female and male. They had no idea how much things would change, however, or that after the four-year intermission that was the Civil War, women of color would once again be forced to negotiate their freedom in a nation where government leaders would claim that all persons were now truly free, regardless of race, color, or previous condition of servitude. Not only did sex remain as a category of difference, however, but these same leaders assiduously looked the other way as legalized segregation rose to give birth to slavery by another name, and made a lie of the Constitution yet again. While some things may have changed, it appeared that black women in the postwar South would have to continue their struggle "to catch the vision of freedom."[9]

NOTES

Abbreviations

ARC	Avery Research Center, Charleston, SC
BFSP	Brown Fellowship Society Papers
HFP	Holloway Family Papers
ZPCR	Zion Presbyterian Church Records, 1854–70
CCPL	Charleston County Public Library, Charleston, SC
1856 CCD	Charleston City Directory, 1856
1859 Tax List	List of the Tax Payers of the City of Charleston, 1859
RICC	Return of Interments in the City of Charleston
CLS	Charleston Library Society, Charleston, SC
1859 CCD	Charleston City Directory, 1859
LCP	Library Company of Philadelphia, Philadelphia, PA
SCSVP	Stevens-Cogdell/Sanders-Venning Papers
RSS	Robert Scott Small Library, Special Collections, Charleston, SC
BFP	Bell Family Papers
1860 Tax List	List of the Tax Payers of the City of Charleston, 1860
SCDAH	South Carolina Department of Archives and History, Columbia, SC
CCEP	Charleston County Estate Papers, 1732–1912
CCIA	Charleston County Inventories and Appraisements, 1783–1846
CCIMB	Charleston County Index to Manumission Books, 1801–48
EDB	Equity Decree Books
1860 Tax Returns	Individual Tax Returns for Free People of Color in St. Philip's and St. Michael's Parishes, 1860
ERB	Equity Report Books
GAP	General Assembly Papers
LGA	Letters of Guardianship and Administration, Probate Records, Charleston
LTA	Letters of Testamentary and Administration, Court of the Ordinary/Probate
MRSS	Miscellaneous Records, Secretary of State, 1729–1825
PRSPEC	Parish Registers of St. Philip's Episcopal Church, 1810–40
SFNCTB	State Free Negro Capitation Tax Books, 1811–1860
TAB	Tax Assessment Books, Office of the Mayor, 1852–56
WBCC	Will Books for Charleston County, 1790–1860
SCHS	South Carolina Historical Society, Charleston, SC
1859 Tax Book	Charleston Capitation Tax Book, Free People of Color, 1859
1861 Tax Book	Tax Book, Free Persons of Color, Charleston, 1861

ESLP	Eliza S. Lee Papers, in Rutledge and Young Collection
TFP	Tunno Family Papers, in the Langdon Cheves Legal Collection
UNCG	University of North Carolina–Greensboro
RSPP	Race and Slavery Petitions Project

Introduction

1. Petition: J. E. Holmes for Catherine, GAP 003 ND00 01751, at SCDAH.

2. Ibid. Similar situations occurred across the nation. There were free blacks in Baltimore who turned over sums of money to slaveowners as payment for family members, only to have the owner not release their loved ones. Fields, *Slavery and Freedom*, 29. In New Orleans, an enslaved woman narrowly escaped being defrauded of the $400 she had given her owner to purchase her freedom. When the man attempted to deny the woman her freedom, she sued him and won her case only because she had saved the receipts he had given her each time she made a payment. J. Schafer, *Becoming Free*, 53.

3. Hunter, *To 'Joy My Freedom*, 2–3.

4. For the purposes of this project, the phrases "Old South," "slave South," "antebellum South," or "pre–Civil War South" refer generally to the years from 1790 to 1860, as distinct from the Colonial or Revolutionary South. I begin this study in 1790 for two reasons. One is that the first national census was conducted that year. Within the census are the names of 267 free black heads of families who resided in South Carolina that year, 60 of whom were women. The census records thus give us a place to begin tracing free black South Carolinians and their families. U.S. Bureau of the Census, *Special List No. 34* (1790), 38–41, CCPL. Additionally, the revolution in Saint-Domingue, which began in the early 1790s, played a significant role in shaping Charleston's free black community in the nineteenth century. Berlin, *Slaves without Masters*, 35–36, 58; Johnson and Roark, *Black Masters*, 33; Powers, *Black Charlestonians*, 28; Wikramanayake, *World in Shadow*, 18, 159.

5. See, for example, E. Brown, "Catch the Vision of Freedom"; Foner, *Reconstruction*; Hahn, *Nation under Our Feet*; and Hunter, *To 'Joy My Freedom*.

6. J. Schafer, *Becoming Free*, xiii–xiv; W. King, *Essence of Liberty*, 3, 32.

7. Johnson and Roark, "Middle Ground"; Koger, *Black Slaveowners*, 19, 35, 181; Senese, "Free Negro and the Courts"; Williamson, *New People*, xi, 2, 18; Wikramanayake, *World in Shadow*, xii–xv, 48–54, 60–63; Powers, *Black Charlestonians*, 61–62.

8. Powers, *Black Charlestonians*, 61–62.

9. See Tera Hunter's examination of the Atlanta washerwomen's strike in *To 'Joy My Freedom*, chap. 4. While Charleston's free black women did occasionally band together to sign petitions, their efforts were, for the most part, familial or individual as opposed to collective. See chaps. 3 and 4 for more on women's petitions.

10. Du Bois, "Talented Tenth." For more on respectability, see works cited in n. 22.

11. Wilma King's work is an excellent synthesis of the literature on free black women, North and South, from the colonial period through general emancipation. W. King, *Essence of Liberty*.

12. See in particular A. Alexander, *Ambiguous Lives*; Bell, *Revolution*; Blassingame, "Negro in Antebellum New Orleans"; Dabel, "Ma Went to Work"; Fields, *Slavery and Free-*

dom; Gould, "Henriette Delille"; W. Johnson, *Black Savannah*; W. Johnson, "Free African-American Women"; W. Johnson, "Free Blacks in Antebellum Augusta"; W. Johnson, "Free Blacks in Antebellum Savannah"; W. King, *Essence of Liberty*; Lebsock, *Free Women of Petersburg*; Phillips, *Freedom's Port*; J. Schafer, *Becoming Free*; and Sumler-Edmond, *Secret Trust*.

13. See, for example, L. Alexander, *African or American?*; Bell, *Revolution*; Fields, *Slavery and Freedom*; Hanger, *Bounded Lives*; W. Johnson, *Black Savannah*; Phillips, *Freedom's Port*; Powers, *Black Charlestonians*; J. Schafer, *Becoming Free*; and Taylor, *Frontiers of Freedom*.

14. See Bynum, *Unruly Women*; Kennedy, *Braided Relations*; Lebsock, *Free Women of Petersburg*; and Pease and Pease, *Ladies, Women, and Wenches*. From these, Cynthia Kennedy's *Braided Relations* must be singled out. Kennedy examines all the women of Charleston, white and black, enslaved and free, working-class and elite, during the entire slave era. *Braided Relations* thus casts a wider net in terms of subject matter, and covers a longer time period, than I do in this book. Additionally, Kennedy's work is more materialist and structural than my own, identifying and quantifying relationships between the groups of women she studies, which is not the goal of my study. Instead, *Forging Freedom* does what *Braided Relations* never aspired to: it offers a close portrait of the women who created, negotiated, and defended their rights as free women of color, with significant attention to change over time. The two studies, then, are complementary in many ways.

15. Hunter, *To 'Joy My Freedom*, introduction. See also E. Brown, "Catch the Vision of Freedom"; Frankel, *Freedom's Women*; and Schwalm, *Hard Fight for We*.

16. See Berry, *Swing the Sickle*; Camp, *Closer to Freedom*; Stevenson, "Marsa Never Sot Aunt Rebecca Down"; and White, *Ar'n't I a Woman?*

17. See Fitchett, "Free Negro in Charleston"; Powers, *Black Charlestonians*; and Wikramanayake, *World in Shadow*. Fitchett's 1950 dissertation focuses on wealthy, light-skinned black men and was never published in monograph form, while Powers's study, a social history of Charleston's black community from 1822 to 1885, focuses largely (six of eight chapters) on the period after the Civil War. Finally, Wikramanayake's work, which contains significant data from the cities of Columbia and Charleston, examines free black life across the entire state.

18. A. Alexander, *Ambiguous Lives*; Dabel, *Respectable Woman*; Dunbar, *Fragile Freedom*. Jessica Millward's forthcoming study of free black women in Baltimore (University of Georgia Press) will be a welcome addition to this field. Free black women are also discussed in a number of studies that examine black communities in other cities. See L. Alexander, *African or American?*; Fields, *Slavery and Freedom*; Hanger, *Bounded Lives*; L. Harris, *Shadow of Slavery*; W. Johnson, *Black Savannah*; Phillips, *Freedom's Port*; and Taylor, *Frontiers of Freedom*. These works were very useful in helping me shape my own work, as were several biohistories of free black women. See Hudson, *Making of "Mammy Pleasant"*; Leslie, *Woman of Color*; Painter, *Sojourner Truth*; D. Schafer, *Anna Madgigine Jai Kingsley*; and Sumler-Edmond, *Secret Trust*. Two anthologies on enslaved and free black women provided substantive additional material: Gaspar and Hine, *Beyond Bondage* and *More than Chattel*. See also works cited in nn. 11–14.

19. See, for example, Bynum, *Unruly Women*; Lebsock, *Free Women of Petersburg*; Pease and Pease, *Ladies, Women, and Wenches*; and K. Wood, *Masterful Women*.

20. See works cited in n. 12.

21. This adds especially to the work of Berlin, *Slaves without Masters*; Curry, *Free Black in Urban America*; and Wade, *Slavery in the Cities*.

22. On racial uplift and respectability, see Gaines, *Uplifting the Race*; Higginbotham, *Righteous Discontent*; Hunter, *To 'Joy My Freedom*; Mitchell, *Righteous Propagation*; Shaw, *What a Woman Ought to Be*; White, *Too Heavy a Load*; and Wolcott, *Remaking Respectability*.

23. Johnson and Roark, *No Chariot*, 10–12.

24. Cynthia Kennedy concludes that Charleston's elite free women of color did not engage in benevolent work in part because they defined themselves as "respectable ladies," which depended to a certain extent on their avoiding contact with poor black women, enslaved women, and laboring white women. Kennedy, *Braided Relations*, 132–35.

25. Wikramanayake, *World in Shadow*, 42–43; Berlin, *Slaves without Masters*, 140, 144.

26. Much of the older literature uses these terms. See Berlin, *Slaves without Masters*.

27. See, for example, W. King, *Essence of Liberty*; Schweninger, *Black Property Owners*; and Schweninger, "Fragile Nature of Freedom."

28. Harper, quoted in Johnson and Roark, *Black Masters*, 54–55.

29. O'Neall quoted in ibid. This is unusual considering that other states, including Maryland, decided as early as 1785 that anyone with a black ancestor in the past two generations of their family tree would be classified as black. Phillips, *Freedom's Port*, 32–33; Kennedy, *Braided Relations*, 124–25.

30. In this I follow the lead of Cynthia Kennedy. See Kennedy, *Braided Relations*, 8.

31. I refer to long-term unions as familial, kinship, common-law, or domestic connections and relationships. Others have called similar partnerships "faithful concubinage" or "moral marriages." A. Alexander, *Ambiguous Lives*, 67; Kennedy-Haflett, "Moral Marriage."

32. Interracial sex was not illegal in antebellum South Carolina. Additionally, interracial marriage was legal as long as both parties were free persons. "*Powers v. McEachern*," in Cooper and McCord, *Statutes at Large*, 7:290, 293–94; Johnson and Roark, *Black Masters*, 52–54; Wikramanayake, *World in Shadow*, 13.

33. Quoted phrase from White, *Too Heavy a Load*, 212.

Chapter 1

1. For Mary Purvis, see chap. 3.

2. This chapter relies in large part on the scholarship of Cynthia Kennedy and Bernard Powers Jr. I am indebted to both these historians for the work they did to compile such detailed material on Charleston's early history. Their efforts meant that I did not have to reinvent the wheel when constructing this chapter. See Kennedy, *Braided Relations*, 16; and Powers, *Black Charlestonians*.

3. Kennedy, *Braided Relations*, 12–13. For the story of Margaret, Barbara, and Adam, see chap. 6.

4. For Eliza Lee, see chaps. 3, 4, and 6.

5. Powers, *Black Charlestonians*, 43–44.

6. In recent years, historians have debated whether the Vesey conspiracy was real or if it was an elaborate fiction designed by the city's white residents to reduce the

rights of free blacks and justify the reprisals against enslaved and free persons of color that followed revelation of the affair. See M. Johnson, "Denmark Vesey and His Co-conspirators." For the purposes of this study, I am less interested in whether the conspiracy was fictitious or not and more concerned with the backlash the city's free people of color experienced in the aftermath of the Vesey affair. For example, while the minister of Charleston's African Methodist Episcopal (AME) church was not thought to be involved in the conspiracy, some of the church's class leaders and members belonged to Denmark Vesey's inner circle. White Charlestonians were already discomfited by the church's existence and had been harassing its congregants since 1818. When news of the connection between Vesey and the church was made public, the parishioners found themselves under direct attack. Reverend Morris Brown fled for his life, and his flock scattered as angry whites destroyed the church building on Hanover at Reid Street. The AME church did not officially return to Charleston until after the Civil War. See chap. 2 for more on the alleged conspiracy. See also Powers, *Black Charlestonians*, 17, 21.

7. Ibid., 27; Kennedy, *Braided Relations*, 13.

8. Sarah Blanch lived at 4 Zig-Zag Alley. See Hagy, *Directories for Charleston, 1830–41*, 97. See also Powers, *Black Charlestonians*, 44; and Pease and Pease, *Ladies, Women, and Wenches*, 53.

9. Berlin, *Slaves without Masters*, 253–56; Johnson and Roark, *Black Masters*, 22; Johnson and Roark, *No Chariot*, 96–97.

10. Powers, *Black Charlestonians*, 25.

11. Ibid., 23–24. For Sophia Cochran and Sarah Blank, see chap. 3.

12. Powers, *Black Charlestonians*, 33.

13. Ibid.

14. Kennedy, *Braided Relations*, 11–12, 18–20, 29.

15. Pease and Pease, *Ladies, Women, and Wenches*, 4.

16. Kennedy, *Braided Relations*, 3, 22.

17. Ibid., 11, 19–20.

18. Ibid., 20, 27.

19. Powers, *Black Charlestonians*, 2–3.

20. Kennedy, *Braided Relations*, 3, 11, 22–23, 26–27.

21. Ibid., 3, 19.

22. The elegant dress of many of the city's enslaved and free blacks, particularly the apparel of black women, became a source of tension between Charleston's white and black residents in later years. See chap. 4.

23. Kennedy, *Braided Relations*, 12, 22, 28–29; Powers, *Black Charlestonians*, 2.

24. Kennedy, *Braided Relations*, 4, 19, 27–28; Powers, *Black Charlestonians*, 2.

25. Kennedy, *Braided Relations*, 26, 29.

26. Powers, *Black Charlestonians*, 13–14; Pease and Pease, *Ladies, Women, and Wenches*, 6.

27. Bremer, quoted in Powers, *Black Charlestonians*, 10.

28. Ibid., 36.

29. Cynthia Kennedy opines that this female majority began as far back as 1790. Kennedy, *Braided Relations*, 4.

30. Powers, *Black Charlestonians*, 3–4, 9.

31. This pattern would hold true for the nineteenth century as well. For more on black female labor in Charleston, see chap. 3.

32. Powers, *Black Charlestonians*, 10–12.

33. Ibid., 12–14. See chap. 2 for more on self-purchase.

34. On black female schoolteachers, see chap. 3.

35. Powers, *Black Charlestonians*, 15–16.

36. Kennedy, *Braided Relations*, 21. For Phillis, see chap. 2.

37. Kennedy, *Braided Relations*, 23. See also Olwell, "Loose, Idle and Disorderly."

38. See chap. 3 for more on black market women and the licensing laws that attempted to eliminate them.

39. Kennedy, *Braided Relations*, 26–27; Johnson and Roark, *No Chariot*, 5–6.

Chapter 2

1. Affidavit: Sophia Mauncaut, MRSS 4G (4 Feb. 1814): 364, at SCDAH. Sophia is called both Sophie and Sophia in this document, and the spelling of her last name is unclear: it could also be Mauncaud, Mauncant, or Mauncand. The affidavits attesting to Sophia's second emancipation were true. In volume 3V there is a deed of manumission for an "Elizabeth Sophie and her children Catherine and Josephine." Written in French, the document gives the emancipator's name as one Josephine Quatreuil. MRSS 3V (4 Sept. 1804): 234, at SCDAH.

2. Camp, *Closer to Freedom*; White, *Ar'n't I a Woman?*, esp. chap. 2.

3. J. Schafer, *Becoming Free*, xiii.

4. Olwell, "Becoming Free," 1.

5. Ibid., 4–9. Olwell's conclusions are based on his examination of all recorded deeds of manumission from across the state, 1737–85. I utilize these same records but use only those deeds that refer to black women in Charleston after 1790. MRSS, at SCDAH; and n. 11. See also Blassingame, "Negro in Antebellum New Orleans," 96; and Dabel, "Ma Went to Work," 221.

6. Black slaveownership has been central to discussions of free black life for almost a century. Forbes, "Colored Slave Owners"; "Free Negro Owners of Slaves." For a comprehensive study of the issue in South Carolina, see Koger, *Black Slaveowners*.

7. Olwell, "Becoming Free," 10–11, 13–15.

8. This "revolutionary fervor" ended by 1800, after which the growth of Maryland's free black population slowed to a more routine pace. Fields, *Slavery and Freedom*, 4–6.

9. Wikramanayake, *World in Shadow*, 33–35. While I use secondary data from a number of sources in this chapter, I draw on the works of four scholars in particular: Berlin, *Slaves without Masters*; Koger, *Black Slaveowners*; Powers, *Black Charlestonians*; and Wikramanayake, *World in Shadow*.

10. U.S. Bureau of the Census, *Negro Population of the United States, 1790–1915*; Sumler-Edmond, *Secret Trust*, 8; Phillips, *Freedom's Port*, 15; Bell, *Revolution*, 37.

11. In addition to wills and other sources, this chapter utilizes information taken from 81 deeds of manumission recorded in the state's Miscellaneous Records (MRSS) that refer to black women who acquired their freedom in Charleston after 1790. Of these, 43 are dated prior to 1800; 7 were recorded after 1810; none date to after 1819; and 24

refer to émigrés from Saint-Domingue. Also critical to this chapter are 96 affidavits of freedom from the MRSS for black women who lived in Charleston after 1790. Three date from before 1801; 24 from 1801 to 1809; 45 fall between 1810 and 1819, and 24 date to after 1820. None are dated after 1824. MRSS, at SCDAH.

12. Affidavits: Catharine, MRSS 4C (26 Aug. 1811): 592; Sally Ford, MRSS 4H (23 July 1814): 85, at SCDAH.

13. Other historians note that free blacks migrated to Charleston from other states and countries but do not focus on women or in-state, rural to urban migration. Curry, *Free Black in Urban America*, 3; Powers, *Black Charlestonians*, 37; Wikramanayake, *World in Shadow*, 8, 18.

14. Many free blacks in rural parts of South Carolina farmed for a living: according to the 1860 U.S. Census, 45% of Edgefield County's black female household heads were agricultural laborers, and 39% of all free black female workers in the area tilled the land. Burton, *In My Father's House*, 213–14. City directories reveal that free black women pursued a variety of occupational endeavors in Charleston. Hagy, *Charleston City Directories*, 1816–29. Numerous free black women moved to Baltimore from rural districts in Maryland for similar reasons. Fields, *Slavery and Freedom*, 33–34; Phillips, *Freedom's Port*, 72–73.

15. Affidavit: Becky Jackson, MRSS 4Y (22 Aug. 1822): 159, at SCDAH; Fields, *Slavery and Freedom*, 33–34; Hunter, *To 'Joy My Freedom*.

16. The Act of 1820, in Cooper and McCord, *Statutes at Large*, 7:459–60. See also A. Alexander, *Ambiguous Lives*, 32, 40; and Lebsock, *Free Women of Petersburg*, 91–92.

17. Black women could find domestic service positions in Baltimore. Phillips, *Freedom's Port*, 73.

18. Fields, *Slavery and Freedom*, 4, 10–12, 15–16.

19. Affidavits: Chasey Travois, MRSS 4Q (1819): 271; Mary A. Allison, MRSS 4Q (5 April 1818): 282, at SCDAH. The free black population of Charleston included a large number of light-skinned blacks, due in part to the selective manumission of biracial children by their white fathers. Powers, *Black Charlestonians*, 37–38. This happened in New Orleans and Savannah as well: "mulattoes" comprised 75% of New Orleans's free population of color by the late colonial period, and 68% of Savannah's free blacks were classified as "mulattoes" in 1860. Dabel, "Ma Went to Work," 221; W. Johnson, *Black Savannah*, 78. This was in direct contrast to the Upper South, where the free population grew more from indiscriminate emancipation during the Revolutionary era, leading to the creation of a darker free black community in Virginia and North Carolina. Berlin, *Slaves without Masters*, 48–49. Baltimore's free blacks were also overwhelmingly (66–75%) dark skinned. Phillips, *Freedom's Port*, 62.

20. See works cited in n. 16. Savannah had 224 free black residents in 1800 and 578 by 1810. In 1826, Chatham County, where Savannah was located, was home to 64 foreign-born free persons of color, 33 of whom were from Saint-Domingue. W. Johnson, *Black Savannah*, 108; Sumler-Edmond, *Secret Trust*, 8.

21. Phillips, *Freedom's Port*, 70–72.

22. Bell, *Revolution*, 37–38; J. Schafer, *Becoming Free*, 130. Petersburg, Virginia, also received a sizeable number of black refugees from Saint-Domingue, which led the state to pass new manumission policies. See works cited in n. 16. On New Orleans, see Curry,

Free Black in Urban America, 5–6. Only in that city did foreign-born blacks ever comprise as much as 10% of the free black population.

23. Berlin, *Slaves without Masters*, 35–36; Wikramanayake, *World in Shadow*, 18.

24. For the Langlois family, see chap. 5. See also SFNCTB, 1811–60, vol. 11-1 (1826–27), at SCDAH; Koger, *Black Slaveowners*, 98; Woodson, *Free Negro Heads of Families*, 156; "Free Negro Owners of Slaves," 72; Rules and Regulations, BFSP, 27, at ARC. The Brown Fellowship Society was founded in 1790 by "free brown" men of St. Philip's Episcopal Church who were refused burial in the church's cemetery. The group's purpose was to create a burial ground for free people of color and to aid poor, widowed, and orphaned people of color in Charleston. Women, slaves, and free blacks were excluded from membership. See Browning, "Beginnings of Insurance Enterprise"; and R. Harris, "Charleston's Free Afro-American Elite." For Aspasia Cruvellier Mirault, see Sumler-Edmond, *Secret Trust*.

25. Deeds: Véronique, MRSS 4C (4 Jan. 1811): 555; Janette and Louise Agathe, MRSS 4C (4 May 1805): 572–73, at SCDAH.

26. Will: Marie Françoise Merceron Petit Bois, WBCC 32 (1807–18): 619; Deed: Cité and Her Child, MRSS 3Q (22 Dec. 1797): 131, at SCDAH.

27. See nn. 67, 73, 74, and 79 for primary sources supporting this conclusion. For secondary discussions, see Berlin, *Slaves without Masters*; W. King, *Essence of Liberty*; Fitchett, "Origin and Growth"; Powers, *Black Charlestonians*, chap. 2; Rothman, *Notorious in the Neighborhood*; J. Schafer, *Becoming Free*; Schweninger, *Black Property Owners*; and Wikramanayake, *World in Shadow*.

28. Deed: Lucie and Baptist, MRSS 30 (14 July 1799): 282; Antoine Plumet, WBCC 33 (1807–18): 1064, at SCDAH.

29. Only 8 of the 24 deeds pertaining to women from Saint-Domingue (many of which were written in French) mention financial or material assistance. Deed: Marie Magdeleine Messive and Her Children; Audré Félix age 8, Jeanne Marie age 4, Ulalie Cartrom age 2, and Elizabeth, MRSS 3Q (1 Nov. 1800): 185–86, at SCDAH.

30. Koger, *Black Slaveowners*, 35; Powers, *Black Charlestonians*, 38; Wade, *Slavery in the Cities*, 141–42. In Maryland, the law defined elderly as being more than 45 years of age. Fields, *Slavery and Freedom*, 32.

31. The Act of 1800, in Cooper and McCord, *Statutes at Large*, 7:442–43; Johnson and Roark, *Black Masters*, 35–36; Wikramanayake, *World in Shadow*, 35.

32. Koger, *Black Slaveowners*, 35, 37; Wikramanayake, *World in Shadow*, 34–35. On free black women and employment, see chap. 3.

33. Berlin, *Slaves without Masters*, 101; Koger, *Black Slaveowners*, 53; Wade, *Slavery in the Cities*, 264–66.

34. Louisiana's "relaxed racial climate" meant that free blacks were 34% of the population of New Orleans by 1805. This alarmed many whites, who believed that free blacks set a bad example for enslaved persons, and led to the passage of the anti–free black immigration law of 1807. Bell, *Revolution*, 37, 75; Dabel, "Ma Went to Work," 220; J. Schafer, *Becoming Free*, 4–5, 129.

35. On gender and skilled trades under slavery, see White, *Ar'n't I a Woman?*, chaps. 2 and 4. The index records the volume in which the manumission deed could be found, the first name of the person being freed (in alphabetical order) the name of the manu-

mitter, the date, and the page number on which the deed was located. The volumes the index refers to have been lost, and the index itself is blank after the D's. See CCIMB, at SCDAH.

36. J. Schafer, *Becoming Free*, 45.

37. Phillips, *Freedom's Port*, 95–96.

38. Bell, *Revolution*, 18; Dabel, "Ma Went to Work," 220–21; J. Schafer, *Becoming Free*, 2–3, 45.

39. Deeds: Phillis Gunter and James, MRSS 3M (24 Feb. 1800): 104; Lydia, Mary, and Ann, MRSS 3M (27 July 1799): 282, at SCDAH. See also Koger, *Black Slaveowners*, 47–48.

40. Deed: Diana, Benjamin, Charlotte, Elizabeth, Samuel, Thomas, and Deborah, MRSS 3Q (23 March 1801): 360, at SCDAH. Diana paid 10 shillings (just over $2) for herself and her 6 children.

41. Barsheba Cattle, WBCC 34 (1818–26): 97; Deed: Sally, MRSS 3Q (15 July 1800): 139, at SCDAH. On women, work, and wages, see chap. 3. See also Dawson and De-Saussure, *Census of the City of Charleston, 1848*, 31–35; Berlin, *Slaves without Masters*, 217–23; Blackburn and Ricards, "Mother-Headed Family"; Johnson and Roark, *Black Masters*, 57–59, 185; Powers, *Black Charlestonians*, 41; and Schweninger, *Black Property Owners*, 85.

42. For more on black slaveownership, see chap. 4. On black women's wages, see chap. 3. Dick Wragg, WBCC 28 (1800–1807): 21; Dick Wragg, CCEP, 23 Feb. 1801, at SCDAH.

43. Phillips, *Freedom's Port*, 95–96; Bell, *Revolution*, 18; Gould, "Henriette Delille," 274; J. Schafer, *Becoming Free*, 4–5, 48–49.

44. Koger, *Black Slaveowners*, 45–46; Deed: Betsey Grimes, MRSS 3W (14 Feb. 1804): 729, at SCDAH.

45. Olwell, "Becoming Free," 10–11, 13–15.

46. Deed: Polly and Beck, MRSS 3S (30 March 1803): 23, at SCDAH. Daniel Ravenel stated he was freeing the women because "this day" Polly had given him 15 pounds 8 shillings, which, with sundry other payments, came to 165 pounds, the full amount of the purchase price for herself and her daughter, Beck. The original agreement was made in 1779. See also Bill of Sale and Deed: Rosetta, MRSS 3Q (24 Oct. 1800) and (31 Oct. 1800): 260–62, at SCDAH.

47. This happened in New Orleans as well. Bell, *Revolution*, 18, 37; J. Schafer, *Becoming Free*, 46.

48. Deed: Sarah Weston, MRSS 3R (10 March 1802): 246; Samuel Creighton, WBCC 30 (1800–1807): 1127, at SCDAH; Koger, *Black Slaveowners*, 46–47.

49. Peter Parler, WBCC 39 (1826–34): 1137, at SCDAH; Koger, *Black Slaveowners*, 47–50.

50. Deed: Kate, MRSS 3R (12 July 1798): 691, at SCDAH.

51. Deed: Nancy, MRSS 4N (12 July 1817): 402, at SCDAH.

52. Delayed manumission was particularly common in Maryland. Fields, *Slavery and Freedom*, 30–31.

53. Introduction, nn. 1 and 2.

54. Legal decisions were only published if they were sent up to the South Carolina Court of Appeals. An examination of the pertinent records (the South Carolina Reports) turned up no material regarding a verdict on this matter, which suggests that the case

was resolved at the district court level. Petition Analysis: Grace, RSPP Series 2 County Court Petitions, Charleston Parish/District, #21381708, at UNCG.

55. Deed: Victoria, MRSS 3Y (21 June 1807): 576, at SCDAH.

56. See works cited in nn. 16 and 51.

57. See works cited in nn. 31–33.

58. Deeds: Grace, MRSS 30 (27 Nov. 1799): 31; Tenah, MRSS 4B (21 Dec. 1790): 109; Sue, Dick, and Chloe, MRSS 3R (20 Aug. 1795): 239, at SCDAH.

59. Jacques Truelle, WBCC 31 (1807–18): 165; Marie Gouvignon, WBCC 36 (1818–26): 1228; Certificate of Freedom: Richard Brewton, Grandson of Phillis, MRSS 3Q (8 Dec. 1802): 668, at SCDAH. This is likely the same fire that demolished more than 300 buildings in Charleston in 1741. See chap. 1.

60. Charles Filben, WBCC 28 (1800–1807): 317, at SCDAH.

61. Samuel Jones, WBCC 31 (1807–18): 189; Charles Pinckney WBCC 36 (1818–26): 1048, at SCDAH.

62. See introduction, nn. 31 and 32.

63. Paul de St. Julien Ravenel, WBCC 34 (1818–26): 257, at SCDAH.

64. Under the Act of 1800, manumitting Beck and Bristol would have meant leaving them some type of financial support. See works cited in nn. 31–33. By leaving them to their daughter, a free woman who now owned a home, land, and livestock, Paul negated the issue of support while ensuring the couple's freedom.

65. S. King, Blue Coat or Powdered Wig, 121.

66. See introduction, nn. 31 and 32; and Petition: John Carmille, GAP 003 ND00 01807, at SCDAH.

67. Chap. 6; TFP, Collection 12-107, at SCHS. See also Myers, "Bettingall-Tunno Family"; Crane, "Two Women"; and Kennedy-Haflett, "Moral Marriage."

68. W. Johnson, Black Savannah, 78. See also discussion of "eyeball estimates" in introduction.

69. Dabel, "Ma Went to Work," 221.

70. Bell, Revolution, 13, 71–72, 77.

71. Deed: Sarah, MRSS 3R (18 April 1801): 76, at SCDAH.

72. Consider the case of Celestine and Philippe Noisette. Philippe, in the same document where he acknowledged Celestine's children as his own, referred to Celestine as his housekeeper. "Housekeeper" was the polite way to refer to a woman who had all the responsibilities of a wife without having any of the legal protections of a wife. Philippe Stanislas Noisette, WBCC 40 (1834–39): 203; Petition: Philippe Stanislas Noisette, GAP 003 ND00 01880, at SCDAH. See also Gould, "Henriette Delille," 274; and S. King, Blue Coat or Powdered Wig, 121.

73. Thomas Branford Smith, WBCC 32 (1807–18): 548, at SCDAH. Men used the term "natural child" to refer to a child who was biologically their own but who was not born of a relationship recognized by the courts or the church.

74. James Douglas, WBCC 33 (1807–18): 1107, at SCDAH.

75. For Lindy, see Thomas Branford Smith, WBCC 32 (1807–18): 548; for Flora, see Charles Filben, WBCC 28 (1800–1807): 317; for Chloe, see Sue, Dick, and Chloe, MRSS 3R (20 Aug. 1795): 239; and for Cyprienne, see Will: Marie Françoise Merceron Petit Bois, WBCC 32 (1807–18): 619, at SCDAH.

76. Berlin, *Slaves without Masters*, 151, 177, 222; Curry, *Free Black in Urban America*, 3–5; Fitchett, "Origin and Growth," 424–25; Fitchett, "Status of the Free Negro," 433–35; Johnson and Roark, *Black Masters*, 31–32, 52–54; Koger, *Black Slaveowners*, 31–32; Powers, *Black Charlestonians*, 37–38; Wikramanayake, *World in Shadow*, 13–14.

77. For more on interracial sex and consent in the Old South, see K. Brown, *Good Wives*; Hodes, *White Women, Black Men*; Hodes, *Sex, Love, Race*; W. King, *Essence of Liberty*; Leslie, *Woman of Color*; Painter, *Southern History*; Rothman, *Notorious in the Neighborhood*; and White, *Ar'n't I a Woman?*

78. See, for example, A. Alexander, *Ambiguous Lives*; and D. Schafer, *Anna Madgigine Jai Kingsley*.

79. See works cited in n. 67 and chap. 6.

80. Fitchett, "Origin and Growth," 421–22.

81. See works cited in nn. 16, 33, and 34.

82. Dawson and DeSaussure, *Census of the City of Charleston, 1848*, 3–4. See also P. Wood, *Black Majority*.

83. Johnson and Roark, *Black Masters*, 35–36; Powers, *Black Charlestonians*, 39; Wikramanayake, *World in Shadow*, 19, 161–62. The Act of 1820, in Cooper and McCord, *Statutes at Large*, 7:459–60.

84. Koger, *Black Slaveowners*, 35–36; Wikramanayake, *World in Shadow*, 36–37, 45.

85. See works cited in n. 16. See also W. Johnson, "Free Blacks in Antebellum Savannah," 418.

86. Bell, *Revolution*, 79–80, 93; J. Schafer, *Becoming Free*, 130–32.

87. See works cited in n. 72 and Petition: Philippe S. Noisette, GAP 003 ND00 01880, at SCDAH.

88. See works cited in n. 66 and Petition: John Carmille, GAP 003 ND00 01807, at SCDAH.

89. Petitions: Claude Rame, GAP 003 ND00 02900; Auguste Genty, GAP 003 ND00 01749, at SCDAH.

90. Petitions: Rebecca Drayton, GAP 003 ND00 02831 and 02832; Special Committee Report: Rebecca Drayton, GAP 004 1827 00158, at SCDAH.

91. Petitions: John Walker, GAP 003 1825 00131 and 00132; Judiciary Committee Report: John Walker, GAP 004 1825 00240, at SCDAH.

92. Koger, *Black Slaveowners*, 57, 60.

93. William C. Doughty, WBCC 40 (1834–39): 436; John M. Hopkins, WBCC 40 (1834–39): 301, at SCDAH.

94. Ann Scott, WBCC 36 (1818–26): 947, at SCDAH.

95. See works cited in nn. 83–84.

96. The exact number of virtually free persons is unknown. Berlin, *Slaves without Masters*, 143–44; Powers, *Black Charlestonians*, 39; Mary Smith, WBCC 42 (1839–45): 260; George J. Logan, WBCC 41 (1834–39): 874, at SCDAH.

97. Berlin, *Slaves without Masters*, 144; Johnson and Roark, *Black Masters*, 44–46; Koger, *Black Slaveowners*, 61.

98. W. Johnson, "Free Blacks in Antebellum Augusta," 14–15.

99. For the full story of Aspasia and the lawsuit, see Sumler-Edmond, *Secret Trust*, esp. chaps. 2 and 6.

100. See documents cited in n. 89. See also Powers, *Black Charlestonians*, 39; Wikrama-nayake, *World in Shadow*, 41; and Auguste Genty, WBCC 36 (1818–26): 1139, at SCDAH.

101. See documents cited in n. 91 and John Walker, WBCC 42 (1839–45): 62, at SCDAH. Ann J. Walker appears in the 1841 city directory as a free person of color living on Wall Street. Hagy, *Directories for Charleston, 1830–41*, 112.

102. See documents cited in n. 93. See also Koger, *Black Slaveowners*, 53, 61; Powers, *Black Charlestonians*, 9; and Molly Neyle, WBCC 39 (1826–34): 912, at SCDAH.

103. Charlotte Kershaw, WBCC 37 (1826–34): 196, at SCDAH.

104. Wikramanayake, *World in Shadow*, 41; Koger, *Black Slaveowners*, 36.

105. Koger, *Black Slaveowners*, 63–65.

106. Wikramanayake, *World in Shadow*, 41.

107. See works cited in n. 15.

108. Affidavit: Martha Sophia Inglis, Wife of Thomas, and Her Sisters Catherine and Elizabeth, MRSS 4Y (6 April 1824): 459, at SCDAH; Rita Reynolds, "Vanishing Images," at ARC. There is a long history of racially ambiguous persons from across the South claiming descent from "Moorish" or "Portuguese" ancestors as a way to avoid enslave-ment, or to escape the social and legal limitations that accompanied the status of "free person of color." Referred to by themselves and others by a host of terms, including Brass Ankles, Melungeons, and Croatans or Lumbee, such persons were often of Afri-can, white, and Native American descent and were called "tri-racial isolates" by some scholars. Triracial persons and communities found they could acquire increased rights and privileges in the South only to the extent that they distanced themselves from people of African descent. See Gross, "Of Portuguese Origin."

109. Deed: Susannah and Catherine, MRSS 3Q (20 June 1800): 427, at SCDAH; Rita Reynolds, "Vanishing Images," at ARC.

110. Native peoples had enslaved each other long before Europeans arrived in the Americas. Once Europeans had established themselves, they began purchasing Native slaves from their Indian allies and made war against other Native tribes in order to ac-quire additional enslaved laborers. In Carolina Colony, an explosive trade in Indian slaves existed from the 1670s to the 1720s, and in 1724, some 2,000 enslaved Indians worked for white masters in South Carolina. Virginia banned the slavery of Native peoples in 1691 (the only southern colony to do so), while in Georgia "Florida Indians" were sold at market as late as 1760. Snyder, *Slavery in Indian Country*, 78. For more on Native Ameri-cans and slavery, see Gallay, *Indian Slave Trade*; and Miles, *Ties That Bind*.

111. Affidavits: Diana Beamer, MRSS 4T (20 Aug. 1821): 502; Charlotte and Joseph Bull, MRSS 4W (12 Aug. 1823): 369; Sarah Fox, MRSS 4Y (29 Jan. 1823): 257, at SCDAH.

112. Affidavits: Levy, Crawford, Beedy, James, Sarah, and Steven Stapleton, MRSS 4Z (28 May and 18 Aug. 1823): 227; Betsey Findlay, MRSS 4Y (3 Aug. 1822): 147, at SCDAH. Contrary to Betsey's declarations, she may have had black ancestry. See n. 108.

113. See chap. 1. See also Powers, *Black Charlestonians*, 21, 60; Eckhard, *Digest of the Ordi-nances of the City Council*; Hagy, *Charleston City Directories, 1816–29*; and Hagy, *Directories for Charleston, 1830–41*.

114. Bell, *Revolution*, 79.

115. In 1830, Baltimore was home to 14,790 free blacks and 4,120 enslaved laborers out of a total population of 80,620. Indeed, while the city's enslaved population had de-

creased since 1810, the free black population had almost tripled in size. Fields, *Slavery and Freedom*, 1–2, 28; Phillips, *Freedom's Port*, 15.

116. Court decisions in the 1820s and 1830s were at odds with the Act of 1820. In *State v. Harden* (1832), Justice John Belton O'Neall ruled that evidence showing a black person had been living as a free person for several years would establish the fact of freedom. In *Monk v. Jenkins*, the court concluded that illegally manumitted slaves had the right to own property. Wikramanayake, *World in Shadow*, 42–43; Berlin, *Slaves without Masters*, 140, 144. See also Johnson and Roark, *Black Masters*, 44–46; Koger, *Black Slaveowners*, 65; and Powers, *Black Charlestonians*, 39.

117. The exact number of enslaved persons denied legal manumission that same year is unknown, although few slaveowners would have petitioned the state in 1850 given that the legislators made it clear after the Act of 1820 that they were opposed to manumitting any enslaved persons. See Koger, *Black Slaveowners*, 66–67; Powers, *Black Charlestonians*, 40; and Wikramanayake, *World in Shadow*, 10, 17, 43–45.

118. Bell, *Revolution*, 80, 87; J. Schafer, *Becoming Free*, 132.

119. Berlin, *Slaves without Masters*, 144–45; Powers, *Black Charlestonians*, 40.

120. Koger, *Black Slaveowners*, 68; Harriet O'Driscoll, WBCC 48 (1856–62): 35, at SCDAH.

121. Jacob Wehlert, WBCC 46 (1851–56): 230; Ishmael Mitchell, WBCC 42 (1839–45): 426; Natt Comings Ball, WBCC 44 (1845–51): 109, at SCDAH.

122. Koger, *Black Slaveowners*, 74–75.

123. J. Schafer, *Becoming Free*, 133–35.

124. Scholars have long noted the benefits that urban condition and white patronage had on enslaved and free men of color, including the skilled apprenticeship opportunities that existed for enslaved men in southern cities, the chances enslaved men had to work for wages (funds that could go toward self-purchase), as well as the impact that white clients had on free black men's shops and businesses. See Berlin, *Slaves without Masters*; Curry, *Free Black in Urban America*; Fitchett, "Free Negro in Charleston"; Powers, *Black Charlestonians*; Wikramanayake, *World in Shadow*; and Wade, *Slavery in the Cities*. Beyond a discussion of "concubinage," however, few scholars have examined the role that urban condition and alliances with white persons played in the lives of enslaved and free women of color, nor have they noted that the dual obstacles of race and gender meant that having a white benefactor was more important, if not most important, for black women.

Chapter 3

1. Will: George Mathews, WBCC 40 (1834–39): 238, at SCDAH.

2. Ibid.

3. See chaps. 2 and 4 for more on manumission and inheritances. On the penalties for unemployed and impoverished blacks, see Berlin, *Slaves without Masters*, 224–26.

4. Cynthia Kennedy also concludes that waged labor in antebellum Charleston was affected by assumptions about both race and gender. Kennedy, *Braided Relations*, 129.

5. Johnson and Roark, "Strategies of Survival," 93.

6. Hagy, *Charleston City Directories*, 1816–29. The 1819 directory was the first to identify free people of color. There are, however, many years for which no directories exist. Addi-

tionally, only the heads of households are listed, and the directories we do have under-count persons. For example, the 1820 federal census records 1,745 free blacks living in Charleston, while the 1819 city directory lists only 333 such persons. U.S. Bureau of the Census, *Negro Population of the United States*. This is likely because many free blacks, such as those in New Orleans, avoided government officials since they did not have manumission papers or were virtually free persons. J. Schafer, *Becoming Free*, xxi. There were also occupations that women chose not to report, such as prostitution, and work that went unrecorded because it remained "culturally invisible." This included a woman's sale of the excess products of her "homework" (from her dairy, garden, chicken coop, etc.) and any labor she may have performed in the family business. See Boydston, *Home and Work*. Still, the directories do reveal many of the jobs that free black women and men held, and they give us a sense of the sex ratio in the free black community. They should not, then, be dismissed entirely.

7. Dawson and DeSaussure, *Census of the City of Charleston, 1848*, 3–4. Although this census also suffers from undercounting, it does provide us with important information on the breadth of jobs that Charleston's free blacks held and contains valuable demographic data on the city's free community of color.

8. *1861 Tax Book*, at SCHS; Blackburn and Ricards, "Mother-Headed Family," 23–24. It is difficult to ascertain the extent of black women's employment: federal census takers did not record women's jobs prior to 1860 and city directories list only the names of heads of households. Still, it is clear that a large number of free black women labored for wages.

9. Wikramanayake, *World in Shadow*, 112.

10. See Dawson and DeSaussure, *Census of the City of Charleston, 1848*, 3–4. See also ibid., 15–16, 29–31.

11. To date, free black women's employment statistics have not been compared across southern cities. See Lebsock, *Free Women of Petersburg*, 100–101, 185. According to city registration books, black women outnumbered black men in Savannah's labor force and, unlike white women, were "as visible in the work force as free black men." W. Johnson, "Free African-American Women," 238; W. Johnson, "Free Blacks in Antebellum Savannah," 428. Cynthia Kennedy also uses data from the *City Census of 1848* but does not calculate the percentages of black or white women who worked for wages. Kennedy, *Braided Relations*, 129.

12. While many scholars have discussed South Carolina's head taxes, none have examined the unique burden they placed on black women due to that group's occupational limitations and wage differentials as compared to black men. See Bellows, *Benevolence among Slaveholders*, 180; Berlin, *Slaves without Masters*, 97; Schweninger, *Black Property Owners*, 64; and Johnson and Roark, *Black Masters*, 44. See also SFNCTB, 1811–60, at SCDAH; *1859 Tax Book*, at SCHS; *1861 Tax Book*, at SCHS; Walker, *Ordinances of the City*, 13. The city's head taxes were $5 for free black men 14–17 years of age and $10 for black men over the age of 18.

13. W. Johnson, *Black Savannah*, 44.

14. Powers, *Black Charlestonians*, 44.

15. It is unknown how many persons were actually enslaved for nonpayment of the capitation tax. Kennedy, *Braided Relations*, 67.

16. Petitions and Committee Reports: Richland County, GAP 003 ND00 01808, 01809, and 01885; 004 1806 00090; 004 ND00 00781, at SCDAH.

17. Petition: Sundry Free Women of Color from Charleston, GAP 004 1841 00069, at SCDAH.

18. The exact amount of money that capitation taxes raised for the state, or the city, is not known. SFNCTB, 1811–60, at SCDAH; 1859 Tax Book, at SCHS; 1861 Tax Book, at SCHS.

19. See chap. 2.

20. "Hagar Cole," 1859 Tax List, 386, at CCPL. In 1801, legislators determined that only free persons of color 15–50 years of age would be liable for the state capitation tax. The note "overage" means Hagar was over the age of 50 in 1840, corroborating statements made by relatives that she was born prior to 1790. Cooper and McCord, Statutes at Large, 9:265, 540; "Hagar Cole," 1840 SFNCTB, at SCDAH; Deposition: Liston W. Barguet, TFP, F4, at SCHS. See chap. 6 for more information on Margaret, Hagar, and Adam.

21. Arrest Warrant: Hetty Barron, Miscellaneous Documents, at ARC.

22. Berlin, Slaves without Masters, 60–61, 192, 217–23. This also happened in rural areas of South Carolina. Burton, In My Father's House, 213–14. In New Orleans, married black women were often compelled to work because of the low wages earned by their free black husbands, many of whom served in unskilled positions as laborers, boatmen, and stewards. Dabel, "Ma Went to Work," 219, 223.

23. Berlin, Slaves without Masters, 219–23; Dawson and DeSaussure, Census of the City of Charleston, 1848, 14–16; Johnson and Roark, Black Masters, 209; Pease and Pease, Ladies, Women, and Wenches, 12; Powers, Black Charlestonians, 41. This sexual imbalance existed in rural parts of the state as well: women headed over two-thirds of the free black households in Edgefield County, South Carolina. Burton, In My Father's House, 213–14.

24. Phillips, Freedom's Port, 54–55; Lebsock, Free Women of Petersburg, 90, 97–101, 185; W. Johnson, "Free African-American Women," 238; Blassingame, "Negro in Antebellum New Orleans," 98; Dabel, "Ma Went to Work," 219, 223; J. Schafer, Becoming Free, 80.

25. Schweninger, "Fragile Nature of Freedom," 107.

26. Dabel, "Ma Went to Work," 219; Phillips, Freedom's Port, 81; Gehman, Free People of Color of New Orleans, 33.

27. W. Johnson, "Free African-American Women," 247; Phillips, Freedom's Port, 93.

28. Johnson posits that enslaved husbands married to free black women in Savannah, Georgia, were the "decision makers, breadwinners, and heads" of their families, despite their legal status, and concludes that women married to such men experienced "normal marital relationships." It is unclear what data Johnson uses to reach this conclusion, or how he is defining "normal." I would submit that without direct evidence, it is difficult to draw conclusions about marital "normalcy," a condition that would have been, at the very least, extremely complicated due to the factors I have outlined in the text. W. Johnson, "Free African-American Women," 247.

29. City tax books reveal that young black girls worked for wages in a variety of occupations. See n. 12.

30. Pease and Pease, Ladies, Women, and Wenches, 12. See also Will: George Mathews, WBCC 40 (1834–39): 238, at SCDAH.

31. Dawson and DeSaussure, Census of the City of Charleston, 1848, 13–16, 29–31; Schweninger, Black Property Owners, 86; Powers, Black Charlestonians, 41. Census data sug-

gests that for most white women in southern cities, marriage meant an exit from the labor force. Lebsock, *Free Women of Petersburg*, 187–88; K. Brown, *Good Wives*.

32. Phillips, *Freedom's Port*, 68, 72–73; W. Johnson, "Free Blacks in Antebellum Savannah," 420; Bell, *Revolution*, 16, 75; J. Schafer, *Becoming Free*, 99–100, 129. See also Wade, *Slavery in the Cities*, 248–49; Wikramanayake, *World in Shadow*, 100; and chap. 2.

33. Phillips, *Freedom's Port*, 74–75.

34. W. Johnson, "Free Blacks in Antebellum Savannah," 420.

35. Bell, *Revolution*, 16, 78.

36. Berlin, *Slaves without Masters*, 97, 230, 270; Curry, *Free Black in Urban America*, 16–18; Schweninger, *Black Property Owners*, 63–67.

37. Fields, *Slavery and Freedom*, 35–36, 79.

38. The license cost $10 if one was a skilled artisan such as a carpenter. Coopers and painters paid $8, as did vendors of small wares, hucksters, and vegetable vendors. These last three professions were practiced mainly by women. Male porters and laborers had to pay $4.50, while women in those same jobs were charged $3. See W. Johnson, "Free Blacks in Antebellum Savannah," 419, 426.

39. During the colonial era, many of New Orleans's free black men were artisans. Black women in the city found work as domestic servants, seamstresses, peddlers, and hawkers, while free blacks of both genders owned a variety of shops. Dabel, "Ma Went to Work," 222.

40. See works cited in n. 36. See also W. Johnson, "Free Blacks in Antebellum Savannah," 419; and Blassingame, "Negro in Antebellum New Orleans," 98.

41. Berlin, *Slaves without Masters*, 217–18, 230–31, 334; Schweninger, *Black Property Owners*, 63–67, 79, 84, 114.

42. Berlin, *Slaves without Masters*, 61–63, 247, 279–80; Johnson and Roark, "Strategies of Survival," 93; Johnson and Roark, *Black Masters*, 57; Wikramanayake, *World in Shadow*, 93–94.

43. Fields, *Slavery and Freedom*, 37–38, 71–72; Phillips, *Freedom's Port*, 32–33, 196–97, 235.

44. J. Schafer, *Becoming Free*, 75–77.

45. Gehman, *Free People of Color of New Orleans*, 68; Bell, *Revolution*, 80, 82; Blassingame, "Negro in Antebellum New Orleans," 96.

46. Berlin, *Slaves without Masters*, 61–63, 192, 234, 344. See also nn. 33–35.

47. Powers, *Black Charlestonians*, chap. 2.

48. Berlin, *Slaves without Masters*, 214, 222–23; Curry, *Free Black in Urban America*, 25–27, 34–35.

49. Wikramanayake, *World in Shadow*, 100–101.

50. Phillips, *Freedom's Port*, 73, 110; Lebsock, *Free Women of Petersburg*, 33–34, 164–66; Lebsock, "Free Black Women"; W. Johnson, "Free African-American Women," 237–39; Dabel, "Ma Went to Work," 223–24; Schweninger, "Fragile Nature of Freedom," 107.

51. Burton, *In My Father's House*, 213–14.

52. Berlin, *Slaves without Masters*, 217–23; Schweninger, *Black Property Owners*, 85; Dawson and DeSaussure, *Census of the City of Charleston, 1848*, 35. My evidence from 1848 coincides with the findings of Michael Johnson and James Roark, who conclude that free women of color were twice as likely as free men of color to labor at the bottom of the

southern job ladder. Johnson and Roark use the 1860 census to calculate the number of black women in menial occupations at 37%. Johnson and Roark, *Black Masters*, 185. Blackburn and Ricards, who also use the 1860 census, estimate the number at 33%. Blackburn and Ricards, "Mother-Headed Family," 23–24. In 1848, 12.8% of the city's free black men enumerated in the census (35 out of 273) worked at the bottom of the occupational ladder. Dawson and DeSaussure, *Census of the City of Charleston, 1848*, 35.

53. Phillips, *Freedom's Port*, 110.

54. W. Johnson, "Free Blacks in Antebellum Savannah," 428.

55. W. Johnson, "Free African-American Women," 239, 243; Dabel, "Ma Went to Work," 223, 225.

56. Johnson and Roark, *No Chariot*, 77, 99.

57. On the benefits and disabilities of laundry work and domestic service, see Hunter, *To 'Joy My Freedom*. Hunter examines the lives of southern black women after the Civil War, but I think it quite likely that many of the advantages and drawbacks she describes held true for free black women's work experiences in the Old South.

58. Hagy, *Charleston City Directories, 1816–29*.

59. The 1822 directory contains the names of 231 black women, 106 of whom listed an occupation. Hagy, *Charleston City Directories, 1816–29*. In 1830–31, only 26 of the 136 black women in the directory gave a job description. In 1835–36, 49 of the 50 black women whose names were recorded appear to have worked outside the home. Hagy, *Directories for Charleston, 1830–41*. See also Table 3.1.

60. Only 13 black women appear in the 1837–38 directory. Hagy, *Directories for Charleston, 1830–41*. See Table 3.1.

61. Dawson and DeSaussure, *Census of the City of Charleston, 1848*, 31, 35; *1861 Tax Book*, at SCHS; Blackburn and Ricards, "Mother-Headed Family," 23–24. I do not include taking in wash or laundry as a "clothing-related" field, unlike the *Census of the City of Charleston, 1848*; I examine it instead as a category unto itself.

62. I agree with Cynthia Kennedy that women of color figured prominently among Charleston's artisans, and that free black women and white women together dominated the city's clothing trade. She concludes, however, that "25% of Charleston's free women of color labored as skilled artisans," which is lower than my calculations. Kennedy, *Braided Relations*, 142–43, 262 (n. 50).

63. Berlin, *Slaves without Masters*, 220–21; Curry, *Free Black in Urban America*, 200–201; Powers, *Black Charlestonians*, 41; Phillips, *Freedom's Port*, 110. Jane Dabel concludes that even in New Orleans, few black women held professional positions due to racism, sexism, and a lack of skills. Although some black women did become artisans, most, she states, were unskilled laborers who worked for low pay: market women, domestic servants, washerwomen, ironers, etc. Dabel, "Ma Went to Work," 223–26.

64. See Phillips, *Freedom's Port*, 110.

65. W. Johnson, *Black Savannah*, 181, 185; W. Johnson, "Free African-American Women," 239, 241; W. Johnson, "Free Blacks in Antebellum Savannah," 421–22, 426. Johnson's data comes from city and county registers of free persons of color for 1817–29, 1819–36, and 1826–35, as well as city and county tax digests for 1810, 1820, 1824, 1837, and 1858, and the city council minutes, 1832–37.

66. Jane Dabel concludes that while sewing required training, and was cleaner and

less physically exhausting than doing laundry, it still garnered low wages. Dabel, "Ma Went to Work," 225. Jane and William Pease maintain that seamstresses "were paid wages that were insufficient on any scale." Pease and Pease, *Ladies, Women, and Wenches*, 53.

67. Even the city's death records support this. Occupations are listed in those records for July, Sept., Oct., and Nov. 1850, and for all of 1860. From these 16 months I culled the names of 60 free black women, 40 (67%) of whom were seamstresses or mantua makers. See RICC, 1819–61, at CCPL.

68. "Venus Deas," in Hagy, *Charleston City Directories, 1816–29*, 38; "Roxanna Niles," in ibid., 92; "Ann Francis," in 1859 CCD, at CLS; "Nancy Eden," in Hagy, *Charleston City Directories, 1816–29*, 40.

69. "Sally Seymour," in Hagy, *Charleston City Directories, 1816–29*, 61, 98; Sarah/Sally Seymour, WBCC 36 (1818–26): 1008, at SCDAH; Powers, *Black Charlestonians*, 42–44; Schweninger, *Black Property Owners*, 132; Wikramanayake, *World in Shadow*, 111.

70. W. Johnson, *Black Savannah*, 181–82; W. Johnson, "Free African-American Women," 240, 243; W. Johnson, "Free Blacks in Antebellum Savannah," 423.

71. Wikramanayake, *World in Shadow*, 108; William Wightman, WBCC 40 (1834–39): 262–65; Jane Wightman, WBCC 46 (1851–56): 258–60, at SCDAH; Powers, *Black Charlestonians*, 42; Margaret and Louisa Noisette, *1861 Tax Book*; Philippe S. Noisette, WBCC 40 (1834–39): 203, at SCDAH. See chap. 2 for more on the Noisette family.

72. Sumler-Edmond, *Secret Trust*, 1–2; W. Johnson, "Free Blacks in Antebellum Augusta," 14.

73. Kennedy, *Braided Relations*, 138–39.

74. Phillips, *Freedom's Port*, 110; W. Johnson, "Free African-American Women," 239; Dabel, "Ma Went to Work," 226; Gehman, *Free People of Color of New Orleans*, 56.

75. Schweninger, *Black Property Owners*, 85; "Kitty Jacobs," in Hagy, *Charleston City Directories, 1816–29*, 47; "Felicity White," in ibid., 103; "Elizabeth Grant" and "Harriet Lazarus," in *1861 Tax Book*, at SCHS.

76. "Mary Purvis," *1861 Tax Book*, at SCHS.

77. Olwell, "Loose, Idle and Disorderly," 102–6.

78. It is unclear how diligently these laws were enforced. 1807 Ordinance, in Eckhard, *Digest of Ordinances*, 461; Statute No. 2639 (1834), in Cooper and McCord, *Statutes at Large*, 7:468–70; Ordinance of 11 April 1843, in Eckhard, *Digest of Ordinances*, 21–23; Wikramanayake, *World in Shadow*, 102.

79. Olwell, "Loose, Idle and Disorderly," 102–6.

80. W. Johnson, "Free Blacks in Antebellum Savannah," 419; W. Johnson, "Free African-American Women," 239.

81. Kennedy, *Braided Relations*, 138–39.

82. Free black women in Savannah who earned the most money were usually seamstresses, pastry cooks, or shopkeepers. W. Johnson, *Black Savannah*, 181–82.

83. Phillips, *Freedom's Port*, 110.

84. "Nancy Burns," in Hagy, *Charleston City Directories, 1816–29*, 35; "Mary Duprat," in Hagy, *Directories for Charleston, 1849–55*, 128; "Betsy Henry," in 1856 CCD, at CCPL; "Sophia Cochran," in Hagy, *Charleston City Directories, 1816–29*, 75; "Sarah Blank," in Hagy, *Directories for Charleston, 1849–55*, 116.

85. Berlin, *Slaves without Masters*, 242–44; Schweninger, *Black Property Owners*, 85. See also works cited in n. 36.

86. Schweninger, *Black Property Owners*, 84, 115–16, 132. There were 5 free black female boardinghouse operators in Charleston in 1848. Dawson and DeSaussure, *Census of the City of Charleston, 1848*, 35. See also Phillips, *Freedom's Port*, 100–102, 110; Dabel, "Ma Went to Work," 223; Gehman, *Free People of Color of New Orleans*, 56.

87. Powers, *Black Charlestonians*, 44. For more on Eliza, see works cited in n. 69 as well as chaps. 4 and 6.

88. Schweninger, *Black Property Owners*, 132; Wikramanayake, *World in Shadow*, 82, 103–6; Ravenel, *Charleston*, 461; Frances Kemble, *Records of a Later Life*, in Vertical Files: Negroes, at SCHS.

89. Berlin, *Slaves without Masters*, 256; Johnson and Roark, *Black Masters*, 22; Johnson and Roark, *No Chariot*, 96–97.

90. Bellows, *Benevolence among Slaveholders*, 135–36. See also Phillips, *Freedom's Port*, 101.

91. In this I disagree with Jane Dabel, who places boardinghouse operators in the category of professional workers (along with nurses and midwives). Dabel, "Ma Went to Work," 223.

92. Johnson and Roark, *Black Masters*, 59; Schweninger, *Black Property Owners*, 85. Blackburn and Ricards calculate the number of nurses in 1860 at 3.35%. Blackburn and Ricards, "Mother-Headed Family," 23–24. Dawson and DeSaussure, *Census of the City of Charleston, 1848*, lists 10 black nurses out of 322 black working women (3.1%), while the *1861 Tax Book* lists 30 black female nurses out of a total 758 black working women (3.95%). "Clarinda Hamilton," in Hagy, *Charleston City Directories, 1816–29*, 45, 82; "Mrs. R. Baird," 1859 CCD, at CLS; "Molly Mathis," in Hagy, *Charleston City Directories, 1816–29*, 52; "Dinah Buchanan," in Hagy, *Directories for Charleston, 1849–55*, 118. Baltimore, Savannah, and New Orleans all had free black nurses and midwives. Phillips, *Freedom's Port*, 110; W. Johnson, "Free African-American Women," 239; Dabel, "Ma Went to Work," 223.

93. W. Johnson, "Free African-American Women," 244–45. See also Statute No. 2639, in Cooper and McCord, *Statutes at Large*, 7:468–70. On Thomas Bonneau, see Johnson and Roark, *Black Masters*, 88, 108–9, 212, 223; Johnson and Roark, *No Chariot*, 23–25; and Powers, *Black Charlestonians*, 52–55. For Jeanette Bonneau, see 1859 Tax List, at CCPL, 384; 1860 Tax List, 316, at RSS; 1860 Tax Returns, at SCDAH; 1861 Tax Book, at SCHS; and chap. 2.

94. Kennedy, *Braided Relations*, 147. For Payne, see Powers, *Black Charlestonians*, 52–55.

95. Amy Akin in Wikramanayake, *World in Shadow*, 103–4; "Sarah Cole," in Hagy, *Charleston City Directories, 1816–29*, 37; "Sophia Ives," in ibid., 46, 84. Mrs. Stromer and Amelia Barnett in Birnie, "Education of the Negro," 19; Frances P. B. Holloway in Johnson and Roark, *Black Masters*, 208, 223; Johnson and Roark, *No Chariot*, 27–28. In Savannah, Mary Woodhouse, a free black seamstress, secretly operated a school for free black children out of her home in the 1850s. W. Johnson, "Free Blacks in Antebellum Savannah," 425–26.

96. W. Johnson, "Free Blacks in Antebellum Savannah," 425.

97. Bell, *Revolution*, 125, 127; Gehman, *Free People of Color of New Orleans*, 74. There were also secret schools in New Orleans that free blacks set up to teach enslaved children.

These schools changed locations every few weeks in order to evade detection and generally met at night, often in alleyways. Bell, *Revolution*, 127.

98. Ann Mitchell in HFP, Box 1, Folder 7, 17 March 1824; HFP, B1/F17, 28 March 1826; HFP, Oversized B1/F23, 7 June 1827, at ARC. See also Kennedy, *Braided Relations*, 150; Fields, *Slavery and Freedom*, 27.

99. "May Flurney," in Hagy, *Charleston City Directories, 1816–29*, 42; "Ashley Bascombe," 1856 CCD, at CCPL; Pease and Pease, *Ladies, Women, and Wenches*, 148; Wikramanayake, *World in Shadow*, 103–6. A number of free black women worked as prostitutes in New Orleans, many of whom were arrested and charged with fraud in addition to using "foul and obscene language," being "lewd and abandoned," running brothels, "keeping a disorderly house," and maintaining houses of "assignation." J. Schafer, *Becoming Free*, 29, 118, 120–21, 129.

100. Pease and Pease, *Ladies, Women, and Wenches*, 54.

101. Salmon, *Women and the Law of Property*, 44–49, 57.

102. Kennedy, *Braided Relations*, 154.

103. Sole Trader Deed: Sherry and Catharine Sasportas, MRSS 40 (16 Oct. 1817): 165–66, at SCDAH.

104. "Catherine Sasportes," in Hagy, *Directories for Charleston, 1830–41*, 25; Woodson, *Free Negro Heads of Families*, 157; "Free Negro Owners of Slaves," 73.

105. There is no indication that the enslaved persons Barbara and Hagar owned were their kin. For Barbara and Hagar's full stories, see chap. 6.

106. Salmon, *Women and the Law of Property*, 45–49.

107. Sole Trader Deed: Jack and Maria Lopez, MRSS 4W (12 March 1822): 185–86, at SCDAH.

108. Sole Trader Deed: Sherry and Catharine Sasportas, MRSS 40 (16 Oct. 1817): 165–66, at SCDAH.

109. Pease and Pease, *Ladies, Women, and Wenches*, 54; Deed of Loan: Dye Waring and Abraham Moise, MRSS 3Y (14 Dec. 1838): 258–60, at SCDAH. Dye/Diana was once enslaved. See Sarah F. Waring, WBCC 39 (1826–34): 842, at SCDAH. See also "Abraham Moise," in Hagy, *Directories for Charleston, 1830–41*, 86.

110. Bellows, *Benevolence among Slaveholders*, 185–86; Lebsock, *Free Women of Petersburg*, 97; Berlin, *Slaves without Masters*, 234–36, 238–41; Powers, *Black Charlestonians*, 41.

111. Berlin, *Slaves without Masters*, 61–63; Fitchett, "Status of the Free Negro"; Fitchett, "Traditions of the Free Negro"; Curry, *Free Black in Urban America*, 30–33; Frazier, *Black Bourgeoisie*, 32–33.

112. Dawson and DeSaussure, *Census of the City of Charleston, 1848*, 31, 35; Powers, *Black Charlestonians*, 41; Johnson and Roark, *Black Masters*, 57–59, 185.

113. In the 1860 Census, 626 of Charleston's 1,251 free black women age 15 to 65 listed an occupation. Grouped into 8 categories, 358 (57%) were in needle trades or "Bench Work." Another 208 (33%) were in service jobs, mainly house servants and washerwomen; 21 (3%) were professional, technical, or managerial persons, generally nurses or storekeepers; 22 (3.5%) were clerks; 5 were in processing; 2 in structural work; and 10 labored in unclassified occupations. Black men's jobs were more widely distributed and involved higher-status, better-paying positions. Six hundred of 627 black men listed a job. Of these, 216 (36%) were in structural work like carpentry; 106 (18%) were

miscellaneous laborers; 78 (13%) did bench work like tailoring; and 83 (14%) were in service positions. Spread across 10 categories, there were also 17 black men who were professionals; 6 clerks; 27 who farmed, fished, or worked in forestry; 25 in processing work; 39 in machine trades; and 3 in unclassified jobs. See Blackburn and Ricards, "Mother-Headed Family," 23–24.

114. Pease and Pease, *Ladies, Women, and Wenches*, 52–53; Dawson and DeSaussure, *Census of the City of Charleston, 1848*, 29–35. Charleston's laboring women, white and black, thus competed against each other for fewer jobs that paid less than male-dominated occupations. This further depressed wages, as did the fact that free black women could always be replaced by enslaved women, many of whom were trained as washerwomen, mantua makers, seamstresses, fruit sellers, pastry cooks, and house servants. Kennedy, *Braided Relations*, 138, 146.

115. Lebsock, *Free Women of Petersburg*, 97–99; Lebsock, "Free Black Women," 275–77.

116. W. Johnson, "Free African-American Women," 238; W. Johnson, "Free Blacks in Antebellum Savannah," 421–22.

117. Dabel, "Ma Went to Work," 223–24. Dabel's conclusions are based on information gathered from the 1850 and 1860 censuses, parish registers of free persons of color, and newspaper advertisements.

118. Curry, *Free Black in Urban America*, 20–25; Berlin, *Slaves without Masters*, 97, 279–80; Lebsock, *Free Women of Petersburg*, 164–66; Lebsock, "Free Black Women," 278, 284–86; Schweninger, *Black Property Owners*, 63–67, 87–88; Wikramanayake, *World in Shadow*, 80, 103–4.

119. On self-purchase and buying kinfolk out of bondage, see chap. 2.

120. See documents cited in nn. 71 and 87–88.

Chapter 4

1. ESLP, Rutledge-Young Collection, at SCHS.

2. For more on Eliza, see chaps. 1, 3, and 6.

3. Berlin, *Slaves without Masters*, 246–47; Curry, *Free Black in Urban America*, 48; Schweninger, *Black Property Owners*, 25.

4. See chap. 3 for employment issues and capitation taxes.

5. W. Johnson, *Black Savannah*, 78; W. Johnson, "Free African-American Women," 240–42.

6. Pease and Pease, *Ladies, Women, and Wenches*, 102–3.

7. Taxable property included real estate, enslaved laborers, and horses. Inventory: Ann Bivet, CCIA, vol. E (1802–19): 10; Margaret McWharter, CCIA, vol. E (1802–19): 17, at SCDAH.

8. Cocuzza, "Dress of Free Women of Color"; Hunter, *To 'Joy My Freedom*, 4.

9. Powers, *Black Charlestonians*, 22.

10. Cocuzza, "Dress of Free Women of Color."

11. I identified 86 estate inventories (1789–1864) belonging to free Charlestonians of color. Of these, 52 (60%) belonged to free women of color. See CCIA, at SCDAH.

12. Louisa Smith, CCIA, vol. E (1857–60): 192; Ann Wilson, CCIA, vol. D (1854–57): 236, at SCDAH. Few free persons of color became prosperous or affluent. If the cost of a

comfortable home in Charleston ($2,000) is used as a benchmark to indicate economic prosperity, only 117 free blacks in the city, 500 including their family members, were affluent. Curry, *Free Black in Urban America*, 43.

13. Sarah Lucas formerly Glen, CCIA, vol. C (1850–54): 44; Mary M. N. Williams, CCIA, vol. C (1850–54): 492, at SCDAH.

14. Fields, *Slavery and Freedom*, 80. The wills from Charleston reveal that except for specific items of great monetary or symbolic value, such as family portraits, jewelry, or certain pieces of furniture (which were left to specific persons), wealthier Charlestonians tended not to list their belongings in such fashion. Instead, they referred to the general division of their household goods among certain heirs. See WBCC, at SCDAH.

15. Will: Esther McIntosh, WBCC 34 (1818–26): 411; Esther McIntosh, CCIA, vol. F (1813–24): 347, at SCDAH. At her death, McIntosh owned 5 cows and 5 calves worth $75; 4 cows valued at $48; 12 head of cattle assessed at $84; 1 horse appraised at $70; 1 mare and 1 colt priced at $130; and 5 hogs totaling $10.

16. Susannah Cart, WBCC 36 (1818–26): 984; Ruth Gardiner, CCIA, vol. F (1813–24): 571, at SCDAH. See also Berlin, *Slaves without Masters*, 236, 244; Curry, *Free Black in Urban America*, 42; Johnson and Roark, *No Chariot*, 6; Lebsock, *Free Women of Petersburg*, 104; Schweninger, *Black Property Owners*, 25, 70; and Wikramanayake, *World in Shadow*, 84, 106.

17. W. Johnson, "Free African-American Women," 239–40; W. Johnson, "Free Blacks in Antebellum Savannah," 426.

18. Probate records include inventories, wills, and other estate papers. I uncovered 41 wills belonging to free black female Charlestonians, 52 estate inventories, and 4 estate documents. Of the 52 estate inventories, 24 are for women who also had wills. Of the 4 estate documents, 3 refer to women with inventories. Not counting any woman more than once then, there are 41 wills, 28 inventories, and 1 estate document. This means there are probate records referring to 70 different free black women. There are likely more inventories and wills pertaining to free women of color, but it is difficult to know how many more since many free blacks did not state their race in the probate records. I was often able to identify the race of these 70 women only because I discovered other records for them in which their race was referenced. See CCIA, WBCC, and CCEP, at SCDAH.

19. See *1859 Tax List*, at CCPL; *1860 Tax List*, at RSS; and *1860 Tax Returns*, at SCDAH.

20. Bella Fenwick, CCIA, vol. G (1824–34): 303; Rosina Dobbins, CCIA, vol. G (1824–34): 275; Rose Dobbins, CCEP, vols. A–H, at SCDAH. See also works cited in n. 12.

21. Phillips, *Freedom's Port*, 98–100.

22. This is in direct contrast to Loren Schweninger, who concludes that free black women across the South owned more real estate, on average, than free black men. Schweninger, *Black Property Owners*, 86, 289–91.

23. In 1859, 134 women controlled about $279,000 in real estate (37% of the city's $758,000 black-owned real estate), or an average of $2,082 per woman. See documents cited in n. 19.

24. In 1860, black Charlestonians collectively owned almost $760,000 in real estate. About $267,000 (35%) of this belonged to 123 black women, or an average of $2,170 per woman. See documents cited in n. 19.

25. Curry, *Free Black in Urban America*, 44; Blackburn and Ricards, "Mother-Headed Family," 23–24. On free black women's occupational struggles, see chap. 3.

26. Lebsock, *Free Women of Petersburg*, 90, 103; Lebsock, "Free Black Women," 281–82.

27. Why Charleston differed from Savannah and New Orleans is unclear. W. Johnson, *Black Savannah*, 76–77; W. Johnson, "Free African-American Women," 239–40; W. Johnson, "Free Blacks in Antebellum Savannah," 423.

28. Gould, "Henriette Delille," 273; Gehman, *Free People of Color of New Orleans*, 49–50. David Rankin argues that census takers underestimated free black wealth in New Orleans, most of which was held in real estate, and concludes that at least half of the city's black real property owners were women. Rankin, cited in J. Schafer, *Becoming Free*, 162.

29. Phillips, *Freedom's Port*, 97, 154; Fields, *Slavery and Freedom*, 79.

30. W. Johnson, "Free Blacks in Antebellum Augusta," 14–15; W. Johnson, "Free Blacks in Antebellum Savannah," 419; Sumler-Edmond, *Secret Trust*.

31. W. Johnson, *Black Savannah*, 76–78.

32. W. Johnson, "Free African-American Women," 240; W. Johnson, "Free Blacks in Antebellum Savannah," 426–27.

33. W. Johnson, *Black Savannah*, 3; Bell, *Revolution*, 81.

34. Gehman, *Free People of Color of New Orleans*, 52–53; Bell, *Revolution*, 81.

35. Bell, *Revolution*, 81; Gehman, *Free People of Color of New Orleans*, 66–68.

36. W. Johnson, *Black Savannah*, 3; Blassingame, "Negro in Antebellum New Orleans," 97.

37. J. Schafer, *Becoming Free*, 162.

38. In 1859, 353 free blacks appeared on the city's list of taxpayers. Only 134 were black women who owned real estate, versus 172 black men, but 170 (48%) of all the black taxpayers that year were women. Eleven taxpayers were listed with an initial instead of a first name and could not be identified as either male or female. In 1860, 123 of the city's 371 black taxpayers were female real estate owners, versus 186 black men, but 156 (42%) of all the black taxpayers that year were women. That year 29 persons were identified by initials instead of first names. See *1859 Tax List*, at CCPL; and *1860 Tax List*, at RSS.

39. Schweninger, *Black Property Owners*, 23–24; Johnson and Roark, *Black Masters*.

40. Johnson and Roark, "Strategies of Survival," 94–95; Curry, *Free Black in Urban America*, 45; "Free Negro Owners of Slaves," 70–74.

41. Phillips, *Freedom's Port*, 93–96.

42. W. Johnson, *Black Savannah*, 79–80; W. Johnson, "Free Blacks in Antebellum Savannah," 427. Johnson posits that free black women outnumbered free black men as slaveowners because they outlived black men and thus inherited real estate and slaves from their deceased husbands. W. Johnson, "Free African-American Women," 244.

43. W. Johnson, *Black Savannah*, 83; Blassingame, "Negro in Antebellum New Orleans," 96; Gehman, *Free People of Color of New Orleans*, 32–33.

44. W. Johnson, *Black Savannah*, 80.

45. Ibid., 79–81; W. Johnson, "Free Blacks in Antebellum Savannah," 427–28.

46. W. Johnson, *Black Savannah*, 81: W. Johnson, "Free Blacks in Antebellum Savannah," 428.

47. I could not estimate if the antebellum decline in black slaveowning paralleled a decline in black real estate holdings. While there is information on slaveholding in Charleston from the 1830 Census, in addition to data from the 1859 *Tax List*, the numbers on real estate ownership come from the 1859 *Tax List* and the 1860 *Tax List*, as well as tax returns from 1860. See works cited in n. 40; 1859 *Tax List*, at CCPL; 1860 *Tax List*, at RSS; 1860 Tax Returns, at SCDAH; and Curry, *Free Black in Urban America*, 47. Why free black slaveholding declined in Charleston is unclear. It may have been because many free blacks left Charleston in the 1850s and moved north to escape the increasing hostility of the city's white working class. It could have also resulted from the passage of new anti-black legislation that decade or the city's reenslavement crisis. Johnson and Roark, *No Chariot*, introduction; Johnson and Roark, *Black Masters*, 186–87, 237–38, 274–75.

48. On free black slaveownership, see Koger, *Black Slaveowners*. See also Berlin, *Slaves without Masters*, 271–76; Johnson and Roark, "Strategies of Survival," 94–102; Curry, *Free Black in Urban America*, 45–47; Frazier, *Black Bourgeoisie*, 31–32; Halliburton, "Free Black Owners of Slaves"; Johnson and Roark, *Black Masters*; Johnson and Roark, *No Chariot*; Pease and Pease, *Ladies, Women, and Wenches*, 102–3, 113–14; Powers, *Black Charlestonians*, 48–50; Schweninger, *Black Property Owners*, 23–24, 104–5; and Wikramanayake, *World in Shadow*, 73–75. See chaps. 1 and 3 for more on the demographics of the city's free black population.

49. I found no slaves assessed at over $1,000 in the city's estate inventories. The vast majority were valued at around $400. See CCIA, at SCDAH. See works cited in nn. 12 and 20 for housing prices. See also Nelly Wilson, CCIA, vol. D (1789–10): 191; Barsheba Cattle, CCIA, vol. F (1813–24): 81–82; Delia Wyatt, CCIA, vol. E (1802–19): 150, at SCDAH.

50. On trusts, see chap. 2. Ann Scott, WBCC 36 (1818–26): 947; Tenah Glen, WBCC 38 (1826–34): 736, at SCDAH. Scott and Glen's inability to free their relations was due to the Act of 1820. See chap. 2.

51. W. Johnson, *Black Savannah*, 79. In 1830, less than 4% of Baltimore's free black households contained enslaved persons, most of whom were kin to the free blacks with whom they lived. Phillips, *Freedom's Port*, 93–96.

52. See works cited in n. 42. On the outlawing of owner manumission in Georgia, see chap. 2.

53. Powers, *Black Charlestonians*, 49–50; Johnson and Roark, *No Chariot*, 6–7. For Sally Johnson, see Robert Stockton, "Free Black Bought Old House," in BFP, at RSS. For Barquet, see Koger, *Black Slaveowners*, 94–95, and chap. 6. This suggests that Whittington Johnson's argument does not hold up when the slaveowners in question are black women as opposed to black men. Based on the wills of three well-to-do, free black men, Johnson posits that in Charleston, unlike Savannah, enslaved persons owned by free blacks were used as personal servants, and that this resulted from socioeconomic differences between the two communities. The free black community in Charleston was older, wealthier, and more aristocratic than the one in Savannah, he states, and had been more successful in narrowing the gap in the standard of living between themselves and their white neighbors than had their peers in Savannah. My data suggests that Charleston's free black women were not only poorer than their male counterparts but also more likely to head their households alone. As such, they worked outside the home and utilized their

enslaved laborers to expand their own small businesses, rented them out to supplement their monthly incomes, or both. W. Johnson, *Black Savannah*, 206 (n. 112).

54. Esther McIntosh, WBCC 34 (1818–26): 411; Charlotte Boon, WBCC 41 (1834–39): 516, at SCDAH.

55. Petition: Mary Douglas, GAP 003 1837 00013, at SCDAH; Pease and Pease, *Ladies, Women, and Wenches*, 114.

56. Juliet Eggart, WBCC 40 (1834–39): 138; Jubah Warren, WBCC 45 (1845–51): 501; Jubah Warren, CCIA, vol. B (1844–50): 492, at SCDAH.

57. Ira Berlin states that the more free blacks acted like wealthy whites, the better their chances of acceptance in the Old South, and the higher their standard of living. Thus some free blacks defended slavery to secure their own positions while others, realizing that economic success in the South depended on owning human laborers, bought and sold black people for profit and used them to expand their commercial endeavors. Berlin, *Slaves without Masters*, 271–76. Michael Johnson and James Roark concur. Wealth was a powerful tool that free blacks could use to gain the respect of whites, and Johnson and Roark argue that southern blacks understood that nothing would inspire more admiration from their white neighbors than slaveownership. No other investment promised as many returns for free blacks, socially or economically. Johnson and Roark, "Strategies of Survival."

58. Marriage of Sarah and George, 31 Oct. 1855, in Trapier, *Private Register*, at CCPL. Grase wanted her servants (a woman and her child, assessed at $300) sold in order to buy her son, John, out of bondage. Grase Snipes, WBCC 32 (1807–18): 628; Grase Snipes, CCIA, vol. E (1802–19): 127, at SCDAH.

59. Molly Neyle, WBCC 39 (1826–34): 912; Charlotte Kershaw, WBCC 37 (1826–34): 196, at SCDAH.

60. Free blacks owned a miniscule portion of Charleston's real estate, and few free people of color became rich. If you include those who owned either $2,000 in real estate or at least one enslaved laborer, then one-sixth of Charleston's 3,000 free blacks were wealthy. These 500 persons possessed all the black-held enslaved workers in the city and three-quarters of the city's black-owned real estate. Pease and Pease, *Ladies, Women, and Wenches*, 105; Curry, *Free Black in Urban America*, 43; Johnson and Roark, *Black Masters*, 204–7; Johnson and Roark, *No Chariot*, 6–7.

61. Johnson and Roark, *No Chariot*, 6; Curry, *Free Black in Urban America*, 48; Lebsock, *Free Women of Petersburg*, 103–4; Schweninger, *Black Property Owners*, 86; Wikramanayake, *World in Shadow*, 50, 56.

62. Schweninger, *Black Property Owners*, 86; Lebsock, *Free Women of Petersburg*, 103–4.

63. These are women for whom I have found probate records or who are mentioned as legatees in the probate records of others. See n. 18 and LGA and LTA, at SCDAH.

64. See n. 58.

65. Berlin, *Slaves without Masters*, 247; Lebsock, "Free Black Women," 279–80; Schweninger, *Black Property Owners*, 86.

66. Schweninger, *Black Property Owners*, 102; Richard Holloway, WBCC 43 (1839–45): 891; Richard Holloway, CCIA, vol. B (1844–50): 141, at SCDAH. See entries for Elizabeth Holloway in 1859 *Tax List*, 392, at CCPL; 1860 *Tax List*, 323, at RSS; 1860 *Tax Returns*, at SCDAH; and 1861 *Tax Book*, at SCHS.

67. See entries for William Pinceel in WBCC 36 (1818–26): 1123 and in CCIA, vol. G (1824–34): 74, at SCDAH. For black male occupations, see chap. 3.

68. See entries for Maria Weston in *1859 Tax List*, 403, at CCPL; *1860 Tax List*, 332, at RSS; *1860 Tax Returns*, at SCDAH; and *1861 Tax Book*, at SCHS. "Sarah Weston: Seamstress," in Hagy, *Charleston City Directories, 1816–29*, 67; "Elizabeth Weston: Mantua Maker, Sarah Weston: Mantua Maker, and Sarah Weston: Seamstress," in ibid., 103; "Lydia Weston: Seamstress," in Hagy, *Directories for Charleston, 1849–55*, 173; Curry, *Free Black in Urban America*, 42; Johnson and Roark, *Black Masters*, 203.

69. Moses Wells, WBCC 34 (1818–26): 139; Moses Wells, CCIA, vol. F (1813–24): 61–62, at SCDAH. Many black legatees were defrauded of their inheritances by corrupt executors. See works cited in nn. 105–7.

70. Emily Benedict, WBCC 42 (1839–45): 716, at SCDAH.

71. Marie Gouvignon, WBCC 36 (1818–26): 1228; Madame Gouvignon, CCIA, vol. G (1824–34): 104–5, at SCDAH.

72. See Fitchett, "Origin and Growth," "Status of the Free Negro," "Traditions of the Free Negro," and "Free Negro in Charleston."

73. See Hanger, *Bounded Lives*, "Desiring Total Tranquility," "Landlords," and "Protecting Property."

74. See Bell, *Revolution*, 81; and chap. 2.

75. Gehman, *Free People of Color of New Orleans*, 38–39.

76. Ibid., 71, 73.

77. See entries for Christopher Smith in WBCC 32 (1807–18): 796 and in CCIA, vol. E (1802–19): 213, at SCDAH.

78. See entries for Martin Damascke in WBCC 41 (1834–39): 506 and in CCIA, vol. H (1834–44): 215, at SCDAH. See also entries for Jacob Wulff in WBCC 40 (1834–39): 367 and in CCIA, vol. H (1834–44): 162, at SCDAH.

79. Onerine Pillot, WBCC 37 (1826–34): 40; Onerine Pillot, CCIA, vol. G (1824–34): 138; Catherine Pelot, LTA, vol. F (1856–60): 278, at SCDAH.

80. Isaac Lewis, WBCC 46 (1851–56): 12; Isaac Lewis, CCIA, vol. C (1850–54): 207, at SCDAH; Pease and Pease, *Ladies, Women, and Wenches*, 107.

81. Curry, *Free Black in Urban America*, 42; William Wightman, WBCC 40 (1834–39): 262–65, at SCDAH. See entries for Jane Wightman in WBCC 46 (1851–56): 258–60, at SCDAH; *1859 Tax List*, 404, at CCPL; *1860 Tax List*, 333, at RSS; and *1861 Tax Book*, at SCHS.

82. See works cited in n. 68.

83. See n. 60. In 1859, 95 of 134 black female taxpayers (71%) owned $1,000–$9,999 in real property. In 1860, 91 of 123 (74%) fell into this category, while in 1861 the percentage was 78% (95 out of 122). See *1859 Tax List*, at CCPL; *1860 Tax List*, at RSS; and *1861 Tax Book*, at SCHS.

84. See entries for John Walker in WBCC 42 (1839–45): 62 and in CCIA, vol. A (1839–44): 40, at SCDAH. See also entries for Ann J. Walker in *1856 CCD*, at CCPL; *1859 Tax List*, 402, at CCPL; *1860 Tax List*, 332, at RSS; and *1861 Tax Book*, at SCHS. See chap. 2 for more on Ann and John's story.

85. See chaps. 5 and 6 for expanded discussions of this issue.

86. See works cited in n. 81.

87. John Bonthron, WBCC 33 (1807–18): 1258; Adam Tunno, WBCC 39 (1826–34): 1242, at SCDAH. See chap. 6 for the complete story of Margaret, Adam, and Barbara.

88. See J. Morgan, *Laboring Women*; and Kennedy, *Braided Relations*, 115–16.

89. I employ the term "wealthy" for those who had property worth over $10,000 and use "affluent" or "prosperous" for those whose estates ranged from $1,000 to $9,999. Over half of these affluent women owned only $1,000–$2,000 in real property. See Table 4.3. Since only real property was assessed, not personal property, it is difficult to draw definitive conclusions about a person's or group's total wealth. The tax lists record only those persons with horses, real estate, and enslaved laborers, and while they note how many bondspersons were owned, they do not list the value of these persons. Still, using the tax lists as a guide, we can draw preliminary conclusions about black female property ownership.

90. See entries for Jennett Bonneau in 1859 *Tax List*, 384, at CCPL; 1860 *Tax List*, 316, at RSS; 1860 *Tax Returns*, at SCDAH; and 1861 *Tax Book*, at SCHS. See entries for Susan Ann Dereef in WBCC 40 (1834–39): 62 and in CCIA, vol. H (1834–44): 46, at SCDAH. For more on the Bonneau and Dereef families, see Johnson and Roark, *Black Masters*; and Johnson and Roark, *No Chariot*. On the BFS, see chap. 2.

91. Gehman, *Free People of Color of New Orleans*, 38–39.

92. Anywhere from 21% to 28% of the city's black female property owners had estates worth under $1,000. See Table 4.3. "Dianah Tresvant" (also Trazvant or Trezevant), in Hagy, *Charleston City Directories, 1816–29*, 65; Hagy, *Directories for Charleston, 1830–41*, 28, 129. See also entries for Dianah Tresvant in TAB, 21, at SCDAH; 1859 *Tax List*, 402, at CCPL; 1860 *Tax List*, 331, at RSS; 1860 *Tax Returns*, at SCDAH; and 1861 *Tax Book*, at SCHS.

93. See 1861 *Tax Book*, at SCHS.

94. See entries for Emma Peronneau in 1856 CCD, at CCPL; 1859 CCD, at CLS; 1859 *Tax List*, 399, at CCPL; 1860 *Tax List*, 329, at RSS; 1860 *Tax Returns*, at SCDAH; and 1861 *Tax Book*, at SCHS. See entries for Catherine Pritchard in 1859 *Tax List*, 399, at CCPL; 1860 *Tax List*, 329, at RSS; 1860 *Tax Returns*, at SCDAH; and 1861 *Tax Book*, at SCHS.

95. Peter Parler, formerly Peter Teasdel, WBCC 39 (1826–2834): 1137; Peter Parlour, CCIA, vol. G (1824–34): 568, at SCDAH.

96. Phillips, *Freedom's Port*, 154.

97. Johnson and Roark, *Black Masters*, 205; Johnson and Roark, *No Chariot*, 6–7.

98. W. Johnson, "Free Blacks in Antebellum Savannah," 428.

99. Schweninger, *Black Property Owners*, 86.

100. In 1859, the average wealth for the city's propertied free black women, once Maria Weston's data was removed, was $1,404. 1859 *Tax List*, at CCPL. In 1860, after removing Maria Weston, the average was $1,462. 1860 *Tax List*, at RSS. In terms of the cause of the differential in Charleston, it appears that the data from states like Louisiana, where the wealthiest free blacks lived, was high enough to distort the overall average of the Lower South. Schweninger, *Black Property Owners*, appendix 5, 281–94. See also Blackburn and Ricards, "Mother-Headed Family," 24–25; and Lebsock, *Free Women of Petersburg*, 111. See chaps. 1 and 3 for demographics of Charleston's black population, and chap. 2 for information on black women's occupational opportunities.

101. Quoted phrase from White, *Too Heavy a Load*, 212.

102. Basch, *In the Eyes of the Law*; Chused, "Married Women's Property Law"; Jensen, "Equity Jurisdiction"; Salmon, "Women and Property in South Carolina." See chap. 6 for a detailed discussion of trust estates.

103. See chap. 3.

104. Pease and Pease, *Ladies, Women, and Wenches*, 100; Schweninger, *Black Property Owners*, 84–85.

105. Schweninger, "Fragile Nature of Freedom," 114.

106. Petitions: Eliza Brown, GAP 003 1838 00083 and 003 1838 00084; Judiciary Committee Report: Eliza Brown, GAP 004 1838 00195, at SCDAH. Sibby Gordon's entire estate consisted of "a colored girl named Susan," who was assessed at $500. Sibby Gordon, CCIA, vol. H (1834–44): 130, at SCDAH. Thomas W. Malone was likely T. W. Malone, listed in the 1835–36 directory as an attorney. See Hagy, *Directories for Charleston, 1830–41*, 50.

107. "O. L. Dobson," in Hagy, *Directories for Charleston, 1830–41*, 39.

108. Kennedy, *Braided Relations*, 180–81.

109. See nn. 1 and 2 for Eliza Seymour Lee.

110. Petitions: Myra Reid, GAP 003 1844 00139 and 003 1844 00033; Judiciary Committee Report: Myra Reid, GAP 004 1844 00213, at SCDAH. Sarah Ferris refers to her husband, Ben Reid, as a "free man of color," so it is possible that he was a virtually free man. Sarah Ferris or Reid, WBCC 40 (1834–39): 18, at SCDAH.

111. See chap. 6 for a detailed discussion of Barbara's life and the lawsuit.

112. Legal decisions were published only if they were sent up to the South Carolina Court of Appeals. An examination of Westlaw, American Century Digests, and South Carolina Reports turned up no material regarding a verdict on this matter, which suggests the case was resolved at the district court level. See Petition Analysis: Theressa Taylor, RSPP Series 2: County Court Petitions, Charleston Parish/District, 21383320, at UNCG.

113. Peter Simpson's widow is the same Hagar Simpson who signed a marriage contract setting aside her premarital property into a separate trust estate before saying "I do" to her next husband, William Johnson. See works cited in n. 104. See also Peter Simpson, WBCC 36 (1818–26): 1157–60, at SCDAH.

114. *Pro confesso*, i.e., it was as if the defendant had confessed. Petition Analyses: Elsey Pyatt, RSPP 21384542 and 21384546, at UNCG. What is interesting is that another, unrelated, petition suggests that Hagar may not have turned the property over to Elsey: despite the judgment against her, and the fact that she held no legal title to the property, Hagar continued to live in the house in question until her death in the 1850s. Petition Analysis: Hagar Simpson Johnson, RSPP 21385752, at UNCG.

115. J. Schafer, *Becoming Free*, 64.

116. Margaret Bettingall, WBCC 42 (1839–45): 67–69, at SCDAH. For more on the attitudes of southern blacks and whites toward the ownership of real estate, see Koger, *Black Slaveowners*; Schweninger, *Black Property Owners*; and Wikramanayake, *World in Shadow*. See also chap. 6.

117. See chap. 3.

Chapter 5

1. Much of the information in this chapter comes from the SCSVP, held at the LCP. The collection encompasses three large boxes with multiple folders in each box. Documents from the collection are referenced as SCSVP, Box#/Folder#/Document#. The papers date from the 1750s to the present, but I focus on the collection's early national and antebellum materials.

2. Richard's date of birth, SCSVP, B1/F1/D1; George's date of death, SCSVP, B1/F5/D12; George and Mary Ann's marriage, SCSVP, B1/F1/D5a, at LCP; "Mary Ann Cogdell," in Hagy, *People and Professions*, 62, 76, 95; Hagy, *Charleston City Directories, 1816–29*, 5, 75, 110.

3. Mary Ann's sketches in SCSVP, at LCP. "John S. Cogdell," in Hagy, *Charleston City Directories, 1816–29*, 5, 75, 110; Hagy, *Directories for Charleston, 1830–41*, 6, 36, 76, 101; Rutledge, *Artists*; Severens, *Selections*, 79; Uncle Harry (Jervis Henry Stevens) in SCSVP, B1/F5/D12, at LCP; Flynn, *Militia*, 80–81; Hagy, *People and Professions*, 20, 32, 46, 70, 86, 109; Hagy, *Charleston City Directories, 1816–29*, 26, 100, 131; Williams, "Eighteenth-Century Organists."

4. "Richard Cogdell," in Hagy, *City Directories, 1803–13*, 99, 143; "Marriage and Death Notices," 336; Pease and Pease, *Ladies, Women, and Wenches*, 11. John was 29 years old when he married in 1806. SCSVP, B1/F1/D27, at LCP.

5. Pease and Pease, *Ladies, Women, and Wenches*, chap. 7. James Walpole, n.d., SCSVP, B1/F1/D1; Richard Clement, 30 Aug. 1812, SCSVP, B1/F1/D10; George Burgess, 24 Oct. 1817, SCSVP, B1/F1/D11; John Walpole, 7 Oct. 1820, SCSVP, B1/F1/D12; Charles Stevens, 15 Aug. 1822, Maria Langlois to Daniel Horlbeck, 1860, SCSVP, B1/F5/D7, at LCP.

6. "Maria Langlois," in Holcomb, *South Carolina Naturalizations*, 20; Hagy, *Charleston City Directories, 1816–29*, 15, 49, 86, 120, 149; Hagy, *Directories for Charleston, 1830–41*, 16, 48, 113. Maria is listed in the white section of the directories. Maria was Cecille's sister, mentioned in Daniel Horlbeck to Richard W. Cogdell, 29 Oct. 1860, SCSVP, B1/F5/D11, at LCP.

7. For more on Saint-Domingue, see chap. 2. See also Berlin, *Slaves without Masters*, 35–36, 58; Johnson and Roark, *Black Masters*, 33; Powers, *Black Charlestonians*, 28; and Wikramanayake, *World in Shadow*, 18, 159.

8. White female Charlestonians from the middle and upper classes married when they were in their late teens or early twenties. Pease and Pease, *Ladies, Women and Wenches*, 10–12, 15–17.

9. Koger, *Black Slaveowners*, 98; "Free Negro Owners of Slaves," 72; Woodson, *Free Negro Heads of Families*, 156; SFNCTB, 1811–60, vol. 11-1 (1826–27), at SCDAH; Rules and Regulations, BFSP, 27, at ARC. See chap. 2 for more on the Langlois family.

10. Register of Baptisms for St. Philip's Episcopal Church, Charleston (1813): 15, in SCSVP, B1/F1/D10, at LCP.

11. See Mary, child of Maria Edwards (adopted) 12 July 1857; Lavinia, child of Eliza Stephens (adopted) 9 March 1860; and Mary Ann, child of Ann Mathewes (adopted) March 1861, all in ZPCR, 1854–70, at ARC.

12. For example, "Baptism of John Pincel and Joseph, the children of John P. and Mary Barquet, free people of color, 18 June 1813," PRSPEC, at SCDAH. See also introduction.

13. On these limitations, see introduction.

14. Richard Walpole had a brother named Clement Burgess and a maternal uncle named Clement Crookblake. Family Tree, SCSVP, B1/F1/D1, at LCP. On sexual relationships in the Old South between white women and black men, see Hodes, *White Women, Black Men*; and Jordan, *White Man's Burden*. Baptismal Certificates of George Burgess Cogdell and John Walpole Cogdell, SCSVP, B1/F1/D11 and D12, at LCP.

15. Richard Cogdell Travel Letter, 27 April 1802, SCSVP, B2/F2/D5, at LCP.

16. Richard Cogdell Commission Papers, SCSVP, B2/F2/D4, at LCP. That Richard was a city warden is mentioned in Killens, *Trial Record of Denmark Vesey*, 140–46. Richard's obituary notes he was a city councilman. SCSVP, B2/F11/D21h, at LCP. Document certifying Richard as a notary public in SCSVP, B2/F2/D6, at LCP.

17. Jordan, *White Man's Burden*, chaps. 1–4; S. King, *Blue Coat or Powdered Wig*.

18. For more on this migration, see chap. 2. See also A. Alexander, *Ambiguous Lives*, 32, 40; Berlin, *Slaves without Masters*, 35–36; Kein, *Creole*; Lebsock, *Free Women of Petersburg*, 91–92; Johnson and Roark, *Black Masters*, 33; Powers, *Black Charlestonians*, 28; and Wikramanayake, *World in Shadow*, 18, 159.

19. See works cited in n. 9.

20. A quadroon was one-quarter black, the child of one white parent and one biracial parent, an octoroon one-eighth black, with one white parent and one quadroon parent. Berlin, *Slaves without Masters*, 365–66; Kein, *Creole*, 57, 103.

21. James Walpole was born before Richard Clement and his baptismal records contain no notations as to color, indicating he was classified as white. See works cited in n. 5. The Cogdells remained married until Cecille's death late in 1831. Richard purchased a coffin for her on 2 Jan. 1832. Receipt Book 2, SCSVP, B2/F2/D9, at LCP. Richard and Cecille had three more sons together, two of whom were baptized at St. Philip's. Neither of these boys (nor their parents) was listed in the baptismal registers as being a person of color. See n. 14.

22. Receipts for the rental and purchase of various slaves, Receipt Books 1, 2, and 3, SCSVP, B2/F2/D8, D9, and D10, at LCP. The Cogdells purchased their first enslaved laborer, John, on 27 Aug. 1817, SCSVP, B2/F2/D8, at LCP.

23. Social engagements, SCSVP, B2/F1, B2/F6, and B3/F4/D9, at LCP. For Richard's political offices, see works cited in n. 16. Receipts for pew rental and school tuition, Receipt Book 1, SCSVP, B2/F2/D8, at LCP. On the limitations of free persons of color, see introduction.

24. Entries in the receipt books record the purchase of claret, port, madeira, ale, cigars, imported furniture, dinnerware, and calfskin-bound books. SCSVP, B2/F2/D8, D9, and D10, at LCP.

25. See documents cited in n. 22.

26. Bill of Sale: Sarah Martha Sanders, MRSS 5K (7 Aug. 1830): 285, at SCDAH; Sarah's date of birth, Family Bible, SCSVP, B1/F1/D14; Receipt Books, SCSVP, B2/F2/D8, D9, and D10, at LCP.

27. "Cecille Cogdell" and "Richard Cogdell," in Hagy, *Directories for Charleston, 1830–41*, 6. On antebellum marriages and separation, see Pease and Pease, *Ladies, Women, and Wenches*. Date of conception for Robert Sanders extrapolated from his date of birth, SCSVP, B1/F1/D14, at LCP.

28. SCSVP, B1/F6/D23, at LCP. By comparing this letter to others in the collection, it

is possible to concretely identify the handwriting as that of Richard W. Cogdell. The contents of the letter are such that it is logical to conclude it was written to Cecille Langlois Cogdell after she left her husband in 1831.

29. On *couverture*, see chap. 3 and Pease and Pease, *Ladies, Women, and Wenches*, 52–53.

30. See Chesnut, *Diary from Dixie*.

31. See n. 21.

32. For George's job and gambling habit, see Receipt Books 2 and 3, SCSVP, B2/F2/D9 and D10; and John S. Cogdell to Richard W. Cogdell, 1840, SCSVP, B1/F6/D16, at LCP. For the duel, see SCSVP, B1/F4/D18, B1/F4/19a and 19b, B2/F1/D22, and B1/F4/D10, at LCP. John's profession in Hagy, *Directories for Charleston*, 1849–55, 9. Charles's job in SCSVP, B2/F1/D21, at LCP. For Richard Clement's position in the Navy, see Richard W. Cogdell to Sarah Sanders, 20 Dec. 1844, SCSVP, B1/F4/D15, at LCP.

33. James's date of death extrapolated from data in Receipt Books 2 and 3, SCSVP, B2/F2/D9 and D10; Robert Sanders's date of birth, SCSVP, B1/F1/D14, at LCP.

34. Upon being accused of fathering a biracial child, John wrote to a former friend, "Know, Sir, that I am the lawful husband of a woman I love; that the small education I have received and the religion I profess has ever taught me to live above so gross, so mean an act as that of placing a negro slave on a footing with a virtuous woman. I hold such an act in so horrid a light that I would not (not even to be the master of ten provinces) wear such a crime about me." John Stevens to Clement Martin, 14 June 1770, SCSVP, B1/F2/D2, at LCP.

35. John Stevens stated he believed his son had fathered the "mulatto boy, (Dick)." Ibid.

36. Mary Ann Elizabeth Stevens Cogdell-Common Place Book, 1805, SCSVP, B1/F3/D3, at LCP.

37. SCSVP, B2/F2/D1; Receipt Book 2, SCSVP, B2/D2/F9, at LCP; Jordan, *White Man's Burden*, 75–79.

38. For more on the nature of such relationships, see, for example, Leslie, *Woman of Color*.

39. See, for example, A. Alexander, *Ambiguous Lives*; and D. Schafer, *Anna Madgigine Jai Kingsley*.

40. On the Act of 1820, see chap. 2. John S. Cogdell was an attorney, a state legislator, comptroller of the state, and president of the State Bank, in addition to being the first secretary of the South Carolina Association. January, "South Carolina Association."

41. See chap. 2.

42. Receipt Book 2, SCSVP, B2/F2/D9, at LCP.

43. Dishes referenced in ibid. "Miss Sarah will have received 29 lessons since our last settlement." A note at the bottom says, "Paid Mr. Garcia on the 25th." James R. Garcia to Richard W. Cogdell, ibid., B2/F1/D1. City directories list James R. Garcia as a "Professor of Music" or "Music Teacher," 1835–41. Hagy, *Directories for Charleston*, 1830–41, 41, 80, 106. Abraham Tobias was listed as a "Vendue Master" and "Auctioneer" throughout the 1830s. Ibid., 27, 62, 70, 92, 129.

44. On black educational restrictions, see chap. 3.

45. In his will, Richard mentions that he educated his children. SCSVP, B1/F4/D23, at LCP. Letters written by the children indicate a high level of schooling, and Sarah's

daughters Julia and Cordelia were teachers. SCSVP, B2/F6/D17 and D18, at LCP. For the education law, see Johnson and Roark, *Black Masters*, 224; Johnson and Roark, "Middle Ground," 261; and Wikramanayake, *World in Shadow*, 168. Richard's cousin, Mary Ann Jane, was married to Lionel H. Kennedy, a prominent attorney and one of the magistrates in the Denmark Vesey trials. SCSVP, B1/F1/D1 and D9, at LCP. See also Hagy, *Charleston City Directories, 1816–29*, 14, 48, 85, 119, 149; Hagy, *Directories for Charleston, 1830–41*, 15, 47; Koger, *Black Slaveowners*, 182; Robertson, *Denmark Vesey*, 98, 110–12; and Wikramanayake, *World in Shadow*, 135.

46. Powers, *Black Charlestonians*, 52–54; chap. 3.

47. See documents cited in n. 33. For more on George, see SCSVP, B1/F6/D16, at LCP. John committed suicide by throwing himself out his apartment window in what was termed "a fit of temporary insanity." Obituary Notice, SCSVP, B2/F11/D21e, at LCP. Both Charles and George supposedly died from mania or dementia. Maria Langlois to Daniel Horlbeck, 1860, SCSVP, B1/F5/D7, at LCP. All of Richard's sons by Cecille died before he did. SCSVP, B2/F4/D4, at LCP.

48. For the children's ages, see SCSVP, B1/F1/D2, at LCP. For information on the inheritance, see SCSVP, B1/F6/D16, D18, D19, and B1/F4/D17, at LCP. A letter from the bank dated 11 April 1844 commemorates Richard's long and faithful service and indicates that he was leaving the bank's employ. SCSVP, B2/F2/D3, at LCP. Concert Program, 24 June 1844, SCSVP, B1/F6/D6; Parisian Bank Statement, Aug. 1844, SCSVP, B1/F6/D4, at LCP.

49. "Call upon Mr. Whitney for anything you may want and I will write to him to pay the same." Richard W. Cogdell to Sarah Sanders, 20 Dec. 1844, SCSVP, B1/F4/D15, at LCP. It is unclear exactly who Mr. Whitney was.

50. Invitation to Tuileries, SCSVP, B1/F5/D8; Invitation/Ticket to the Opera, SCSVP, B1/F4/D6, at LCP.

51. Richard Cogdell to Sarah Sanders, 20 Dec. 1844, SCSVP, B1/F4/D15, at LCP.

52. Letter of Alfred Huger to his nephew in M. Johnson, "Planters and Patriarchy," 49. Alfred was a close friend of Richard W. Cogdell.

53. Receipt for French Perfume, SCSVP, B1/F6/D3; Sophia Elizabeth's birth, SCSVP, B1/F1/D2, D14, at LCP.

54. John's date of death, SCSVP, B1/F1/D27; Will of John Cogdell, SCSVP, B1/F6/D2 and B2/F4/D1, at LCP.

55. See n. 34. See also Will of Mary Ann Cogdell, SCSVP, B2/F3/D6 and B2/F5/D1; Notarized Document of Richard W. Cogdell, Philadelphia, 8 May 1858, SCSVP, B2/F6/D16, at LCP.

56. On Richard's breathing problems, SCSVP, B1/F4/D14, D17, D20, and B2/F1/D7, at LCP. For information on trust agreements, written and verbal, see chap. 2. There are many letters in the collection to and from Alfred Huger.

57. On the Act of 1841, see chap. 2.

58. On natural children, see chap. 2.

59. Miranda's date of birth, SCSVP, B1/F1/D2, at LCP. The events of the 1840s and 1850s are referenced in all U.S. history survey texts.

60. Florence's date of birth, SCSVP, B1/F1/D2; Sarah's date of death, SCSVP, B1/F1/D15, at LCP.

61. Purchase of Cemetery Plot for Sarah Martha Sanders, SCSVP, B1/F1/D24; Epitaph,

SCSVP, B3/F1/D15; Florence's date of death, SCSVP, B1/F1/D15, at LCP. The epitaph on Sarah's headstone notes that the stone next to Sarah's is for her daughter and is marked "Florence."

62. Richard Clement was alive in 1846 and was mentioned in his uncle John's will. See n. 58. Only his youngest son by Cecille, Charles, is mentioned in Richard's will, implying that the other sons died before their father did. The earliest copy of Richard's will is dated 24 Sept. 1856. SCSVP, B2/F4/D2, at LCP. For John W. Cogdell's suicide, see n. 47. George's aunt discussed his afflictions in a letter. Maria Langlois to Daniel Horlbeck, 1860, SCSVP, B1/F5/D7, at LCP. For more on John W. and George B. Cogdell, see Hagy, *Directories for Charleston, 1849–55*, 9, 59.

63. Charles S. Cogdell to Richard W. Cogdell, SCSVP, B2/F1/D21, at LCP.

64. Will of Richard W. Cogdell, 1856, SCSVP, B2/F4/D2, at LCP.

65. Charles S. Cogdell to Richard W. Cogdell, SCSVP, B1/F4/D22, at LCP.

66. For more on this conflict, see chap. 3. See also Johnson and Roark, *Black Masters*, chap. 5; Johnson and Roark, *No Chariot Let Down*, introduction; and Powers, *Black Charlestonians*, 62–65.

67. For Robert's date of birth, see documents cited in n. 33. Cordelia taught school in Brooklyn and Julia in Philadelphia. SCSVP, B2/F6/D17, D18, and B3/F1/D5, at LCP. Robert and Martha were married 18 April 1857. SCSVP, B1/F1/D4 and D17, at LCP. The family was in Philadelphia by April 1858. John Irving to Richard Cogdell, 30 April 1858, SCSVP, B2/F1/D3, at LCP.

68. Johnson and Roark, *No Chariot*, 14; Johnson and Roark, *Black Masters*, 274–75. There are many letters from old friends in Charleston that date from after Richard and his children moved to Philadelphia, many of which attest to how homesick the family was. SCSVP, Box 2, at LCP.

69. Maria Langlois to Daniel Horlbeck, SCSVP, B1/F5/D7, at LCP.

70. See documents cited in nn. 54 and 55. Richard Cogdell to Sarah Ann Sanders, SCSVP, B2/F6/D16, at LCP.

71. Will of Richard W. Cogdell, Aug. 1860, SCSVP, B1/F4/D23, at LCP.

72. Will of Richard W. Cogdell, Oct. 1860, SCSVP, B1/F6/D1, at LCP.

73. Marriage Certificate of Edward and Julia, SCSVP, B1/F1/D4; Letter of Reference for Edward W. Venning, Charleston, 20 April 1830, SCSVP, B2/F9/D8, at LCP. Box 2, Folder 9 contains material on the Venning family during the antebellum era and beyond, including business cards from the carpentry firm and data on the family's social status.

74. Miranda Cogdell Venning, born 8 June 1862, christened 27 July 1862, St. Thomas Church, Philadelphia, SCSVP, B1/F1/D16 and B1/F11/D2; Will of Richard W. Cogdell, 1863, SCSVP, B2/F4/D4, at LCP.

75. Richard Cogdell to David C. Levy of Charleston, SCSVP, B2/F1/D9 and D18; Richard Cogdell to Major James Ferguson, SCSVP, B1/F4/D20; Daniel Horlbeck to Richard Cogdell, SCSVP, B2/F6/D9; Richard Cogdell to Daniel Horlbeck, SCSVP, B2/F1/D11, at LCP.

76. Sophie's date of death, SCSVP, B1/F1/D15 and B2/F11/D21b; Birth of Sophia Sanders Venning, SCSVP, B1/F1/D2; 1865 Codicils to the 1863 Will of Richard W. Cogdell, SCSVP, B2/F4/D4, at LCP.

77. John Irving to Richard W. Cogdell, SCSVP, B2/F1/D13; sale of railroad bonds,

23 Oct. 1865, SCSVP, B2/F1/D16; Delia Sanders to Richard W. Cogdell, 10 Feb. 1866, SCSVP, B2/F6/D17, at LCP.

78. Richard's death of "apoplexy," SCSVP, B1/F1/D3 and D15, at LCP. "Apoplexy" was the term used for a stroke. Daniel Horlbeck's telegraph, SCSVP, B2/F1/D19, at LCP. Richard asked to be buried next to his mother. SCSVP, B2/F4/D4, at LCP.

79. Daniel Horlbeck to Sarah Ann Sanders, SCSVP, B2/F3/D1, at LCP.

80. That Sarah's children remained in Philadelphia is evidenced by the late nineteenth and twentieth-century materials in the SCSVP, at LCP. Letters, church and work records, educational materials, diary entries, and a wide range of ephemera all record the continued story of Sarah and Richard's descendants down to the present day.

81. Marriage of Cordelia Sanders to William Chew, SCSVP, B1/F1/D4, D17, D19; Richard Sanders Chew, SCSVP, B1/F1/D16, at LCP.

Chapter 6

1. For a detailed examination of the lawsuit, see Crane, "Two Women." On marriage contracts, see chap. 4.

2. Much of the information in this chapter comes from the TFP, seven folders of documents within the Langdon Cheves Legal Collection, held at the SCHS. Documents from the collection are referenced as TFP, Folder#. See *Elizabeth M. Hamilton per pro ami Henry D. Cruger v. General James Hamilton et al.* (Hamilton v. Hamilton), in Charleston Court of Equity Records Bill 105 (1843), at SCDAH; William Harper's Report, in Court of Equity Reports, 1839–45, vol. 40 (3 March 1842), at SCDAH. Harper was ordered to discover the amount, nature, and order of precedence of all liens against the estate. The report listed $155,000 in debts, almost $50,000 of which was mortgages on Rice Hope Plantation and $30,000 in mortgages on Pennyworth Plantation. Barbara held the third mortgage on Rice Hope.

3. Depositions: Thomas N. Holmes and Theodore E. Mitchell, TFP, F3; Deposition: Liston W. Barguet, TFP, F4, at SCHS. See also Easterby, *History of the St. Andrew's Society*, 21, 30, 34.

4. Mitchell and Holmes, TFP, F3; Barguet, TFP, F4, at SCHS. Will: Margaret Bettingall, WBCC 42 (1839–45): 67–69; Adam Tunno, WBCC 39 (1826–34): 1239–43, at SCDAH.

5. See documents cited in n. 4.

6. For manumission documents, see MRSS, CCIMB, and WBCC, at SCDAH. See also Bettingall Will in n. 4; Holmes, TFP, F3, at SCHS; SFNCTB, at SCDAH.

7. Barbary, CCIMB 1, p. 151, at SCDAH. Barbara's marriage certificate refers to her as Barbary. 1814: Marriage of John P. Burget and Barbary Tunno, PRSPEC, at SCDAH.

8. Holmes and John Gregg, TFP, F3, at SCHS; Dalcho, *Historical Account*, 246, 585.

9. Holmes, TFP, F3; Letter: Langdon Cheves, TFP, F1, at SCHS.

10. Holmes, TFP, F3, at SCHS; *Powers v. McEachern*, in Cooper and McCord, *Statutes at Large*, 7:290, 293–94. See also introduction and Kennedy-Haflett, "Moral Marriage."

11. See chap. 5.

12. For Thomas Cole, see Bettingall Will, in n. 4; Hagy, *Charleston City Directories*, 1816–29, 37; Koger, *Black Slaveowners*, 15, 142–43; and Schweninger, *Black Property Owners*, 20–21, 247–48.

13. If Margaret was a virtually free person, then Hagar, and her children, would, by law, be legally enslaved. For more on free blacks and marriage, see Powers, *Black Charlestonians*, chap. 2; and Fitchett, "Free Negro in Charleston." See also Tunno Will, in n. 4.

14. On head taxes, see chap. 3.

15. In 1830, Hagar Cole, aged between 36 and 55, lived in Ward 4 and headed a household of 13 people. Woodson, *Free Negro Heads of Families*, 156; "Free Negro Owners of Slaves," 72. Jehu Jones, the free black hotel owner, avoided paying capitation taxes due to the influence of his white guardians, John L. Wilson and William Lance. Petitions: Jehu Jones, GAP ND00 01871, 1823 00130, 1823 00138, and 1827 00102, at SCDAH.

16. Hagar paid $15 on $1,000 worth of real estate in 1859. *1859 Tax List*, 386, at CCPL.

17. On *feme sole* and *feme covert*, see chap. 3.

18. See n. 15. Margaret mentions Thomas in her will, written in 1838. See documents cited in n. 4. No death records have been found for Thomas up to and including the year 1860. See RICC, at CCPL. A Thomas Cole also paid property taxes in Charleston in 1859 and 1860. Thomas Cole, *1859 Tax List*, 386, at CCPL; Thomas Cole, *1860 Tax List*, 317, at RSS.

19. See Bettingall Will, in n. 4. In 1853, Hagar's grandson bequeathed to her "one share in the Bank of Charleston." Alexander Forrester, WBCC 46 (1851–56): 280, at SCDAH. In 1860, Hagar paid taxes on her own real property, including a house and lot inherited from her mother. See n. 16. See also "Hagar Cole," 1860 Tax Returns, at SCDAH.

20. See chap. 3 and Sole Traders Deeds, in MRSS, at SCDAH.

21. See Basch, *In the Eyes of the Law*; Chused, "Married Women's Property Law"; Jensen, "Equity Jurisdiction"; Salmon, "Women and Property"; and Salmon, *Women and the Law of Property*.

22. Eliza spent years cooking and cleaning for other people in order to become a success. Equally important was the inheritance she received from her mother, which allowed Eliza and her husband to open their first hotel more quickly than if they had had to depend on their savings alone. This legacy also made Eliza a wealthy woman in her own right, as well as a *feme sole* who managed her own estate, apart from her husband. See chaps. 3 and 4.

23. Barbara Barquet, WBCC 44 (1845–51): 23; Letter: John C. Tunno, TFP, F1; Barguet, TFP, F4; Holmes, Mitchell, and John Johnson, TFP, F3, at SCHS; Marriage of Burget and Tunno, in n. 7; Tunno Will, in n. 4.

24. See documents cited in n. 7 and Johnson and Mitchell, TFP, F3, at SCHS. John likely came to Charleston during the Haitian Revolution. For more on this topic, see chap. 2; Berlin, *Slaves without Masters*, 35–36, 58; Johnson and Roark, *Black Masters*, 33; Powers, *Black Charlestonians*, 28; and Wikramanayake, *World in Shadow*, 18, 159.

25. Mitchell and Barguet, TFP, F3 and F4, respectively, at SCHS; Hagy, *Directories for Charleston*, 1816–29, 1, 33, 70, 137. On the BFS, see chap. 2.

26. Barbara's age calculated from the federal census of 1830, where she is listed as being between 24 and 36 years of age. Woodson, *Free Negro Heads of Families*, 156; "Free Negro Owners of Slaves," 71–72. See also 1813: Baptisms of John P. Barquet, Joseph Barquet, and William Barquet, PRSPEC, at SCDAH.

27. Parish records list John's last name on his wedding day as Burget. When he and

Barbara attended a baptism in 1815, however, they were referred to as Barquet, and city directories list the couple as Barguet and Barquet at different times. See documents cited in n. 7. See also Johnson, TFP, F3, at SCHS; 1815: Baptism of Eliza Tunno, PRSPEC, at SCDAH; and Hagy, *Directories for Charleston, 1816–29*, 1, 33, 70, 137.

28. See documents cited in n. 26. William Pincel was likely William Pencil, who exposed the alleged Vesey Rebellion to authorities in 1822. Powers, *Black Charlestonians*, 32. For Thomas Bonneau, see chap. 3; Koger, *Black Slaveowners*, 98, 166; and Schweninger, *Black Property Owners*, 129.

29. On the size of Charleston's elite free black community, see chap. 4. The city's death records do not begin until 1819, and the registers of St. Philip's Church are not extant, so we do not know the date of Mary's death. It would have been after 26 Nov. 1813, when she attended her son William's baptism, and before 6 July 1814, the day Barbara married John. See documents cited in nn. 7 and 26; RICC, at CCPL; and PRSPEC, at SCDAH.

30. Liston W. Barguet, Barbara and John's eldest son, recorded the names of every child his parents had, the names of the people each of his siblings married, and the names of all his nieces and nephews, but he never mentioned his father's first wife or his half siblings. See Barguet, TFP, F4, at SCHS.

31. Bleser, *In Joy and in Sorrow*, esp. chap. 6; Pease and Pease, *Ladies, Women, and Wenches*, 38; Powers, *Black Charlestonians*, chap. 2.

32. Rules and Regulations, BFSP, at ARC. On p. 25 is a list of persons admitted to the BFS between 1 Nov. 1790 and Nov. 1844. Number 40: John P. Barquet admitted 1 Jan. 1807. The "D" beside his name indicates he was deceased when the pamphlet was published in 1844. If Barquet Sr. had resigned there would be an "R" next to his name; if he had been excluded there would be an "E." Number 102: Jonathan P. Barquet admitted 4 Nov. 1830.

33. See documents cited in n. 26.

34. Barguet, TFP, F4, at SCHS.

35. Hagy, *Directories for Charleston, 1816–29*, 70; Deposition: Mary Louisa Enburg, TFP, F3; Barguet, TFP, F4, at SCHS.

36. Woodson, *Free Negro Heads of Families*, 156; "Free Negro Owners of Slaves," 71–72. On black female slaveowners, see chap. 4; Johnson and Roark, *No Chariot*, 128–130; Koger, *Black Slaveowners*, xiii, 7, 30, 87–88, 98, 164–72, 214–18; and Wikramanayake, *World in Shadow*, 2, 73, 80–81, 87, 94. For taking in boarders, see chap. 3.

37. See Sole Trader Deeds, in MRSS, at SCDAH. In addition to the census, Barbara's name appears in other public records including Letters of Guardianship, in LGA, at SCDAH. Barbara, like many other black female slaveholders, rented out some of her enslaved laborers to supplement her monthly income. Koger, *Black Slaveowners*, 94–95.

38. See chaps. 1 and 3 on the sexual imbalance among Charleston's free blacks.

39. On the structures of southern families, see Bleser, *In Joy and in Sorrow*, xviii; Clinton, *Plantation Mistress*, xv; Elizabeth Fox-Genovese, *Within the Plantation Household*, 52, 406 n. 27; M. Johnson, "Planters and Patriarchy"; and Lebsock, "Free Black Women."

40. See introduction. See also Johnson and Roark, "Middle Ground"; Wikramanayake, *World in Shadow*, xiii; and Williamson, *New People*, xi, 2.

41. See Barguet, TFP, F4, at SCHS. For more on *feme sole* and *feme covert* status, see chap. 3.

42. Memorial of Adam Tunno: *Charleston Courier*, 28 Dec. 1832, TFP, F5; Letter of J. C. Tunno, TFP, F1, at SCHS; Tunno Will, in n. 4.

43. In antebellum Charleston, most women would have fallen under the protection of some man, whether it was a husband, father, brother, or other male guardian. In using the words he did, Adam differentiated between his slaves, who were his property, and his family of color, who were under his protection. See Tunno Will, in n. 4.

44. Ibid. On the cost of homes in antebellum Charleston, see Curry, *Free Black in Urban America*, 43; Johnson and Roark, *Black Masters*, 204–7; Johnson and Roark, *No Chariot*, 6–7; and Pease and Pease, *Ladies, Women, and Wenches*, 105. See also chap. 4.

45. See Tunno Will, in n. 4.

46. On interracial relationships, see chaps. 2 and 4. Quotation from the *Mercury* in Kennedy, *Braided Relations*, 118.

47. Presidency in Easterby, *History of the St. Andrew's Society*, 21, 30, 34; *Courier* memorial, TFP, F5, at SCHS.

48. See Tunno Will, in n. 4.

49. Hagy, *Directories for Charleston, 1830–41*, 2.

50. I use "wealthy" to refer to persons who possessed property valued at over $10,000 and "affluent" or "prosperous" for those whose estates were assessed between $1,000 and $9,999. See chap. 4.

51. Hagy, *Directories for Charleston, 1830–41*, 32, 73; Koger, *Black Slaveowners*, 94–95.

52. Letter of Guardianship: William and Mary Cole, LGA 2B (27 May 1834): 39, at SCDAH.

53. Ibid.; Tunno Will, in n. 4. See chap. 3 for more on husbands, creditors, and *feme sole* traders. On guardianship, see Berlin, *Slaves without Masters*, 215; and Wikramanayake, *World in Shadow*, 42–44, 55, 59, 65, 151.

54. See introduction and Bettingall Will, in n. 4.

55. See chap. 4.

56. Letters of Guardianship: Sarah and Margaret Reid, Maria Bentham, and Alexander Forrester, LGA 2C (6 Aug. 1838): 35, at SCDAH; Tunno Will, in n. 4. We do not know if or how these children were related to Adam and Margaret.

57. Bettingall Will, in n. 4.

58. Ibid.; Margaret Bettingall, CCIA, vol. A (1839–44): 47, 570, at SCDAH.

59. Jane Wightman and Maria Weston controlled real property in excess of $10,000. See *1859 Tax List*, 403–4, at CCPL; *1860 Tax List*, 332–33, at RSS; *1861 Tax Book*, at SCHS; and chap. 4.

60. Bettingall Will, in n. 4.

61. "R. F. Henry," in Hagy, *Directories for Charleston, 1830–41*, 109; "L. L. Levy," in ibid., 115; "Alexander McDonald," in ibid., 117. All of these men were listed as white persons.

62. There is no Isabella Simmons in the 1840 directory, but there is a listing for a free person of color named Bella Simons. "Bella Simons," in Hagy, *Directories for Charleston, 1830–41*, 126. See n. 58 for Bettingall inventory. The inventory lists other moveable property Margaret owned, including furniture from her Bedon's Alley home. Worth $70,

these items would have gone to Barbara, Hagar, and four of Margaret's grandchildren, in accordance with her will. See documents cited in n. 4.

63. "Arthur G. Rose," in Hagy, *Directories for Charleston, 1830–41*, 124; "J. G. Moodie," in ibid., 119. See Tunno and Bettingall Wills, in n. 4. See also Crane, "Two Women," 214.

64. For more on land ownership, see chap. 4. See also Schweninger, *Black Property Owners*, chaps. 3 and 4; and Wikramanayake, *World in Shadow*, 78–80, 105–9.

65. See chap. 2.

66. See nn. 56 and 57. See also Salmon, *Women and the Law of Property*; and Bettingall Will, in n. 4.

67. For James Moodie as Barbara's advisor and guardian, see Bettingall Will, in n. 4. See also Answer of Barbara Barquet, *Hamilton v. Hamilton*.

68. Gantt Register #10, in Court of Equity Decree Book (1841): 152–55, at SCDAH; Johnson Decree, *Hamilton v. Hamilton*, 25 March 1843.

69. Affidavits of Alexander Mazyck, *Hamilton v. Hamilton*, 2 and 25 Jan. 1844.

70. William Harper's Order, *Hamilton v. Hamilton*, 27 June 1845; Harper, "Memoir on Slavery."

71. Richardson, *Report of Cases at Law*, vol. 2: 355–67. See also ERB (1843–44): 15–17; ERB (Feb. 1845–July 1846): 142–43; *Records of the Court of Appeals*, 28 Jan. 1845; EDB (April 1843–Feb. 1844): 112–13, at SCDAH.

72. Barquet Will, in n. 23; Barbara Barquet, RICC, Feb. 1846, at CCPL; Rules and Regulations, BFSP, at ARC.

73. Barquet Will, in n. 23; Elizabeth Hamilton, WBCC 50 (1862–65): 27, at SCDAH.

74. Barquet Will, in n. 23; Barbara Barquet, CCIA, vol. B (1844–50): 207–8, at SCDAH; Koger, *Black Slaveowners*, 94–95.

75. Barquet Will, in n. 23; Inventory of Barquet, in n. 74. If the seven enslaved persons are factored in, Barbara, like her mother, likely left behind an estate worth over $10,000.

76. See Crane, "Two Women."

Epilogue

1. Much of the information in this section draws on the wonderfully rich and detailed reconstructive work done by historians Michael Johnson, James Roark, and Bernard Powers Jr. See Johnson and Roark, *Black Masters*, chap. 5; Johnson and Roark, *No Chariot*, introduction; and Powers, *Black Charlestonians*, 62–66.

2. Johnson and Roark, *Black Masters*, 186–87.

3. Alfred Huger, quoted in ibid., 192–93.

4. Johnson and Roark, *No Chariot*, 7.

5. Ibid., 8; Johnson and Roark, *Black Masters*, 237–38; Powers, *Black Charlestonians*, 64.

6. Johnson and Roark, *No Chariot*, 9, 13.

7. Ibid., 14; Johnson and Roark, *Black Masters*, 274–75.

8. Wikramanayake, *World in Shadow*, 170; Petitions: Lucy Andrews, GAP 003 ND00 02811, 003 1860 00026, and 003 1861 00017; Committee on the Colored Population: Reports on Lucy Andrews, GAP 004 ND00 02535 and 004 1861 00096, at SCDAH.

9. E. Brown, "To Catch the Vision of Freedom."

BIBLIOGRAPHY

Primary Sources

MANUSCRIPT COLLECTIONS

Avery Research Center, Charleston, SC
  Hetty Barron Arrest Warrant, Miscellaneous Documents
  Brown Fellowship Society Papers
  Centenary Methodist Episcopal Church Records
  Virginie A. Ferrette Deed of Conveyance, Miscellaneous Documents
  Free Blacks: Vertical File
  Free Blacks in the Antebellum Era: Folder
  Friendly Union Society Papers
  Holloway Family Papers
  Eugene Hunt Collection
  Jane and William Pease Collection
  Dorothy Richardson Collection
  St. Peter's Church Records
  Trinity United Methodist Church Records
  Zion Presbyterian Church Records, 1854–1870
Charleston City Archives, Charleston, SC
  Charleston City Police Records
  Charleston City Poor House Records
  List of Taxpayers of the City of Charleston, 1858
Charleston County Public Library, Charleston, SC
  Cemeteries: Vertical File
  Charleston City Directory, 1856
  List of the Tax Payers of the City of Charleston for 1859
  Lowcountry Church Records
  Mayor's Report on City Affairs, 1857
  Return of Interments in the City of Charleston
Charleston Library Society, Charleston, SC
  Charleston City Directory, 1859
  City of Charleston Report of Interments
  Hinson Clippings: Negroes
  Police Department Record Books
  Statement of Receipts and Expenditures by the City Council of Charleston from
      1st July 1849 to 1st July 1850, with a List of Taxpayers of the City for 1850
Library Company of Philadelphia, Philadelphia, PA
  Stevens-Cogdell/Sanders-Venning Papers
Robert Scott Small Library, Special Collections, Charleston, SC

Bell Family Papers
Charleston City Council Proceedings
Friendly Moralist Society Papers
List of the Tax Payers of the City of Charleston for 1860
South Carolina Department of Archives and History, Columbia
Charleston County Estate Papers, 1732–1912
Charleston County Index to Manumission Books, 1801–48
Charleston County Inventories and Appraisements, 1783–1846
Equity Decree Books
Equity Report Books
General Assembly Papers
Guardianship Bonds and Bond Books, Court of Equity and Master Collection,
    1810–81
Individual Tax Returns for Free People of Color in St. Philip's and St. Michael's
    Parishes, 1860
Letters of Guardianship and Administration, Probate Records of Charleston
    County
Letters of Testamentary and Administration, Court of the Ordinary and Probate
    Court
Miscellaneous Records, Secretary of State, 1729–1825
Parish Registers of St. Philip's Episcopal Church, 1810–40
Records of the Court of Appeals
St. Stephen's Chapel Records
State Free Negro Capitation Tax Books, 1811–1860
Tax Assessment Books, Office of the Mayor, 1852–56
Will Books for Charleston County, 1790–1860
South Carolina Historical Society, Charleston
Benjamin Berry Papers, in William S. Elliott Collection
Charleston Capitation Tax Book, Free People of Color, 1859
Peter Desvernay Papers
Education: Vertical File
Thomas Hunter Forrest Papers
L. Louis Green Collection
Hagar Johnson Papers, in Edward McCrady Sr. Legal Collection
Ladies Benevolent Society: Vertical File
Ladies Benevolent Society Records
Eliza S. Lee Papers, in Rutledge and Young Collection, #24/269/5
Charles Legare Papers, in Rivers Collection, George Buist Legal Papers
Sydney A. Legare Autobiography
Henry D. Lesesne Diary
Miscellaneous Antebellum History: Vertical File
Negroes: Vertical File
William Remley Papers
Hagar Richardson Papers, in Arnoldus Vanderhorst Collection
Statement of Receipts and Expenditures by the City Council of Charleston from 1st Sept. 1850

to 1st Sept. 1851, with a List of Taxpaying Citizens in the Upper and Lower Wards—
Separated

Tax Book, Free Persons of Color, Charleston, 1861

Tunno Family Papers, in Langdon Cheves Collection

University of North Carolina–Greensboro
Race and Slavery Petitions Project

GOVERNMENT DOCUMENTS

DeBow, J. D., ed. *Compendium of the Seventh Census of the United States, 1850*. Washington, DC: Nicholson, 1855.

U.S. Bureau of the Census. *Return of the Whole Number of Persons within the Several Districts of the United States*. Washington, DC: Duane, 1801.

———. *Aggregate Returns for the United States Census for 1820*. Washington, DC: Gales and Seaton, 1821.

———. *The Seventh Census of the United States: 1850*. Washington, DC: Robert Armstrong, 1853.

———. *Population of the United States in 1860, Compiled from the Eighth Census*. Washington, DC: Government Printing Office, 1864.

———. *A Century of Population Growth, from the First Census of the United States to the Twelfth, 1790–1900*. Washington, DC: Government Printing Office, 1909.

———. *Negro Population of the United States, 1790–1915*. Washington, DC: Government Printing Office, 1918.

———. *Special List No. 34: Free Black Heads of Families in the First U.S. Census*. Washington, DC: National Archives and Records Service, 1973.

PUBLISHED WORKS

Bremer, Fredricka. *The Homes of the New World: Impressions of America*. Vols. 1 and 2. Trans. Mary Howitt. New York: Negro Universities Press, 1968.

Catterall, Helen Tunnicliff, ed. *Judicial Cases Concerning American Slavery and the Negro*. Vol. 2, *Cases from the Courts of North Carolina, South Carolina, and Tennessee*. Washington, DC: Carnegie Institution of Washington, 1929.

Chesnut, Mary Boykin. *A Diary from Dixie*. Boston: Houghton Mifflin, 1949.

Cooper, Thomas, and David J. McCord, eds. *The Statutes at Large of South Carolina*. 10 vols. Columbia: State Company, 1930.

Dawson, J. L., and H. W. DeSaussure, eds. *Census of the City of Charleston, South Carolina, for the Year 1848, Exhibiting the Condition and Prospects of the City, Illustrated by Many Statistical Details*. Charleston, SC: J. B. Nixon, 1849.

Eckhard, George B., ed. *A Digest of the Ordinances of the City Council of Charleston from the Year 1783–Oct. 1844*. Charleston, SC: Walker and Burke, 1844.

Ford, Frederick A. *Census of the City of Charleston, South Carolina, for the Year 1861, Illustrated by Statistical Details*. Charleston, SC: Evans and Cogswell, 1861.

Grimke, Sarah M. *Letters on the Equality of the Sexes, and the Condition of Woman*. Boston: Isaac Knapp, 1838; rpt., New York: Source Book, 1970.

Hagy, James W., ed. *The People and Professions of Charleston, South Carolina, 1782–1802*. Baltimore: Clearfield, 1992.

———. *City Directories for Charleston, South Carolina, for the Years 1803, 1806, 1807, 1809 and 1813.* Baltimore: Clearfield, 1995.

———. *Charleston, South Carolina, City Directories, for the Years 1816, 1819, 1822, 1825, and 1829.* Baltimore: Clearfield, 1996.

———. *Directories for the City of Charleston, South Carolina, for the Years 1830–31, 1835–36, 1836, 1837–38, and 1840–41.* Baltimore: Clearfield, 1997.

———. *Directories for the City of Charleston, South Carolina, for the Years 1849, 1852, and 1855.* Baltimore: Clearfield, 1998.

Holcomb, Brent H., ed. *South Carolina Naturalizations, 1783–1850.* Baltimore: Clearfield, 2000.

Horsey, John R., ed. *Ordinances of the City of Charleston from the 14th of September 1854 to the 1st of December 1859.* Charleston, SC: Walker, Evans, and Co., 1859.

Killens, John Oliver, ed. *The Trial Record of Denmark Vesey.* Boston: Beacon, 1970.

Olmsted, Frederick Law. *A Journey in the Seaboard Slave States in the Years 1853–1854.* New York: G. P. Putnam and Sons, 1904.

———. *The Cotton Kingdom: A Traveller's Observations on Cotton and Slavery in the American Slave States.* New ed. New York: Knopf, 1953.

Payne, Daniel A. *Recollections of Seventy Years.* New York: Arno, 1968.

Ravenel, Harriott Horry Rutledge. *Charleston: The Place and the People.* New York: Macmillan, 1931.

Richardson, J. S. G. *Report of Cases at Law in the Court of Appeals and Court of Errors.* Columbia: A. S. Johnston, 1847.

Smith, D. E. Huger, and A. S. Salley, Jr., eds. *The Register of St. Philip's Parish, 1754–1810.* Columbia: University of South Carolina Press, 1971.

Trapier, Paul. *The Private Register of the Reverend Paul Trapier.* Charleston: Dalcho Historical Society of the Diocese of South Carolina, 1958.

Walker, H. Pinckney, ed. *Ordinances of the City of Charleston from the 19th of August, 1844, to the 14th of September, 1854.* Charleston, SC: A. E. Miller, 1854.

Secondary Sources

BOOKS

Alexander, Adele Logan. *Ambiguous Lives: Free Women of Color in Rural Georgia, 1789–1879.* Fayetteville: University of Arkansas Press, 1991.

Alexander, Leslie M. *African or American? Black Identity and Political Activism in New York City, 1784–1861.* Urbana: University of Illinois Press, 2008.

Bancroft, Frederic. *Slave Trading in the Old South.* Columbia: University of South Carolina Press, 1996.

Bardaglio, Peter W. *Reconstructing the Household: Families, Sex, and the Law in the Nineteenth-Century South.* Chapel Hill: University of North Carolina Press, 1995.

Basch, Norma. *In the Eyes of the Law: Women, Marriage and Property in Nineteenth-Century New York.* Ithaca, NY: Cornell University Press, 1982.

Bell, Caryn Cossé. *Revolution, Romanticism, and the Afro-Creole Protest Tradition in Louisiana, 1718–1868.* Baton Rouge: Louisiana State University Press, 1997.

Bellows, Barbara L. *Benevolence among Slaveholders: Assisting the Poor in Charleston, 1670–1860.* Baton Rouge: Louisiana State University Press, 1993.

Berlin, Ira. *Slaves without Masters: The Free Negro in the Antebellum South.* New York: New Press, 1974.

Berry, Daina Ramey. *Swing the Sickle for the Harvest Is Ripe: Gender and Slavery in Antebellum Georgia.* Urbana: University of Illinois Press, 2007.

Bleser, Carol, ed. *In Joy and in Sorrow: Women, Family, and Marriage in the Victorian South, 1830–1900.* New York: Oxford University Press, 1991.

Bowes, Frederick P. *The Culture of Early Charleston.* Chapel Hill: University of North Carolina Press, 1942.

Boydston, Jeanne. *Home and Work: Housework, Wages, and the Ideology of Labor in the Early Republic.* New York: Oxford University Press, 1990.

Bracey, John H., August Meier, and Elliot Rudwick, eds. *Free Blacks in America, 1800–1860.* Belmont: Wadsworth, 1971.

Broussard, Albert S. *African-American Odyssey: The Stewarts, 1853–1963.* Lawrence: University Press of Kansas, 1998.

Brown, Kathleen M. *Good Wives, Nasty Wenches, and Anxious Patriarchs: Gender, Race, and Power in Colonial Virginia.* Chapel Hill: University of North Carolina Press, 1996.

Burton, Orville Vernon. *In My Father's House Are Many Mansions: Family and Community in Edgefield, South Carolina.* Chapel Hill: University of North Carolina Press, 1985.

Bynum, Victoria E. *Unruly Women: The Politics of Social and Sexual Control in the Old South.* Chapel Hill: University of North Carolina Press, 1992.

Camp, Stephanie M. H. *Closer to Freedom: Enslaved Women and Everyday Resistance in the Plantation South.* Chapel Hill: University of North Carolina Press, 2004.

Campbell, Edward D., and Kym S. Rice, eds. *Before Freedom Came: African-American Life in the Antebellum South.* Charlottesville: University Press of Virginia, 1991.

Clinton, Catherine. *The Plantation Mistress: Woman's World in the Old South.* New York: Pantheon, 1982.

Curry, Leonard P. *The Free Black in Urban America, 1800–1850: The Shadow of the Dream.* Chicago: University of Chicago Press, 1981.

Dabel, Jane E. *A Respectable Woman: The Public Roles of African American Women in Nineteenth-Century New York.* New York: New York University Press, 2008.

Dalcho, Frederick. *An Historical Account of the Protestant Episcopal Church in South Carolina.* New York: Arno, 1972.

Dunbar, Erica Armstrong. *A Fragile Freedom: African American Women and Emancipation in the Antebellum City.* New Haven, CT: Yale University Press, 2008.

Easterby, James H. *History of the St. Andrew's Society of Charleston, South Carolina, 1729–1929.* Charleston, SC: St. Andrew's Society, 1929.

Edgar, Walter. *South Carolina: A History.* Columbia: University of South Carolina Press, 1998.

Fields, Barbara Jeanne. *Slavery and Freedom on the Middle Ground: Maryland during the Nineteenth Century.* New Haven, CT: Yale University Press, 1985.

Flynn, Jean Martin. *The Militia in Antebellum South Carolina Society.* Spartanburg, SC: Reprint Co., 1991.

Foner, Eric. *Reconstruction: America's Unfinished Revolution, 1863–1877*. New York: Harper and Row, 1988.

———. *Nothing but Freedom: Emancipation and Its Legacy*. Baton Rouge: Louisiana State University Press, 2007.

Fox-Genovese, Elizabeth. *Within the Plantation Household: Black and White Women of the Old South*. Chapel Hill: University of North Carolina Press, 1988.

Frankel, Noralee. *Freedom's Women: Black Women and Families in Civil War Era Mississippi*. Bloomington: Indiana University Press, 1999.

Fraser, Walter J., Jr. *Charleston! Charleston! The History of a Southern City*. Columbia: University of South Carolina Press, 1989.

Frazier, E. Franklin. *The Free Negro Family*. New York: Arno, 1968.

———. *The Negro Family in the United States*. Rev. ed. Chicago: University of Chicago Press, 5th printing, 1969.

———. *Black Bourgeoisie*. New York: Free Press, 1997.

Gaines, Kevin K. *Uplifting the Race: Black Leadership, Politics, and Culture in the Twentieth Century*. Chapel Hill: University of North Carolina Press, 1996.

Gallay, Alan. *The Indian Slave Trade: The Rise of the English Empire in the American South, 1670–1717*. New Haven, CT: Yale University Press, 2003.

Gaspar, David Barry, and Darlene Clark Hine, eds. *More than Chattel: Black Women and Slavery in the Americas*. Bloomington: Indiana University Press, 1996.

———. *Beyond Bondage: Free Women of Color in the Americas*. Urbana: University of Illinois Press, 2004.

Gatewood, Willard B. *Aristocrats of Color: The Black Elite, 1880–1920*. Fayetteville: University of Arkansas Press, 2000.

Gehman, Mary. *The Free People of Color of New Orleans: An Introduction*. New Orleans: Margaret Media, 1994.

Giddings, Paula. *When and Where I Enter: The Impact of Black Women on Race and Sex in America*. New York: Quill William Morrow, 1984.

Gilmore, Glenda E. *Gender and Jim Crow: Women and the Politics of White Supremacy in North Carolina, 1896–1920*. Chapel Hill: University of North Carolina Press, 1996.

Gould, Virginia Meacham, ed. *Chained to the Rock of Adversity: To Be Free, Black, and Female in the Old South*. Athens: University of Georgia Press, 1998.

Hagy, James W. *This Happy Land: The Jews of Colonial and Antebellum Charleston*. Tuscaloosa: University of Alabama Press, 1993.

Hahn, Steven. *A Nation under Our Feet: Black Political Struggles in the Rural South from Slavery to the Great Migration*. Cambridge, MA: Belknap Press of Harvard University, 2003.

Hanger, Kimberly S. *Bounded Lives, Bounded Places: Free Black Society in Colonial New Orleans, 1769–1803*. Durham, NC: Duke University Press, 1997.

Harris, Leslie M. *In the Shadow of Slavery: African Americans in New York City, 1626–1863*. Chicago: University of Chicago Press, 2003.

Henry, H. M. *The Police Control of the Slave in South Carolina*. New York: Negro Universities Press, 1968 [1914].

Higginbotham, Evelyn Brooks. *Righteous Discontent: The Women's Movement in the Black Baptist Church, 1880–1920*. Cambridge, MA: Harvard University Press, 1993.

Hindus, Michael. *Prison and Plantation: Crime, Justice, and Authority in Massachusetts and South Carolina, 1767–1878*. Chapel Hill: University of North Carolina Press, 1980.

Hine, Darlene Clark, and Kathleen Thompson. *A Shining Thread of Hope: The History of Black Women in America*. New York: Broadway, 1998.

Hodes, Martha. *White Women, Black Men: Illicit Sex in the Nineteenth-Century South*. New Haven, CT: Yale University Press, 1997.

———, ed. *Sex, Love, Race: Crossing Boundaries in North American History*. New York: New York University Press, 1999.

Horton, James Oliver. *Free People of Color: Inside the African American Community*. Washington, DC: Smithsonian Institution Press, 1993.

Hudson, Lynn M. *The Making of "Mammy Pleasant": A Black Entrepreneur in Nineteenth-Century San Francisco*. Urbana: University of Illinois Press, 2003.

Hunter, Tera. *To 'Joy My Freedom: Southern Women's Lives and Labors after the Civil War*. Cambridge, MA: Harvard University Press, 1998.

Johnson, Michael P., and James L. Roark. *Black Masters: A Free Family of Color in the Old South*. New York: W. W. Norton, 1984.

———, eds. *No Chariot Let Down: Charleston's Free People of Color on the Eve of the Civil War*. New York: W. W. Norton, 1984.

Johnson, Whittington B. *Black Savannah, 1788–1864*. Fayetteville: University of Arkansas Press, 1996.

Johnston, James. *Race Relations in Virginia and Miscegenation in the South, 1776–1860*. Amherst: University of Massachusetts Press, 1970.

———. *Miscegenation in the Antebellum South*. New York: AMS, 1972.

Jordan, Winthrop. *The White Man's Burden: Historical Origins of Racism in the United States*. New York: Oxford University, 1974.

Kein, Sybil, ed. *Creole: The History and Legacy of Louisiana's Free People of Color*. Baton Rouge: Louisiana State University Press, 2000.

Kennedy, Cynthia M. *Braided Relations, Entwined Lives: The Women of Charleston's Urban Slave Society*. Bloomington: Indiana University Press, 2005.

King, Stewart R. *Blue Coat or Powdered Wig: Free People of Color in Pre-revolutionary Saint Domingue*. Athens: University of Georgia Press, 2001.

King, Wilma. *The Essence of Liberty: Free Black Women during the Slave Era*. Columbia: University of Missouri Press, 2006.

Koger, Larry. *Black Slaveowners: Free Black Slave Masters in South Carolina, 1790–1860*. Columbia: University of South Carolina Press, 1985.

Lebsock, Suzanne. *The Free Women of Petersburg: Status and Culture in a Southern Town, 1784–1860*. New York: W. W. Norton, 1984.

Leslie, Kent Anderson. *Woman of Color, Daughter of Privilege: Amanda America Dickson, 1849–1893*. Athens: University of Georgia Press, 1995.

McCurry, Stephanie. *Masters of Small Worlds: Yeoman Households, Gender Relations, and the Political Culture of the Antebellum South Carolina Low Country*. New York: Oxford University Press, 1995.

Miles, Tiya. *Ties That Bind: The Story of an Afro-Cherokee Family in Slavery and Freedom*. Los Angeles: University of California Press, 2006.

Mitchell, Michelle. *Righteous Propagation: African Americans and the Politics of Racial Destiny after Reconstruction.* Chapel Hill: University of North Carolina Press, 2004.

Morgan, Jennifer L. *Laboring Women: Reproduction and Gender in New World Slavery.* Philadelphia: University of Pennsylvania Press, 2004.

O'Brien, Michael, and David Moltke-Hanson, eds. *Intellectual Life in Antebellum Charleston.* Knoxville: University of Tennessee Press, 1986.

Painter, Nell Irvin. *Sojourner Truth: A Life, a Symbol.* New York: W. W. Norton, 1996.

———. *Southern History across the Color Line.* Chapel Hill: University of North Carolina Press, 2002.

Pearson, Edward A., ed. *Designs against Charleston: The Trial Record of the Denmark Vesey Slave Conspiracy of 1822.* Chapel Hill: University of North Carolina Press, 1999.

Pease, Jane H., and William H. Pease. *The Web of Progress: Private Values and Public Styles in Boston and Charleston, 1828–1843.* New York: Oxford University Press, 1985.

———. *Ladies, Women, and Wenches: Choice and Constraint in Antebellum Charleston and Boston.* Chapel Hill: University of North Carolina Press, 1990.

Phillips, Christopher. *Freedom's Port: The African American Community of Baltimore, 1790–1860.* Urbana: University of Illinois Press, 1997.

Powers, Bernard E., Jr. *Black Charlestonians: A Social History, 1822–1885.* Fayetteville: University of Arkansas Press, 1994.

Robertson, David. *Denmark Vesey: America's Largest Slave Rebellion, and the Man Who Led It.* New York: Alfred Knopf, 1999.

Rothman, Joshua D. *Notorious in the Neighborhood: Sex and Families across the Color Line in Virginia, 1787–1867.* Chapel Hill: University of North Carolina Press, 2003.

Rutledge, Anna Wells. *Artists in the Life of Charleston: Through Colony and State, from Restoration to Reconstruction.* Philadelphia: American Philosophical Society, 1949.

Salmon, Marylynn. *Women and the Law of Property in Early America.* Chapel Hill: University of North Carolina Press, 1986.

Saville, Julie. *The Work of Reconstruction: From Slave to Wage Laborer in South Carolina, 1860–1870.* New York: Cambridge University Press, 1996.

Schafer, Daniel L. *Anna Madgigine Jai Kingsley: African Princess, Florida Slave, Plantation Slaveowner.* Gainesville: University Press of Florida, 2003.

Schafer, Judith Kelleher. *Becoming Free, Remaining Free: Manumission and Enslavement in New Orleans, 1846–1862.* Baton Rouge: Louisiana State University Press, 2003.

Schwalm, Leslie A. *A Hard Fight for We: Women's Transition from Slavery to Freedom in South Carolina.* Chicago: University of Illinois Press, 1997.

Schweninger, Loren. *Black Property Owners in the South, 1790–1915.* Chicago: University of Illinois Press, 1997.

Severens, Martha R., ed. *Selections from the Collection of the Carolina Art Association.* Charleston, SC: Carolina Art Association, 1977.

Shaw, Stephanie J. *What a Woman Ought to Be and to Do: Black Professional Women Workers during the Jim Crow Era.* Chicago: University of Chicago Press, 1996.

Snyder, Christina. *Slavery in Indian Country: The Changing Face of Captivity in Early America.* Cambridge, MA: Harvard University Press, 2010.

Sterkx, H. E. *The Free Negro in Antebellum Louisiana.* Rutherford, NJ: Fairleigh Dickinson University Press, 1972.

Sterling, Dorothy. *We Are Your Sisters: Black Women in the Nineteenthth Century*. New York: W. W. Norton, 1984.

Sumler-Edmond, Janice L. *The Secret Trust of Aspasia Cruvellier Mirault: The Life and Trials of a Free Woman of Color in Antebellum Georgia*. Fayetteville: University of Arkansas Press, 2008.

Taylor, Nikki M. *Frontiers of Freedom: Cincinnati's Black Community 1802–1868*. Athens: Ohio University Press, 2005.

Wade, Richard C. *Slavery in the Cities: The South, 1820–1860*. New York: Oxford University Press, 1964.

White, Deborah Gray. *Ar'n't I a Woman? Female Slaves in the Old South*. Rev. ed. New York: W. W. Norton, 1999 [1985].

———. *Too Heavy a Load: Black Women in Defense of Themselves, 1894–1994*. New York: W. W. Norton, 1999.

Wikramanayake, Marina. *A World in Shadow: The Free Black in Antebellum South Carolina*. Columbia: University of South Carolina Press, 1973.

Williamson, Joel. *New People: Miscegenation and Mulattoes in the United States*. New York: New York University Press, 1984.

Wolcott, Victoria W. *Remaking Respectability: African American Women in Interwar Detroit*. Chapel Hill: University of North Carolina Press, 2001.

Wood, Kirstin. *Masterful Women: Slaveholding Widows from the American Revolution through the Civil War*. Chapel Hill: University of North Carolina Press, 2004.

Wood, Peter H. *Black Majority: Negroes in Colonial South Carolina from 1670 through the Stono Rebellion*. New York: W. W. Norton, 1996.

Woodson, Carter G. *Free Negro Heads of Families in the United States in 1830*. Washington, DC: Association for the Study of Negro Life and History, 1925.

———. *The Education of the Negro Prior to 1861*. New York: Arno, 1968.

ARTICLES, ESSAYS, AND DISSERTATIONS

Berlin, Ira. "The Structure of the Free Negro Caste in the Antebellum United States." *Journal of Social History* 9, no. 3 (1976): 297–318.

———. "Time, Space, and the Evolution of Afro-American Society on British Mainland North America." *American Historical Review* 85 (1980): 44–78.

Birnie, C. W. "The Education of the Negro in Charleston, South Carolina, Prior to the Civil War." *Journal of Negro History* 22, no. 1 (1927): 13–21.

Blackburn, George, and Sherman L. Ricards. "The Mother-Headed Family among Free Negroes in Charleston, South Carolina, 1850–60." *Phylon* 42, no. 1 (1981): 11–25.

Blassingame, John. "The Negro in Antebellum New Orleans: Background for Reconstruction." In *Not a Slave! Free People of Color in Antebellum America, 1790–1860*, ed. Lacy Shaw Jr., 91–102. New York: American Heritage, 1995.

Brown, Elsa Barkley. "To Catch the Vision of Freedom: Reconstructing Southern Black Women's Political History, 1865–1880." In *Unequal Sisters: A Multicultural Reader in U.S. Women's History*, ed. Vicki L. Ruiz and Ellen Carol DuBois, 124–46. 3rd ed. New York: Routledge, 2000.

Browning, James B. "The Beginnings of Insurance Enterprise among Negroes." *Journal of Negro History* 22, no. 4 (1937): 417–32.

Buckley, Thomas E. "Unfixing Race: Class, Power and Identity in an Interracial Family." *Virginia Magazine of History and Biography* 102, no. 3 (1994): 349–80.

Burton, Orville Vernon. "Anatomy of an Antebellum Rural Free Black Community: Social Structure and Social Interaction in Edgefield District, South Carolina, 1850–1860." *Southern Studies* 21, no. 3 (1982): 294–325.

Bynum, Victoria. "On the Lowest Rung: Court Control over Poor White and Free Black Women." *Southern Exposure* 12 (1984): 40–44.

Cameron, Diane. "Circumstances of Their Lives: Enslaved and Free Women of Color in Wethersfield, Connecticut, 1648–1832." *Connecticut History* 44, no. 2 (2005): 248–61.

Chused, Richard. "Married Women's Property Law: 1800–1850." *Georgetown Law Journal* 71 (1983): 1359–425.

Cocuzza, Dominique. "The Dress of Free Women of Color in New Orleans, 1780–1840." *Dress* 27 (2000): 78–87.

Collier-Thomas, Bettye, and James Turner. "Race, Class and Color: The African American Discourse on Identity." *Journal of American Ethnic History* 14, no. 1 (1994): 5–31.

Crane, Virginia Glenn. "Two Women, White and Brown, in the South Carolina Court of Equity, 1842–45." *South Carolina Historical Magazine* 96, no. 3 (1995): 198–220.

Dabel, Jane E. "'My Ma Went to Work Early Every Mornin': Color, Gender, and Occupation in New Orleans, 1840–1860." *Louisiana History* 41, no. 2 (2000): 217–29.

Dickerman, G. S. "A Glimpse of Charleston History." *Southern Workman* (1907): 15–23.

Du Bois, W. E. Burghardt. "The Talented Tenth." In *The Negro Problem: A Series of Articles by Representative Negroes of Today*, ed. Booker T. Washington, W. E. Burghardt Du Bois, and Paul Laurence Dunbar, 32–75. New York: James Pott, 1903.

Everett, Donald. "Free Persons of Color in New Orleans, 1803–65." PhD diss., Tulane University, 1952.

Fitchett, E. Horace. "The Traditions of the Free Negro in Charleston, South Carolina." *Journal of Negro History* 25, no. 2 (1940): 139–51.

———. "The Origin and Growth of the Free Negro Population of Charleston, South Carolina." *Journal of Negro History* 26, no. 4 (1941): 421–37.

———. "The Status of the Free Negro in Charleston, South Carolina, and His Descendants in Modern Society." *Journal of Negro History* 32, no. 4 (1947): 430–51.

———. "The Free Negro in Charleston, South Carolina." PhD diss., University of Chicago, 1950.

Forbes, George. "Colored Slave Owners and Traders in the Old Days." *American Methodist Episcopal Review* 29 (1913): 300–303.

"Free Negro Owners of Slaves in the United States in 1830." *Journal of Negro History* 9, no. 1 (1924): 41–85.

Gould, Lois V. Meacham. "In Full Enjoyment of Their Liberty: The Free Women of Color of the Gulf Ports of New Orleans, Mobile, and Pensacola, 1769–1860." PhD diss., Emory University, 1991.

Gould, Virginia Meacham. "Henriette Delille, Free Women of Color, and Catholicism in Antebellum New Orleans, 1727–1852." In *Beyond Bondage: Free Women of Color in the Americas*, ed. David Barry Gaspar and Darlene Clark Hine, 271–85. Urbana: University of Illinois Press, 2004.

Gross, Ariela. "'Of Portuguese Origin': Litigating Identity and Citizenship among the 'Little Races' in Nineteenth-Century America." *Law and History Review* 25, no. 3 (2007): 467–512.

Haber, Carole, and Brian Gratton. "Old Age, Public Welfare and Race: The Case of Charleston, South Carolina, 1800–1949." *Journal of Social History* 21, no. 2 (1987): 263–79.

Hagy, James W. "Black Business Women in Antebellum Charleston." *Journal of Negro History* 72, no. 1–2 (1987): 42–44.

———. "The Death Records of Charleston." *South Carolina Historical Magazine* 91, no. 1 (1990): 32–44.

Halliburton, R. "Free Black Owners of Slaves: A Reappraisal of the Woodson Thesis." *South Carolina Historical Magazine* 76, no. 3 (1975): 129–42.

Hanger, Kimberly S. "Protecting Property, Family, and Self: The *Mujeres Libres* of Colonial New Orleans." *Review Interamericana* 22, nos. 1–2 (1992): 126–50.

———. "'Desiring Total Tranquility' and Not Getting It: Conflict Involving Free Black Women in Spanish New Orleans." *Americas* 54, no. 4 (1998): 541–56.

———. "Landlords, Shopkeepers, Farmers, and Slave-Owners: Free Black Female Property-Holders in Colonial New Orleans." In *Beyond Bondage: Free Women of Color in the Americas*, ed. David Barry Gaspar and Darlene Clark Hine, 219–36. Urbana: University of Illinois Press, 2004.

Harper, William. "Memoir on Slavery." In *The Ideology of Slavery*, ed. Drew Gilpin Faust, 79–135. Baton Rouge: Louisiana State University Press, 1981.

Harris, Jr., Robert L. "Charleston's Free Afro-American Elite: The Brown Fellowship Society and the Humane Brotherhood." *South Carolina Historical Magazine* 82, no. 4 (1981): 289–310.

January, Alan F. "The South Carolina Association: An Agency for Race Control in Antebellum Charleston." *South Carolina Historical Magazine* 78, no. 3 (1977): 191–201.

Jensen, Carol. "Equity Jurisdiction and Married Women's Property in Antebellum America: A Revisionist View." *International Journal of Women's Studies* 2 (1979): 144–51.

Johnson, Michael P. "Planters and Patriarchy: Charleston, 1800–1860." *Journal of Southern History* 46, no. 1 (1980): 45–72.

———. "Denmark Vesey and His Co-conspirators." Forum: The Making of a Slave Conspiracy, Part 1. *William and Mary Quarterly* 58, no. 4 (2001): 915–76. Forum: The Making of a Slave Conspiracy, Part 2. *William and Mary Quarterly* 59, no. 1 (2002): 135–202.

Johnson, Michael P., and James L. Roark. "'A Middle Ground': Free Mulattoes and the Friendly Moralist Society of Antebellum Charleston." *Southern Studies* 21, no. 3 (1982): 246–65.

———. "Strategies of Survival: Free Negro Families and the Problem of Slavery." In *In Joy and in Sorrow: Women, Family, and Marriage in the Victorian South, 1830–1900*, ed. Carol Bleser, 88–102. New York: Oxford University Press, 1991.

Johnson, Whittington B. "Free Blacks in Antebellum Savannah: An Economic Profile." *Georgia Historical Quarterly* 64, no. 4 (1980): 418–31.

———. "Free Blacks in Antebellum Augusta, Georgia: A Demographic and Economic Profile." *Richmond County History* 14, no. 1 (1982): 10–21.

————. "Free African-American Women in Savannah, 1800–1860: Affluence and Autonomy amid Adversity." In *We Specialize in the Wholly Impossible": A Reader in Black Women's History*, ed. Darlene Clark Hine et al., 237–52. New York: Carlson, 1995.

Kennedy-Haflett, Cynthia. "'Moral Marriage': A Mixed-Race Relationship in Nineteenth-Century Charleston, South Carolina." *South Carolina Historical Magazine* 97, no. 3 (1996): 206–26.

Klebaner, Benjamin Joseph. "Public Poor Relief in Charleston, 1800–1860." *South Carolina Historical Magazine* 55, no. 4 (1954): 210–20.

Kotlikoff, Laurence J., and Anton J. Rupert. "The Manumission of Slaves in New Orleans, 1827–1846." *Southern Studies* 19, no. 2 (1980): 172–81.

LaChance, Paul. "The 1809 Immigration of Saint-Domingue Refugees to New Orleans: Reception, Integration, and Impact." *Louisiana History* 29 (1988): 109–41.

————. "The Limits of Privilege: Where Free Persons of Color Stood in the Hierarchy of Wealth in Antebellum New Orleans." *Slavery and Abolition (Great Britain)* 17, no. 1 (1996): 65–84.

LaFoy, D. C. "A Historical Review of Three Gulf Coast Creole Communities." *Gulf Coast Historical Review* 3, no. 2 (1988): 6–19.

Lebsock, Suzanne. "Free Black Women and the Question of Matriarchy: Petersburg, Virginia, 1784–1820." *Feminist Studies* 8 (1982): 271–92.

Lempel, Leonard. "The Mulatto in United States Race Relations." PhD diss., Syracuse University, 1979.

"Marriage and Death Notices from the *Charleston Courier*, 1806." *South Carolina Historical Magazine* 29 (1928): 336.

Moore, John Hammond. "The Abiel Abbot Journals: A Yankee Preacher in Charleston Society, 1818–1827." *South Carolina Historical Magazine* 68, no. 3 (1967): 115–39.

Morgan, Philip D. "Black Life in Eighteenth-Century Charleston." *Perspectives in American History* 1 (1984): 187–232.

Morton, Patricia. "From Invisible Man to 'New People': The Recent Discovery of American Mulattoes." *Phylon* 46, no. 2 (1985): 106–22.

Murray, Gail S. "Charity within the Bounds of Race and Class: Female Benevolence in the Old South." *South Carolina Historical Magazine* 96, no. 1 (1995): 54–70.

Myers, Amrita Chakrabarti. "The Bettingall-Tunno Family and the Free Black Women of Antebellum Charleston: A Freedom both Contingent and Constrained." In *South Carolina Women: Their Lives and Times*, ed. Marjorie Julian Spruill et al., 1:143–67. Athens: University of Georgia Press, 2009.

Olwell, Robert. "Becoming Free: Manumission and the Genesis of a Free Black Community in South Carolina, 1740–90." *Slavery and Abolition (Great Britain)* 17, no. 1 (1996): 1–19.

————. ""Loose, Idle and Disorderly": Slave Women in the Eighteenth-Century Charleston Marketplace." In *More than Chattel: Black Women and Slavery in the Americas*, ed. David Barry Gaspar and Darlene Clark Hine, 97–110. Bloomington: Indiana University Press, 1996.

Phillips, Ulrich B. "The Slave Labor Problem in the Charleston District." *Political Science Quarterly* 22 (1907): 416–39.

Provine, Dorothy. "The Economic Position of the Free Blacks in the District of Columbia, 1800–1860." *Journal of Negro History* 58, no. 1 (1973): 61–72.

Rankin, David C. "Black Slaveholders: The Case of Andrew Durnford." *Southern Studies* 21, no. 3 (1982): 343–47.

Reinders, Robert C. "The Free Negro in the New Orleans Economy, 1850–1860." *Louisiana History* 6 (1965): 273–85.

Ribianszky, Nik. "'She Appeared to Be Mistress of Her Own Actions, Free from the Control of Anyone': Property-Holding Free Women of Color in Natchez, Mississippi, 1779–1865." *Journal of Mississippi History* 67, no. 3 (2005): 217–45.

Salmon, Marylynn. "Women and Property in South Carolina: Evidence from Marriage Settlements, 1730–1830." *William and Mary Quarterly* 39 (1982): 655–85.

Schafer, Judith Kelleher. "New Orleans Slavery in 1850 as Seen in Advertisements." *Journal of Southern History* 47, no. 1 (1981): 33–56.

———. "'Open and Notorious Concubinage': The Emancipation of Slave Mistresses by Will and the Supreme Court in Antebellum Louisiana." *Louisiana History* 28 (1987): 165–82.

Schweninger, Loren. "A Slave Family in the Antebellum South." *Journal of Negro History* 60, no. 1 (1975): 29–44.

———. "Antebellum Free Persons of Color in Postbellum Louisiana." *Louisiana History* 30, no. 4 (1989): 345–64.

———. "Black-Owned Businesses in the South, 1790–1880." *Business History Review* 63, no. 1 (1989): 22–60.

———. "Property Owning Free African-American Women in the South, 1800–1870." In *"We Specialize in the Wholly Impossible": A Reader in Black Women's History*, ed. Darlene Clark Hine et al., 253–79. New York: Carlson, 1995.

———. "The Fragile Nature of Freedom: Free Women of Color in the U.S. South." In *Beyond Bondage: Free Women of Color in the Americas*, ed. David Barry Gaspar and Darlene Clark Hine, 106–24. Urbana: University of Illinois Press, 2004.

Senese, Donald J. "The Free Negro and the South Carolina Courts, 1790–1860." *South Carolina Historical Magazine* 68, no. 3 (1967): 140–53.

Stavisky, Leonard P. "The Negro Artisan in the South Atlantic States." PhD diss., Columbia University, 1958.

Steckel, Richard H. "Miscegenation and the American Slave Schedules." *Journal of Interdisciplinary History* 11, no. 2 (1980): 251–63.

Steen, Ivan D. "Charleston in the 1850's: As Described by British Travelers." *South Carolina Historical Magazine* 71, no. 1 (1970): 36–45.

Stevenson, Brenda E. "'Marsa Never Sot Aunt Rebecca Down': Enslaved Women, Religion, and Social Power in the Antebellum South." *Journal of African American History* 90, no. 4 (2005): 345–67.

Ware, Lowry. "Reuben Robertson of Turkey Creek: The Story of a Wealthy Black Slaveholder and His Family, White and Black." *South Carolina Historical Magazine* 91, no. 4 (1990): 261–67.

Williams, George W. "Eighteenth-Century Organists of St. Michael's, Charleston." *South Carolina Historical Magazine* 53 (1952): 219–20.

INDEX

Act of 1800, 47–53

Act of 1820, 53, 159–60, 195; passage of and similar legislation, 60–62; impact on manumission, 62–65; and freedom trusts, 65–67; and development of virtual freedom, 67–72. *See also* Freedom: virtual freedom; Trusts

Act of 1841, 72–74, 166

African Church, 23, 71

Alexander, Adele, 9

American Revolution, 27, 28, 30, 31, 35, 41, 49

Baltimore, 7, 28; free black population of, 32, 42–44, 83; owner-initiated manumission in, 49; employment of free blacks in, 85–87, 91–92; property ownership by free blacks in, 117–20, 138; free black slaveowners in, 122–23, 125

Barbados, 26–28

Barquet, Barbara Tunno, 23, 56, 60, 176–78, 205; as slaveowner, 105, 125, 184, 189, 200, 230 (n. 105); and Adam Tunno, 135, 186–88, 201; and courts, 142–43, 176, 196–99; marriage to John Barquet, 182–84; as *feme sole*, 185–86, 191–95, 202; death and will of, 199–200

Barquet, Mary, 183–84

Berlin, Ira, 88

Bettingall, Margaret, 17, 21; and Adam Tunno, 56, 60, 82, 135, 176–82, 186–89, 201; will and estate of, 191–96

Blank, Sarah, 25, 98

Bonneau family, 34; Thomas S., 24, 101, 136, 183–84; Jeanette, 24, 136–37;

Frances Pinckney Bonneau Holloway, 101

Boston, 27, 30

Bremer, Fredricka, 31

Brown, Kathleen, 85

Brown Fellowship Society, 45, 101, 136–37, 152, 154, 182–84, 199, 218 (n. 24)

Burton, Orville, 90

Calhoun, John C., 166

Calvary Episcopal Church, 4

Capitation taxes. *See* Taxes: capitation taxes

Cattle, Barsheba, 50, 124

Charleston Neck, 24–26, 104, 134

Church, 13, 31, 33, 43, 56, 127, 149; freedom to attend, 4, 17, 26; free blacks and elite white churches, 5, 11–12, 23, 34, 114, 136, 173, 201–2

Citizenship, 73, 81, 100, 124, 141–42, 153, 158, 204–5; fluid definition of, 2, 8; "denizenship," 4, 154, 205; black women's construction of, 4–6, 8, 9, 12, 18, 113; earned citizenship, 6; rights of, 10, 59, 111, 115, 129, 146, 153–54, 157, 173, 175, 195, 198; and protections of law, 113; and wealth, 113–46

Civil rights. *See* Citizenship: rights of

Civil War, 2–33 passim, 43, 55, 87–88, 94, 101, 107, 203, 208–9

Cochran, Sophia, 25, 98

Cogdell, Cecille Langlois, 17, 160, 173–75; and Richard Walpole Cogdell, 149–58; uncertain heritage of, 153–54; sons of, 162–64, 166–69

Cogdell, Mary Ann Stevens, 150, 158, 165

{ 263 }

80, 188, 195–96, 201–2; and employment opportunities, 32, 43, 82–84, 90–91, 106–9; and means of acquiring freedom, 40, 59, 75–76; and marriage opportunities, 83–84, 145, 185; and slaveholding, 118, 122–28; and real estate ownership, 118–20; and value of real wealth, 138–39
Goose Creek conspiracy, 33
Gourdin, Henry, 113, 190
Gouvignon, Marie, 54, 131

Hamilton, Elizabeth, 176, 196–98, 200
Hamilton, James, 142, 176, 196–98, 200
Harper, William, 14, 198
Harpers Ferry, 207
Head taxes. See Taxes: capitation taxes
Holloway family, 34; Richard Jr., 101; Frances Pinckney Bonneau, 101–2; Elizabeth, 102, 129–30; Richard Sr., 102, 130
Horlbeck, Daniel, 168–69, 172
Huger, Alfred, 166, 168, 207

Jackson, Becky, 43, 69
Johnson, Michael, 79
Johnson, Whittington, 84, 91, 92–93, 123
Jones, Ann (Walker), 64, 66–67, 127, 135
Jones, Jehu, 23, 99, 245 (n. 15)
Jordan, Winthrop, 158

King, Wilma, 3

Langlois family: Joseph, 45, 151–52, 154; Maria (sister of Cecille Langlois), 45, 151–52, 168–70; Antoinette, 151. See also Cogdell, Cecille Langlois
Law. See Legal system
Lebsock, Suzanne, 108
Lee, Eliza Seymour: as businesswoman, 23, 94, 99–100, 182, 190; lawsuit against Henry Gourdin, 112–13, 115, 142–43

Legal system: lawsuits involving black women, 1–2, 4–6, 53, 75, 105, 113–15, 142–44, 176, 196–99; role in defining black women's freedom, 3, 6–8, 10, 40, 53, 75–76, 82, 115; petitions filed by free black women, 4, 6, 75, 105, 111, 140–43; affidavits obtained by free black women, 4, 16, 39–40, 69–71, 75, 82, 111, 203; and path to manumission, 7–8, 40, 53, 64–69, 70–72; feme sole laws, 10, 79, 103–6, 140, 181, 185–86, 189, 201–2; statutory regulations imposed on free blacks, 16, 34, 78–79, 86, 88, 96–97, 110–11; wills belonging to free black women, 40, 67, 75, 117–18, 125–26, 145, 178, 182, 191–93, 199–200; coverture laws, 103, 156, 173; and protection of assets, 115, 139–44
Liberty. See Freedom
Licensing regulations. See Legal system: statutory regulations imposed on free blacks
Literacy, 17, 33, 89, 135, 141, 161, 170, 175, 178, 182, 201

Mansion House Hotel, 23, 94, 99
Manumission, 1, 3, 9, 35; limitations of, 4, 40, 115; irregularly manumitted persons, 12–13, 65–70, 72–74; means of achieving, 16, 40, 50–51, 53, 59; and heroic acts, 33, 40, 46, 48, 54, 61, 74, 159; affidavits of, 39–40, 42; and sexual/kinship relationships, 41, 46, 54–60, 62–63, 135–38; purchasing freedom, 41, 49–52, 60, 64, 127, 212 (n. 2); regulation of, 47–48, 53, 60–74, 159
Marriage: interracial marriage, 55, 137; opportunities for, 83–85, 185; benefits and constraints of for free black women, 103–6, 137, 190, 195; remarriage, 143, 150, 159, 183–84, 186, 189. See also Contracts: marriage contracts (premarital)
Mathews, Dye, 77–78, 84–85

and Richard Walpole Cogdell, 155–65; children of, 165–67; death of, 167

Sanders family: Robert, 158–60, 163, 169–70; Sarah Ann, 163, 165, 169–70, 172; Cordelia, 163, 170, 172, 174; Julia Sanders Venning, 163, 170–72, 174

Savannah, Georgia, 7, 45; free black population in, 42–44, 56; restrictions on free blacks in, 65–66, 95–96; employment in, 80, 83, 85–86, 91–94, 109; black schools in, 101–2; property ownership by free blacks in, 115, 119–21, 139; slaveholding in, 122–23

Schafer, Judith, 3

Schools: regulation of black schools, 4, 101, 161; free black teachers, 24, 92–93, 101–2, 151–52, 169, 174; underground schools, 33, 101; prominent free black schools, 60, 101, 136, 153, 182–84; boarding schools, 101, 150

Segregation: of free blacks, 4, 24, 101, 108, 209

Seven Years' War, 28, 30

Sexual relationships: terminology for, 15. See also Race: interracial sexual relationships

Simpson, Hagar, 140, 143–44

Slaveholders: free black women as, 5, 11–12, 17, 122–28, 132, 145, 195; ownership of family members, 49–52, 64, 67, 127. See also Barquet, Barbara Tunno: as slaveowner; Enslaved laborers: owned by free black women; Freedom: and slaveholding; Property: black female ownership of enslaved laborers

Slavery: threat of reenslavement, 8, 12–13, 39–40, 69, 76, 112, 128, 144–45, 149, 174, 181, 208; urban slavery, 10, 31–34, 49; Charleston and African slave trade, 28, 33–34; "slave hiring," 31–34, 48. See also Contracts: and enslaved persons; Enslaved laborers; Freedom; Manumission; Slaveholders: free black women as

Snipes, Grase, 127, 129

South Carolina General Assembly, 1, 2–3, 8, 14, 16, 44, 62–63, 72, 81–82, 89, 102–3, 110, 115, 123, 126, 140–42, 159–60, 208–9

Stono slave rebellion, 33

Taxes, 62, 114, 130, 140; capitation taxes, 4, 5, 12, 67, 71, 78–84, 110, 112, 137, 152, 157, 179, 181, 206; property taxes, 4, 12, 66, 82, 115, 118, 120–21, 135, 137, 140, 181; avoidance of payment of, 17, 78, 80, 82, 181, 201

Trusts, 16, 40, 65–67, 69, 72–73, 75, 125, 140, 166, 186–88, 194. See also Act of 1841

Vesey, Denmark, 23, 25, 64, 71, 141, 168, 214–15 (n. 6)

Walker, John, 64, 66–67, 135

Weston family, 24, 34; Sarah, 51; Lydia, 67–69; Nancy, 68; Anthony, 130; Maria, 130, 134

Wightman, Jane, 94, 112, 130, 134–35

Zion Presbyterian Church, 23

Made in the USA
Columbia, SC
22 June 2020